Introduction to Witchcraft

Thirteen Lessons in the Practice of Magic

About the Author

Sara L. Mastros is the author of *The Big Book of Magical Incense, Orphic Hymns Grimoire,* and *The Sorcery of Solomon: A Guide to the 44 Planetary Pentacles of the Magician King*. Recognized by her peers as a brilliant and original thinker, an engaging and inspiring teacher, a compelling and clever writer, and a generally decent human being, Sara spends a lot of time dreaming, thinking, enchanting, writing, and teaching about witchcraft, magic, and myth. But, her true passion is raising up an army of inspired, educated, empowered witches prepared to weave weird new ways of Being in a world that desperately needs us.

Sara L. Mastros
Foreword by Mat Auryn

Introduction to Witchcraft

Thirteen Lessons in the Practice of Magic

Paperback ISBN: 978-1-964537-57-3
Hardcover ISBN: 978-1-964537-70-2
eBook ISBN: 978-1-968185-39-8

Library of Congress Control Number on file.

Published by:
Crossed Crow Books, LLC
518 Davis St, Suite 205
Evanston, IL 60201
www.crossedcrowbooks.com

Printed in the United States of America.
IBI

Dedication

This book is for, and from, the great Teacher of Teachers, and particularly for Ibis-Headed Thoth, the Great Scribe. May his light make the way to learning clear. As he says in my head, *"Learning how to learn is the greatest of all knowledge! Honk, honk!"*[1] We will learn more about him in Chapter Twelve.

1 My human mouth cannot replicate the weird squeaky-raspy bird-voice in which I hear him, but he honks like a goose. I expect he is actually honking like a sacred ibis *(Threskiornis aethiopicus),* his animal-form, but I have never encountered a living ibis, as they do not live in the same ecosystem as me.

Dedication

[illegible]

[illegible]

Acknowledgments

So many people have helped me learn witchcraft that I couldn't possibly name them all, but special thanks to all my beloved teachers and witch-siblings whose hands I have held while we worked magic together, especially JM, MG, AC, MK, CF, BC, MV, CK, and so many others. Many students, colleagues, and co-teachers helped with this book, but special thanks are owed to my beloved student, friend, witch-sister, and co-teacher Monica Herald, whose keen editorial eye was invaluable in transitioning this material from lesson to book.

Table of Contents

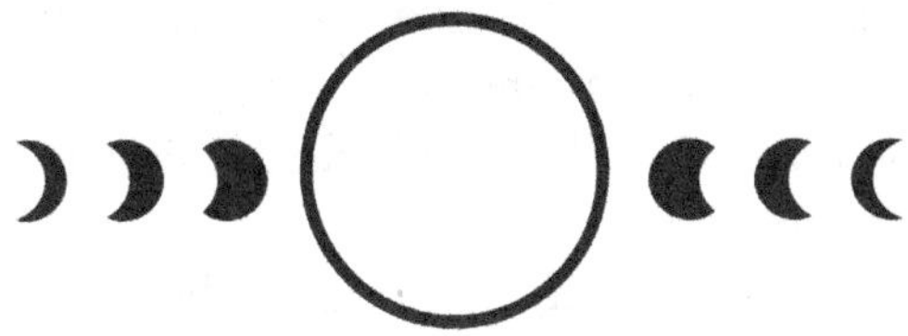

Foreword

After decades of studying and practicing witchcraft, few beginner-focused books both impress me and offer something genuinely new, especially when they are intelligent without talking down to the reader. It comes as no surprise that Sara Mastros accomplishes exactly that with this book. Sara is a witch's witch. Her work speaks to those who live the Craft as a daily reality. She writes with a clarity that arises through practice, trial, spirit encounters that leave a mark, and scholarly study of occultism. Her perspective comes from direct engagement, offering techniques rooted in use, language lived in fully, and insights earned through committed experience.

She acknowledges the importance of structure while moving freely within it, understanding the dynamic balance between discipline and wildness. Her writing displays deep fluency with the forces she engages. It becomes clear she writes from within the work. She is also one of the most brilliant modern occultists I have had the pleasure to know. With a foundation in both the magickal arts and teaching, she brings the clarity of a seasoned educator, shaped by her experience as a high school teacher and university professor.

Introduction to Witchcraft: Thirteen Lessons in the Practice of Magic delivers precisely what it promises, with many welcome surprises. Readers familiar with Sara's earlier works, such as *The Orphic Hymn Grimoire*, *The Big Book of Magical Incense*, and *The Sorcery of Solomon*, will find their expectations met. New readers will discover an excellent starting point. What Sara offers here is both rare and valuable: a beginner's guide that remains richly useful for experienced witches. This is an instructional manual grounded in clarity, respect, and depth; it's the kind of book that draws readers back repeatedly, each visit revealing fresh insight. It provides steady guidance and substantial content, each chapter drawn from lived experience and skillful application.

Sara has crafted something exceptional, a book that blends theory and practice through long, focused dedication. This is magick built through direct engagement. Her imagination and insight shine, but the strength of her work lies in its foundation: years of applied, embodied experience. That depth brings meaning. Much contemporary material feels hollow, assembled from fragments without spirit, will, or tradition. Sara's voice rises above that. It feels immediate, human, and real. She writes with the confidence of someone who knows magick through experience, shaped by study and revealed through direct contact.

Sara understands what great teachers recognize: beginners often struggle due to a lack of clear guidance, not complexity. Magick rests on intuitive understanding, yet benefits immensely from precision. Her teaching succeeds through clear explanation and thoughtful pacing. She encourages personal experience and insight, preparing readers for every stage of the journey. Many new practitioners face their greatest challenges after the ritual, in moments of uncertainty or lapses in will. Sara meets these with practical wisdom.

The scope of this book is impressively expansive for an introductory text, offering a broad and solid foundation. That's because witchcraft, as Sara teaches it, connects deeply with many magickal traditions, being a somewhat magpie practice. From planetary magick to trance, dark mirror work to dream incubation and shapeshifting, she shows how every practice exists in relationship with others. Magick flows between systems, opening space for discovery. Her "fuck around and find out" attitude remains one of my favorite aspects of her work. It is bold, inquisitive, and grounded. She provides a clear entry point that leads toward ceremonial magick, folk traditions, ancestral communion, divination, spirit work, and more. Her rituals and methods offer beginners lasting tools that support long-term practice.

What distinguishes Sara's teaching is her voice. In a culture saturated with surface-level enchantments and quick solutions, her careful, thoughtful work shines. Her convictions matter because they reflect experience. Every spell and technique she offers comes from a practice that is tested, refined, and proven. That clarity, rooted in authenticity, holds real power.

One topic that receives too little attention in modern magickal writing is the central role of imagination and altered states of consciousness. These elements shape my own practice and the work I offer. With imagination and deep awareness, casting, conjuring, and communicating gain essential vitality. Imagination gives form to vision. It molds intention and empowers the will before any ritual begins. This is structured psychic work, not idle daydreaming or delusion.

Reading *Introduction to Witchcraft*, I felt deep resonance with Sara's perspective. Although our crafts differ in form (as they should from witch to witch), we share an understanding of imagination as a power in itself. Her writing explores liminal states, dream logic, and inner theater. She presents magick as a process shaped by direct experience and treats subjective immersion as a purposeful strategy. Her work clearly shows how states of consciousness influence magickal results. I found this deeply affirming. She approaches the inner sensorium as sacred space, not mere decoration.

I often say I can teach someone witchcraft and magick, but I cannot teach them to be a witch. Only they can do that. I firmly believe that witchcraft itself is a spirit. This spirit is to be encountered, befriended, and eventually embodied by the witch. All I can do is reveal the path and trust the student to walk it. This is exactly what Sara offers. Her method allows magick to guide the practitioner's journey, fostering attention to self, to spirit, and to the intuitive rhythm of the work. Her approach blends inspiration with grounded practice. She shows that real magick thrives where will, imagination, and the material world converge. She invites students to explore freely, trust their experiences, and stay anchored in the everyday.

As I said earlier, strong teachers remain rare. Traditionally, witches learned from the spirits themselves. One of the most powerful elements of *Introduction to Witchcraft* is Sara's use of "guest teachers," spirits introduced throughout the book who participate in the student's education. This choice creates a collaborative structure, inviting readers to meet and engage these spirits as active teachers. They appear with presence and intention. Readers are encouraged to forge bonds, learn from them, and include these relationships in their development.

This approach honors the animist heart of witchcraft, sharpening awareness and deepening sensitivity to spiritual contact. The book encourages a fully embodied way of learning, where each guest teacher appears as a genuine presence, not a symbolic archetype. These spirits act as entry points into immersive, lasting spirit work. Sara's thoughtful structure makes this path accessible while preserving its richness. For those who engage sincerely, the spirits introduced here can continue to offer insight well beyond the final chapter.

Whether your practice spans years or is just beginning, this book offers lasting support. Set aside space, open your journal, prepare to get your hands dirty, and learn from a teacher who knows magick through lived experience and shares that knowledge with precision and care. This is the book I needed at the beginning of my journey, and one that still offers value now. You are sure to find the same by the final page.

—Mat Auryn, Author of *Psychic Witch, Mastering Magick,*
and *The Psychic Art of Tarot*

writing explores internal states, dream work, and much more. The present [illegible] by direct experience and [illegible] as a purposeful [illegible] how [illegible] [illegible] more [illegible] sacred space, not merely a location.

I [illegible] some [illegible] and [illegible], but [illegible] Only they can [illegible]. Let us believe that [illegible] itself [illegible] by the words. [illegible] to guide the participant's journey [illegible] attention [illegible] to write [illegible] that [illegible] practice. She knows that real magic thrives where [illegible] imagination and the material world [illegible] she invites students to [illegible] their experiences [illegible] in the everyday.

A [illegible] storytellers [illegible] Traditions [illegible] themselves. One of the most powerful elements of [illegible] teachers [illegible] who participated in the [illegible] education. [illegible] to speak [illegible] with presence and intention. Readers are encouraged to [illegible] sounds, learn from them, and include them in [illegible].

This [illegible] honors the [illegible] in [illegible] writing [illegible] embedded in [illegible] language [illegible] teacher [illegible]

[illegible] spirit [illegible] and make [illegible] possible [illegible] who engage students [illegible] and continue to [illegible] well beyond the final chapter.

Whether your path is [illegible] this book offers [illegible] support [illegible] and learn from a teacher who knows [illegible] experience [illegible] and one that will [illegible] the final page.

[illegible]

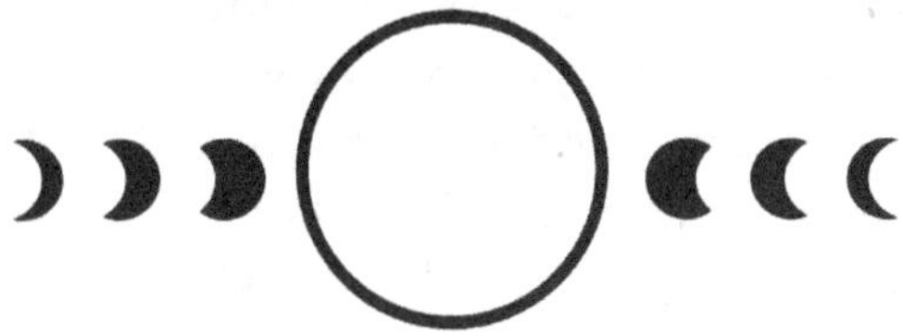

Author's Prologue[1]

I am often asked how I became a witch, but that's not really a question I can answer. As soon as I knew what witches were, I knew a witch was what I was. Since I can't answer that question, instead, I'm going to tell you the story of how I found out I wasn't the only witch in the world. Like most Americans, my first introduction to witchcraft was in fairy tales and other stories. When I was very little, my mother was in graduate school, studying early childhood education. Her specialty was teaching kids to read, and so I had an especially rich exposure to children's literature, including not just the "standard" fairy tales most American children hear, but also a diverse sampling of tales from around the world. I feel very lucky for this.

When I was about ten, my mostly estranged grandfather sent me a gift certificate and a mail-order book catalog for my birthday. There, in the catalog, under nonfiction, was a section titled "Witchcraft." I knew what nonfiction meant; that meant it was true! Alight with excitement, I ran to my mother: "Mom, Mom! Are witches real?"

She blinked a few times. "There are people who think they're witches," she replied.

I showed her the catalog. "Can I get a book about witchcraft?"

"You can get any book you want, but I think you're going to be disappointed with those. Wouldn't you rather get a book of witch folklore?"

"No! I want to be a real witch in the real world!" I declared, and stamped my foot. But, of course, I already was, and so was she.

---

1 Normally I would have called this "Author's Introduction," but since the whole book is called Introduction, that felt weird.

I chose two books—Ray Buckland's classic *Complete Book of Witchcraft* and Paddy Slade's *Encyclopedia of White Witchcraft.* Neither was really what I wanted them to be, but together, they were enough to get me started. The Buckland book was an introduction to American Wicca. It had lots of interesting information in it, but felt altogether lacking in the "real magic" I was hungry for. This was a book on religion, which I had very little interest in. This was especially true since it seemed to me to be a religion invented by and for Christians, with just a thin veneer of fun on top of what seemed more or less identical to what my Christian friends' parents believed and did. I felt deeply cheated! Where were the devils? Where were the ghosts? Where were the fairies and familiars and flights by night? Where was the witchcraft?!? Worst of all, I had to admit my mother had been right!

However, I did learn many valuable things from that Buckland book. To my mind, the most important lessons I took away from it were (1) witchcraft is real, and you can learn to be a witch, but it requires study and hard work, and (2) witchcraft is real, and it's written between the lines of nature and history and stories if you have eyes to see it. Those two lessons have served me very well in the intervening decades. However, I also learned a lot of other lessons that I wish I hadn't, in particular a kind of strictly heteronormative "Lord and Lady" paganism I found a bit baffling. I was instructed that, in order to be a witch, I had to pick one He-God and one She-God, which, even then, seemed like Christian mishegas.

My late mother, like me, was Jewish, and my late father, like me, was Greek. I knew quite a lot of Greek mythology for a ten-year-old, and I also knew that the overwhelming majority of people I encountered thought that I, and everyone I loved, were all going to Hell as punishment for not accepting Christ. Thus, I already knew which gods—the witch gods—were mine. I swore myself to Hermes and Hekate—gods of learning, crossroads, liminality, and magic. Looking back as an adult, I now realize that in choosing the queerest gods I could lay hands on, I completely misunderstood the point of the Lord and Lady of Wicca, but I was pretty much bang on for learning witchcraft.

As I practice it, witchcraft is, in its essence, a crossroads practice, practiced by and for and in solidarity with crossroads people—refugees, thieves, sex workers, heretics, the unhoused, the mentally ill, slaves, Jews, Romani people, strangers, weirdos, queers, freaks, and witches. I have never, for even a moment, regretted swearing myself to them, or to the other powers of the Cosmic Crossroads and the Eternal Witches' Sabbat.

The second book, *Encyclopedia of White Witchcraft*, was also disappointing, but in almost the opposite way. It focused on a very friendly and child-appropriate version of witchcraft similar to what is now called British

Traditional. This book felt real, but didn't teach much. It did, however, have gorgeous full-color illustrations of nature and enrapturing pathworkings (guided imaginings) that woke up things inside me. Whereas the Buckland book had no style but substantive content, this book had the "vibe" I was looking for, but lacked much in the way of systematic teaching. Between the two books, I charted my own path, and never looked back.

However, even more than those two books, the great privilege of my early education in witchcraft was that, from the very beginning, I had someone to witch with. My friend M, whom I met in Girls Scouts, was a half-Jewish nerdy weirdo, just like me! Our interests in magic were different—she was very much into psi and plants, whereas I preferred spells and spirits. But I couldn't have wished for a better partner. Our different focuses meant we both had to learn to "speak each other's language," and we invented our own magics to fill in the gaps in our disappointing books. My number one piece of advice for beginners to witchcraft is that a real co-magician, with whom you can hold hands while working magic, is more valuable than any book or any teacher. Find one.

I have never once regretted those first steps along the Witches' Path. At times, it has been hard. At times, it has hurt. But, it's always, always, always been worth it. I have kept journals of my magic since the very beginning of that road. Doing so has let me look back over those journals, seeing patterns that I missed at the time, reminding myself of how much I've learned, and most importantly, remembering that the amazing life I now live was "just" a wish when I made it. However, perhaps more instructive have been the times when I *didn't* take good notes. I will tell but one funny[2] story about such a time. Partly, this is so that you can learn from my mistakes, but even more than that, so when you make your first spectacularly stupid mistake, you can remind yourself that the road to learning is paved with such mistakes. There's no path to being right that doesn't go through being wrong.

When I was in high school, my co-magician's grandmother had a small cabin near a lake about an hour outside town. It was not in the best of repair, but it was beautiful, and the land was deeply magical. Many of my early magical experiments took place there, especially those with land spirits. At one point, it looked like their family was going to have to sell it, and so they and I enchanted to prevent that. We did a type of traditional folk magic called "nailing down" a property, which involves driving railroad spikes into the

2 It didn't feel funny to me at the time, but I acknowledge that it would have been hilarious if it had happened to someone else!

four corners of the property.[3] Almost twenty years later, that co-magician and I were trying to buy the property from their grandmother, and the entire process was just one snag after another. A quick tarot reading reminded us that we had spiked it. Sadly, because we had not recorded where exactly we put those spikes, we spent a very unpleasant, cold, wet night digging for spikes in the rain. We never found the fourth one; thankfully, my magic had gotten much better in those intervening years, so I managed to undo the spell even without removing that spike, but I do not think beginner me could have done that. So, if you learn nothing else from this story, *please* learn to write things down. Your future self will thank you.

Your Magic Journal

If you take no other practice from this book, I hope you make yourself a magical journal. In this section, I'll provide a little bit of guidance, but over time, you'll work out a magical journal practice that works best for you. My early journals were composition books that I covered in leather. Today, I keep most of my magical journals digitally, but also handwrite talismanic books. The biggest reason I prefer digital journals is that they are keyword searchable, but I also like the ability to insert non-written media (like audio files and pictures), to hyperlink passages to related passages, and to automatically track dates and changes. However, many people prefer to handwrite their magic journals, and that's great too!

Throughout this text, you'll find several "writing prompts" intended to help you connect more deeply with the material. Even if you don't think of yourself as a writer, I encourage you to experiment with them. I've framed them all as writing exercises, but you can, of course, also engage with them in other ways. Consider making audio recordings, drawings, or any other kind of expression. Make your journal your own!

From experience, I have a few tips for keeping your magical journals, especially if you choose to write them by hand. These are things I wish I'd done from the beginning, but implemented slowly, as I learned, over many decades. The first is not to get too precious about it. I always wanted a beautiful, artistic "Book of Shadows" like I saw in movies, and for that reason, was reluctant to write or draw anything until I was sure it was "good enough." Fuck that! Keep two journals, if you want, one for scribbling and sketching

3 You can read two variations of this spell on pages 233–235 of *The Big Book of Magical Incense.*

and recording everything in, and another into which you copy only the best of things. Leave space at the beginning to add a table of contents after you fill the book, and number the pages. Use only the front of every page—that way, you have extra space to go back later and add additional information about how things turned out.

Finally, always date your entries, including the year. When I was a teenager making my own early journals, I couldn't really conceive of the idea that I'd be looking back at them three decades later, trying to figure out when I wrote what, but here I am. On that same note, take the time to remind future-you what you're talking about. Don't just write about the magic, write about the situation in which it is occurred. Over the years, I have discovered helpful patterns by also noting the weather and my general health when I cast.

Finding Your Place in Witchcraft

There are as many kinds of witchcraft as there are witches. Instead of trying to decide what kind of witch you are, I think it's a much better strategy to experiment with many different types of witchcraft, and with non-witchcraft magical styles as well. Choosing a style someone else made for you is, in my opinion, a sucker bet. Take the time to play and experiment and develop your own personal style. Over the years, I've tried many, but by no means all, styles of magic. In this book, I've tried to present you with a sampler of many different magical practices from a variety of styles. However, the only witchcraft I can teach you is mine. Instead of trying to learn to do witchcraft the way I do it, I encourage you to read this book as a structured set of teaching examples, intended as a structural framework upon which to scaffold the construction of your own witchcraft, taught only by your own inner teacher. When you're ready, burn my scaffold down, allowing only that made of your own witchfire to remain.

How This Book Came to Be

As I mentioned, throughout my magical life, I have always had amazing co-magicians, and that meant I was always both learning and teaching others. However, starting around 2001, I began teaching small classes, first in my living room and then, once there were too many people, after hours in at my university's math tutoring center, which I was then managing. I continued teaching individuals and small groups locally wherever I was living. In 2017, I quit my day job as a high school math teacher in order to pursue magic and witchcraft full time. I began teaching more. In March of 2021, in response to COVID-19, I moved classes online. Since they were online anyway, I opened them to non-local people. I was astonished at the response! Almost overnight, I had almost one hundred students. Over the next several years, I reformulated the class to suit its new online medium. This book is the product of that work. At the time of publication, nearly one thousand students have taken this course with me, and their questions, feedback, and magical fellowship has deeply enriched this work. This book is dedicated to all my students and teachers, both past and future, and to the divine Teacher of Teachers, who has always lit my path.

How To Learn with This Book

Obviously, you are welcome to use this book however you like. However, it was organized with certain uses in mind. If you have not yet done so, go look over the table of contents now, and see what catches your attention. If you like, go look at those sections now. The ability to learn with ease and joy is the natural state of all sentient creatures. However, we live in a culture that doesn't like it when people learn too much, and so many of us have been trained not to learn.

If you prefer a steady and methodical approach, just keep reading. Personally, I am a big believer in the traditional method of studying a magical text, which is to copy it out, word for word, in your own handwriting. I often do this when studying a new magical text, but my experience is that most students are unwilling to even try this method. You do you.

On behalf of the great Teacher of Teachers, whose student I am, I promise you this: the only teacher you need is your own intuition, your Inner Teacher. Many witches never have a living human teacher. I had been witching for decades before I found a geniune teacher. However, that is not an ideal experience! It is vastly easier to learn in person, with a human teacher whose breath you can hear and whose hand you can hold. But if you can't do that, books like this are also good.

Having taught this material to hundreds of students,[4] I believe that everyone learns best on their own path. However, for most people, I find the path that best balances maximizing learning with minimizing hard work is to read the whole

4 And as an experienced mathematics teacher with thousands of past students.

book, in order, at a rate of one chapter per month, taking notes and doing the exercises as they go. That's why I arranged this book as I did.[5] However, some people (particularly readers who are not strictly beginners) will do better skimming through the whole book, pausing to investigate whatever strikes their fancy.

Risk takers, nerds, and those who enjoy games might try opening the book to random sections, and building their own system of witchcraft by figuring out how to understand the material in the order it is presented. This style of reading more closely mimics the experience of being "spirit taught" instead of learning from a human teacher. Learning in this less controlled way is harder than reading the book in order, but if you're into it, it's also a lot more fun. I recommend combining both methods.

A Warning

As a person religiously devoted to the goddess of learning, I have never in my entire life regretted learning anything, but I am given to understand that is not most people's experience. Learn at your own pace, in your own way, in whatever way seems best to you. Learning should be fun! If it isn't, slow down, and write about what you've been reading. Learning can sometimes be frustrating, but it shouldn't hurt. If it does hurt, stop reading until you can explain to yourself what happened and make an informed decision about whether to continue.

To the best of my ability as a witch, a writer, and a teacher, with the help of many gods, angels, demons, ghosts, and other spirits, as well as the help of many human students, colleagues, and editors, I have written this book to light a magical fire in you. But once your witchfire is ignited, you'll need to keep feeding and tending it. The exercises in this book will help you strengthen your ability to do that. For beginners, I recommend choosing only those exercises that seem most appealing. The beginning of learning is curiosity. Curiosity is your best guide to learning. For more experienced witches, I suggest you lean into those exercises that seem the worst. Sadly, while the beginnings of learning are on the other side of play, deep learning is often on the other side of work.

Keep track of your experiences with the exercises as if they are experiments (which they are). Monitor your progress. However, don't push yourself too hard. These are gentle exercises intended for beginners. They shouldn't hurt while you're doing them, and you should not be experiencing any sort of hangover or recovery period that is not cured by drinking water, eating a meal, and taking a nap.

---

5 Readers who have already been my student in this material will notice that I've slightly rearranged some things. This is owing to the differences between text and video media.

In my experience, most magical hangovers are due to dehydration and/or sleep deprivation. If you are having magic hangovers, slow down; drink more water; get several full nights of healthy, uninterrupted sleep; and give yourself time to adjust before doing more. In rare cases, you may experience some unpleasant side effects, especially if you:

* are very dehydrated
* are very sleep deprived
* are an adolescent
* are newly on artificial hormones (including hormonal birth control)
* are intoxicated
* have a predisposition to mania or psychosis
* have ever had a grand mal seizure
* ignore my directions

Specifically, you may have a cluster of unpleasant side effects including something I call the "too-much-magic-crazies," which are sometimes also called "light sickness," "kundalini syndrome," or "qi gong madness." In extreme cases, the too-much-magic-crazies can look like spirit possession, but it almost never is.

If any of the above criteria apply to you, especially if more than one applies, it's best to use "the buddy system" and have a caring, stable grown-up in the room to babysit you. They don't need to be a witch, but you should explain to them what's going on. All that being said, I have done magic while simultaneously doing/being all of the above "bad" things, and many times suffered the too-much-magic-crazies. Personally, I have never regretted it, even when it sucked. Crazy is a harsh but very effective teacher.

For most humans, the too-much-magic-crazies typically begin as a sinus pressure headache accompanied by some combination of muscle twitching/spasms, a feeling of shooting/tingling up and down your spine, a feeling of being too hot and itchy, or confusing or racing thoughts that make it hard to focus.

For some lucky people, there is an early warning sign that can help you avoid even these symptoms: you may begin to unexpectedly weep even though you are not sad.

I am a such crier, but for many, many years, I did not know it was a warning sign. I was embarrassed by it, because I thought I was just a whiny baby who didn't want to work. When I cried, I just pushed harder. (Bad idea.)

The first time I did it in front of a genuine magic teacher, she explained, and called them "tears of power." Now that I recognize them, I have never once caught the too-much-magic-crazies, because they tell me when to slow down.

If you keep pushing through the early symptoms, the pain can get much worse, the confusion can slip into hallucinations, and you might even have a seizure or a full-blown psychotic episode.

However, for almost everyone, even if you get the too-much-magic-crazies, things will resolve themselves in a day or two. Here are some things that can help the natural healing process:

* Get out of the sun and turn indoor lights off, or at least down.
* In the shade, lay directly on the earth, ideally with a lot of skin touching the ground. Do not do this under strong sunlight.
* Drink at least sixteen ounces of room temperature water.
* Eat some protein, fat, and salt.
* Take a sensible dose of iron and calcium supplements. Do not megadose!
* Take a cool bath in salt water.
* If you don't have a bathtub, take a shower and/or soak your feet in cool salt water.
* Make direct skin-to-skin contact with a trusted, stable, compassionate adult human who knows you're learning witchcraft. Seriously, call a friend or family member, and tell them you are not ok and need them to come over immediately.
* If you do not have such a human, a combination of talking to such a human online or over the phone while in direct contact with a mature tree can also help. Don't try to stabilize with a living creature much smaller than a human, like a dog or cat or potted plant. If it's too much for your body to process, it almost is certainly too much for their much smaller body.

Most importantly, however, *go to sleep!* Sleeping is the human equivalent of rebooting a computer to fix things. If you don't feel better after a full night (or day) of sleep, consult a competent witch or other magician. In an emergency, if you have no one else to consult, and you've already tried to sleep it off, you or your buddy may email me at Sara@WitchLessons.com, but, obviously, I cannot promise to be on-call all the time.

Learning Circles

I believe that, for beginners, this book is best studied with at least one study partner. As Talmud[6] says, studying alone just makes you stupider. Is there a witchy book club in your area? Perhaps a local bookstore that would help you organize one? Who in your life would think it was fun to study witchcraft? Who in your life would think it was fun to *pretend* to study witchcraft? If you are learning with a partner, course, book club, or learning circle, I recommend learning at a pace of one lesson per month. Read the chapter. As you go, write down any questions you have. Ask your learning circle your questions, and try to answer theirs.

Try the exercises and discuss them with your learning circle. Did that help you answer any of your questions? If not, can you think of an experiment you can perform that might help? Discuss. Take notes. At the end of the month, move on to the next chapter. As you read on, I believe things will become clearer.

A Solo Wishing Rite Before Beginning to Learn

Although I wrote this spell specifically for this book, it could be easily adapted for use with any textbook. With more thought and care, it can also be adapted for almost any purpose.

Go outside, at night, preferably somewhere you can see stars; take this book with you. If you absolutely cannot go outside, you can do this inside, ideally while looking out a window. If you cannot see the sky, for whatever reason, to the best of your ability, believe that you are outside under a starry sky. You may want to look up what is happening in the sky above you to help your imagination.

Spend thirteen minutes considering what you hope to get out of this book. Condense your wish down to a single, clear, evocative sentence like "I wish to learn real magic" or "I wish to know I am a witch" or "I wish to hone my craft" or "I wish to meet a co-magician" or "I wish to know this book as a living creature, a spirit teacher of witchcraft." Hold the book close to your heart.[7] Close your eyes, and take seven long, slow, deep breaths. Turn your head to the sky, spin around in a circle three times counterclockwise, open your eyes, and stare intently at whichever star they first fall upon. Speak your wish out loud.

---

6 Talmud Berachot 63a

7 Literally if you have a physical book, metaphorically if an ebook.

Author's Prologue

A Group Wishing Rite for Learning Together

In just a moment, I'll show you how to expand the single-player ritual you just learned into a group practice. As you read, think about how each part of this ritual mirrors the single-player ritual, and try to formulate some theories about a general method of translating rituals from solitary to group and vice versa.

Basic Instructions for Group Ritual

Before I talk about this specific rite, I'm going to give a little bit of advice on group ritual, more generally. This advice, like this book, is intended for beginners. Experienced magicians should adapt everything to suit their own needs, styles, and skillsets.

Unless your group has been working magic together for a long time, it's generally better to have at least a general outline in mind before beginning. Spontaneous ritual is very fun and exciting, but it's also a recipe for getting into trouble. And, certainly, witches would never want to be thought of as troublemakers. Right?

Groups of beginners who do not know each other should talk through the whole ritual before starting and get everyone's enthusiastic consent. Although it's not always necessary for very short rituals like the one below, it's generally a good practice to rehearse a ritual at least once before working it for real.

Some groups might want to choose a "magic safeword" that any participant can call at any time to immediately put a stop to all magic in progress. Personally, I am not a fan of this practice, because the secret subtext to any magical safeword is "Magic isn't real!"

As you'll learn in this book, witch-power moves like a wave through a fluid. If you just hold still, it will usually settle down on its own. However, slapping the surface of the lake in an attempt to swat out the waves is counterproductive, especially for people who don't know what they're doing.

Instead, I recommend a ritual safeword (like "Stop!" or "Pause!") that anyone can yell out at any time to tell everyone to stop pushing, keep quiet, hold still, and be chill until the person who called "Stop!" tells you it's ok to talk. Once everyone feels the magical current has settled down, discuss what happened before deciding what to do next. The most typical decision in most groups is to either close the ritual down and depart, or try again immediately, but you can decide on whatever you want.

As I said, all of these suggestions are best practices for group ritual, but the ritual below is quite simple, and unlikely to cause any problems. Don't be so casual about it as to be disrespectful, but don't take it so seriously that you never get around to actually doing the magic.

Group Wishing Ritual

Each of you should probably have already done the solo ritual before working this one together, but that is not strictly necessary. Go outside together, at night, preferably somewhere you can see stars. If you absolutely cannot go outside, you can do this inside. If you cannot see the sky, for whatever reason, to the best of your ability, imagine that you are outside under a starry sky. In theory, this ritual can be done over a live video chat instead of in person, but that is a relatively sophisticated magic that is probably outside the skill of most beginners. However, I encourage you to try virtual ritual now, and also after you finish the whole book. I think you'll be able to feel a difference in effectiveness.

Spend some time discussing what you hope to get out of learning together. As in the single-player ritual above, condense your wish down to a single sentence. For example, "We come together to learn and grow" or "Power shared is power doubled!"[8] Practice saying your wish out loud together thirteen times, to make sure you're all "on beat" together.

Hold hands in a circle, facing inward. Close your eyes, and take seven long, slow, deep breaths together. Spin around in a circle three times counterclockwise, open your eyes, and stare intently at the person opposite you. Speak your wish out loud.

If you wish, you can deepen the effect of this ritual by repeating it at every meeting. If you're not up for all that, you could just join hands and repeat your wish three times. To "level up" this ritual, repeat the wish thirteen times while focusing on sending trust, love, and witchpower out through your right hand, and accepting the same from your partner through your left.[9] If you're not sure how to do that, just pretend for now; you'll learn in more detail in Chapter Seven. As you learn and grow together, adapt the ritual to suit your own needs, style, and rapidly expanding skill.

Writing Prompt: Wishing Ritual

If you wish to go deeper, before or after performing either spell, try to answer the following questions. The goal is not to understand why I wrote it the way I did. Rather, the goal is to understand why *you* are doing it that way. For some of the questions, an answer might be immediately clear. For others, you might need to spend some time imagining an answer. If you're really stuck, try dreaming on them.

---

8 Doubled for two people. Tripled for three or more. Even though it's tempting, don't do *"power shared is power squared,"* as power is generally measured as a percent.

9 This can be quite emotional for some people because it "activates your heart circuit," a phrase that will make more sense after Chapter Seven. If you feel like crying, do so.

* Why at night?
* Why hold the book close to your heart? / Why hold hands?
* Why thirteen?
* Why seven breaths?
* Why three turns?
* Why counterclockwise?

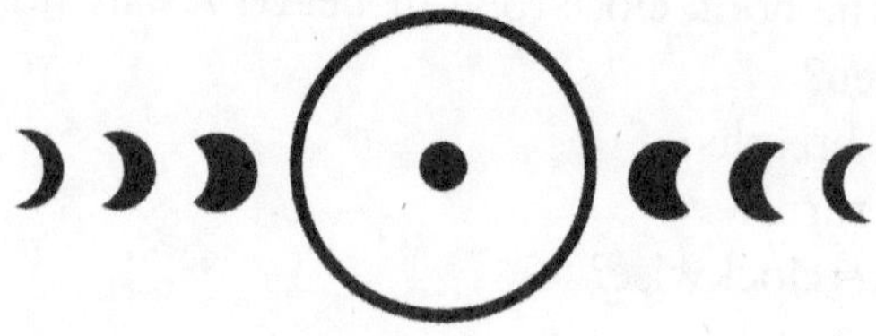

CHAPTER ONE:

A Spell Is a Wish the Will Makes

In this chapter, we'll begin to explore what witchcraft and magic are, and experiment with a few simple forms of magic, including color magic, candle magic, and petitions. In order to encourage you to read with a beginner's mind, I have written some pieces of this chapter as if I were teaching a small child. Other sections, I have written adult to adult, trying to remind you of things you knew when you were a child.

Make Believe as a Magical Tool

I am not the magic pope—I don't believe magic has rules, and I'm not here to try to make you believe anything. That said, I encourage you to approach this book, particularly the exercises, *as if* you believe magic is real and this book is good teaching on magic, and simply see what happens. Stop reading when you stop having fun.

As beginners, it is most important to approach learning as little children do: as a side effect of play. In this book, the primary kind of play we'll engage in is "Make Believe"—a kind of imaginative "playing pretend" that children (and adults!) use to make sense of the world. When we Make Believe, we set aside our fears, doubts, and shame, and explore things with an open mind, an open heart, and a sense of fun.

Make Believe is one primary method by which human children learn to be sentient. Theorists of learning categorize make believe into three primary kinds. In small children, who are still learning how to play, these different kinds of make believe tend to develop in stages. However, as adult magicians, we are generally mixing all of the kinds together.

* *Non-literal actions* are a kind of make believe play about what objects are. Many children[10] are around two or three when they start to really get good at this.
  * Simple: Substitute one object for another similar one. For example, make believe an apple is a tomato.
  * Complex: Pretend your bed is a magic carpet you can ride into the Dream Place.
* *Socio-dramatic play,* also called "role play," is make believe about who you are. This can be individual (you are the only "character" in your Make Believe) or collaborative (multiple characters). Playing make believe with other people is fun, but you can also engage in collaborative socio-dramatic play by yourself by simply playing more than one role. Playing with dolls and action figures is a common example of this, which we'll discuss in great detail in Chapter Two, when we learn to make and work with magic dolls.
  * Simple: Pretend you are in a simple situation that you have experienced.
  * Intermediate: Pretend you are in a situation that you have never experienced.
  * Complex: Pretend you are someone else in a situation that you have experienced.
  * Advanced: Pretend you are someone else in a situation that you have never experienced. Many children are around five when they begin to develop a sophisticated understanding of other minds sufficient for this kind of play.
* *Fantastical play* is imagining that the world is different than it is. Most kinds of magical play are rooted in fantastical play.
  * Simple: Pretend trees can talk and you can understand them.
  * Complex: Pretend you don't have a body. Pretend bodies don't exist, and people (humans and otherwise) are simply constantly changing fields of information.

Please set your fear, shame, and doubt aside, and come play Make Believe with me as we learn magic together!

---

10 Delays in the emergence of make believe play are often used as an early diagnostic for autism, although this is by no means definitive, and many autists (including myself) engage in deep, complex, rich make believe as both children and adults.

WTF Are We Even Talking About When We Say "Magic"?

Even though this is the first question we will tackle in this book, it is, in many ways, the most difficult one. Because this book is intended for beginners, I do not feel it necessary to get too bogged down in technicalities here at the beginning. We will revisit this question several times over the course of this book, and hopefully our shared understanding will grow and change over that time. After all, if your understanding of magic is the same on page one as it is on page three hundred and forty then what will you really have learned from this book? However, just to make sure we're all on the same page, I'd like to take a few minutes to talk just a little bit of theory.

The first thing you need to keep in mind at all times when reading this book (or any other book on magic) is that we Anglophones have spent almost the entire history of the English language murdering anyone who dared to speak or write about magic. For that reason, English is very much lacking a robust technical vocabulary for discussing magic. As we shake off our old cultural shackles, and begin to more openly engage with things that most cultures never stopped doing, we are beginning to develop such a vocabulary, but it is not yet fixed. What that means is that, when I speak with other magicians about magic in English, I often find that we all have our own idiosyncratic ways of talking about things that we've cobbled together ourselves, and the first step in any kind of collaboration is to hammer out a shared vocabulary.

I'm not the magic police, and I'm not here to lay down the law about what witchcraft is or how you should practice. What I am, however, is a teacher of magic and witchcraft, and I take that role, which I consider to be a sacred calling from the gods of magic,[11] very, very seriously. As part of my role as teacher, I want to make sure we're all on the same page about what we're talking about as we learn together. Before you read my definitions, however, I'd like you to spend some time thinking about your own.

---

11 My personal call to teaching comes from Thoth Hermes, Teacher of Teachers, in whose service I taught mathematics for decades before I quit to teach witchcraft. My call to teach magic, specifically, comes from She of the Krokopeplos. You'll get to know both of those spirits by the end of this book.

Writing Prompt: WTF Are You Doing Here?

Set a timer for fifteen minutes. During that time, write[12] continuously, even if you're just free-associating words. Answer the following questions:

* Why are you reading this book?
* What do you expect to learn from it?
* What is witchcraft to you, and why are you interested in it?
* What is magic to you? Why do you care about it?
* What is the difference between the words "witchcraft" and "magic"?

What Is Magic?

The British occultist Aleister Crowley (1875–1947) defined *magick*[13] as "the Science and Art of causing Change to occur in conformity with Will." Personally, I find this definition absurd. What human actions are not intended to cause change in conformity with will? A more traditional English definition, historically, would be something like: "Rituals or actions intended to subdue or manipulate supernatural beings and forces in order to have some benefit from them." While I like this definition better, I still have some issues with it, particularly with the coercive implication and because of the word "supernatural." I do not believe in the existence of the supernatural. I believe visible (to humans) nature and invisible (to humans) nature to be one beautiful, complex, coherently interconnected thing—the only thing. I believe that the best way to understand invisible nature (what some might call the "supernatural") is close observation of visible nature.

When I use the word *magic* in this book, I mean "a body of practices and techniques by which human beings, often in alliance with nonhuman spirits,[14]

---

12 As I mentioned in the introduction, your journal doesn't need to exclusively be written. You can also draw, record audio or video, etc. However, for simplicity, I'm going to always talk about them as written.

13 He added the *k* to distinguish "real" magic from stage magic. This spelling has largely fallen out of favor today but is still used by many magicians (magickians).

14 When I use the word *spirit,* I mean any coherent being capable of communication. I am a spirit. You are a spirit. A tree is a spirit. The wind is a spirit. The great god Dionysus is a spirit. The planet Mars is a spirit. Indeed, as an animist, I believe everything, even the pile of old tires in the alley behind my house, is a spirit.

direct the action of insensible[15] forces in order to bring about observable[16] change in the world." In magic, we engage in specific activities (often called "rituals") here in the observable world that, through an occult (unobservable) chain of causation, produce seemingly unconnected changes in the world. These occult (hidden) chains of causation are, to me, the defining characteristic of magic.

In order to be able to perceive these hidden chains of causation, some kinds of magic are done in a non-normal states of consciousness (trance). As we move through this book together, you'll learn many different kinds of magical states of consciousness, but for now, I'm going to call them all generically "magical space/time/consciousness."

Entering Magical Space/Time/Consciousness

As you doubtless understand from fairy tales and other depictions, magic is often cast from a special "frame of reference" that includes delineating a special "temple" built in both space and time.[17] In fiction, this is usually depicted as a circle, which is drawn around the caster and then unwound in the other direction when the magic is over. That's certainly one way to do it, and you'll learn all about that method in Chapter Seven.

For now, we'll learn only the simplest way to enter magical space/time, which is to occupy the Sacred Center. More importantly, you'll begin to learn about the special states of consciousness used in magic. In these, too, there is variety. From folklore, we learn some of the most common: visionary experience (like seeing spirits in a crystal ball), heavy drug trance (think of a seeress swaying above a brazier of sacred smoke), fully out-of-body travel (like a witch riding a broom to the magic sabbat). You'll learn more methods like that later in the book, but for now, let's begin with simpler and lighter trances.

---

15 I don't mean *nonsensical*. Magical actions make sense. I mean invisible to normal human senses.

16 Whenever I use words like *visible* or *observable*, I mean "appreciable by any sense." What is visible to one person might be invisible to another.

17 If you're not sure what it means to build a temple in time, I recommend the classic article by the Jewish theologian Abraham Heschel, "Shabbat as a Sanctuary in Time."

Our First Trance: Childlike Wonder, a.k.a. Make Believe

For most people, the easiest trance state to learn for magic is the one we'll be working with in this chapter: the open-minded and playful state of childlike wonder called Make Believe. I strongly encourage you to approach all these exercises in that frame of mind. Very little will block your ability to do magic as powerfully as shame or embarrassment at the things you are doing. Let go of your shame and play like a child. Play like no one is watching. As my friend and co-magician, the poet Simon Zealot, says:

> "*We dance to grow stronger.*
> *We play to finish the Work.*
> *That Game is all that matters,*
> *disregard if you're a jerk.*"

Exercise: Wander the Wild

This is among the most important exercises in this book, and you should be doing it as often as you can manage. It will take you about three hours and is excellent to do with co-magicians, children, dogs, or other company, but it is also good to do by yourself. Before you jump in, you'll need to do a little planning. First, you need to choose where to go. Ideally, pick the wildest place you reasonably can go. However, it's better to go to a local park tomorrow than to a state park in a month. Obviously, the best thing to do is to frequently visit a local wild place, and also sometimes travel further. If you're outdoorsy, feel free to wander far afield, but I do this in the park, and that's more than sufficient.

Before beginning, you will need to gather some supplies. At minimum, you'll probably want a backpack, a trash bag, a full water bottle, an empty water bottle, a notebook, a pencil or pen, several plastic bags,[18] a permanent marker, a pocket knife, and comfy shoes. You might want other things.

Head into the wilds. Put your phone in your bag and set it to "do not disturb." Spend at least an hour wandering, but *don't get lost.* Gather things that seem cool, like feathers, sticks, pretty rocks, dirt from special locations, pine cones, leaves, berries, mushrooms, or whatever else catches your attention. This is what the bags are for; label them with the marker. If you find trash, pick it up to dispose of properly.

---

18 They don't need to be new or even all that clean. This is good for bags you wouldn't want to put food in, but don't need to throw out yet.

As you wander, begin to hum or sing a song about finding the magic heart of the wild. This is a song every human knows, but it might take you a while to figure it out. It will sound different every time you sing it. Just hum, and keep humming, until it blossoms into a song. It might have words, or it might not. If it has words, they'll probably describe the things you are seeing, a sort of series of landmarks that guide your way. Keep wandering and singing until you find a magical place. Don't stress about it, just stop where your song naturally comes to a stop.

Sit for at least half an hour. In the notebook, list everything you see. Do your best to identify species, but *do not* look things up. Stay in the moment. It's ok to give things your own names; you can look up their proper names later (for example, as a kid, I called sparrows "brown bush birds"). Sketch some pictures if you want, but *do not* take photos. When you're done listening, pour out a little water as an offering to the creatures (seen and unseen) you've shared this space with.

You can also do this exercise in crowded or loud environments, but it's slightly more dangerous because there's a lot more going on in a small area. Pay attention!

Exercise: Standing at the Sacred Center

The goal of this exercise is to change your frame of mind so that you stand at the exact center of the universe.

Begin by getting up and moving around for a few minutes, so you are fully present in your body. The first few times you do it, this exercise is easiest when standing. Whenever you feel fully "aerated," stand up as straight as you can, close your eyes, and take several deep breaths. Make a fist with your right hand and put it on your sternum, thumb side up. Put your left hand over it, palm inward. Push hard. Say or sing an *"ahhhhhhh"* sound loud enough to feel it vibrate in your chest. Do this several times, holding the sound as long as you can, until you are fully out of air.

Next, reach upward, as high as you can, with your palms facing up, and say or sing *"eeeeeeeeeeeee"* in a higher pitch. Feel it vibrate in your head. Do so several times, holding the sound as long as you can, until you are fully out of air.

Sweep your hands down, palms down, until they are as low as you can get them while keeping your back straight. Push your heels down into the ground; try to keep your weight off your toes. Bend your knees a little, but do not bend at the waist or lean forward. Say or sing *"ohhhhhhhhhh"* in a deep tone. Feel it vibrate in your lower torso. Do this several times, holding the sound as long as you can, until you are fully out of air.

Reach your hands up, and when your arms have reached their maximum extension, keep reaching with your mind and spirit and everything you have.

Reach up, up, up to the depths of space. Reach up, up, up to the "edges" of the universe. And when you have reached up as far as you can, vibrate *"eeeeeeeee"* and yank down the energy you find there, bright, sparkling and scintillating like starlight. If you can't feel the energy, that's ok. Just pretend that you can. Energy sensitivity grows with practice.

Continue pulling it down, down, down through the top of your head and down, down, down through your chest and down into your hips. It should "paint" your spine, going down through the center of your body, leaving a trail of starlight. Down through your legs and down, down, down into the center of the earth, where you should fling the energy as hard as you can.

Now, reach down, down, down as far as you can (keep your back straight) and vibrate *"ohhhhhhh"* as deep and rumbly as you can. Grab some of the energy you find there, cool and calm and still as the deep, dark sea. Pull it up, up, up through the earth, through your feet, up your legs, through your pelvis, and up into your chest. It should "paint" this energy through your lower body. Leave it in your core, where it mingles with the starlight already there. Put your hands on your chest again, and push. Vibrate *"ahhhhhhhhhh"* there, and let the two mingle. Unless you already have a lot of experience with energy work, this should feel like hard work. You should be tired. If it is easy, you're doing it wrong.

Next, repeat the three sounds up and down a few times, in different orders. Try all the combinations. However, the last one you do should be *"eeeee, ahhhh, ohhhh"*[19]—Above, Here, Below.

Plant yourself as firmly into the ground as you can with that last sound. Rest all your weight on your heels, and none on your toes. Now, reach out in the four directions: front and back, left and right. Just like you did with up and down, push out and pull in, collecting yourself very firmly at the center. There are no fixed vocalizations for the directions, but you might try other sounds until you find something that feels right for you.

Finally, open your eyes, and be confident in the knowledge that you stand at the omphalos, the Sacred Center of the universe, and that from this position, your will makes things happen. To release, simply feel the energy you have gathered sink into your body and come to rest. You're actually always in this state; you simply need to release your awareness of it.

It is a good idea, when you are new, to practice this exercise every day, if

---

19 This is normally written in Greek: iota, alpha, omega = IAO = ιαο. In addition to representing the sounds *"eeee ahh ohh,"* this is also a divine name used commonly in ancient Greek sorcery. Most scholars believe it to be a corruption of the Hebrew Most Holy Name, יהוה (YHVH). For now, concentrate on it simply as sounds—shapes made out of your breath.

possible. However, do not do this exercise more than twice in a row without taking a break to be "in the real world" for at least half an hour.

Practice until you can do the whole thing in under three minutes, while still putting attention and effort into each step and keeping them all discrete. Eventually, you should be able to do it in a single breath, but that takes practice. Eventually, learn to do it without moving (so you can do it stealthily in public).

Colors of Magic

In the previous exercise, you experimented with three different vibrations: *eeeeeee, ahhhhhh,* and *ohhhhh*. Speech is a shape made with the vibration of our breath. Similarly, color is made from the vibrations of light.

You can choose to understand colors as colors of energy, as spirits of the colors, as "elements" of magic which combine in complex ways,[20] or in any other way that works for you. It doesn't really matter. They are simply colors. If you cannot see colors, I am sorry. The rest of the chapter might be less interesting for you than others. However, seeing colors is not a necessary skill for magicians; read about it, but don't worry about it and just move on. We will work with lots of other kinds of magic throughout the course. Try to focus on the descriptions of the colors and how they feel in your body. It doesn't actually matter if you can perceive them with your senses; the colors are "real" whether you can see them or not. As I've said before, there is a common misconception that magic relies on your belief in it. That is simply not true. Just like colors still exist, and are still accessible to color-blind (or fully blind) magicians, spirits and energy exist and are accessible whether you can perceive them or not, whether you believe in them or not.

What follows is narrated by our first guest teacher, a seven-year-old witch named Sofia Solomon; she's one of many teachers you'll meet as you move through the course. Each of them teaches magic from a different frame of reference; Sofia teaches Make Believe. That's how easy magic is; kids do it all the time. Do your best to be in a childlike state of mind while reading this. The child-mind trance is, for most people, the easiest magical trance to obtain. In my opinion, this is the best framework from which to learn color magic, and it is a good choice for most kinds of magic.

We'll go back to a more grown-up style of learning after Sophia teaches us the color spectrum. As we progress through the following chapters, we'll

20 This is usually how I think about it.

try out a wide variety of magical styles, ranging from "childlike delight" to "Paleolithic shaman covered in red ochre and bear fat"[21] to "pretentious wizard in an ivory tower."[22] I love them all! A skilled witch can work in any style, but everyone naturally gravitates toward some over others. If childlike magic isn't for you, that's ok. We'll do lots of other kinds. But I urge you to give it a try. It's very powerful. Be sure to answer the questions and make believe the prescribed imaginings as you go. It might help your play if you take the notes for this section using crayons or markers. I encourage you to draw pictures to illustrate each color. Remember, *none* of this is a metaphor; it is important to imagine everything as carefully and in as much detail as you can, exactly as I've written it. Feel free to experiment with your own additions, but do not make changes until you understand *why* I've asked you to imagine what I did.

Sophia Solomon's Seven Color Imaginings

Red Magic

Red is the first color in the rainbow. Red smells like chilies and tastes like strawberries or apples or blood. Red is the color of blood, and also of Valentine's Day hearts. Red is the color that the center of the earth is, where it's so hot that rocks melt! It sometimes feels hot and angry like a volcano. Other times, it's exciting and fun, like riding a bike very fast! Red magic is very strong; it works hard to keep people safe. That's why fire trucks and stop signs are red. Red magic fights for good and protects people, like a superhero or a knight. When I do red magic, I imagine that I'm riding on a giant red dragon! The dragon is breathing fire. Can you feel the heat rising up from their back? Do you feel the deep rumble of their breath between your legs? Riding a dragon is what red magic feels like! When you want to be strong, so that you can fight for good and protect people, use fire-breathing red magic!

Orange Magic

Orange comes next. Marigolds are a kind of flower that are orange. Did you know that flowers are fancy costumes that plants wear so that bees will come visit them? Bees carry messages from one plant to another, so flowers always want a visit! Bumblebees have orange butts, and they know all the best stories. Orange is a funny color. It's the color of ideas and making new things! It feels warm like a cozy blanket, and it tastes like pumpkin or citrus or curry

21 This is my favorite.

22 This is what people think my favorite is, because I write a lot of books about it.

or carrots. Orange is the color of construction cones. "Construction" means building new things. Making new things that didn't exist before is an orange sort of thing to do. Orange magic is very fast, it goes *buzzzzzoooooom,* like a flash! Orange magic helps you think and move and learn.

When I do orange magic, I like to pretend that I am a fairy, dressed all in orange, riding on a bumblebee. I can fly fast, and I know all the best stories. Can you imagine riding on a bumblebee? The bee's whole body buzzes while you ride them; can you feel the orange magic *zzzzzzzz* just below your belly button? Try saying "Bumblebee Buzz Belly Button" as fast as you can! When you want to make up a story, when you want to go fast, and when you want to learn things, use buzzy orange magic.

Yellow Magic

Yellow is the next color. It's the color of sunshine, and it makes people happy and healthy! Yellow feels warm like sunshine, and it tastes and smells like honey and pears. Did you know that flowers eat sunshine like people eat food? They turn it into nectar, and the bees use that to make honey! When I do yellow magic, I imagine that I'm like a plant, and I eat sunshine too! I feel it all warm, shining down on me from the sun, and eat it, so it's in my tummy, where it still shines!

Outside in the sun, close your eyes, and put your face up to the sun with your mouth open. Imagine that you're a sunflower, tall and straight and reaching up to the sun to drink. What is your sunflower name? Feel the warmth of the sunshine. Taste it. It tastes like honey and sunflower seeds and butter and egg yolks. Feel it radiate down your throat and into your tummy, making you happy and healthy. Feel the warmth of the sun in the exact center of your body. That's what yellow magic feels like!

When you are sad or sick or tired, you can use yellow magic to help make you feel better. If you practice eating sunshine, like a sunflower, you'll learn how to shine, and then you can help other people be happy and healthy too!

Green Magic

Green is the next color. Green is the color of gardens. Gardens are beautiful and full of plants and insects and birds and life! If you had a garden, what would you want to grow in it?

Everything works together to make the garden beautiful; the plants and trees, and the birds and bees, and the rabbits and me! Green smells like plants and feels like love. How do you feel about your favorite people? Do you feel the tug in your heart? That's what green feels like!

One of my favorite green plants is clover. Clovers have three green leaves with white splotches that make a triangle. Some clovers have four leaves that make a square. Four-leaf clovers are especially lucky. Clovers grow in big patches, with lots of little plants all connected to each other. Together a patch of clover is very strong. You can even walk on it, and it won't get hurt! Each clover is connected to the other ones, but they're all different! Next time you see clovers, look hard until you find a four-leafed one—the white splotches will make a square.

When I do green magic, I like to pretend that I'm a clover. I feel my leaves all big and green, soaking up sunshine. I feel my roots that go down into the ground and connect to other clovers. I feel love in my heart for all my clover friends. When you want to make new friends, or you want people to like you, remember what it's like to be a clover and feel green love in your heart. When you want to be lucky, try being a four-leaf clover!

Blue Magic

Blue is the next color. Blue is the color that the sky is. Blue feels very calm, and very big and powerful, like the sky. Blue feels like soft wind, and it smells like rain. My fairy godmother says that Sophia, the wisdom goddess who has my name, wears a blue cloak, because she's a Queen of the Sky. When I do blue magic, I imagine that I'm Queen[23] of the Sky, flying through the air like Superman. I am wearing a big blue cape, and it flutters around in the wind. I hold my back very straight, and my head up high. I streeeeeeetch my neck up, up, up. What sound do you think the Queen of the Sky sings? Hum along with her! Can you feel it hum in your throat? That's blue magic!

Blue magic is good for helping you be nice to people, even when you're angry. It's also good for helping you be calm when you are worried or scared. Blue magic can also help you go to sleep and have good dreams. Whenever you need blue magic, remember what it was like to be a Queen of the Sky.

Indigo Magic

Indigo is the next color in the rainbow, and it's a secret color that not everyone knows the name of, even though they can see it. Indigo is dark blue, like the sky at twilight, or a thunderstorm, or very dark blue jeans. It is named after a plant that makes dark blue dye. Indigo feels like waiting and it smells like fruit.

---

23 Because we will later build on this exercise to connect with specific goddesses, I encourage everyone, regardless of sex or gender, to imagine themselves as queen (not king) of the sky, but you do you.

It tastes like blueberries or blue corn. Indigo is the color that time would be, if time were a thing that had a color. Indigo is the taste of water. Indigo is the sensation of being immersed in natural living water, like a lake or the rain.[24]

When I do indigo magic, I imagine that I'm a wizard—in a long indigo robe, with a pointy indigo hat. I have a staff, and there is an owl on my shoulder. Can you imagine being a wizard? What kind of bird is on your shoulder? What's their name?

Do you feel the hat, tight around your forehead, and going up to a point above your head? That's what indigo magic feels like!

Indigo magic is a little bit of a secret, but I'll teach you how to learn it. Just like the color indigo, it's all around you, even if not everyone knows about it. When you're in bed, almost asleep, imagine the dark blue indigo sky above you. Imagine that you're a space wizard, wearing a pointy hat, floating up into the sky. Practice that when you're falling asleep, and soon enough, you'll have a dream where you learn indigo magic!

Violet Magic

The last color is violet. Violet is my favorite color, except for all the other colors, which are also my favorites! Violet feels like wisdom, and it tastes like the flower named violet.[25] Violet is the color of the dream world, where anything is possible. Violet is what color imagination would be if imagination were a single color. Violet magic is what lets you do all the other kinds. Violet magic will help you learn from fairies and other friendly spirits.

When I do violet magic, I like to pretend that I am an angel or a fairy, wearing a long, violet robe, with shimmering violet, rainbow, iridescent wings. I am very, very tall, and I have big shiny white wings, and there is violet-colored light shining down onto the top of my head, and tickling my brain. Can you imagine what it's like to be a violet angel? Can you feel the light on the top of your head? Do you have a special angel name?

Sometimes, everyone makes mistakes or does bad things. I feel bad after I do something bad, because I want to be good. Do you want to be good too? Use violet magic to help you know what is the right thing to do, and to help you be good—just remember what it felt like to be a violet fairy-angel, with light shining into your head.

---

24 In general, the ocean is not indigo, but green, in this kind of magic. (And also in many, perhaps most, physical oceans.)

25 If you don't know what violets taste like, I recommend a type of candy called Choward's Violet Mints, which also makes a lovely offering for the Fair Folk.

Writing Prompt

Write and/or draw more about each imagining. I've gotten you started with some questions about the red imagining. Write your own questions (and answer them) for the other colors.

* What is on the banner your red knight form holds?
* What's your red dragon's name?
* What sound does your dragon make when they breathe fire?
* Who knighted your knight? What power(s) do they serve?

Exercise: Make Believe

Sofia has taught you a make believe for each of the colors. Practice imagining each one until you have made yourself believe it. Make sure you know what you see, what you hear, what you smell, what you taste, and what you feel. For example, for red, you should be seeing a red dragon. You should be hearing the roar of its fire breath. You should be smelling chiles. You should be tasting strawberries. You should feel the dragon you are riding, the heat and motion between your legs. You should know who you are in the imagining, and who everyone else (including plant-people and animal-people) is in the imagining, by both name and description.

Practice imagining with all your senses. Draw pictures. Make up songs. Know what it is like to be in each situation. Act each situation out like a child playing make believe. Describe the situation to yourself until it blossoms into sensory awareness. When you have properly imagined it, you should feel yourself filled with the color, beginning to radiate it like an aura.

Practice each make believe until you can make yourself believe it at will. Some colors will come more easily than others; make note of which ones were easier for you and which ones were harder. Once you have successfully felt each color, you may develop your own imaginings to prompt them, if you prefer; however, I strongly encourage you to work with the ones I have provided, which I have very carefully constructed for you. The goal is to be able to summon forth each color almost instantaneously, but you don't need to be that fast to continue the chapter. You'll get faster and better with time.

The Lesser Ritual of the Rainbow Star (LRRS)

After she discusses the individual colors, Sofia teaches her readers a "spell," although it's really more of a prayer or a magical ritual than a proper spell. That is to say, it's not exactly operative magic, because it doesn't have a clear goal. However, it is an excellent preface to more practical spell work, and also a nice way to end spells. Please remember that this spell is designed to be performed by children, or by adults in a childlike state of consciousness.

Now that you know all the colors, I can teach you the magic rainbow star spell. Here's how it works: First, draw a seven-pointed star. Draw the very best star you can. Next, color the points in with the seven colors, starting with red at the top, and continuing along the star in whichever direction you drew it.

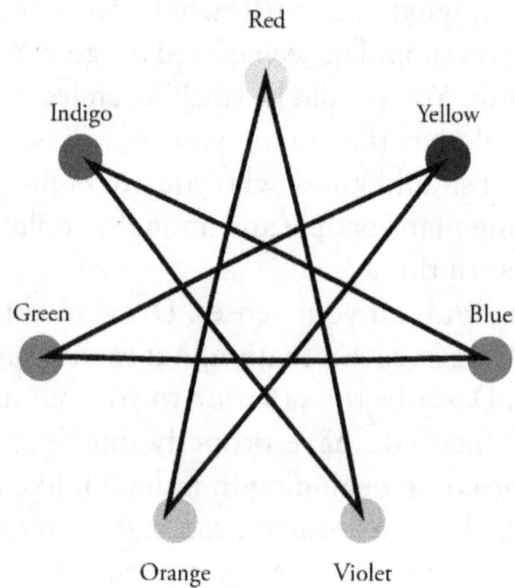

After you have a good picture, put it on top of your head. Say all the color names in order, and call to mind each imagining as you do. Then, say this rhyme:

"Roy G. Biv,[26] *Roy G. Biv:*
Seven-pointed rainbow star,
All the colors that there are,
Even the ones that are in between,
Even the ones that remain unseen,
All the colors of the light,
Come to me, shining bright!
Seven-pointed rainbow star,
I'm the magic that you are!"

While you say the rhyme (you might need to say it more than once), imagine all seven colors inside you at the same time. Feel them balancing out, so that you are a glowing rainbow pillar, with red at the bottom and violet at the top. Abide in this for a while, and when you're done, let go of the imagining.[27]

Sofia is leaving us now. I encourage you to make believe that she is playing with your child-self. Ask her questions to learn more from her. I encourage this with all the guest teachers.

The following table summarizes Sofia's teaching, and adds some other details, which we'll discuss further in later chapters, particularly Chapter Six, on planetary magic, which is closely related but not identical to color magic. When I was a beginner to magic, I used to be very excited by tables like this, and take them *very seriously*. Don't do that; nothing about the real world can be adequately summarized in a table.

26 Roy G. Biv is an acronym for "Red Orange Yellow Green Indigo Violet" that is commonly taught to American children when we learn our colors. Here, we're using him as an anthropomorphization of the color spectrum.

27 These powers are always in you, so there is no need to "dismiss" the ritual.

Color Associations							
	RED	ORANGE	YELLOW	GREEN	BLUE	INDIGO	VIOLET
Person	Will	Intellect	Spirit	Emotion	Order	Intuition	Conscience
Action	Wanting	Thinking	Doing	Feeling	Creating	Knowing	Being
Body	Genitals/ Tailbone	Womb	Solar Plexus	Heart	Throat	Forehead	Crown of the Head
Magical Goals	Conflict, Sex, Verve	Communication, Travel	Healing, Wholeness	Love, Friendship	Status, Wealth	Insight, Foresight	Boundaries, Wisdom
Ally	Dragon	Bee	Sunflower	Clover	Queen of Heaven	Wizard	Angel
Scents/ Tastes	Hot Pepper, Strawberry	Nutmeg, Cloves, Allspice	Saffron, Turmeric, Honey	Cut Grass, Green Herbs	Blueberries, Frankincense	Milk, Violets	Licorice, Salt
Planet	Mars	Mercury	Sun	Venus	Jupiter	Moon	Saturn
Weekday	Tuesday	Wednesday	Sunday	Friday	Thursday	Monday	Saturday
Metal(s)	Iron, Steel	Mercury, Aluminum	Gold, Brass	Copper	Tin	Silver	Lead
Angel	Gabriel[28]	Raphael	Michael	Aniel	Zadkiel	Auriel	Zafkiel
Weakness	Oppression	Ignorance	Hunger	Loneliness	Poverty	Insecurity	Pain
Mastery	Mercy	Humility	Harmony	Completeness	Kingship	Egolessness	Wisdom
Virtue	Patience	Bravery	Temperance	Nobility	Magnanimity	Benevolence	Experience
Vice	Wrath	Cockiness	Waste	Rapacity	Greed	Envy	Laziness

White and Black

In addition to the seven colors we learned above, you've actually dealt with two other colors already, although you might not have thought of them as colors. Remember the scintillating star energy you pulled down from above in the LRRS? That's white. It can be used for purification, peace, truth, or drawing in energy from above. Similarly, the energy we drew up from below, deep and cool and refreshing, is black. It can be used for banishing, binding, protection, absorption, and enforcing boundaries. Black and white are also used in some kinds of malefica (cursing), which we'll discuss further in Chapter Nine.

Because both black and white, in some sense, contain all the other colors, you

28 Many people would disagree with this and make Gabriel the angel of the violet ray. Based on decades of experience with Hebrew magic, angelic invocation, an ongoing relationship with the angel Gabriel, and the fact that his name literally means "divine manliness," I think they're wrong.

can usually substitute either white or black[29] for any other color, but why would you? Unless you are color-blind, I think it is almost always a missed opportunity to not introduce color into a spell in some form. There are almost limitless ways to work color into a spell. For example, I usually only have white candles "in stock," but if I want red energy in a candle spell, I can still dress in red, decorate the working space with red, or write the petition in red ink.

Our First Spell

Soon, we'll be casting our first spell together. But first, we need to talk about appropriate goals for magic. Like in anything, as you get better at magic, you'll be able to break more of the rules, because you'll have a better intuition about what will and won't work. But for these first few lessons, I strongly recommend that each spell have only a single, clearly worded goal. Goals should be measurable; that is to say, you should be able to evaluate whether or not they worked.

For example, "Make me rich" is not a good goal. First, it's too vague; what does *rich* mean? Compared to people starving in the third world, you're probably already rich. It also has no deadline; if you're poor for decades, but then win the lottery and die the next day at age eighty, technically the spell still worked. "By New Year's Day of [year], I will have at least $100,000 in savings" is a much better goal. It's clear. It has a deadline. It may or may not be reasonable, depending on your personal circumstances. Perhaps you already have far more than that (good for you!). Perhaps you are $100,000 in debt and currently unemployed. In that case, this would be a difficult goal for a beginner spell, because it isn't a viable extension of the current circumstances.

As a general rule of thumb, beginner magical goals should be things that, when they come true, will seem improbable enough that people ask how you did it, but not so impossible that people are deeply suspicious. *Magic can work miracles,* but your first spell, which will take about twenty minutes to perform, probably won't. As we move through the book, you'll learn to do bigger and more complicated magic that is more appropriate for addressing bigger, more complicated situations. For now, think about things in your life that could use a little nudge. In everything that follows, I'll be using the example of a spell to help a friend, whom I'll call Mike, get a job for which he already has an

29 Most people find it much easier to radiate white energy than black, so I generally recommend white over black for beginners.

interview scheduled.[30] This same method can be applied to much more complex situations, but for now, try to stick with something simple. I encourage you to read the rest of this chapter before beginning your first spell.

The Polya Problem-Solving Method

My first great nerd-love, and my academic specialty before I found out that magic was a viable career, was theoretical mathematics. I believed, when I was young, that mathematics is, as Galileo would have it, "a language by which God has written the universe," and in some important ways, I still believe that to be true. Over the course of this book, you'll see many mathematically inspired methods and techniques. The method that I'm about to teach you, I first learned from a classic text on mathematical pedagogy called *How to Solve It,* by George Polya, which I strongly recommend to nerds, even non-math nerds. Although Polya's method was originally designed for solving mathematical problems,[31] I find it applicable to all kinds of problems in life, both theoretical and personal. We will return to these four stages many times over the course of this book.

1. First, you have to understand the problem.
2. After understanding, make a plan.
3. Carry out your plan.
4. Look back on your work. How can you do better next time you encounter a similar problem?

When we apply this method to magic, it looks something like the following:

1. Understand the current situation, and in what ways you want it to change.
2. Make a "recipe" for a spell to fit the situation.
3. Cast the magic.
4. Analyze your results and improve your recipe for next time.

The most important stage of spellcraft—and the place where most people go wrong—is not in the execution of the spell, but rather the first stage. I often see beginners (and even experienced magicians) dive into magic without

30 He did, indeed, get the job.

31 More accurately, it was designed to teach non-mathematicians how to solve mathematical problems. If you went to high school in the US, you were probably taught this method. However, most people were taught it so badly that you might not even recognize it.

actually figuring out what they want their magic to do.[32] Unsurprisingly, this often leads to unfortunate results.

Step One: Understand the Current Situation

Carefully examine the situation from your current point of view. Write at least a full paragraph, in complete sentences, describing the situation you would like to witch. If you are having trouble explaining the situation, it can help to ask yourself the following questions. You may wish to do (or purchase) some divination (such as a tarot reading) to help you answer all these questions. We'll learn more about divination in Chapter Four. I find that most situations take about an hour of investigation. If it's not worth spending an hour thinking about, it's probably not worth enchanting either.

* Who is involved?
* Where is the situation physically located in space and time?
* How do you feel about the situation, emotionally?
* How do others feel about it?
* How is this situation operating? What is sustaining it?
* How will the current pattern play out over time if uninterrupted?
* Why is this situation happening?
* What was the original cause?
* Who benefits from the current situation?
* What forces in the world work to keep this status quo?

Next, write a full-page description of the situation as you would like it to be. Ask yourself all the same questions you asked before. It's ok if you don't know all the answers. Be as specific as you can about the situation, but try to avoid describing the path from here to there. Be sure to think about who and what, other than you, would benefit from the situation being as you wish it to be. Also, think about what people (human and otherwise) might be opposed to your goal. Who loses when you win? Be sure to think about the timing—when do you want these changes to happen? Be specific. The longer you can wait, the easier it will (probably) be, but fix a deadline. As a rule of thumb, most beginner spells should be showing some kind of results in a month or less, and be fully manifest in three months or less. If your deadline is more

32 This is also where most people go wrong in math. I see an astonishing number of students start trying to solve a word problem before they've even read the whole thing.

than a month away, consider splitting it into several shorter-term goals. Below are some questions to ask yourself. Answer them in your magical journal.

* Can I describe the desired change in a single sentence?
* What similar changes have I been able to make in the past?
* What have I tried that didn't work?
* Can I break this problem into several smaller, more manageable problems?
* What is a simpler version of this problem that I already know how to solve?
* Who do I know who has solved this problem before? Can I ask them how they did it?
* Start with the goal and work backward; what will it look like as it unfolds?

Step Two: Make a Plan—Single Color Candle Spell Template

Now, to step two: make a recipe to fit the current situation. You can use the following simple "template" to cast a spell for almost any purpose. After the spell, we'll discuss the "theory" behind this spell a little more so you can learn how it works, and I'll show several methods by which it can be "leveled up." However, I think all that will make more sense after you've done it at least once, so let's jump right in.

In this example, our goal is "Mike gets offered the job[33] before the next full moon." Decide on your own goal. Like the example, it should be clear, concise, specific, measurable, and bounded in time.[34] Next, you need to choose what color you think would most benefit the situation you are enchanting. That can be tricky.[35] For example, to get Mike the job, we could use green to make the interviewer like him. We could use yellow to help him feel confident, so he does well in the interview. We could use blue, on the theory that, at the end

33 This spell is to get a specific job, but could easily be modified to get any job which that meets a list of specified criteria.

34 I usually set deadlines to coincide with specific, observable natural phenomena, like "when the moon is full" or "when the sun enters Gemini," because it ties your spell to the implacable momentum of the heavens.

35 In fact, as we'll discuss later in this chapter, it's sometimes better to work with multiple colors at once, or to do multiple spells of different colors. However, for our first spell, we'll just pick one.

of the day, what Mike really wants from that job is money, and if it comes some other way, that's probably ok too. In fact, it's often best to do several small spells, each centered around a different color, all working together. At other times, you'll want to use several colors all together in the same spell. We'll discuss both options later, but those sorts of more complicated spells are built out of the basic structure of this one-color spell.

In this example, I think orange is the best choice. Orange is communication magic; it's the magic of merchants, mathematicians, translators, teachers, thieves, and anyone else who survives by their wits. Since an interview is fundamentally about communication, orange is often a good choice for job interviews. The example was specifically a job doing orange type things,[36] so I think it is especially good here. Additionally, orange magic is fast, which would be helpful in this case, because the interview is already scheduled.

You will need:

* About half an hour of undisturbed time on two different days. You can also perform the spell straight through, if you'd prefer, with just a short break in the middle.
* A candle[37] of the appropriate color. You can use white if you don't have a candle the right color. The candle will need to remain burning. If you feel safe allowing it to burn in a place where it will not be tampered with or knocked over, I recommend seven-day jar candles, which can be easily sourced in a variety of colors. If your living situation (such as pets or kids) makes burning such candles ill-advised, you can use a small tea light, which usually burns for one to three hours, or even a birthday candle.

---

36 Many modern jobs, including retail, are orange in nature, being essentially about either communication or commerce.

37 If you cannot burn a candle at all (for example, in a dorm room or prison cell), that's also ok. Find another source of energy for your spell, such as wind, moving water, or even feeding it a chemical battery. Most spells can be worked with no material components at all, but doing so will make the spell much more difficult, because its only path into and out of the physical world will be through your body. If you routinely find yourself having to do entirely internal/mental magic, you should start working to develop your internal energy reserves by doing something like tai chi, qi gong, or pranayama. Running magical power through your body without developing your internal energy body is not healthy; it will leave you depleted and can eventually make you sick. We'll discuss this in much greater detail in Chapter Seven. For now, use a candle unless you absolutely can't.

* A pen and paper. If you have a piece of paper appropriate to your goal (such as a printed job ad, in our example), that is even better. Appropriately colored ink and/or paper are nice, especially if you aren't using a colored candle.
* Before beginning the spell, write a petition describing what you want. Make it beautiful, both in the language and in the craftsmanship. If you feel called to do so, decorate it. Address it to "Beneficent spirits of the color ______" or "Blessed Ones of the ____ Ray" or "Powers of ______" or some such.

In our example, the petition says:

"Beneficent spirits of the color orange, you are as beautiful as the glow of sunset and as refreshing as a creamsicle. You are the power of the tiger and the heat of the flame. Awaken within me, and spill your warmth upon me, and upon Mike's quest to get a job. Make his tongue clever and his mind quick. Let him be well favored by all who hear him speak. Let him be hired! Let him succeed! Let him become the [JOB TITLE] he wants to be!"

* A glass of water. A special, pretty cup you only use for magic is nice to have, but any container is fine.
* Olive or other oil. For extra potency, scent the oil in a way that resonates with the color you're working with. For example, I added some pumpkin pie spice to mine.

Step Three: Execute Your Plan[38]

Phase One

1. Prepare the space: Arrange your space so that the candle is the main point of focus, with the water and oil flanking it. If you wish, decorate the space (and yourself) with the color you'll be working with.
2. Prepare yourself: If you wish, take a special bath and dress in the appropriate color. Enter magical time, space, and consciousness by standing at the Sacred Center, or by any other method. Get your mind

38 Because this is a book, it's sort of hard to distinguish between making the plan and executing the plan. But when you are actually doing magic, they are clearly distinct steps.

and heart into a place of calm, collected power. Beginners should not cast magic while in a state of desperation, fear, anxiety, or rage, because those emotions make you sloppy. Sloppy magic (rather than some kind of universal judgment/punishment) is what causes "monkey's paw" style blowback. Be clean and precise in your casting.

3. Perform Sofia's Lesser Ritual of the Rainbow Star or any other conjuration of the seven rays.
4. Imagine the conjuring Sofia taught you for the color until you feel the color glowing inside of you. In the case of our example, that imagining is of yourself as a fairy or other spirit clad all in orange, riding on a bumble bee. Feel the orange glow growing inside you, just below your belly button. Maintain the imagining throughout what follows.
5. Imagine the colored glow spreading throughout your body and pouring out of your hands.
6. Anoint the candle with the oil, beginning in the middle of the candle and working your way out to both ends.[39] While you do this, speak to the candle, telling it what you want. Read your petition out loud. Feel the color flowing out of your hands and into the candle. This process is sometimes called "dressing" a candle. You'll learn some ways to "level up" this practice later, but this is the basic method.
7. When you have poured as much of the color into the candle as you can, and you are feeling too tired to continue, thank the candle, and put it back between the water and the oil. Trace a seven-pointed star over it with your hands to seal in the energy you have dressed it with.
8. Exit magical space, time, and consciousness. Stand up and move around. Drink some water. Take a break, however long you like. Eat some food. Take a nap. If you are not tired, you've done it wrong.[40] Do it over.

There's no need to do the two phases of conjuration on the same day. The candle will retain its charge for several weeks, at least.[41] Whenever you're ready, begin phase two.

---

39 This is a traditional instruction for dressing candles, but I prefer to anoint them in different ways for different purposes. Sometimes I spiral. Sometimes I go top to bottom, other times bottom to top. Sometimes I jack the candle off. We'll discuss these sort of symbolic movements in Chapter Three, when we talk about poppets.

40 This is targeted at beginners. Once you're accustomed to magical work, you'll be able to do significantly more before tiring. However, if you don't feel like you have less energy than when you started, you did it wrong. Start over.

41 Much longer, once you get better at this.

Phase Two

1. Enter into magical space, time, and consciousness. Get your head and heart right for magic.
2. Perform the Lesser Ritual of the Rainbow Star (or any other invocation of the seven rays).
3. Light[42] the candle.
4. Assume the imagining of the relevant color.
5. Read your petition out loud several times, in your very best magician voice. You may find yourself slipping into song or glossolalia. Those are excellent signs. You're doing it right!
6. Place the still-lit candle on top of the petition. In a candle holder is fine.
7. As the candle burns, allow the power in it to permeate into the petition, and from there, into the situation you are enchanting. Imagine the situation being bathed in colored light and everything working out the way you want it to. In our example, I imagine Mike succeeding in the interview, being offered the job, and finally, being happy and successful doing the job. If you are using a long-acting candle, exit magical space, time, and consciousness whenever you are ready to do so, but do not put out the candle. Each time you pass the candle, greet it, and thank it for working on your behalf. If you are using a short-action candle, try to maintain your trance and make believe until the candle is completely out.
8. Record what you did, and how it felt, in your magical journal. Leave space after your notes for analyzing results after the deadline. Once the spell is done, don't obsess about it. This sort of obsessing is sometimes called "lust for results," and it can cause problems because when you mentally/emotionally "grasp" at the spell, you can unintentionally drag it back toward you, preventing it from getting where it needs to go. However, it's ok to keep thinking about the situation, as long as your thoughts are productive rather than anxious. In fact, you may want to separately enchant on many fronts. Once the deadline is up, move on to step four.

Step Four: Analyze Your Results

Do not move on to this stage until the deadline you specified in your spell has come and gone, but if your wish comes true early, make note of when. In

42 I prefer not to light magic candles directly from a match or lighter, because I do not like the smell of either in my magic. I often light a birthday candle, and then light my magic candle from that. That being said, I am fussier than most people about smells.

your journal, write down any results, both good and bad, that you attribute to the spell. Write about how you feel about the results. Look back over your notes from step one. Answer the following questions in complete sentences.

If it succeeded...

* Be sure to say thank you to the powers of the color, and to any other powers who may have helped!
* Celebrate! Then get down to work, analyzing...
    * When you were working, what parts felt the best? The worst?
    * How can you parlay this result into even better results?
    * How could you have simplified the spell and still gotten the same results?

If it failed...

* Don't worry! This is only lesson one! You're going to get better at this! Chuck Jones, the animator of Bugs Bunny, says that every artist has thousands of terrible drawings in their hands, and they have to get all of them out to get to the good ones. It's the same with magic, and with everything else worth learning. The road to success goes through failure, and there's no way out but through.
* When you cast, were there parts that didn't feel right? What did you do about that? What might you do differently next time?
* Even if you didn't get what you wanted, might you have gotten what you asked for? Spell failure is often caused by sloppy planning.
* What paths were available to your spell work to unfold along? For example, if it was a spell to attract a new romantic partner, did you go out and meet people?
* Were there any "supernatural" effects, like light bulbs bursting or some such? This is usually a sign of sloppy casting—the energy leaked out of your spell instead of getting to its target.
* Were you "in the zone" when you cast the spell, or were you just going through the motions?
* Did you cast from a place of fear or anxiety? Were you sick or especially tired? In my experience, this is a common reason for spell failure.
* What powers opposed your objective? How can they be avoided, placated, defeated, or converted next time?
* What have you learned from your failure? What would you do differently next time?

How to Level Up This Spell

There are a variety of ways to improve this spell, many of which you'll learn over the next twelve lessons. They can be broken into several categories. The first, and the one where I think you will see the most "bang for your buck" is including *sympathetic links* to the situation you are enchanting. We will extensively discuss this in the next chapter.

Another way to add some oomph to your magic is to include *magical materials*, like plants, metals, incenses, and such. We'll learn a lot more about magical materia in the next chapter, but materia related to the colors are particularly easy. You don't have to be a learned witch to make some guesses about what kind of materials are, for example, good for orange magic: oranges (the fruit), saffron, allspice, "pumpkin[43] spice," carnelian, citrine, marigolds, calendula, and most other orange flowers.

Casting from a *place of power* can make a significant difference in your color spells. There are, broadly speaking, four kinds of places of power: those personal to you, those related to your situation, those that resonate with the color of magic you are casting, and those awesome places that simply hum with power, such as temples, dance clubs, and places of great natural beauty. These are often good for many kinds of magic, but use your common sense. A dance club is not ideal for magic intended to calm a fever. Similarly, a calm Zen garden is not an ideal place to enchant to get laid.

In our example of a job interview, the best choice would almost certainly be the location of the job and/or the interview. Crossroads (associated with the exchange of ideas), markets, and libraries, all of which resonate with the purposes of orange magic, would also be good choices, as would most places of awesome power.

Identifying places that are good for magic can be tricky. Some are obvious from the geography, folklore, or history of the location: mountaintops, river confluences, and cemeteries, for example. You'll need to experiment and talk to local witch elders and other experienced magicians to find others.[44]

Witching at an opportune moment is another way to add power to spell-casting. There are, broadly speaking, two kinds of magical timing. The first is choosing times especially appropriate to your specific situation. For example,

43 Pumpkins, surprisingly, are not ideal for most orange magic. Like most fruits, they're better for green magic.

44 In my experience, even non-magicians who have lived in the same place for a long time are generally eager to tell stories about places like this. Ask them to tell you about their favorite places, places that make them "feel close to God," or spooky places. Ask them to tell you any local ghost stories they know. You don't have to explain why you want to know.

in the case of helping Mike get a job, it would be especially powerful to cast the spell during the interview. This is one reason why it's advisable to enchant the candles in advance, and to use long-acting candles, since sometimes these "magic moments" are very short or inconvenient. The other type of timing is astrological: choosing a time based on the positions of celestial bodies in the sky. Astrological timing is complicated; we'll discuss it a little bit in Chapter Six, on planetary magic, but I am not especially good at astrology. To learn more, I recommend Ivo Dominguez's book, *Practical Astrology for Witches and Pagans: Using the Planets and the Stars for Effective Spellwork, Rituals, and Magickal Work*. For now, here are some simple things to try:

* Cast spells designed to increase something when the moon is waxing (growing).
* Cast those designed to decrease something when the moon is waning (getting smaller).
* Cast on the appropriate day of the week (see the table on page 173).
* Cast spells that target external actions and situations during the day.
* Cast those related to internal emotions and thoughts by night.

Almost any special skill you have mastered can be leveraged to improve the efficacy of a spell. If you're a musician, sing. If you're a gardener, grow witching herbs. If you're a coder, make magical servitors. Throughout the course of these chapters, you'll learn many, many ways to do so, and (more importantly) you'll learn how to safely and effectively experiment to find your own methods.

Color Theory for Magicians

Once you've mastered working with one color at a time, you can begin to work with them in combination. If you don't remember how to mix primary colors to get secondary colors, or what things like "complementary colors" are, you should go google "basic color theory" and relearn it before proceeding. It is important, when working with multiple colors of magic at once, that you keep them separate; once they begin to blend together, your magic will get messy and muddy, and lose a lot of power.

Combining Colors

Before we get into combining colors, I want to remind you that, far from there being only seven colors, when we call *all* the colors, we mean "Even the ones that are in between,[45] Even the ones that remain unseen."[46] However, in this section, when I talk about combining colors, I am not talking about "mixing" magical colors the way you mix paints, which I generally do not recommend to beginner magicians.[47] Instead, I recommend working with multiple colors in the same spell, but keeping the individual colors separate. When working with multiple colors in the candle spell we learned, it is usually easiest to charge each candle individually, and then activate them in the same spell. To get a feel for any particular combination of two (or more) colors, try to very rapidly switch between the color imaginings until they collapse into a single imagining. Obviously, I can't talk about every possible combination. However, here are some basic pairs to get you started:

Red and blue magics, when worked together, are excellent for protection, politics, and work to support the status quo. In general, by combining two out of three of a triad[48] of colors, you get a very material manifestation of the third. So, in this case, red and blue together call a material manifestation of yellow/sunny energy, like Superman.

Red and green magics, when worked together, are an excellent combination for fertility, vitality, familial love, and luxurious growth. Think of Christmas, apple trees, or the Red Devil of the Woods. This combination can be so quick-growing that it's invasive. Use it with caution. This is typical of complementary[49] colors—what they produce grows almost explosively.

Red and orange is the athlete's combination. It is excellent for healing, or anytime you need to produce spectacular results from your body. *Do not* use this for healing fever.

Red and yellow magics, when worked together, are powerful and fiery. They are excellent for burning away things you don't want. They produce a hot version of blue magic, perfect for both casting and clearing political malefica.

Teal and saffron magics, when worked together, are good for projecting confidence and acquiring status, as well as for business, leadership, and authority. This color combination is common in advertising.

---

45 In general, "in between" colors have qualities similar to those they are in between. So, for example, aqua is sort of like green and sort of like blue.

46 Like, say, infrared or ultraviolet.

47 Unless you are especially good at color theory, for example, if you are a painter.

48 By triad, I don't mean any three colors, I mean three colors evenly spaced around a color wheel.

49 Directly opposite each other on a color wheel.

Purple and yellow magics together are excellent for insight, clarity, and psychism. Imagine the sun king wearing an imperial purple robe, or the lavender moon glowing gold through the clouds. We will revisit this combination in Chapter Five when you get to know Phoebe Chrysostephanos—the Golden Crowned Moon.

Green and purple magics, when worked together, are great for sex, intoxication, artistic inspiration, criminality, and trickery. Think about the Muses, grapes on the vine, or comic book supervillains. This is one of my personal favorite combinations.

Green and indigo magics, worked together, are excellent for trauma healing and forming or repairing deep, intimate connections. This is also an excellent combination for ancestor work.

Blue and green magics, when worked together, are good for strengthening a marriage, blessing a garden, or calming the mind.

Black and white magics, when worked together, are good for reversing and dispelling other magic, such as in curse breaking. We will discuss this further in Chapter Nine, on malefica (cursing).

In the next ritual, we'll work all seven "basic" colors simultaneously.

The Greater Ritual of the Rainbow Star (GRRS)

This ritual is primarily designed to balance and attune your energy body, and is excellent preparation for magic. It can also be used to balance and attune the energy of a space. Additionally, it can also be used to create a "bubble" of psychic protection around yourself, which can be good in miasmically dense or sensorily overstimulating environments. However, it is quite noticeable to anyone with eyes to see such things, so I do not recommend doing it if you're trying to fly under the radar.[50] This practice also helps exercise your energy channels, which we will discuss further in Chapter Seven. However, the most typical use of this kind of ritual is as a sort of "frame" around other magic, especially work that is a bit delicate or complicated, or which you worry might be vulnerable to outside interference.

---

50 In general, I recommend against too much prophylactic magic protection. Going about regular life wearing a lot of magical protection makes it seem like you're spoiling for a fight, as if you wore a Kevlar vest to the grocery store. In my circle, we call this "wearing plate mail to a picnic."

1. Begin by entering magical space, time, and consciousness by any method.
2. Perform the Lesser Ritual of the Rainbow Star, which is on page 28. However, you really should have practiced that one enough to not need to look it up before trying this one.
3. Focus on the star atop your head. Imagine it growing until it surrounds you, and slowly spinning, clockwise (i.e., going from left to right across your forehead, and right to left behind your head).
4. Slowly allow it to descend your body, while still orbiting your body. You may find a similar physical motion helps; I rotate my hips like I'm hula hooping, but see what feels right in your body.
5. As the spinning star descends, feel all the energy in your body turn to scintillating white. You should be radiating brilliance like a star.
6. When you get to your feet, allow the star to reverse, now spinning widdershins (counterclockwise) and ascending your body. As this happens, feel the star splitting the white energy into a rainbow spectrum, like a prism. Each point of the star is like a lens that shoots out a highly focused laser beam of a particular color, so the whole color wheel is glowing around you. Say, "Seven-pointed rainbow star, all the colors that there are, even the ones in between, even the ones that remain unseen." This radiance is a powerful energetic blast that is excellent for rebalancing the energy of an unpleasant space.
7. Bring the star up to your forehead. In this position, the lasers can be turned on and off, so you can emit either a single color at a time or several colors together, flashing but not mixing.
8. If you are using this ritual as a "frame" for other magic, this is where the other magic goes. Try to keep your focus split between the rainbow crown and the magic you're doing, but that can be hard as a beginner. If you have to choose, pay attention to what you are doing, and trust the star to keep itself moving. If you are using this ritual to clear a space or rebalance your body, pause here for several breaths. If you're using it as an exercise, hold it as long as you can without losing focus.
9. When you are done, return the seven-pointed rainbow star to the top of your head, and allow the energy to sink back into you. Remove the paper from the top of your head. Eventually, after you're good at this, the paper will not be necessary, but it will make it easier while you're learning.

10. Make some notes in your journal about how the ritual went. In particular, note which colors seemed to be absorbed by different parts of your body, and by different parts of the space. If you are routinely "hungry" for a certain color in a certain part of your body, try to determine why. Similarly, if a space seems hungry for a color, try to understand why.

CHAPTER TWO:

Sympathetic Magic

A classic joke:

Nikola Tesla[51] visited Henry Ford[52] at his factory, and a certain machine was having difficulties. Ford asked Tesla if he could help identify the problem. Tesla closed his eyes, listened, and sniffed the air. He then walked up to a wall of boilerplate and tapped it gently with a hammer. The machine clanged, and chugged, and came back online. Ford was thrilled, and told him to send an invoice. The bill arrived, for $10,000. Ford was shocked, and asked an itemized bill. Tesla sent another invoice, indicating a $1 for the tap, and $9,999 for knowing where and how to tap.

What Is Magical Sympathy?

Some people will tell you that magic is "all about intent." They are wrong. For the most part, magic is about knowing where and how to direct that intent. In this chapter, we're going to talk about sympathetic magic, which is one of the broadest and most universal types of magic. In fact, the color magic we did in the previous chapter is really just a particular type of sympathetic magic.[53]

Sympathetic magic is magic that relies on the simple fact that everything that exists is connected by complex, interwoven strings of sympathy. A skilled

51 Widely reputed to be a magician.

52 Widely reputed to be a poser.

53 It is also a particular type of energy magic, and a particular type of spirit magic. Its versatility and simplicity are why I teach it first.

witch, by knowing just where to "tap," can send gentle ripples through that "net" to effect change in the world. This "net" is similar, but not identical, to the specific culturally bound concepts of the "Web of Wyrd" (or "Web of Weird") and "Indra's Net," both of which I encourage nerds who want extra homework (like me!) to research.

The word *sympathy* (from *sym-pathos*) means "feeling together." When we say that two things are in magical sympathy, we mean that there is a difficult-to-explain causal link of "spooky action at a distance"[54] between them; things done to one also affect the other. The phrase "sympathetic magic" was coined by George Frazer in his classic (speculative) study of comparative religion, *The Golden Bough*. Although this book is grotesquely colonialist and (to put it charitably) not up to modern standards of scholarship, its importance to the development of modern Anglophone witchcraft cannot be overstated. I recommend at least skimming it. Parts of it are very inspiring when read with an open mind and several grains of salt. The rest, you should just ignore. That is to say, it is best to understand it as well-written mythopoetry, not poorly researched anthropology. In that text, Frazer writes:

> *"If we analyze the principles of thought on which magic is based, they will probably be found to resolve themselves into two: first, that like produces like, or that an effect resembles its cause; and, second, that things which have once been in contact with each other continue to act on each other at a distance after the physical contact has been severed. The former principle may be called the Law of Similarity, the latter the Law of Contact or Contagion. From the first of these principles, namely the Law of Similarity, the magician infers that he can produce any effect he desires merely by imitating it: from the second he infers that whatever he does to a material object will affect equally the person with whom the object was once in contact, whether it formed part of his body or not."*

Although Frazer's writing discusses first similarity and then contagion, I think they will make more sense if we discuss them in the other order.

54 A phrase coined by Albert Einstein to describe certain kinds of quantum entanglement. You can google "Einstein–Podolsky–Rosen paradox" to learn more. However, I strongly caution people who do not have advanced training in math and physics to avoid using quantum mechanics as an explanatory metaphor for magic. In my experience (as a mathematician/magician), people who do usually just look like idiots.

The Laws of Contagion and Similarity

Law of Contagion and Magical Links

We spoke very briefly at the end of the last chapter about the importance of magic links. Let's expand on that discussion. The Law of Contagion (and other "magical laws") should not be understood as a "law of nature," but rather as a generalization of how magic is performed cross-culturally. Here is a more modern and casual way I could explain the same rule: "When two objects are in close physical connection over a long period of time, they 'infect' each other with their 'vibes.'" And here is a slightly more formal modern one: "If a pair or group of particles are spatially close in such a way that the probabilistic state of each cannot be mathematized independently of the state(s) of the other(s), then they will retain that entanglement even when they are separated by a large distance." As magicians, we can use that connection to our advantage to enact a sort of "spooky action at a distance."

Our goal, as sympathetic magicians, is to build a chain of sympathetic connections from the act of magic to the desired goal. The Law of Contagion is one easy way to fill in the gaps in such a chain, using objects that have been "infected" by the people/places/objects/events/situations the spell is trying to affect. For example, among the strongest links to humans are pieces of their body: hair, nails, skin, blood, ejaculate, etc. A person's hand-written signature is good, as is a recording of their voice. Next best are items they have worn or handled—the more often and intimately, the better. Underclothes are good, as are other unwashed clothes or jewelry.

Sometimes, you'll want to link to a place. There are many reasons for this, but most fall into one of two categories: drawing energy in from a place of power, or targeting magic to operate at a specific location. In either of these circumstances, living dirt (dig down several inches) or living water that includes a representative sample of the chthonic biome is best, but inorganic materia like pebbles are also ok.

If you can't get a material link, then you can also use symbolic links: things that are not entangled by physical proximity, but rather by informational proximity. For example, a person's full name, a photo, their birth date, or "secret" information about them can all be used as "targeting" links. The internet has dramatically expanded the size, depth, and complexity of our informational landscape; if you can't find a symbolic link to someone or something, you're probably not trying hard enough. Physical links will almost always provide more oomph than symbolic ones, but a combination of both is best. It is essentially impossible to have too much linkage when you are linking to a spell's main target.

In addition to people and places, sometimes you'll want to link to more abstract things. Use your imagination, but follow the general rule: you are looking for things that have been in close physical proximity and causal entanglement with the situation you are looking to enchant.

You can also use the Law of Contagion "backward" by intentionally handling an object intensely so that it becomes "infected" with your "vibes," and then planting it somewhere you'd like to influence. For this use, I am especially fond of coins, which I will discuss on page sixty. This is because it is very easy to "accidentally" drop a coin almost anywhere, and also very easy to get people to pick up an "infected" coin and put it in their pocket.

Law of Similarity

Simply put, the Law of Similarity (also called the Law of Imitation) says that symbolic representations and ritual reenactments of activities allow us to access the power of the thing being mimicked. In this way, we can throw red paint to represent blood when we hex for animal rights, or use a gold coin to represent the sun's nourishing light and warmth. We can sew up a cow's tongue to stop a gossiper or smear honey across a photograph's lips to draw in a kiss. It is why we witches might tell a barren woman to lie down in a field and press her belly to the biggest melon on the vine, and why we can call the dead on old rotary phones. The variations of this sort of magic are almost limitless, and are best discovered by experimentation and play.

At the end of this chapter, we'll combine the Laws of Contagion and Similarity into perhaps the most archetypal example of sympathetic magic: a poppet. However, first we'll learn about some typical items used in sympathetic magic, often called *materia magica* (which is really just a pretentious way of saying "magical materials"). Our guest teacher for that is a spirit I call Grandmother Winter, who is also known as Frau Holle (Mrs. Hell). She lives in the Underworld, so to meet her, you'll need to learn a new kind of trance, good for simple travel below.

The Granny Trance

The trance state I call *Granny Trance* has many variations. What all share is the induction technique; one attains Granny Trance by small, repeated motions, usually swaying back and forth (like in a rocking chair), but sometimes from side to side, or in circles. This motion is combined with a faster, smaller, and perpendicular motion of the eyes and concentration. For example, you might knit or spin in a rocking chair, or read while swaying back and forth, or grind corn while bobbing your head.

The name Granny Trance comes from the association of these activities with "women's work," particularly the work of older and/or less physically able women, but the trance is available to everyone. In Yiddish-speaking Jewish communities, where this trance accompanies prayer and religious study, it is called *shuckling* (which means "swaying") and is said to mimic the quivering of a candle flame, because during prayer, the soul is on fire. In addition to producing a light magical trance, it also improves reading comprehension and retention. I find a tempo of about one hundred beats per minute best for the larger motion, but it varies from person to person.

1. Begin to rock (or whatever movement you use), and as you do, focus your concentration on a perpendicular movement. For example, if you are swaying front and back, move your attention either side to side (as you would if you were reading, for example) or in a circle.
2. The first time you practice, don't add any intention at all, just really concentrate on feeling the sensations in your body. Sometimes it can help to "label" them, like "I feel an itch on my nose," "I feel a pain in my right knee," "I feel dizzy," etc.
3. After a while, you should begin to feel the rhythm of the motion "take hold" of you, the same way that some songs compel you to dance. Let go, and just feel.
4. This might make you dizzy until you get used to it. Build up to practicing for at least ten minutes at a time.
5. Practice a few times until you've mastered the physical part, and you can easily maintain your swaying tempo for the whole ten minutes.
6. Once you've managed that, add the following imagining: Feel yourself getting smaller inside your body; that is, your body stays the same size, but your "you-ness" concentrates into a ball at your center.
7. When your imagination seems firm, send your you-ness down your spine, out your bum, and into the ground.
8. Keep going down, down, down until there is no more down to go.
9. If you like, you can imagine that you are going down stairs, riding in an elevator, or climbing along tree roots. I imagine I'm Alice going down the rabbit hole into Wonderland. I also use the mnemonic phrase "Down, down, down I go, into the Great Below!"

10. Your breathing and heart rate should slow down, and you might feel cold or heavy.
11. Keep rocking, and keep going down until you "land." There should be a distinct physical sensation of downward movement, like in an elevator.
12. The first several times you practice, you might still be going down when your ten minutes ends, but with practice, it will get faster.
13. Most likely, the place you'll end up in will be some kind of cave or other small, enclosed place, but for right now, it doesn't really matter where you land. We'll learn more about this place in later chapters. For now, the goal is to simply go down until you run out of down to go.
14. Once you're at the bottom, open your eyes, and prepare to work magic. Remember to come back up and grow back to full size when you're done.

Once you've gotten the hang of the Granny Trance, you're ready to meet this chapter's teachers: Granny Winter and her bard, Jacob Grimm.

Granny Winter

Like Sofia in the previous chapter, Granny Winter is a spirit teacher of mine who has agreed to teach all of you as well.[55] In addition to the teachings on magical materia here, she also teaches healing[56] and a variety of other kinds of witchcraft. If you would like to interact with her more, you can ask her to appear in your dreams.

Granny Winter is one avatar of the White Lady, who is also sometimes called Frau Holle (Mrs. Hell), Mother Hulda, Grandmother Frost, Mother Goose, the Witch of the Northern Wood, and many other names. She is a traditional fairy tale character, and her magic is the magic of fairy tales. I will tell you her tale in a moment, but first let me introduce the man who first told it to me.

Jacob Grimm

Jacob Grimm is our first teacher among the dead. He is a real person, who was born in 1785, near Frankfurt, Germany (then in the Holy Roman Empire). Whether you know his name or not, if you're reading this book in English, he has undoubtedly shaped your connection to magic. Famed in his own day as

55 In fact, like Sofia and I (and most teachers), she's a bit of an attention whore, so I'm sure she'd love a visit!

56 There is a ritual for seeking her aid in healing on page 109 of my book *The Big Book of Magical Incense.*

jurist and linguist,[57] he is best known today for the work he did with his brother, preserving and interpreting the stories he called *Children and Household Stories*. Today, that collection is normally called *Tales of the Brothers Grimm*. As the Grimms were among the first to write down these tales, and the first to popularize them outside Germany, they "modernized" the tales in many ways, forever changing the way we interact with them. That is the nature of story magic—it changes with every new telling, and every new teller.[58] Similarly, in the twentieth century, Disney retold and modernized many of them again, once again changing the way they work in magic. However, to the best of my knowledge, there is no Disney version of the tale most relevant to our work in this chapter, that of Frau Holle.[59] My version of her story, closely modeled on Jacob Grimm's, is as follows:

Once upon a time, a widow lived with her two girls, one her biological daughter, and the other the daughter of her late husband's first wife. She treated her stepdaughter very badly, making her do all the work, berating her, while her biological daughter was spoiled quite thoroughly. One day, the stepdaughter took her spinning outside, where she could work in peace. She sat at the side of the well, spinning, her mind traveling free in fancy as she worked. Then, all of sudden, splash! She dropped her spindle into the well. Oh no! She knew her stepmother would beat her for her carelessness, and, in a panic, she jumped into the well after it.

She fell and fell and fell, far further than any fair physics should have allowed. Eventually, she landed in a beautiful meadow. She walked a bit, through the meadow, looking for her lost spindle, to no avail. Eventually, she came upon a large brick oven with no one attending to it. The smell of fresh-baked bread made her mouth water, and she lingered near the oven.

A voice cried out, "Save me! Oh, save me! I am beginning to burn!"

She opened the oven and found that it was the bread itself speaking to her, which seemed just a little bit strange. But she didn't want the bread to burn, and so she wrapped her skirts around her hands and snatched it from the oven.

---

57 He helped develop the Proto-Indo-European reconstruction.

58 Making substantial changes to the magic of well-known stories (for good or ill) requires a high level of skill in bard-craft. I don't always appreciate the way Disney changes stories, but I always appreciate their skill as storytellers.

59 To be super "well actually" about it, the character of Hele from Thor comics/movies is a version of Frau Holle, and Marvel is owned by Disney, so I guess technically there is a Disney version of her.

"Thank you, oh thank you! You saved me from burning all up!" said the bread. "Is there anything I can do for you?"

"I have lost my spindle," said the girl, almost in tears, "and I need to find it before I can go home."

"I haven't seen your spindle," said the bread, "but my sister, Apple Tree, lives high on the hill, where she can see everything that passes by. Perhaps she can help find your spindle."

"Thank you!" said the girl, and she headed up the hill.

Atop the hill was a beautiful apple tree, heavy with both blossom and fruit. The girl went up to the tree and asked, "Sister Apple Tree! Sister Apple Tree! So beautiful with your flowers and fruit! I have lost my spindle down the well, and I must find it before I can go home. Have you seen my spindle?"

"Oooooh!" said the wind whistling in the leaves of the tree "Oooooh. I haven't seen your spindle, but my boughs are so heavy and laden with fruit, I am afraid they might break off. Can you harvest some apples and lighten my load, little human child?"

And so, the girl shook the tree, and she collected the apples, tucking a few into her apron. When the sweet juice touched her tongue, she smiled, and was not so afraid anymore.

The tree said, "Thank you! Oh, thank you, for picking my fruit. Thank you for lightening my load. I have not seen your spindle, but Mrs. Hell lives in yonder cottage. Perhaps she can help you find it."

"Thank you," said the girl, and she set on her way, munching and crunching an apple.[60]

She walked through the meadow and came to a house, and she knocked upon its door. An old woman answered the door and asked what she wanted. "Frau Holle, Gracious Grandmother, Sister Apple Tree has sent me to you. I have brought you some apples, and I ask for your help. I was spinning by the well, and my head flew away in fancy. I dropped my spindle down the well, and now I have come here to find it."

"I can help you get your spindle back, but first, you must help here in my house. Will you stay a while and help me?"

So, the girl stayed, and she helped Frau Holle and learned many, many things. She swept the floors and did the cooking. She made the beds and shook out the featherbeds, causing the snow to swirl. For almost a year, she lived with Frau Holle and learned many things from her. Finally, however, the girl missed her home, and asked if she could return.

60 Unless you know what you are doing, do not eat food in the Underworld.

"Of course, my dear, I will send you home, but first, I must give you what you deserve." They walked back across the meadow, past the apple tree, past the oven, until they came to a cool, clear pond, which was also the well in the world above. Frau Holle gave the girl back her spindle and kissed her once on the forehead. "Do not say a word," she cautioned, "until you are back at your stepmother's house."

Following Frau Holle's instruction, the girl dove into the pool, and found herself rising up, up, up. When she found herself beside the well, she touched the grass and shook off her trance, and ran all the way home, surprised to find she had been gone only a few hours. When she got there, she began to tell her tale, but when she opened her mouth to speak, a shower of golden coins fell from her lips. Her stepmother demanded to know where she had gotten them, and so she related the whole tale. Stepmother, always covetous and mean, immediately thought to get more of such riches.

Stepmother took her daughter to the well, dropped in a spindle, and then pushed Stepsister into the well after it. Like her sister, Stepsister fell and fell and fell and found herself in the meadow. She set off for Frau Holle's house. She saw the oven, but ignored the bread's cry. She saw the apple tree, but did not help her. She came to the Frau Holle's house, where she offered to help with the housework. However, she soon reverted to her lazy and selfish ways. Frau Holle grew frustrated with her, and took her to the pond to send her home. "But first," said Frau Holle, "I will give you just what you deserve. I warn you, you mustn't speak until you return to your mother's house."

The lazy stepsister swam through the pond, and up, up, up the well. She ran home, and when she got there, she opened her mouth, awaiting her gold. However, from this sister's lips fell nothing but swamp muck and frogs—just what she deserved!

There are many, including Jacob Grimm and myself, who believed Frau Holle to be an inheritor of an ancient Germanic goddess gone into hiding, one whose home lies on the other side of the well. He remarks on several of her features, not all fully apparent in this telling of the story, including her association with the Winter Solstice.

In addition to the commonly known tale I related above, scholars have identified at least eleven medieval sources from the region that reference Frau Holle, the oldest dating from the thirteenth century.[61] "She loves to haunt

61 Cat Heath, "From Fairytale to Goddess: Frau Holle and the Scholars That Try to Reveal Her Origins."

the lake and fountain; at the hour of noon she may be seen, a fair white lady, bathing in the flood and disappearing; a trait in which she resembles Nerthus. Mortals, to reach her dwelling, pass through the well...."

Jacob Grimm believed that, following the coming of the Romans, the goddess who would become Frau Holle was associated with their goddess Diana, particularly in the region surrounding Würzburg. "The Passion of St. Kilian," written between 788 and 800 CE, describes Killian's struggles to Christianize the area. In Würzburg, the peasants are quite adamant that they wish to continue in their old ways, saying, "*Volumus servire magnae Dianae, sicut et anteriores nostril fecerunt patres, et prosperati sunt in eo usque in praesens*," meaning, "We want to serve the great Diana, as our fathers did and in doing so, have prospered well to this day." In addition, in five of those eleven sources I mentioned earlier, Frau Holle and Diana are explicitly equated.

So, who was this goddess whose land lies on the other side of the well, before she was called Frau Holle, before she was called Diana?[62] Many, including Grimm, think it is Frija (a.k.a. Freya), a Germanic goddess of love and domesticity. Grimm says of her: "We gather from all this, that the forms and even the meanings of the two names border closely on one another. Freyja means the gladsome, gladdening, sweet, gracious goddess, Frigg the free, beautiful, loveable; to the former attaches the general notion of frau (mistress), to the latter that of frî (woman)."

Whomever this goddess is—perhaps many related goddesses—we know where she lives: down, down, down the well. And so, it is there that we must go. Frau Holle's story is, at least in the way I understand it, a secret lesson in the Granny Trance. There are three features to the story that are classically associated with the Granny Trance: The first is spinning. The next is the entrance into an opening in the earth. Many people learn to enter the Underworld by entering into the hollow of a tree and following its roots into the earth. However, in many traditions, one goes down a well instead. The third is that when the traveler returns, having had a long, complex, and grandiose journey, they find almost no time has passed in the "real world."

---

62 Diana, in this underworld guise, is often also called Hekate, whom we will discuss further in Chapter Three.

Seven Materials for Magic

There are a lot of kinds of magical materials. In fact, all materials have their own magic! Instead of attempting to make a catalog of materials with just a little bit about each, I'll let you look online for such lists, and instead talk in detail about a few of my favorite materials. As we move through the examples, pay careful attention to how the magical properties of each material are extensions of its physical/chemical properties and its historical/cultural contextualization. We learn the "virtue" of a thing by careful observation. I have not included any plant materials on the list below, because I cover them very extensively in *The Big Book of Magical Incense.* If I were to pick seven favorite plant materia, they would be mugwort, frankincense, rose, dittany of Crete, cinnamon, cedar, and saffron, all of which I discuss in the incense book.

Water

Oh water, blessed water! Water is the very fluid of life! Water is the foundation of most potions, and water from different sources has different magical qualities. For example, thunder-water (water collected during a thunderstorm) is excellent for martial magic, or anything else that needs a lot of power released all at once. River water is excellent for travel and communication magic, but really only has much power within its own watershed. Underground water, such as from a well or spring, retains its association with the Underworld, and so is an excellent scrying medium in which to call the dead, and especially lovely for working with Grandmother Winter. Moon water (rain gathered during a full moon)[63] is excellent for all types of lunar magic, particularly as a scrying medium.[64] I strongly advise you to collect water from special places you visit and from different kinds of weather. Water is also an excellent link to magically potent places. Whenever friends visit bodies of water, I always ask them to bring me back some.

Salt

Plain table salt, NaCl (sodium chloride), is one of the most important substances on Earth, a cornerstone of all life. The most ancient humans, who ate a diet rich in animal products, did not usually need to supplement their diet with salt, although they still prized it as a flavoring and preservative. However, the grain-based diets that rose to prominence in the Neolithic age cannot sustain

63 You can also just set out water under a full moon to charge, but that is not as strong.

64 You'll learn more about scrying in Chapter Four, and more about planetary (including lunar) magic in Chapters Five and Six.

human life without additional sources of salt. As agricultural civilization spread, salt became an important trading commodity; it was so valuable that our word *salary* derives from "salt."

Salt's crystalline structure makes it excellent at absorbing and diffusing magical energies, and its potent taste makes it a great trigger for snapping out of trance. It purifies and preserves foods, and by sympathetic extension, it also functions magically as a purifier and protector. A circle of salt around you will protect against most incoming malefica (but also any incoming blessings), and a line of salt on the doorstep serves a similar function. Carry fast food packets of salt in your pockets to ward off ill luck, and keep a big bag of sidewalk salt on your porch to ground out the pollution and miasma of the world. Bathe in saltwater[65] for a deep cleansing to break curses, diffuse negativity, and rebalance the energy body.

When salt appears to me in anthropomorphic form, it is often in the form of Amphitrite (Ἀμφιτρίτη), a very ancient sea goddess who becomes, in later myths, the Nereid wife of Poseidon. Her name means "to wear out around," for she is the inescapable wave that erodes every shore and smooths every corner. Later Greek poets make her the personification of salt water, and Romans compared her to their saltwater goddess, Salacia.

In my personal practice, I work with Amphitrite as a personification of the salubrious cleansing power of salt. She appears to me most often as a salt-white mermaid with white hair and pearlescent scales on her lower half. She has piercing blue eyes. She is often holding a large scallop shell full of sea salt. I find her an excellent ally for all types of work with saltwater, but particularly cleansing or banishing work. At other times, Salt appears to me as a dark-skinned dwarf, wearing white overalls and a white pit helmet, covered in white crystals, and carrying a pickax.

Railroad Spikes, Horseshoes, and Other Iron Stuff

Almost as long as we have been forging iron, people have been using it for magic. It is associated with smith gods (for obvious reasons), and also with warrior gods (because iron weapons changed the course of history), and thus with the planet Mars (also because Mars is rust colored.)[66] Iron is considered extremely apotropaic (averting evil magic) and is thought to be proof against malicious djinn, fae, and trolls alike. However, iron is also understood to ward

65 Note that Epsom salt (MgSO4), while lovely to bathe in, is not magically interchangeable for table salt (NaCl). I typically use both when I bathe.

66 Indeed, the Red Planet acquires its red color from the iron oxide that makes up much of its surface.

off beneficent nature spirits, who shrink from its touch as if burned. Is this remembrance of the days when iron plows and iron blades raped and pillaged their way across Europe, conquering the indigenous populations and spirits as they went? I guess we'll never know.

In his *Natural History*, the famous ancient Roman scholar Pliny says that iron nails hung above a door serve to protect the home against hungry ghosts and other malicious spirits, a practice also common in India. In China, the points of iron plowshares are used, and here in the United States, horseshoes are the preferred iron door charm (more on this shortly). As I mentioned in the prologue, iron railroad spikes can be used to "nail down" a property to prevent it from selling.

Cast iron cauldrons (or Dutch ovens) make excellent fortresses or prisons; their iron forms a barrier to many forms of magic. Magics too delicate to be exposed to the currents and tempests of the world may be kept inside, as can things you would like to hide from view. Similarly, they can be used to keep hostile magic from getting out. If you have a need to store a cursed object or something else magically dangerous or unsavory, put it in an iron Dutch oven, completely bury it in salt, and then tie the iron lid on.

For those doing more advanced magical work, cauldrons are an easy place to create a connection to the void and a receptacle in which energies or spirits that need to be sent away can be cast. Fill the cauldron with sea water[67] and ask Okeanos (or your favorite deep-ocean spirit) to pull the bad thing down, down, down and away to the black, cold, salty depths, there to be encased as a pearl. If you use your cauldron for unsavory magic, be sure to clean it *very* well before using it for food again.

Horseshoes over the Door

Hanging a horseshoe over your door for luck is an old custom, practiced in many countries and cultures. It is unclear when the tradition originated, but it is likely that it grew out of a very ancient tradition of iron talismans made in the shape of a crescent moon or a pair of horns. The antiquity of the moon/horn shape as a protective amulet cannot even be guessed. All over the world, including at the most ancient of Paleolithic sites, we find this motif used; it is doubtless among the oldest of human amulets. The horseshoe, then, combines the luck-drawing magic of the horned moon and the evil-averting power of iron into a singular amulet for the door.

---

67 Be sure to wash the cauldron when you're done, or the cauldron will rust.

Many people date the tradition to the legend of the tenth-century English saint Dunstan, the blacksmith. This is most likely a retelling of a pre-Christian tale, as the real St. Dunstan was not a blacksmith, but a monk who become abbot of Glastonbury, and was "skilled in making a picture and forming letters," a level of education likely unavailable to most blacksmiths.

As the story goes, one night Dunstan was working late in his smithy, singing a song to himself while he worked. Drawn by the sound of the music, the devil appeared, in all his red-skinned, hoof-footed glory, and demanded that Dunstan make him a pair of new shoes. Dunstan did so, affixing the shoes with red-hot nails, making the devil dance, begging Dunstan to remove them. Before agreeing to do so, the good saint extracted a promise from the devil to never bother a home that hung a horseshoe above its door.

No matter the origin of the myth, hanging a horseshoe over the door is a very old and storied magic. I have always been taught that horseshoes ought to be hung with the points facing up, so that the good luck can't "spill out," as it would if the horseshoe was hung with the opening facing down. However, opinions on this matter vary. It is better to hang a used horseshoe than a new one, the repeated poundings by the horse's foot having driven out all evil from the shoe. Finally, it is unwise to hang a horseshoe above a metal door, as the luck will simply bounce off the door and away into the world. If your front door is metal (as mine is), it is better to hang the horseshoe over the front window.

Horseshoes can also be hung in a single person's bedroom to attract a lover. For this purpose, horseshoes with seven nail holes are considered the luckiest. Traditional teachings say that they should be hung opening up in a man's bedroom and opening down for a woman (the sex and/or gender of desired lovers does not matter). I don't know what direction people of other sexes and/or genders should hang them. No matter your assigned gender, you are free to do what seems best to you.

Embroidery Floss and Other Threads

Embroidery floss is one of my favorite materials to work with. It comes in a huge variety of colors and is small, cheap, and easy to store. Additionally, it can be worked with in a variety of ways, including sewing, braiding, knotting, and making tangles or nests. Personally, I prefer to work with natural materials in my magic. In embroidery floss, that generally means cotton, or occasionally silk. However, I also use rayon thread[68] when that's what I have handy. I

68 Rayon is the "normal" material for embroidery floss.

don't use yarn as often, mostly because I do more embroidery than yarn-based crafts, but floss, yarn, ribbon, and other kinds of thread are all more or less the same from a magician's point of view.

I encourage you to google "knot magic" to learn a wide variety of thread-based magic. Here is an example I learned from a "fairy friend" as a kid;[69] it's a variant of a large class of spells called "witch's ladders." It can be performed with embroidery floss, hair, or any other kind of thread. Slowly tie thirteen knots while saying the following rhyme, and then hang the string from a tree branch (do not tie it around the tree):

"Thirteen knots, all in a row,
Sun knot, moon knot, star knot, glow!
Earth knot, tree knot, flower knot, grow!
Rabbit knot hops, Crow knot flies.
Rock knot sits, Wind knot sighs.
Squirrel knot climbs, Cloud knot skies.
Final knot, Elf knot, makes it come true!
Alacazam! Alacazoo![70]
Final knot, Elf knot, makes it come true!"

Coins

Some of my favorite materials to work with are coins. Like all metals, they are easy to charge, but also easy to discharge. They are ubiquitous and inconspicuous in almost any setting. They are beautiful and inherently valuable. They are inscribed with lots of awesome symbolism. Basically, they're very cheap, readily available, small metal talismans with beautiful pictures on them. What could make a better material for magic?

Coins have a long history of being used as amulets and spell components. I'm mostly only familiar with US coins, but by learning the method, you can extend it to the coins of any nation. Older coins usually have established folklore attached to them. For newer coins (like euros), you might need to make your own judgments based on the materials they are made from and the images they feature.

69 I have slightly edited it from the rhyme I used as a child, to improve the poetic meter.

70 As far as I know, these particular magic words are from the 1960s cartoon *The Flintstones,* but many others, such as *abracadabra,* are very ancient.

There are lots of ways to use coins after they've been enchanted. The easiest way is to just carry one in your pocket as a "lucky coin." You can also drill a hole[71] or wrap them in wire to wear as jewelry. You can put them in small charm bags or put them on an altar. You can also give them to other people to target them with your magic. Slipping someone magical material in order to activate a spell is a very traditional technique sometimes called "laying a trick," especially when discussing curses. Getting someone to put a quarter in their pocket is much easier than slipping most magical talismans onto their person, and no one is suspicious if they find some pennies under their bed.

Pennies (and all copper things) are sacred to the goddess Aphrodite, as well as most other Indo-European emanations of the Evening Star. Aphrodite's connection with copper is very ancient. Our English word *copper* derives from the Greek κυπριο (Kyprus), which is both the name of the metal and the island where it was mined, today called Cyprus. Additionally, in the ancient world, mirrors were usually made of copper, polished to a reflective sheen. For this reason, very clean, shiny pennies are especially good for love spells. To attract romance, carry seven blessed pennies in your right pocket. To attract sex, carry them in your left. In addition to their use in Venereal[72] magic, because they feature Abraham Lincoln, they are excellent for political magic aimed at liberation, freedom, or defeating white supremacy.

All dimes, but particularly old silver Winged Liberty dimes (often called "Mercury dimes"), are obvious tokens for magics associated with the Roman god Mercury, or any other Indo-European emanation of the quickest of planets. They make excellent lucky coins, as well as charms for gamblers and travelers.

---

71 How do you drill a hole in a coin? Older coins, which were made of softer metals like silver, can be bored by hand or by pounding a nail through them. However, it is very difficult to drill through modern US coins without a powered drill. In a powered drill, use a small diamond-tipped "twist" drill bit. These are often labeled as a "jeweler's bit." You'll also want a small file to smooth it. These are often labeled "needle files." Do not hold the coin in your hand while drilling; it will get very hot (from the friction). Use pliers or (better yet) vice grips or a small C-clamp to clamp the coin to a block of wood. If you show this list to someone at a small, independent hardware store, they can help you pick out exactly what you need. With the exception of the drill, these are all very inexpensive (and useful!) tools. You don't have to tell them about the magic if you don't want; making jewelry from coins is something everyone understands. But wouldn't it be more fun if you did tell them?

72 Venus-y. The traditional adjectives for the planetary gods are: Lunar, Mercurial, Venereal, Solar, Martial, Jovial, and Saturnian. We'll talk about this more in Chapter Six, "Planetary Magic."

Hung from the rearview mirror, or even just kept in the glove compartment, they are excellent as a car blessing. While you may occasionally get a Mercury dime as change (I consider such events powerful omens of Hermes-Mercury's presence), they can also be bought at any coin shop for slightly more than the cost of the silver. As of May 2025, a Mercury dime should run you about $4.

Just as the Fleet-footed One guides us on our earthly travels, he also holds our hand when it is our time to walk the Long Road, and for this reason, dimes are the traditional coin of the dead. Leave dimes on gravestones to "pay" for any dirt you take or any deals you make. On the Greek side of my family, finding dimes is understood as a message from our recently dead kin that they are watching over us. I sent my parents to the crematory with Mercury dimes on their eyes.

The classic style of quarters, featuring George Washington on one side and an eagle on the other, are excellent tokens for Jupiter or any other Indo-European emanation of the greatest of planets. They are excellent for political magic to ensure just and good leaders, any magic dealing with management or leadership generally, and magic designed to acquire power (like a promotion at work). While they also can be used for wealth magic, for that, I prefer the gold-colored Sacajawea dollars I'll discuss below.

There are now many, many different backs on US quarters, and new ones come out every year. Many feature American sacred locations (such as national parks), animals and trees native to North America, and American heroes among the Mighty Dead (like George Washington and Sacajawea). Think about the symbols on them and use your imagination to make up spells to accompany each of them! For example, in a few pages, you'll learn a spell using the Vermont state quarter, which features maple syrup making, along with maple syrup (another great materia indigenous to North America!) for a kind of sweetening spell.

Gold (colored) Sacajawea coins with the Three Sisters on the back are a relatively new addition to my magic. As you might imagine, golden coins featuring a mother and child on one side and the bounty of the earth on the other are excellent for drawing wealth, fecundity of womb or field, and all kinds of luxury, joy, and good things. There are twenty-three other types of Sacajawea coins to experiment with.

Red Ochre

Red ochre is a special kind of dirt that's full of hematite[73] (Fe_2O_3). Red ochre is dark red, ranging from brick to dried blood. It is very common worldwide, and has been extensively used in ritual in all times and places there have been humans. Pieces of ochre inscribed with abstract designs more than 75,000 years old have been found in Africa, and red ochre was used in burials as early as 40,000 years ago in Australia. In prehistoric Europe, its use was both ubiquitous and multi-mysterious:

> *"The use of ochre is particularly intensive: [at some sites] ... practically all the loose ground seems to consist of ochre. One can imagine that the Aurignacians regularly painted their bodies red, dyed their animal skins, coated their weapons, and sprinkled the ground of their dwellings, and that a paste of ochre was used for decorative purposes in every phase of their domestic life..."*[74]

In my personal practice, a salve of red ochre and ghee[75] connects us to our deepest witch-ancestors—and to the Great Goddess. By covering ourselves in it, we reconnect with the blood of birth, the blood of death, and the sorceress heartbeats in between. I also make a similar salve, of red ochre and the rendered fat of an American black bear, for connection to the Great Bear of the North, Ursa Major. You will learn a related spell in Chapter Ten.

Origami Paper

Origami paper is a very easy way to weave the powers of the colors into any kind of spell. In my opinion, almost every kind of magic benefits from the

73 Although this means "bloodstone" in Greek, this is not the same gem as bloodstone.

74 André Leroi-Gourhan, *The Art of Prehistoric Man in Western Europe* (Thames and Hudson, 1968), 40.

75 I sometimes make it with olive oil instead. If you've seen me do an ecstatic Hekate ritual at an outside festival, you may have watched me pour a bottle of red sludge over my head. That was red ochre in olive oil (with some additional herbs and scents).

application of color. Sometimes I use origami paper to fold votive offerings, poppets (which you'll learn about below), and other spell components. Most of the time, however, I just use it for writing petitions, sigils (see Chapter Three), pentacles (see Chapter Four), and other kinds of written magics. Below, you can see some instructions for folding a paper crane, traditionally used in wish spells.

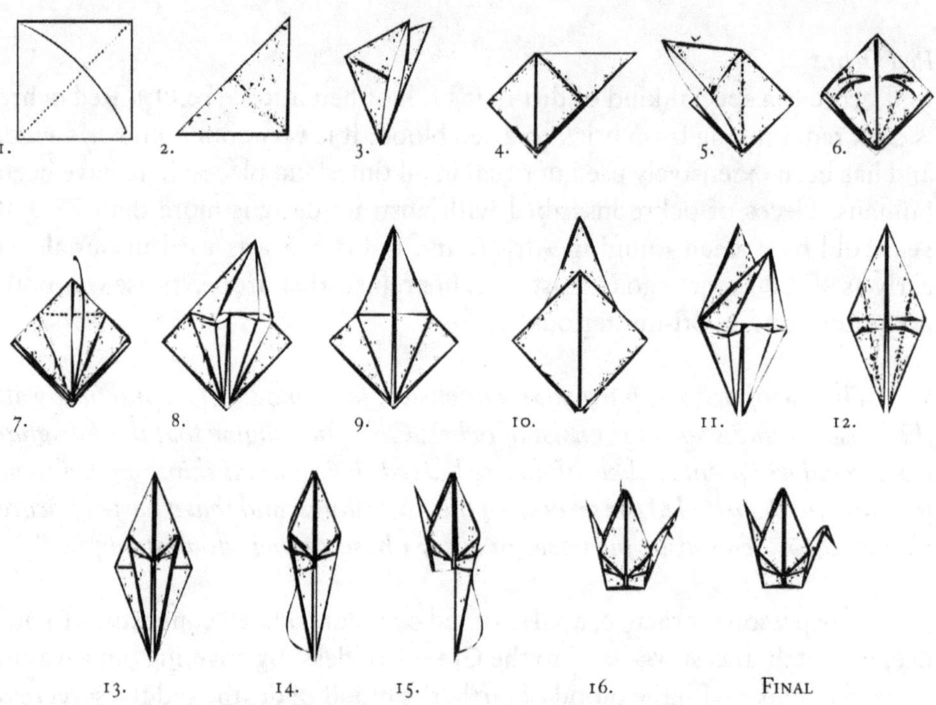

Lesser Ritual: Awakening Magical Materials

What I call *awakening* materia, and some others call *charging* or *blessing* them, is at its most basic the magic that turns objects into people. Of course, as an animist, I believe they were people all along, which is why I think of the process as less of a transformation than simply a change of state. That's why I call it *awakening*—to remind us that the spirit was always there. You've actually already done a kind of awakening—"dressing" candles is a special case of awakening. In the examples below, I'll talk about salt, but you can use the same method for any kind of material. As always, we'll begin with our four-step method. When applied to awakening materia, that looks like:

1. **Understand:** What material are you using? What do you know about it? Why did you choose it? Examining it very carefully. How is it like/unlike other versions of the same material? (For example, how is mountain salt different from sea salt? What sea is your sea salt from?)
2. **Plan:** Make a list of specific magical virtues you want to awaken in the material. Ideally, write a little poem or charm that calls them forward.
3. **Execute:**
    * Enter magical space/time/consciousness.
    * Raise power (for example, with the LRRS).
    * Speak your charm in your best magician voice.
    * Push energy into the materia, just like you did with the candle (you can push energy that is of an appropriate color, rainbow, or uncolored).
    * Greet them by name. ("Hello, Salt! Welcome! I am so happy to meet you! I have awakened you for the purpose of....")
4. **Analyze:** Examine the material again after awakening. Can you sense any differences? Listen to the materia—is it trying to say anything to you? How did it work in the spell?

As examples, let's look at two different charms to awaken salt as a curse breaker. The first is an ancient Mesopotamian spell that I lifted from my seventh-grade history textbook.[76] That book did not cite a source, but now, with more exposure to Mesopotamian spells, I suspect this is probably a Thorkild Jacobsen translation of the Maqlû tablets.

"*O Salt, created in a clean place,*
For food of gods did Enlil destiny thee.
Without thee, no meal is set out in Ekur,
Without thee, god, king, lord, and prince cannot smell incense.
I am NAME, child of NAME,
held captive by enchantment,
held in fever by bewitchment.
O Salt, break my enchantment! Loose my spell!
Take from me the bewitchment!
And, as my creator, I shall extol thee!"

76 Marvin Perry, *Western Civilization: Ideas, Politics, and Society,* Volume I: To 1789.

Notice the specific qualities of salt which are called forth in the beginning of the spell:

* Purity ("created in a clean place")
* Sacredness ("for food of gods...")
* Indispensability ("without thee...")

Now, let's look at a different spell, which uses salt to dispel a curse (in this case, the evil eye). This one was taught by a Sefardic (Iberian Jewish) women in Sarajevo in the 1980s.[77]

"Just as the salt dissolves in the water
So will the evil eye dissolve in this body.
To the depths of the sea it will go
And not return to the body."

Although the intentions of the two spells are very similar, the specific qualities being awoken are very different. In the second, the spell awakens salt's solubility in water and its connection with the sea. It then sympathetically suggests that the evil eye is likewise soluble and to send evil into the ocean. Just like salt, almost all materia have many different qualities that can be awakened, even for the same kind of work. In the example spell below, we'll use the pictured coin and maple syrup. Can you guess what qualities we'll awaken before you read the spell?

Spell: Vermont Quarter Sweetening Spell

The 2001 Vermont quarter depicts a man tapping maple trees for syrup. In the background of the coin is Camel's Hump Mountain. In this spell, we'll use the coin to lay a trick as part of a sweetening spell. Sweetening spells, in general, are used to make someone feel favorably toward you and want to help you. This "good feeling" isn't necessarily (or even usually) romantic in nature. Sweetening spells are often worked on a boss, parent, or neighbor as well. They're also good to mend hurt feelings in existing relationships with family, friends, or lovers. The version I'm presenting here is all-purpose; you should have no trouble adapting it to your specific situation.

77 Tamar Alexander and Eliezer Papo, "On the Power of the Word: Healing Incantations of Bosnian Sephardic Women," Menorah 2 (2011), 57–117.

You will need:

* 2001 Vermont quarter
* Maple syrup
* A small candle (birthday candles are a good size for this)
* A picture of the intended target
* Paper
* Scissors
* A pen or marker
* A small saucer or bowl
* Additional links to the target are great, but not strictly necessary

Steps:

1. To begin, cut out a circle slightly smaller than the saucer or bowl you are using.
2. Next, write your target's full name three times in the middle of the circle.
3. Turn the paper so that their name is upside down, and write your full name over top of the target's three times.
4. Now, around the edge of the circle, write your exact wish. For example, if you want your boss to be impressed by you, you might write: "*[Boss's name] will be impressed by the quality of my work and give me a promotion and a raise.*" You need to write it in script without picking your hand up. If there is extra space, complete the circle before lifting your hand. It's really important that the script makes a complete circle. If you mess up, throw it out and start over. After completing the circle, you can go back to cross your t's, etc.
5. Put the circle of paper, writing side up, in the saucer. If you have material links, put them on the circle of paper.

6. Next, put the picture of the person on top of that. If you don't have a picture, then get better at internet stalking.
7. Pour a small pool of maple syrup over the photo and petition paper.
8. Place the coin, tree side up, in the center.
9. Light the candle and drip a few drops of melted wax onto the coin. Use that to stick the candle to the coin.
10. Tell your exact wish to the candle at least three times, out loud.
11. Continue speaking from your heart to the candle aloud the entire time the candle is burning.
12. Once the candle has burned out, remove it, and put the coin in your mouth, syrupy side down.
13. With it in your mouth, say (as well as you can around the coin), *"As the coin has been made sweet to me, may I be sweet to [NAME]."*
14. Finally, contrive to give the coin to the target. If that is not possible, leave it in their office or somewhere else associated with them.

Greater Ritual: Awakening a Poppet or Idol

Perhaps the most archetypal example of sympathetic magic is piercing a doll with pins, or burning an effigy, in order to bring injury and affliction on the target. While such dolls are often colloquially called *voodoo dolls,* that is an offensive and inaccurate name for them. They're a cross-cultural phenomenon and entered modern American witchcraft by way of Britain. In modern American witchcraft, they are most often called *poppets,* which is basically just an old-timey way to say *puppets*. Here in Appalachia, they're often called *dollies*.

Poppets can be made from a wide variety of materials. The most common are fabric, beeswax, and clay, but I also make them from paper, yarn, bread dough, apples, mud, and many other materia. In this example, I'll be talking about making a fabric doll, but you can easily adapt the method to whatever kind of doll you like.

Step One: Assemble Links

Begin by assembling as many links as possible to the person whom you're duplicating. Hair, nail clippings, used condoms, clothes, pillowcases, used napkins, jewelry, etc. Anything with their DNA on it. Anything they've kept close to their body. Also collect as many symbolic links as possible: their name, their parents' names, their phone numbers, photos, birthday—any identifying information you can collect.

Step Two: Make the Doll

The simplest possible form of poppet for a human is a photo of the person (without other people in it) around which you write other information (such as their name and birthdate). However, if you have access to clothing they've worn, I encourage you to use it to make a fabric poppet. Here's how:

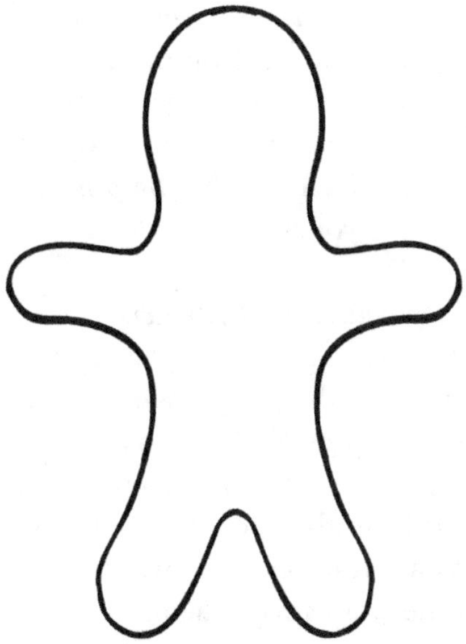

1. Lay the fabric out smooth, and fold it over so it's doubled, with one layer on top of another.
2. Sketch a doll shape like the one shown here. I find that about six inches tall (around the size of a dollar bill) is just right for most purposes, but you can make your poppet any size.
3. Cut the shape out of the fabric. You should now have two identical pieces.
4. Sew around the edges, but leave one side open. I was taught to do this with red silk embroidery floss, but I don't really think it matters. I use a blanket stitch, which you can ask the internet to teach you.
5. Once the doll is mostly sewn up, pack it full of all the links you collected, mixed into some kind of soft filler (I often use dryer lint). You can also mix in herbs or other materia appropriate to your cause (rose petals for love, hot peppers for a curse, lavender for sleep, etc.). Use the eraser end of a pencil to help shove the filling into the limbs and head if needed.
6. Once the doll is full, sew it fully closed. I often embroider a face, because I'm extra, but you can also draw one with a permanent marker or leave it blank.

Step Three: Baptize the Doll

There are many, many methods for awakening a poppet. I encourage you to develop your own. Here is one bare-bones method:

1. Enter into magical space, time, and consciousness by any method.
2. Light a white candle and some frankincense or other "churchy" incense.
3. Make a small bowl of saltwater.

4. Directly address the poppet, speaking from your heart, and saying something like:[78] *"You are no longer a creature of cloth and thread. You are [NAME]. What happens to you will happen to them."*
5. Wave the poppet above the candle flame. Be careful not to accidentally light it on fire! *"…I baptize you [NAME] by fire and light!"*
6. Wave the poppet through the incense smoke. *"…I baptize you [NAME] by sweet-smelling smoke!"*
7. Flick a drop or two of saltwater on the poppet. Don't get it soggy. *"…I baptize you [NAME] by the salty sea!"*
8. Breathe into the poppet, and feel it come to life. *"…I baptize you [NAME] by the power of my breath, which is no longer mine, but yours!"*

Step Four: Ritual Theater

Now you're ready to play with your doll(s)! Compose a small ritual where you enact on the poppet whatever you'd like to have happen to the target. Piece it with pins or thorns as a curse. Write on it with a magic marker. Put it in the freezer to chill someone out. Kiss or fondle the doll for obvious reasons. Move it about on a map to draw the target toward a place (or send them away from one). Crown it for success. Make multiple poppets, and play out little stories with them.

78 If you're looking for inspiration, check out Ezekiel 37:1–10.

Chapter Three:

Symbols, Seals, and Sigils

First, an apology: this chapter gets a little more philosophical than others. Sorry if you're not into that. I also want to say right up front that this chapter on symbols was brought to you by a mathematician and poet. I am a symbol artist, but in a very different way than an illustrator is. This chapter would be very different were it written by a visual artist (for example). I know this because I spent a lot of time discussing this chapter with my BFF, co-magician, and illustrator,[79] Brian Charles, who is also a professional art educator. Visual communication does not come naturally to me.[80] In fact, when I was coming up in magic (in the late 1980s and early 90s), pop books on magic relied almost exclusively on visualizations, and for many years, I lamented that much magic would be impossible for me. However, eventually I remembered that many, many mythic and folkloric witches and wizards were blind, and so visualization couldn't possibly be necessary for all magic, no matter what pop witchcraft books said!

Symbolism: Signatures, Seals, and Signets

The first kind of symbols we'll talk about are seals, or signatures. How did our deep ancestors keep track of whose arrow brought down the ibex? How did they know whose basket was whose? How did they make their mark?

---

79 For example, the ikons in *Orphic Hymns Grimoire* are his work.

80 In fact, I have a neurological condition called *aphantasia;* I am wholly without inner imagery. My thoughts are usually in words, and also sometimes in smells or music or physical sensations, but almost never in pictures.

They used a symbol that, to members of their immediate tribe, identified them. This is equivalent to the modern "signature" or the less modern (but still quite new in terms of deep ancestry) "seal."

Seals, often in the form of signet rings, were pressed into wax and used not just to "sign" documents, but also to show that a scroll (or etc.) had not been opened. Perhaps the most famous of these is the seal of Solomon, a magical signet ring legendarily possessed by King Solomon, used to impress his commands to the djinn and angels. Opinions differ on the exact design, but most agree that it is based around a hexagram or pentagram, and included at least one Holy Name of G-d.

In modern magical parlance, a *seal* is almost always the design itself, rather than the mold that forms it. Seals are uniquely identifying "names" for specific spirits. One very common type consists of the so-called *Solomonic seals,* which come in two flavors. The first are the planetary pentacles, which I teach in great detail in my book *The Sorcery of Solomon: A Guide to the Forty-Four Planetary Pentacles of the Magician King.* We'll learn more about planetary pentacles in Chapter Six. The other type are the demonic seals, which I'll talk about more below. These seals (and these spirits) are often referred to as *goetic* because the text they are from is titled *Ars Goetia*. The Latin translates to "Art of Sorcery." The word *goetia* derives from the Greek γόης, which means "enchanter" (or "sorcerer" or "wizard" or "magician"). Although many uneducated magicians use the word otherwise, *goetia* describes a type of magician or a style of practice, not a type of spirit.

Ars Goetia is a mid-seventeenth century European textbook on Christian demon conjuration and command. There are seventy-two demons named in *Ars Goetia*. For each one, the book includes a short description and a seal. There are also very brief conjuration instructions. Similar (but not identical) lists of spirits and similar (but not identical) instructions appear in many other extant texts of the same period. We'll learn to do this sort of conjuration in Chapter Thirteen.

Seals are not essential characteristics of a spirit; the same spirit can have many, many seals. There are many other types of seals in addition to the Solomonic ones. Logos, for example, are seals for corporate egregores, just as coats of arms are seals for ancestral egregores.

Exercise: Construct a Magical Seal for Yourself

The image at right is the magical seal of the artist Anansi Akan, a friend and co-magician. You can see several features right away:

* The overlapping capital *A*'s.
* The full sentence "A is A" (which, to Anansi, is a statement about the tautological nature of all truth).
* The spider shape, which becomes an eye when turned sideways.

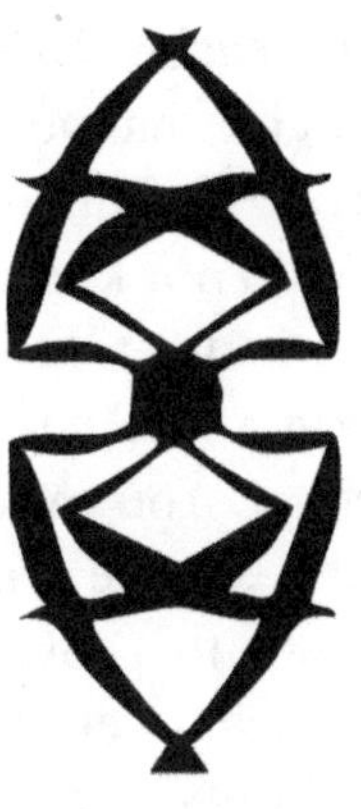

There are several other features more deeply embedded as well. Construct your own personal signature seal, including whatever features feel, at this point in your journey, most important to your identity as a witch. There are no rules for how to do this. If you are feeling at a loss, try reading or watching some online tutorials about designing logos.

Numbers and Letters

The oldest symbols we can still read are number-symbols. The oldest convincing evidence of number-symbols we have yet encountered is the so-called Wolf Bone Tally. Approximately thirty thousand years ago, someone who lived in Dolní Věstonice, in what is now the Czech Republic, cut marks that appear to count the days of a lunar cycle into the calf bone of a young wolf. Were these people counting the days until the moon was full? The days until their monthly blood came again? We'll likely never know. And yet, it seems hard to argue that they weren't counting something.

Guest Teacher: Ugg the Caveman

Our guest teacher now is Ugg, a deep ancestor, who lived around forty thousand years ago in a region we today call Cantabria, Spain. Ugg was a storyteller, a traveler, a painter, a healer, a spirit-speaker, and what we would now call a scientist, but Ugg's people would probably call a Wise One or Teacher. In this lesson, Ugg will teach us about the invention of symbolic reasoning and the symbolism of numbers, but once you get to know her, you can learn many things from her. Ugg is not intended to be a historical personage, but rather a window into early human ways of thinking. Similarly, the story below is not intended as a lesson about the history of counting, but rather a lesson on the essential nature of numbers.

Ugg Teaches: How Did Humans Learn to Count?
Imagine that you live in the long, long, long ago. Your name is Ugg, and you have seven children, Moot, Shem, Zok, Tov, Boka, Nim, and little Tee. However, you do not know that there are seven of them, because counting hasn't been invented yet. One day, as you make your way through the wilds, you come upon a tree heavy with apples. The apples are beautiful—shiny, red, and perfect. You eat one, and the sweetness explodes in your mouth. You gather some to take home to your children, but then you pause. As every parent knows, this could be a problem! If there are not enough apples, the children will fight over them. If there are any extra, the children will fight over them.

You sit at the base of the tree and think long and hard, and finally, inspiration awakens inside of you.

Writing Prompt: What Was Ugg's Insight?
How can Ugg be sure she has the right number of apples? Surely you, so modern and well educated, know what counting is. Define it before moving on. You may find doing so more difficult than you imagined. See the footnote for my definition.[81]

"For Moot" you say, and put an apple in your basket. "For Shem," and you take another apple. "For Zok, for Tov, for Boka and Nim," you recite, putting apples in your basket. "And finally for little Tee!"

You give praise to the Apple Tree, the inspirer of science, and return to your cave, where you produce exactly one apple for each child, much to the wonder of all. In the days that follow, you explain your method to all your people. Days follow days, and the moon grows and shrinks many times. You apply your new method not just to apples, but to days, and then to moons, and then to everything. You know when the moon will shine and when she will hide her face, even when the clouds hang heavy and low. You know when your blood will come and when the baby in your womb will be born. You learn to predict all the cycles of nature. You know when the rains will come, when the cold will abate, when the river will flood its banks, and when the apples on your beloved Teacher will ripen. You know how many bison are coming up the river and how many hunters should go.

You become a great teacher, a Wise One. The number-wisdom you learned from Apple Tree has given previously unfathomable prosperity and security to

81 Counting is the process of creating a one-to-one mapping between a finite collection of objects and a finite subset of an infinite ordered set of "number-words." The total number of objects (the "count") is the largest number that has such a partner. The modern English number-words are: {one, two, three, four, five, six…}.

your people. You grow old. The number-wisdom has spread far; these days, nearly everyone you meet can count a little, although few but other Wise Ones have the training to count once they've run out of fingers. Even the other Wise Ones cannot number as high as you have counted.

You are old now, the oldest among your tribe. You and Apple Tree have had to invent new ways of counting just to number your days. Days almost beyond reckoning—but you have reckoned them. You have counted higher than anyone alive.

Five fingers to a hand. Four hands (including feet) to a person. A person plus two hands less one finger is how many days are in a moon cycle. Three hands less two fingers is how many moons make a year. This, any apprentice knows. But Ugg knows more! Every day since that first, you give thanks to Apple Tree, and you count one more number. You have never run out of numbers, and now you know that you will die before you do. There was a beginning, but there will be no end! Such is the divine teaching of Apple. You have thanked Apple, and named a new number every day for three people and three years, six moons, and two days. How high have you counted?[82]

Apple Tree has taught you many mysteries and given many gifts, but there are ones you still cannot comprehend. Which are there more of, breaths in the sky or drops in a river? Who has more children, Mother of Grassblades or Mother of Stones? How high can a person count? You sit beneath your beloved teacher one last time, and as your vision fades, you begin to number the stars.

What Is Counting?

In this parable, we start off with Ugg counting to seven as a teaching example. However, humans and many other animals can recognize small numbers without counting. For example, if there is a pile of four coins, most humans (and a variety of other animals as well) can recognize how many coins there are without counting them.[83] This is sometimes called *number sense* or *numerosity* or even *approximation*. It is not proper counting and is of limited value in dealing with large numbers. Counting, on the other hand, is a human technology that allows those who have been taught to precisely reckon with numbers larger than our natural numerosity permits.

If you have ever taught a child to count, you probably have an intimate understanding of the difference between number sense and counting. Even very young children can recognize small numbers. However, very, very few

82 (3*20+3)*365 + 6*29 + 2 = 23,171 days, almost 63.5 years

83 The upper limits of how many things a person can recognize without counting varies, but for most humans, it tops out before eight.

humans learn to count without being explicitly taught. We first teach them about ordinal numbers by teaching them to say counting words in order. Most children master this by age two or three. However, there is often at least a year of further instruction and cognitive development required for them to master cardinal numbers—that is, to use the process of deploying counting words in order to answer "How many?" questions for collections larger than about ten. Most children begin to develop this skill around age four and master it by five. By age seven, most children who have been introduced to modern place-value counting can count indefinitely high. This ability to, as Ugg would say, "number the stars" is a complex and hard-won technology which humans developed over many millennia. In many ways, counting is the foundation of all modern science.

Tally marks are the oldest abstract symbols we can still read, and very likely some of the first humans ever produced. We still count this way ourselves. English speakers generally make a diagonal tally mark every five, just like a thumb, but other cultures have other systems.

When we want to count higher, we need to invent more complicated symbols. Building from tally marks, we humans eventually invented numerals,[84] and then accounting with symbols to denote units (fifth millennium BCE), and from there, symbols to stand for sounds (late fourth millennium BCE).

How to Count to Ten

English, like most modern languages, arranges numbers in groups of ten.[85] This almost certainly grows out of our method[86] for counting on fingers, counting each finger (including each thumb) once. It is for this reason that we call our base-10 system of counting *digital,* after the digits of the hand.

As we investigate the symbolism of the numbers, it is important to remember that, for the most part, number symbolism is profoundly similar across cultures. Numbers really are our most universal language. However, the ways we under-

---

84 Our modern place-value notation of numbers, which relies on the complex concept of "zero," was not developed until the seventh century CE. To learn more about this, I strongly recommend the excellent book *Finding Zero: A Mathematician's Odyssey to Uncover the Origins of Numbers* by the mathematician, historian, and mystic Amir Aczel. Indeed, I recommend all his work.

85 The Aztec and the Brythonic counted in base 20. The ancient Babylonian system—which underpins modern timekeeping, including astrology—used base 60, or sometimes base 12. Some African and Asian languages use a base 12 system. Native Californian and Mexican systems use base 8. However, worldwide, base 10 is far and away most common.

86 Cultures with base 12 systems usually use the thumb to point to each of the three "segments" of each finger, yielding twelve total segments. Cultures who reckon in base 8 often count the spaces between fingers, instead of the fingers themselves.

stand and talk about the essence of numbers can be deeply influenced by our cultural point of view. In the following discussion, I will be speaking primarily from the cultural conception of numbers in which I was trained, that of modern theoretical mathematics. That framework incorporates material from many cultures, but I understand its central roots to be in the work of the famed Greek philosopher, mathematician, theologian, and magician Pythagoras of Samos (c. 570–c. 495 BCE). I do not have time, in this book, to tell you much about him, but I encourage you to investigate on your own. He was much, much cooler and witchier than high school may have led you to believe.

One: Beginnings

One is the most fundamental number. When we count, we (usually) begin at one, and then successively add one more at each step. For this reason, nearly all numerological systems agree that one represents the fundamental unity of the cosmos, what Pythagoras[87] called the *Divine Monad*. Many later Christian philosophers equated the Divine Monad with a singular god, but that is not really what Pythagoras meant when he described it. Rather, he meant what we today might today call a *singularity*—a (largely non-physical) origin from which all things flower. As the Tao Te Ching begins:

> *"Tao produced the One.*
> *The One produced the two.*
> *The two produced the three.*
> *And the three produced the ten thousand things."*[88]

Two: Polarity

To get two, we introduce an Other to the One; suddenly, there is interplay where before there was only homogeneity. Change, the essence of creativity, becomes not just possible but desirable. The universe is, as Crowley's *Book of the Law* has it, "divided for love's sake, for the chance of union. This is the creation of the world, that the pain of division is as nothing, and the joy of dissolution all." The Jewish theologian Martin Buber says it differently in his seminal work *I and Thou*: "Love is responsibility of an I for a You: in this consists what cannot consist in any feeling—the equality of all lovers."

---

87 For simplicity, at numerous times in this discussion, I will ascribe to Pythagoras things he may or may not have said, but which were attributed to him by later Pythagoreans and Neopythagoreans. For a more detailed history of Pythagoras, I recommend the Wasserman/Gunther edition of the classic *Pythagoras: His Life and Teachings.*

88 Lao Tzu, *The Way of Lao Tzu,* trans. Wing-Tsit Chan, (Bobbs-Merrill Co., 1963) 176.

Pythagoras calls this dynamic tension the *Dyad;* today we often refer to it by its Chinese name, *yin/yang*. That tension is often symbolically represented by such pairs as night/day, female/male, hot/cold, and in/out. However, because we are currently speaking about numbers, allow us to delve into what I think of as the most fundamental expression of the Dyad's polarity: even/odd.

As the first even number, two is balanced in a way that odd numbers are not. Visually, we can understand whole numbers as rows of dots, like this:

5= ●●●●●

8 = ●●●●●●●●

Odd numbers, like five, have something in their center, whereas even numbers, like eight, have an open space.[89]

5= ●●●●●

8 = ●●●● ●●●●

That is to say, while odd numbers have only a tenuous balancing point around which to pivot, even numbers balance more easily, "folding" around an empty center. This steadiness is a central feature of the number two, and all its "children" (the even numbers) also partake in it.

Three: Tension, Instability

Three is the first odd number; like all odd numbers, it is not entirely stable. For the most part, when a three (or any other odd number) appears, the situation or quality it speaks of will be transient. Three is also prime; that is to say, the only counting numbers that evenly divide it are one and itself. Prime numbers are, in some sense, the building blocks for all other counting numbers. Prime numbers are the essential "notes" that blend together to form harmonious chords of composite numbers. Every counting number can be made by multiplying prime numbers. Even more wonderfully, each counting

89 Thus, Pythagoras calls odd numbers male and even numbers female.

number has only a single unique "recipe" of prime numbers from which it can be composed! That insight is so profound that we mathematicians call it *The Fundamental Theorem of Arithmetic.*

Interpreting this magically, we can understand three as one of the essential building blocks of creation (i.e., prime), but one that is a little bit unstable (i.e., odd). Magically, the number three—as well as other odd prime numbers[90] like five, seven, eleven, etc.—is often (but not always) associated with relationships between two people and the world around them. The threes always represent an escalation of the current situation, for better or worse.

Unsurprisingly, the symbol most associated with number three is the triangle. When, in magic, triangles appear point down, like ∇, they often represent the Great Mother, the Sacred Feminine, or the yin principle. This is due to the resemblance to a vulva. When they appear point up, like Δ, they are generally associated with the Great Father, the Sacred Masculine, or the yang principle. Triangles can also be understood as a symbol of initial manifestation. Just as any three points define a plane, three is the number at which things "begin to get real."

Four: Foundation, Stability

Like all even numbers, four is steady and reliable. However, even more so, four is doubly even.[91] It is the first square number ($4 = 2^2$). Like all square numbers (such as nine, twenty-five, etc.), it represents support and security. However, in some circumstances, this can be too much of a good thing—four is also the number of stagnation.

Like the strong foundation of a building, four embodies practicality and structure. In magic, the number four is very often associated with the four elements—Earth, Air, Fire, and Water. It is important to remember that these are "philosophical" or "mystical" elements—we are not talking about actual earth, air, fire, and water, but about spiritual forces named after them.

90 For obvious reasons, two is the only even prime number. If that is not obvious, define "even" and then define "prime."

91 That is, divisible by two twice. "Doubly even" is really just an old-fashioned way to say "divisible by four."

Earth ▽	Earth is the densest element and generally represents the body, money, housing, and other physical things. Anthropomorphic ambassador spirits of the Earth include the gnomes, pygmies, dwarves, dryads, and many types of Good Neighbors. The salt dwarf I mentioned in the last chapter is an Earth elemental. These spirits are often patient and reliable, but sometimes inflexible or closed-minded. Earth's weapon is the shield, and its tool is the spade or shovel. Earth's symbolic animal is most often the bull, but sometimes the elephant or turtle are also used.
Water ▽	Water is associated with the heart, the emotions, and relationships between people. Anthropomorphic ambassador spirits of the Waters include the undines, nereids, mermaids, and many types of sea people. Amphitrite, the salt goddess I mentioned in the previous chapter, is a water spirit but not a water elemental.[92] Water spirits are often compassionate and wise, but they can also be irrational and vicious. Water's weapon is the chalice, and its vessel is the cauldron. Water's symbolic animal is most often a fish, but sometimes a dolphin, whale, human, or mermaid is used.
Fire △	Fire is associated with the spirit and the passions; it often represents art, sex, and magic. Anthropomorphic ambassador spirits of the Flames include djinn, salamanders, vulcans,[93] and many other types of Fire beings. Fire spirits are usually brave and passionate. Personally, I find them exciting to work with, but they can also be belligerent and short-tempered. Fire's weapon is the staff, and its tool is the torch. Fire's symbolic animal is usually the lion, but sometimes a dragon or salamander is used.
Air △	Air is associated with the mind and all the activities thereof, including communication, invention, and academics. Anthropomorphic ambassador spirits of the Air include the sylphs, sylvestris, satyrs, and many other types of Fair Folk. Air spirits are most often smart and quick, although they can also be flakey and condescending. Air's weapon is the sword, and its vessel is the drum. Most often, the symbolic animal of air is the eagle, but sometimes other birds are used. In modern work, butterflies are sometimes used.

92 What exactly constitutes an elemental spirit is complicated and much debated, but gods are not elementals. To grossly oversimply, if a spirit has a name and a personality and a "biography," they are not an elemental.

93 Not the Star Trek aliens, who are quite airy. In traditional magic, "vulcans" are a kind of fire elemental that live in volcanoes.

Five: Hand, Strength

Five is a delightful number with many important properties. Like all odd numbers, it is an ephemeral waystation. Like all prime numbers, it is an essential building block of reality. Furthermore, five is a Fibonacci number. The Fibonacci sequence starts with two ones. From there, the next number is determined by adding the two previous numbers together, like this:

1
1
1+1=2
1+2=3
2+3=5
3+5=8

And so on. The Fibonacci sequence, including all of the later numbers, can be determined using the formula:

$$F_{n-2} + F_{n-1} = F_n$$

The first few[94] Fibonacci numbers are:
1, 1, 2, 3, 5, 8, 13, 21, 34, 55, 89, 144, 233, 377, 610, and 987.

For reasons that are not yet entirely understood by humans, both the Fibonacci sequence and individual Fibonacci numbers appear very frequently in nature, and are intimately related to the human sense of beauty.[95] In magic, Fibonacci numbers are often connected to a simultaneous sense of slowly unfolding beauty and near-instant flashes of inspiration. This can be literal, like the blossoming of a flower or the swelling of a fruit, or more metaphorical, like the five-seeded apple teaching Isaac Newton about gravity, or the five-seed "star" in the apple teaching Pythagoras about incommensurability.

Five is even more intimately connected to beauty than are other Fibonacci numbers, because of its special relationship with the number we call the "golden ratio." The golden ratio is a magical proportion that appears in natural shapes that are especially pleasing to humans, such as flowers and human faces, as well as spiral shells and spiral galaxies. It frequently appears

94 Thirteen might not seem like "few," but relative to the number of Fibonacci numbers (which are infinite), it is.

95 We'll discuss that more as follows, when we talk about the relationship of the number five to the so-called golden ratio.

in great art. In ancient Greece, that number was named after the great Pheidias, the fifth century sculptor, architect, and mystery initiate who designed and oversaw construction of the Athenian Parthenon.[96] In his honor, we call the golden ratio by the Greek letter Φ, also written as ϕ or φ. In English, the name of the letter is written "phi" and said[97] "fye" (rhymes with "my"). Phi makes the f/ph sound that begins the name Pheidias (Φειδίας).

One example of the golden ratio and its connection to human sensations of beauty and proportion can be found in the pentagram.

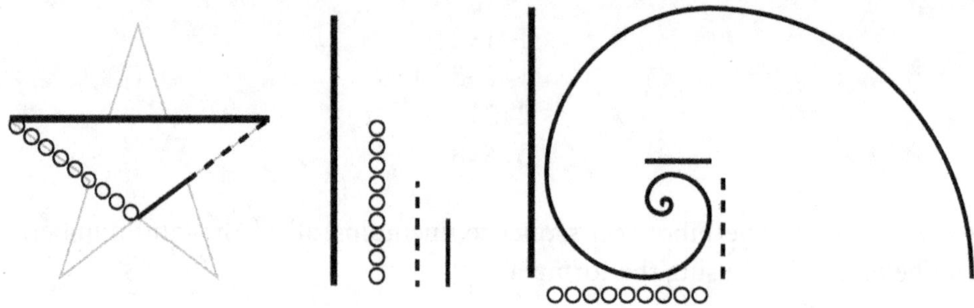

In the diagram above, the proportion of the short black line to the dashed line, and of the dashed line to the dotted line, and of the dotted line to the thick black line, are all the golden ratio, and thus fit onto the so-called golden spiral. Using the pentagram, we can calculate an exact value for the golden ratio.[98] That value is $\frac{1+\sqrt{5}}{2}$, which clearly shows the intimate connection between five and the golden ratio. The golden ratio is an irrational[99] number—it does not have a finite decimal form. It is slightly more than 1.618.

Combining all these properties together, we learn that five is one of the essential building blocks of nature, one associated with beauty and cosmic harmony, particularly the dynamic and unstably beautiful harmonies of nature.

---

96 Among many other things, he is famed for having introduced the three-formed iconography of Hekate to Athens. We will discuss this further later in this chapter.

97 By Americans.

98 If you'd like to understand why, google "compass straightedge pentagram construction golden ratio."

99 In mathematics, *irrational* doesn't mean *nonsensical.* It means that the number cannot be represented as a ratio (fraction) of whole numbers. The fact that in English, a word for "non-fraction-able" came to mean "not-understandable" is because of the deep and pervasive influence of Pythagorean number theology, and Pythagorean mysticism more broadly, on modern theories of mind.

Five is also associated with the so-called *quintessence*,[100] the mystic fifth element[101] often called "spirit" or "void" or "aether," which is the "secret sauce" that animates physical creatures with beauty, harmony, and life.

Six: Composition, Harmony

Six is the first number whose factors are two different prime numbers ($6 = 2 \times 3$). It represents the combination of even and odd, and symbolically, the resolution of all opposites. Six is the number of alchemy and anything where the whole is greater than the sum of its parts.

This union of opposites is often represented by the hexagram which combines the upward- and downward-facing triangles, as well as the four elemental symbols. This shape is also called the Shield of David (דָוִד נֵגֵמְ), particularly in Jewish and kabbalistic contexts. Today, the Shield of David is very closely entwined with both Jewish and Israeli identity, but it has never been an exclusively Jewish symbol. The Shield of David has many layers of symbolism. Legendarily, the design was painted on King David's war shield. Its six points represent the six sacred directions and the three sacred axes (up/down, front/back, left/right) surrounding the Sacred Center. It can be expanded into three (or more) dimensions. When in three dimensions, it presents as two overlapping tetrahedra (triangular pyramids) and is often called a *merkaba* or *merkavah*. *Merkavah* (הבכרמ) means "chariot"[102] and almost always refers specifically to the angelic chariot described in the book of Ezekiel. Based on the technique taught in that book, merkavah also gives its name to a category of kabbalistic trance journey techniques.

Seven: Challenge

The number seven is, to my way of thinking, one of the most magical of the digits. It is both odd and prime. As we've learned, that means it is one of the ephemeral, unstable, primal building blocks of reality. There are seven celestial bodies[103] that move through the ecliptic and are visible from the Earth—Sun, Moon, Mercury, Venus, Mars, Jupiter, and Saturn. There are seven days in a week. There are seven primary chakras.[104] As we've already discussed, in this

100 In modern English, *quintessence* is usually used to mean a "perfect example" of a thing. For example, "Gandalf is the quintessence of wizardry."

101 As you can probably tell from the sound, *quintessence* literally means "fifth element."

102 More literally, it means "thing for riding in."

103 The Greek word for these is *planetes,* which means "wanderers." We'll discuss them in substantially more detail in Chapter Five, "Planetary Magic."

104 We'll discuss this further in Chapter Seven, "Circles and Centers."

book, we use seven colors as our fundamental "flavors" of magic. Of course, as Sofia taught us in Chapter One, color exists along a spectrum; there are not seven colors but infinitely many: "Even the ones that are in between, Even the ones that remain unseen." So, if that is the case, why does our culture divide the spectrum into seven fundamental colors? The answer is deeply magical!

When Isaac Newton was developing our modern theories of light and color, he originally divided the spectrum into five colors (red, sky blue, yellow, green, and purple). However, he later added orange and indigo in order to match the color spectrum to the planets.[105] The table below summarizes those relationships. However, as with all tables, you should beware! Colors, planets, and days are not entirely interchangeable. We'll discuss all of this in much more detail in Chapter Five, "Planetary Magic."

Red	Orange	Yellow	Green	Blue	Indigo	Violet
Mars	Mercury	Sun	Venus	Jupiter	Saturn	Moon
Tuesday	Wednesday	Sunday	Friday	Thursday	Saturday	Monday

Eight: Stability

Eight is the first cube ($8 = 2^3$). In many ways, eight has the same symbolism as four, but more so. It is the cube built up from four's square—not just a stable foundation, but an entire building. Eight is generally a "lucky" number, associated with fortune, victory, and prosperity. Eights have overcome the challenges presented by seven and matured into a wiser state of being.

Because eight is two cubed, there are a total of eight numbers that can be expressed in three binary digits. In modern mathematics, we often represent the binary digits as zero and one, but in Chinese mathematics, they are often called yin (emptiness) and yang (fullness).

In trigram notation, yin is represented by a broken line (Pythagoras would call it a hole), and yang by an unbroken one. In Chinese, the eight three-digit binary numbers are called the *Bagua*, or *Eight Trigrams,* each of which is associated with a particular natural formation.

105 Learn more about this in Brent Berlin and Paul Kay, *Basic Color Terms: Their Universality and Evolution* (University of California Press, 1991).

0	000	☷	Kūn = Receptive	Earth
1	001	☶	Gèn = Still	Mountain
2	010	☵	Kǎn = Abyssal	Water
3	011	☴	Xùn = Gentle	Wind (Air)
4	100	☳	Zhèn = Arousing	Thunder
5	101	☲	Lí = Clinging	Fire
6	110	☱	Duì = Joyous	Lake
7	111	☰	Qián = Creative	Sky (Heaven)

Combining these trigrams in pairs generates a set of sixty-four hexagrams, which are the foundation of the *I Ching*, or *Book of Changes*. To learn more, I recommend Benebell Wen's excellent book *I Ching, the Oracle: A Practical Guide to the Book of Changes: An Updated Translation Annotated with Cultural and Historical References, Restoring the I Ching to Its Shamanic Origin.*

Nine: Completion

Nine, like four, is a square number—the first odd one. Indeed, it is the first odd non-prime number. These qualities tell us that while it is not entirely stable, it is also not especially dynamic. However, most of the properties of nine that we use in magic are due to it being the last single-digit number before our base-ten counting system rolls over to two digits. For these reasons, nine is sometimes called the *wishing number,* standing as it does as the last dynamic/odd outpost between the stable "end stage" of eight, and the "ultimate ending" of ten. Nine is the number of wishes fulfilled, but also of desperate pleas. This liminality means nines are also fabulous numbers for magic. One charm I use for closing spells runs like this: "By the power of the three times three, bound around this work shall be."

Perhaps my favorite association of the number in magic is the Heliopolitan Ennead, a group of nine gods from the ancient city of Heliopolis, now the northeast suburbs of modern Cairo. Below are just the tiniest snacks of information about them. If you find them as delicious as I do, I encourage you to learn more. Because my goal here is to present them as they occur in modern Anglophone witchcraft, my descriptions are slightly biased toward a somewhat Hellenized (Greek-ified) version, rather than the original, indigenous Egyptian versions.

* **Atum**, the evening sun, is a god of primordial creation from whom arises all that is. His name means "The Complete One" or "He Who Is Complete of Himself." He emerges from (and is) the primordial egg at the beginning of the world.[106] He is generally pictured holding a was scepter (the scepter of power) and wearing a crown.
* **Tefnut**, a goddess of moisture, was created by Atum from his spit (some say his semen). The meaning of her name is unclear, but some people think it is simply the sound of spitting.[107] She is generally pictured with the head of a lion with the sun on top of her head and carrying ankhs, which we will discuss later in this chapter.
* **Shu**, Tefnut's twin and husband, is a god of air, wind, and emptiness. Atum created him from his mucus in a great sneeze. Unlike his hotheaded sister-wife, he is generally understood to be a pretty chill guy, and often called upon when diplomacy is necessary. However, like us all, he also has a "hot" side, a warrior-form sometimes called Anhur

106 Similar to Phanes in Orphic myth.

107 While Anglophone cultures usually understand spitting as undignified, that is an unusual take, globally.

or Onuris. He is normally depicted as a human man carrying the was and wearing an ostrich feather on his head.

* **Nut,** also modernly called Nuit,[108] is the daughter of Tefnut by Shu. She is the sky and stars. In addition to her role in ancient Egyptian myth, she is also a very important figure in Thelema, a modern magician religion. Nut is generally depicted as a blue- or black-skinned woman (or sometimes a cow) covered in stars arched above...
* **Geb,** the twin and husband of Nut, is the land. He is normally depicted in human or goose form, but understood to be the mythic father of snakes. Geb is the god of all land, both fertile and barren. He is often depicted as lying on his back, with an erect penis, yearning toward Nut above him.

  Nut and Geb have four children, two female (Isis and Nephthys) and two male (Osiris and Set). In a Greek understanding, which permeates modern Anglophone witchcraft, the girls, like their mother, are celestial—Isis the goddess of celestial light, including both sun and moon,[109] and Nephthys the goddess of darkness. However, for Egyptians, it would be more accurate to say that Isis and Nephthys represent life/death or day/twilight. Similarly, the boys, like their father, are earthy. Osiris is the god of agricultural land[110] and Set the god of the barren desert.
* **Isis,** as I mentioned above, is the daughter of Nut by Geb. She is a goddess I adore, as do many magicians. In addition to her role as celestial illuminator, she is also a goddess of magic and fate. While many other Egyptian gods (including her sister Nephthys and brother Set) were closely associated with sorcery, Isis is almost universally understood to be the most powerful magician in the Egyptian pantheon. Among many other feats, she (temporarily) resurrected her husband Osiris from the dead, after he was slain by their brother Set. She is most often depicted as a human woman, sometimes with wings, and often holding an ankh (a symbol we will discuss later in this chapter).

---

108 This name for her, a cognate for the French word for "night," is quite modern. It was first applied to her by the occultist Aleister Crowley around the turn of the last century.

109 The relation of Isis to the moon is almost entirely Greek in origin. In Egypt, lunar gods, like Thoth, were almost exclusively male. We talked a bit about Thoth in the last chapter in relationship to his role as inventor of writing, and will discuss him much more fully in Chapter Twelve. He is the divine patron of this book.

110 It is only when he's dead (which, honestly, is most of the time, mythically) that he is agricultural. He is not just the land, but specifically the threshed grain.

* **Osiris**, the brother-husband of Isis and twin of Set, is the god of the grain, the cycle of the Nile's flooding and receding, the cycle of death and reincarnation, and the pharaoh. Indeed, pharaohs were understood to be the representatives of Osiris.[111] As in the image shown here, he is generally depicted as a green-skinned human pharaoh, often holding a shepherd's crook and grain-threshing flail. However, this is a Hellenized understanding of those symbols. In Egypt, the crook is a hieroglyph meaning "rulership" and the flail is a fly-whisk, like you see used in other African royal regalia. In later days, both acquired agricultural associations, perhaps as a subtle propaganda campaign to undercut the mytho-political power of Egypt once it became a Roman vassal.
* **Nephthys**, the twin of Isis and sister-wife of Set, is a goddess of night, mysteries, liminality, death, mourning, and magic who is sometimes syncretized with Persephone (as is Isis). Like her sister, she is a magician, specializing in healing. While Isis was the goddess of birth, Nephthys was the goddess of nursing and nurturance, and also maternal death during childbirth. Her name means "She of the Temple." She is generally depicted in human form, often with a house and basket on her head, but at other times as a hawk or other bird of prey.[112] While I love Isis, I have a more personal and devotional relationship with Nephthys.
* **Set**, also called Seth, is the twin of Osiris and the brother-lover of Nephthys (though he also has two other lovers). He is the god of storms and thunder, of the desert, and of all things strange and foreign. His animal form is a mysterious creature, often called the "Set Beast" or "Typhonic Beast," which does not entirely correlate with any known animal. Some believe it is a canine, a donkey, or an aardvark, but other experts believe it is intended to be a mythic creature and not a real animal at all. The Set Beast is generally depicted as some kind of canine (rather like a greyhound) with a forked tail and square ears. His mythology is complex, political, and very different in different time periods. In some periods, he was the chief of the gods, and in others, the archetypal villain. In addition to his role in ancient Egyptian myth, Set plays an important part in many varieties of modern Satanism. As shown, he is generally depicted as a red-skinned[113] human with the head of a Set Beast.

---

111 More accurately, living pharaohs are representatives of Horus (Osiris's and Isis's son), and become Osiris at death. Indeed, we all become Osiris in death, which is, of course, the great leveler.

112 Isis also takes this form, but less often as time goes on.

113 Red is the color of the desert in Egyptian iconography.

My friend and collaborator, the Egyptologist, Coptic magician, and all-around amazing person Dr. Tamara Siuda offered many helpful suggestions on this section. If you'd like to learn more, I strongly recommend her book *The Complete Encyclopedia of Egyptian Deities: Gods, Goddesses, and Spirits of Ancient Egypt and Nubia.*

Ten: Culmination

Because humans have ten fingers, most human counting systems use a base of ten. That is to say, after nine, we "roll over" to double digit numbers. Digital notation (writing numbers as place values) is usually understood to be a relatively new invention in human history. It is unclear when and where it was first developed. It is an amazing technology that engenders an almost magical ability to calculate easily.[114] The kind of digital notation we use today probably originated in India around the sixth century of the Christian era. However, there is good reason to believe that an early version was known to the Greek mystical-magical-mathematics genius Pythagoras in the sixth century BCE. The following is a translation of a Pythagorean prayer to the spirit of the number ten.

The Holy Tetractys

"Bless us, divine number, thou who generated gods and men! O holy, holy Tetractys, thou that containest the root and source of the eternally flowing creation! For the divine number begins with the profound, pure unity until it comes to the holy four;[115] then it begets the mother of all, the all-comprising, all-bounding, the first-born, the never-swerving, the never-tiring holy ten, the keyholder of all."

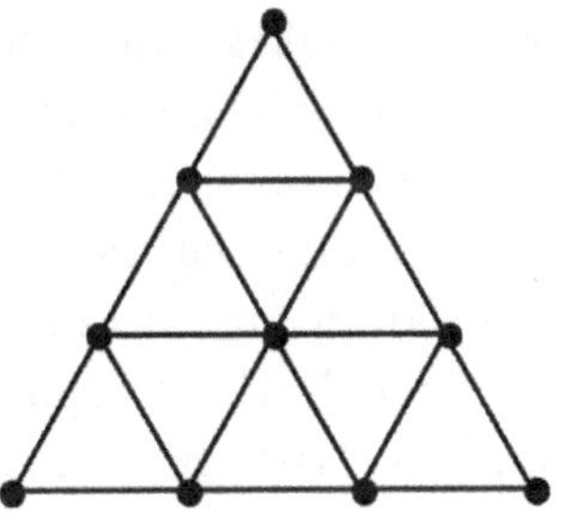

114 If you don't believe me, I encourage you to try doing some complicated arithmetic using only Roman numerals.

115 1+2+3+4=10

The Tree of Life

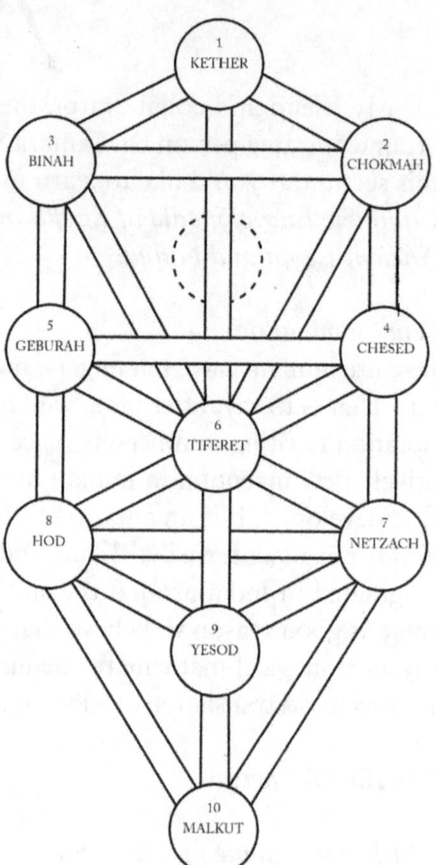

TREE OF LIFE

A note Kabbalah and cultural appropriation: The word "Kabbalah" (הָלָבַּק) means "what has been received," not in the sense of divine revelation, but in the sense of what is passed from master to apprentice. If you're learning it from a book, it's not really Kabbalah, it's just kabbalistic. While Judaism and Kabbalah are both closed practices, the kabbalistic teaching I'm about to give you was always intended to be taught to anyone who earnestly desires to learn. Moreover, the famed twentieth century activist, community organizer, theologian, mystic, and kabbalist Menachem Mendel Schneerson (1902–1994), also known as the Lubavitcher[116] Rebbe,[117] taught that some Kabbalah was kept secret in olden times, because the world was so simple that even small sparks of holiness could accidentally light a soul on fire, much to their detriment. These days, we live in an ocean of complexity, and it takes a blow torch to kindle such flame. So, we teach everyone, and know that only those who should understand will. If it makes your head hurt to read, skip to the section called "Magic Alphabets," which begins on page one hundred. True mysteries keep themselves.

116 Lyubavichi is a place in eastern Russia, where his ancestors were from. However, he and his family fled Europe during the Holocaust. He did most of his teaching in Brooklyn, where the headquarters of the movement he founded still operates. Today, his students together with their students number almost 100,000. I am not one of them.

117 *Rebbe* is the Yiddish form of the word "Rabbi." It means "Teacher."

Etz Chaim (סייחה ץע), or Tree of Life, is a classic[118] kabbalistic[119] map of the cosmos that can be interpreted in many ways. For our purposes, the most useful characteristic of the Tree of Life is that provides a detailed schematic of creation, tracing the paths[120] through which the Divine flowed into the universe, the way that Being became. As you can see in the diagram provided, the Tree of Life has ten "nodes" called *sefirot*.[121] *Sefirot* (ספירות) is the plural of *sefira* (ספירה), which literally means "enumeration" or "counting," but in the context of Kabbalah, is usually translated as "emanation." The word arises from the root ספר (sefer). From this root arises a large family of words related to books, scribes, writing, letters, counting, and numbers. As we learn about them, keep this "one weird trick" in mind: this is the same teaching on "How to Count to Ten" as you just read, just at a higher degree of mystic detail. If facts about numbers are real, they have to be the same when Pythagoras teaches them as when Isaac Luria does. Numbers are not culturally determined, even though the ways we explain them are.

1. Keter, כתר, Crown (not King)
2. Chokmah, חכמה, Wisdom
3. Binah, בינה, Understanding
4. Chesed, חסד, Mercy or Compassion or Loving-Kindness
5. Gevurah, גבורה, Strength or Might (literally, "Manliness")
6. Tiferet, תפארת, Beauty or Adornment or Harmony
7. Netzach, נצח, Victory or Eternity

118 Kabbalah is not ancient. It is a specific style of mystical/magical practice that was first developed in the eleventh century CE, in large part due to the fusion of Pythagorean number-theology, Arabic mathematics techniques, and Jewish theology. The Tree of Life is a Jewish teaching built upon the Pythagorean mystery of the Tetractys, which we just discussed. It is a much more sophisticated version of the same "how to count to ten" number mysticism I just taught you.

119 Although some (uneducated or appropriative or both) people use the word "Kabbalah" to mean either any kind of symbol-mysticism and/or any kind of Jewish mysticism, it does not mean either of those things. Kabbalah is a specific type of modern Jewish oral teaching. If you learned it from books, and not from living human teachers, it's not really Kabbalah, it's just kabbalistic.

120 In addition to the so-called "lightning path" of walking through all the sefirot in order, you will also sometimes hear about a "Pillar of Severity" or "Left Hand Path" that runs down the left-hand side of the tree (1-3-5-6-8-9-10) and a "Pillar of Mercy" or "Right Hand Path" along the right (1-2-4-6-7-9-10). While they are similar, these are not identical to the right- and left-hand paths of tantra, although I often see them equated. Many other paths exist, but are outside the scope of this book.

121 Older transliterations sometimes spell it *sephiroth*.

8. Hod, דוה, Splendor or Brilliance
9. Yesod, דוסי, Foundation (also a euphemism for genitals)
10. Malkut, תוכלמ, Kingdom (not King)

What follows is an extremely brief and simplified understanding of the sefirot, specifically their roles as "way stations of creation." While I've told the story as if it progresses linearly through time (how else could I tell it?), all of these things are happening at once, all the time. Within every sefira is a whole tree, and within that tree are others, and so on, fractally ad infinitum.

Before that, it's worth noting that I have noticed gentile authors often try to understand the tree starting in Malkut and working their way up, which seems quite backward to me, because the sefirot are quintessentially "countings," and the numbers start at the top. I'm going to count them in order.

Three Veils: Nameless Mother(s) of the Ten Thousand Things

In Hebrew, we say that the universe was created ןיאמ שי (yesh me-eyn), literally "something from nothing." In Latin, we would say *ex nihilo*. Before the Tree of Life came to be, beyond its reach and beneath its roots, are Three Veils, which separate the unfathomable, unknowable, undifferentiated *none=all* from the chaotic complexity of Creation. The Hebrew name *Ein*, or *Ain* (ןיא), means literally "not," but I understand it in the context of "Without Quality." It is the primordial state of the universe. On the other side of Nothingness, in perfect dynamic tension with it, is Ein Soph (ףוס ןיא), the transcendent and eternal Divine. *Ein Soph* means, literally, "without limit" or "infinity."[122] When Ein and Ein Soph come together, a third thing is formed, the Ein Soph Aur (רוא ףיס ןיא), or "Limitless Light." Often equated with the Big Bang, Ein Soph Aur is an essentially radiant force that powers creation, moment by moment, breathing Becoming into Being.

1: Keter

The transcendent light of Ein Soph Aur is mediated through the Divine, emerging as an emanation we call Keter (רתכ), or "Crown." Please take note: *Keter* does not mean "King"; it means "crown," from a root meaning "encircle." Keter is a dwelling place of G-d,[123] but it is not G-d themself. Keter is the lens through which the light of Ein Soph Aur is filtered into the universe. Keter is the ultimate

122 In modern Israeli mathematics, it means "transfinite."

123 For complicated kabbalistic reasons that are mostly just about showing respect, I (and many Jews) write "god" when we mean a category of spirit, and "G-d" when we mean the word as a proper name for the specific god of Israel.

and complete unity of creation, past all illusion and separation. When G-d speaks the universe into being, Ein Soph Aur is the air all around Them. Keter is the breath with which They speak. Keter is the first utterance, the sound of breath just before a word begins—this is also the sound[124] the letter א (aleph) makes.[125]

The Hebrew Name of Power[126] most often[127] associated with Keter is Ehyeh Asher Ehyeh.[128] This is a difficult name to translate, partly because Hebrew verb tenses do not entirely correspond to English ones. Like many Hebrew Names of Power, it is built from a root word meaning "to be." This name is often rendered in English as "I Am That I Am," although it is closer to "I Will Be That I Will Be." Personally, I prefer a slightly looser and more poetic translation—"I Am Being, Becoming." This name appears in Shemot (Exodus) 3:14. When Moses asks the burning bush who it is, "Ehyeh Asher Ehyeh" is the cryptic response. It can be understood in many ways. Perhaps G-d is just ducking the question. Perhaps they mean "I Am the One Who Is," implying they are all that exists? Maybe they meant "I Am the One That Just Is," referencing their quality-less-ness? Maybe it's a sort of "Who's on first" situation?—"My Name Is 'I Become.'" A plurality of simultaneous meanings is an essential feature of Jewish holy texts, and (in my opinion) all sacred writing.[129]

When an angel is associated with Keter, Metatron is the most common choice. Metatron is a sort of uber-angel or lesser-god who serves as the scribe, mouthpiece, or translator mediating between G-d and humans. He is sometimes understood as an ascended form of Enoch, the antediluvian patriarch whose name means "initiate." The origins of the name Metatron are unclear, and probably not Hebrew. Some say that it is from the Greek *meta-thronos* ("before the throne"), others that it derives from the Indo-Iranian god Mitra the "Oath Binder," who is also the origin of the Roman god Mithras. I am of this second opinion.

---

124 When I first learned this, I was taught that the sound between the two syllables of "uh-oh" is the sound of an aleph.

125 I know that if you learned "Kabbalah" from someone who didn't speak Hebrew, they told you it makes an A sound, but I assure you, it does not.

126 As witches, we could also just call them "magic words."

127 Despite what some people seem to think, the attribution of names and angels to sefirot varies widely between sources, even in traditional Jewish contexts.

128 I have chosen to not write the Holy Names of Power in Hebrew, because books containing such names have special ritual restrictions on them. In particular, they must not be thrown out. When they are worn out, they should be buried like a person. Because this is an introductory book, I don't want to put that responsibility on you. If you'd like to see them in Hebrew, just look the English name up on Wikipedia.

129 To learn more about this, google "PRDS Exegesis."

2: Chokmah

After Keter lies Chokmah (המכח), or "Wisdom." Every time Tanakh[130] praises Wisdom, it is Chokmah about whom they speak. More than any other sefira, Chokmah is often anthropomorphized into a divine figure in her own right. For example, in one of my favorite passages, King Solomon the Magician says, "Chokmah has been my love. I courted her when I was young and desired to make her my lover. I burned for her beauty."[131] In Greek, she is called "Sophia" and is the goddess of (among many other things) philosophy.

The second utterance, Chokmah is the first thing spoken into being. Chokmah is the first manifestation of the Divine. This is where the One becomes two, and it is also where two become one. This is the universe "divided for the sake of union." Chokmah is the spark of creation that, in Binah, will light the fire of the world.

When I am doing the assigning, the angel of Chokmah is Raziel, the angel of secrets. The divine name of Chokmah is usually the Most Holy Name, YHVH. The origins of the Most Holy Name are deeply unclear—it is probably related to the being verb הָיָה (hayah). Indeed, most Hebrew roots are verbs, rather than nouns, which gives a subtle animist flavor to anything you say in Hebrew. Although some Christians and Pagans pronounce the Most Holy Name as *Yahweh* or *Jehovah*, many Jews (including me) find it gross and deeply appropriative to pronounce it at all. Certainly, as a magician, it is deeply inappropriate to do so outside of magical space/time/consciousness. Indeed, Jews and magicians use a variety of apotropaic cryptonyms,[132] like Adonai ("Lord") or HaShem ("The Name") or "Most Holy Name" to avoid saying this name. I am particularly fond of *Tetragrammaton*, which is Greek for "Four-Lettered Word." In American English, "four-lettered word" is also a euphemism for "naughty word," which I find extremely delightful.

3. Binah

Next is Binah (הניב), or "Understanding."[133] In classic kabbalistic texts, Binah is sometimes referred to as a palace of mirrors, reflecting and refracting the ONE light into a million scintillating points of light. It is the Womb of Being, where the "ten thousand things" of the Tao gestate. Its Hebrew Name of

---

130 TaNaKh is an acronym for Torah, Nevi'im (Prophets), and Ketuvim (Writings). It is a non-appropriative name for the Hebrew texts that Christians call the "Old Testament."

131 Wisdom of Solomon 8:2

132 That is, nicknames used to turn away undesirable spirit powers. Like calling the Furies the Eumenides (a.k.a. the "Good-Minded") or saying "Good Neighbors" instead of the f-word.

133 Binah is a difficult word to translate. The root means "intellect."

Power is Elohim, which is a plural of Eloah, itself is a form of El. El is both the proper name of several Levantine gods, including the god of Israel, and the generic word for "god" as a species of spirit. The word *Eloah* is the female version of the word *El*, the same way *goddess* is the female version of *god*. Elohim is not the normal plural for Eloah. Rather, it is a male plural of a female word, a very unusual grammatical construction in Hebrew. In most mainstream modern Jewish teachings, this is understood to be because G-d is without quality, including the quality of gender.

Why is this plural name used for the singular god of Israel? Opinions, as always, differ. Ibn Ezra, in his commentary on Genesis 1:1, presents a very mainstream opinion, saying, "Elohim (God) is a plural.... Elohim is employed stylistically. Every language has honorific terminology... it is considered a sign of dignity to employ the plural when speaking of a superior." However, another opinion is elucidated by the Kuzari of Yehuda Halevi, a twelfth century CE Judeo-Arabic text which describes how the eighth century CE king of the pagan Khazar (Turkic) people gathered great thinkers and teachers of all faiths to teach him, so he could determine which faith was the true one:[134] "The word has a plural form, because...every deity was invested with astral and other powers. Each of these was called Elōah; their united forces were, therefore, called Elōhim.... These deities were as numerous as are the forces which sway the human body and the universe." This is closer to my own belief—I mostly understand Elohim as a collective singular, a council of gods acting in unity. I sometimes poetically call this "The Circle of Stars," but I don't really mean "stars" in any kind of astrological or even astronomical sense.[135]

Binah's common angel is Tzaphkiel (צפקיאל), whose name means "Knowledge of El." In Hermetic Kabbalah, Binah is associated with Saturn, but personally,

134 This is the "frame story" of the text, but it is generally understood to actually be a metaphor for the complex religious pluralism of medieval Al-Andalus (Muslim-controlled Iberia), where it was written.

135 It is only as I write this that I realize I may have inherited this metaphor from George Bush Sr. (who was president of the United States when I was young). He used "a thousand points of light" as a metaphor for how everyone could do good in the world, and how both faith-based and irreligious charities worked together: "A brilliant diversity spread like stars, like a thousand points of light in a broad and peaceful sky." The phrase really struck me because as part of that political theater, he named tons of specific charitable organizations as "points of light," and one of them was the daycare for homeless kids my mother then ran. It feels important for me to add, for young people who don't understand that the world they see is not "politics as usual," that my mother was a very loud and public opponent of George Bush Sr. in particular, and conservatism/capitalism in general, but President Bush still honored her and her good work.

I often think the planetary associations of the sefirot occlude more than they clarify. Many people are overly quick to equate them. While Binah and Saturn share associations, they are not the same.

Binah is the last of the "supernal" emanations. From here, the divine light passes through a sort of pseudo-sefira, the veil of Knowing called Da'at (תעד), and pours into the fourth emanation.

4: Chesed

Chesed (דסח) is notoriously difficult to translate. In modern English, it is usually rendered as "Loving-Kindness," but I'm partial to "Compassion." In older translations, "Mercy" is commonly used. Chesed is considered the central ethical value of Judaism, the highest moral calling. It is the impulse behind charity and the protective love one feels for a child. More than anything else, Chesed is the love and reciprocal obligation that binds Creator and Creation. As I mentioned before, "Love is responsibility of an I for a You: in this consists what cannot consist in any feeling—the equality of all lovers...."[136]

An alternate name for Chesed is Tzedek (קדצ), which has no direct English translation. It is often rendered as "Charity" or "Righteousness" or "Saintliness." Tzedek is also the Hebrew name for the planet Jupiter. Another alternate name is Gedulah (הלודג), which means "Greatness" or even "Bigness." The traditional Hebrew Name of Power here is El, which we discussed above.

Traditionally, Tzadkiel, a.k.a. Tzedekiel (לאיקדצ), the angel of Tzedek, is often given as the angel of Chesed, but Sandalphon is also excellent for Chesed work. In Hermetic Qabala, Chesed is associated with the god Jupiter, particularly his role as Patriarch. In Christian Cabala, Chesed is closely associated with the Virgin Mary, particularly in her role as a merciful intercessor.

5: Gevurah

After Chesed, creation proceeds in Gevurah (הרובג), which most closely translates in English as "Strength" or "Might." However, it literally means "Manliness." Gevurah is the fire of creation, the passion and the will. Sepher Bahir[137] says, "What is the fifth (utterance)? Fifth is the great fire of God, of which it says 'let me see no more of this great fire, lest I die' (Deut. 18:16). This is the left hand of God." In Kabbalah, the phrase *left-hand path* refers to Gevurah-work in particular, although it can also mean work involving the entire left-hand side of the tree: Hod, Gevurah, Binah. In modern Anglophone magic, how-

136 Martin Buber, *I and Thou* (T. & T. Clark, 1958).

137 A classic kabbalistic text first published in the twelfth century.

ever, the use of that phrase owes more to tantra than to Kabbalah, although people often erroneously conflate them. In Gevurah, creation first manifests into separate things; Gevurah is our power to discriminate "this" from "that." Hermetically, Gevurah is associated with Mars.

The traditional god name here is Elohim Gibor,[138] "Mighty God(s)." Personally, I often also use Aish Kodesh, or "Holy Flame," in the context of Gevorah. The angel of Gevurah is, obviously, לאירבג (Gevuriel), a.k.a. Gabriel, although many Christian and Pagan sources place him in Yesod (see the ninth sephira) for reasons I do not fully understand. לֵאוּמַח (Kamuel, a.k.a. Camael), the "Warming El," is the usual Hermetic/Christian assignment. Camael is also a great choice for working in Gevurah, as is לֵאָמַס (Samael), the angel of poison. Although Christians often consider Samael "evil" or "fallen" (whatever that means), in Judaism and pre-Judaic Middle Eastern paganism(s), he is an angel in service to heaven, head of a category of angels called סינָטְש (satans) or "prosecutors." In Jewish late antiquity and early medieval Judaism, he was usually understood as the angel of Rome and thus also the angel of Christianity.

6: Tiferet

Tiferet (תראפת) is usually translated as "Beauty" in Hermetic texts and "Adornment" in Jewish ones. Personally, I'm partial to the less literal "Harmony." Tiferet is the halfway point between Keter (Crown) and Malkut (Kingdom); it is the balancing point of the universe. It is very closely associated with the Sun, both literally—as the ultimate source of the heat, light, and energy that fuel all life on Earth—and also figuratively, as the shining star at the center of Being. Tiferet is the "light" G-d speaks into being, saying "Let there be light…."

The Hebrew Names of Power assigned to Tiferet vary widely between sources. Often the Most Holy Name is placed here. Personally, I often use Oseh Shalom, or "Peacemaker." The angel of Tiferet is generally given as לעירוא (Auriel, a.k.a. Uriel), the angel of light; לאפר (Raphael), the angel of healing; or לאכימ (Michael), whose name means "Who Is Like El." I generally think of Michael here. In Christian Cabala, Tiferet is the domain of Christ, in his role as intermediary between Earth and Heaven.

7: Netzach

Below Tiferet is חצנ (Netzach), which is often translated as "Victory" or "Eternity," but which can also mean "Perfection" or "Sincerity," from a root word meaning "to endure." In Netzach, purposes are not always clear. Here, for

138 As you can probably hear, *gibor* and *geborah* are different grammatical forms of the same word.

the first time, the Divine light can remain hidden. Netzach is associated with the Book of Esther and its heroine, called "the hidden star." The name (and the character) of Esther is generally understood to be closely related to Ishtar, the Near Eastern love/war goddess of the planet Venus. Traditional angels of Netzach include לאינה (Haniel), the angel of grace; לאירוא (Auriel), the angel of light I mentioned above; and לעירא (Ariel), the Lion of El. Personally, I mostly work with Ariel as the angel of Netzach.

One traditional Hebrew Name of Power here is Adonai Tzevaot, the "Lord of Hosts," however, I prefer El Shaddai, which is my personal favorite name for G-d. The name is extremely difficult to translate, although it is often glossed as "God Almighty." "Shaddai" can mean "Demon," "Breast," or "To Destroy." It is a very feminine name of G-d, and one closely associated with sexual reproduction. In Bereshit (Genesis) 49:25, Jacob is blessing his sons. He says, "By the El Aveinu [God of Our Father(s)] who helps you, and El Shaddai who blesses you, Blessings of the heavens from above, Blessings of the deep lying under, Blessings of breasts and womb, Blessing of ancient mountains, Blessing of everlasting hills..."

However, read differently, the same Name of Power can be Sh'dai, or "The Self-Sufficient One" or "The One Sufficient for All." It can also be read as an acronym for לארשי תותלד רומש (Shomer Daltot Yisrael) which is normally translated as "Guardian of the Gates of Israel," although I prefer "Sentry of the Doors of Israel" because it preserves the SDI acronym. My personal favorite folk etymology is presented by the prophet Ezekiel, who characterizes it as an onomatopoetic rustle, followed by a crash—like rain punctuated by thunder—*Shhhhhhhh-DAI!* "I heard the noise of their wings like the noise of great waters, like the voice Shhhhhh-DAI...."[139]

8: Hod

After Netzach, we come to דוה (Hod), which is usually translated as "Splendor," although it can also mean "Majesty." I prefer "Brilliance" as a translation, because I like the interplay of light-related connotations it evokes. Brilliant can mean "shiny" but it can also mean "smart." *Hod* is much the same. Action in Hod is calculated, circumspect, and often counterintuitive. Hod is associated with truth-telling, divination, teaching, trickery, and lies. In modern Chassidus (the kabbalistic teachings of the Lubavitcher Rebbe, whom I mentioned earlier), Hod is closely correlated with sincerity, supplication, and acceptance.

139 Ezekiel 1:24

Language originates in Hod, and it is in Hod that praise and thanksgiving come into the world. Why? Because in Hod, sentience is attained. Prior to Hod, the universe was full and alive, but there were no people[140] to be conscious of the universe. There was no one to appreciate it because there was no one capable of understanding. Hermetically, Hod is associated with Mercury, with symbol and intellect in general, and with magic, mathematics, and written language specifically. This chapter is, really, all about Hod. The Golden Dawn confusingly cites Michael as the angel of Hod, but I prefer Auriel. Others would say Rafael (Raphael) the healer.

9: Yesod

The penultimate sefira is Yesod, or "Foundation." Yesod is the womb in which the physical world gestates. In both medieval Kabbalah and modern Chassidus, Yesod is overtly sexual in nature. Yesod is also closely associated with the Abrahamic covenant, and with blood-covenants and genetics more broadly. Yesod is where the idea of physical instantiation takes shape, the interface between the seen and the unseen.

El Shaddai is the typical god name here, but I prefer El Chai, "God of Life," or Elohim. As I previously mentioned, many people place Gabriel in Yesod, but I think that's silly. For me, good angels in Yesod are Auriel; לאוגר (Raguel), the angelic shepherd; or (my preference) לאירש (Sariel), the Prince-El.

10: Malkut

The "final" sefira is Malkut, which means "Kingdom." Shekhina, or "Indwelling Presence," is an alternate name. For our purposes, Malkut is the physical world, both in a broad sense of things studied in physics and also in a very specific "the land beneath us" way.

The Hebrew Name of Power usually given here is Adonai HaAretz, "Lord of the Earth," or Malach HaOlam, "King of the Forever," but I always use Shekhina. Many feminist Jews have taken to using םלוע תכלמ (Malkat HaOlam), "Queen of the Forever" or "Queen of the World," as a divine name in Yesod, but I think that name is better in Netzach. ץראה תכלמ (Malkat HaAretz), "Queen of Earth," would be a good Hebrew "Earth Mother" option, if you're into that kind of thing. The "traditional" angel here is Sandalphon, which I don't think is a good fit. Personally, I never work with angels in Malkut, but if I were going to, I guess it would probably be Michael.

140 Human or otherwise

Magic Alphabets

As I mentioned at the beginning of the "Numbers and Letters" section, at least as far as we can determine, writing was used almost exclusively for bookkeeping for many generations before anyone thought to use it for anything like literature, which is perhaps a rather sad commentary on humanity. I believe this movement from counting (which developed as a way to track moon cycles) to writing is why, in cultures where writing developed (rather than being imported), Moon is almost always the deity that taught humans to write. For example, although modern Hermeticists (and ancient Greek colonizers) often associate the scribal god Thoth with the planet Mercury, in ancient Egypt he was unquestionably a lunar god, particular in his role as the teacher of hieroglyphics. However, in cultures such as ours, where writing is imported (that is, those where it is first learned from travelers and traders), mercurial gods like Hermes or Mercury teach writing.

Letters are extremely powerful symbols; they give permanence to speech. They make ephemeral ideas, transmitted as sounds (shapes made of breath), into visible marks. This is what distinguishes a symbolic representation from an illustration.[141] A painting of a bison[142] on a cave wall is a mark that represents a bison. But its referent (the thing it represents) is a specific physical thing. It doesn't mean "bison" as an abstract idea. It's a portrait of a particular bison. It's drawn differently by each artist.

Ugg's genius was this: *numbers don't actually represent anything*, and so you can use them to represent everything. There is nothing in the world you can point to and say, "That's a seven!" That is to say, numbers are purely syntactic, without reference to any semantic content. Symbols are, as Ugg and her people learned, extremely powerful. Their magic is so powerful that it has reshaped the world. So powerful that we usually don't even call it magic anymore.

I mentioned at the beginning of the chapter that I used to be a mathematician. Today, I am a writer. Like mathematics, writing is an extraordinarily sophisticated kind of symbol magic; *all alphabets are magic alphabets*. I will not say too much more about magic writing here. This is because, as a book of magic, and also a magic book, *this entire book is a lesson on written magic.*

However, many people, including me, find the use of ancient, foreign, imaginary, or otherwise extra-mundane alphabets powerful in their practice,

141 As with all such distinctions, there's a fuzzy boundary in between. I am simplifying and highlighting the differences to clarify, but (obviously) this is a *super* deep and complex subject that I am not doing justice to in this brief summary.

142 Or, as in the case of the Lascaux caves, an aurochs.

and that is what people typically mean when they say "magic alphabet." This is something I did a lot when I was first learning magic. Perhaps unsurprisingly for a witch who became first a cryptographer and then a writer and translator, I was particularly interested in "witch cyphers." My favorite at the time was the "ancient Theban alphabet" (which is neither ancient nor Theban, but I

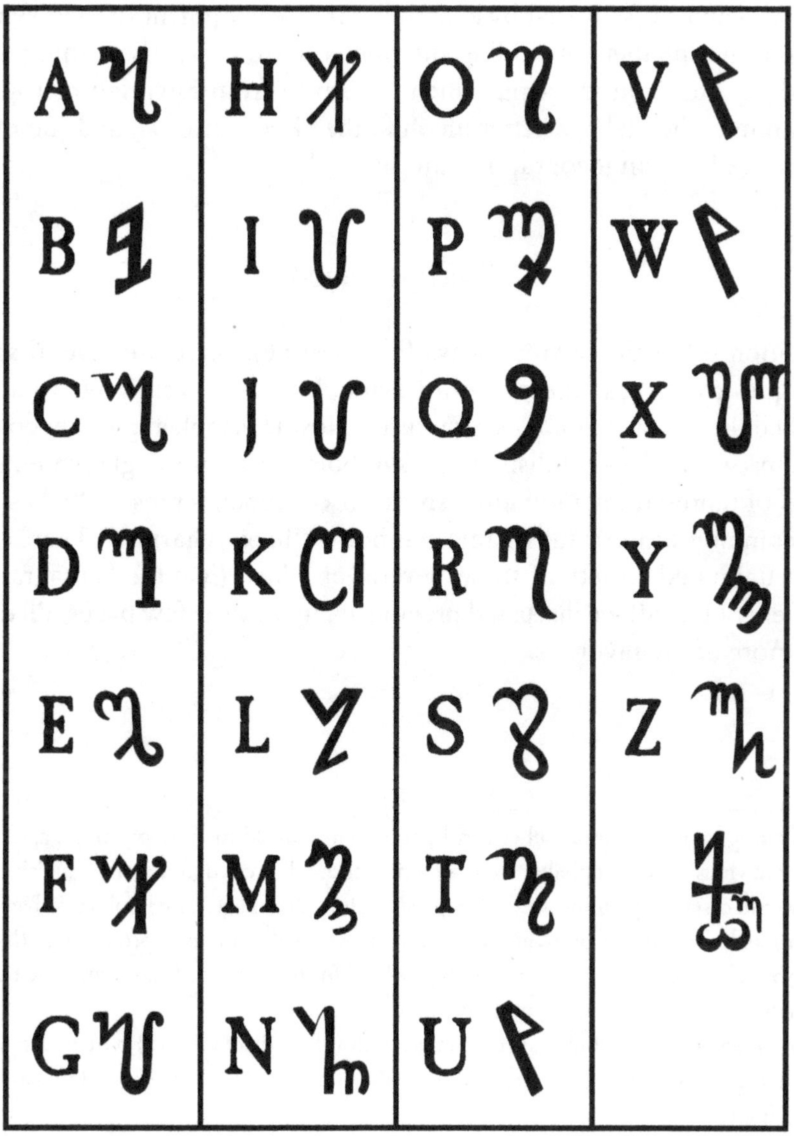

A	H	O	V
B	I	P	W
C	J	Q	X
D	K	R	Y
E	L	S	Z
F	M	T	
G	N	U	

didn't know that then). I used its letters both to encrypt my magic journals[143] and as magical symbols in their own right. The origins of the "ancient Theban alphabet" are unknown to me, but it was popularized by Heinrich Cornelius Agrippa, whom we will discuss later in this chapter.

As I said, every alphabet is a magic alphabet—a set of very powerful symbols, in which each letter has its own ideographic[144] meaning as well as its standard phonographic[145] one. The ideographic meanings of modern alphabets can be discovered by examining the development of their symbols. All Western alphabets, including the one you are currently reading, derive from the proto-Sinaitic script, which is derived from Egyptian hieroglyphs. For example, the Hebrew letter aleph א, the Greek letter Α, and the English A all derive from an ideograph of an ox head.

Talismanic Symbols

In addition to all the obvious ways (like writing), there are several specific techniques to harness the power of symbols in witchcraft. We've already discussed the use of symbols as signatures. Now let's look at another common way to use symbols—as talismanic[146] symbols. These are single symbols that, instead of representing individual spirits or concepts, represent "vibes." The most common kind of talismanic symbol is "lucky charms." There are an almost unlimited variety of these, several of which (like the Pentagram and the Shield of David) we discussed previously. In the next few pages, I'll discuss a few more of my favorites.

143 Looking back, it is not at all clear why fourteen-year-old me thought that pages written in a very obviously weird alphabet were somehow more discreet than regular English writing, which would certainly go unnoticed among the thousands of pages of school work, bad poetry, poorly thought-out short stories, and interminably whiny diaries I also produced at that time. Having both been a teenager and taught high school for many years, I can assure you that even very smart teenagers do all kinds of dumb stuff.

144 An *ideograph* is a symbol that represents an idea. Emoji are (almost) purely ideographic.

145 A *phonograph* is a symbol that represents a sound. English letters are (almost) purely phonographic.

146 While some people have strong opinions on the differences between amulets and talismans, I do not think that those distinctions are universal; most witches and magicians I know use the words mostly interchangeably.

Writing Prompt: Lucky Charms

Make a list of all the lucky charm symbols you can think of. If you have less than twenty, try harder.

Choose one, and write a little report on it, modeled on the entries that follow. Ideally, share your report with your study group, if you have one.

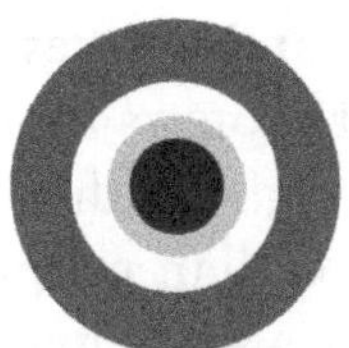

Eye Against Evil

Belief in the "evil eye," a type of curse thrown (usually unintentionally) by malevolent or jealous gazes, exists all over the world, but it is particularly common in the eastern Mediterranean, the Near and Middle East, and the Indian subcontinent. In Chapter Two, you learned a quick salt charm to dispel it, and you will learn more sophisticated methods in Chapter Nine, "Malefica and Curse Breaking." I will never teach you how to cast the evil eye, but it's so easy as to be difficult to avoid for many jealous witches with poor impulse control.

Doubtless you are familiar with the blue glass eye charms used as wards against the evil eye all across the Mediterranean. Such a talisman is often called often called a *nazar* (نظر), which is Arabic and means "sight." The nazar is a glass disk (or sometimes a sphere or bead), mostly cobalt blue, with concentric circles of white, light blue, and dark blue (like an eye). Even if you are not familiar with it, I assure you, it is very common. It's so common there's an emoji for it, U+1F9FF,[147] which appears at the top of this section. When I use the emoji as a digital talisman to ward off the evil eye, which I often do on social media, I generally use six eyes to surround the words I think might prompt it. For example:

Being me is great, I low-key don't understand
why everyone doesn't want to be me.

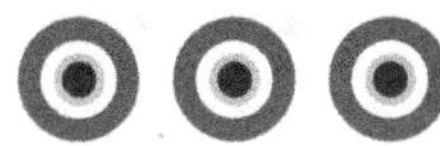

147 In fact, if you're looking for a list of symbols, the Unicode "miscellaneous symbols" block is a good place to start.

There are several important magical features to the design of the Eye Against Evil. The first is the color. Various shades of blue are globally understood as apotropaic colors, often related to the sky or the sea. For example, in the American South, one will find many, many shutter, porches, and especially porch roofs painted a lovely shade of pale blue-green. Some folks have forgotten the original reason and choose the color as a traditional or even just as an aesthetic choice, but old-timers and witches still know why it is done. This color is called *haint blue*, and it protects against visitations from the restless and hungry dead. Although the origins of this practice are shrouded in mystery, most believe it began with the Gullah people, a community of historically enslaved Black people in South Carolina and Georgia who have managed to preserve much of their African heritage. Many of the Gullah people originally came from Angola. Most scholars think *Gullah* is a dialectic form of that name.

In this context, *haint* is a form of the word *haunt*, and describes a type of ghost. Haints are a kind of restless dead who have lost most of their personality and exist primarily as scavengers and parasites, "eating" human warmth and feeling. In my circle, these are sometimes called "hungry ghosts," although we've also started to call them "hangry[148] ghosts," which I think is more accurate. In the African lore, and in many other cultures' lore as well,[149] haints cannot cross running water. The blue-green shades called *haint blue* mimic water, and are thought to provide a similar ward against haints when painted on porches, shutters, and fences.

In addition to the blue color, concentric circles are also apotropaic; they function as a "trap." In this sense, the nazar is like a labyrinth (another very, very powerful symbol, which I encourage you to research and explore).

Finally, eyes are extremely powerful symbols in every culture. Most literally, eyes represent sight, and from there, their meanings expand metaphorically. Eyes convey insight and wisdom, clarity and clairvoyance, and (by extension) intelligence and truth. In the nazar, however, the eye mostly functions simply as a reflective device of the eye that casts the curse.

---

148 Hangry = Hungry + Angry. I don't know where this word originated, but it was popularized by a series of American commercials for the candy bar Snickers.

149 For example, it figures in both the *Iliad* and Washington Irving's classic American horror tale "The Legend of Sleepy Hollow."

Ankh

The next symbol I want to talk about is the ankh, an ancient Egyptian symbol that means, more or less, "life." Ankhs are closely associated with many Egyptian gods, particularly Isis. The origins of the symbol are not clear. Some say it is a kind of knotted rag called a *tyet*, or "knot of Isis," used as an ancient tampon. However, the ankh and the tyet have different hieroglyphs, so I find that explanation uncompelling. Some people say it represents a mirror (like the symbol of Venus, which we'll discuss in the next lesson). Others say that it is a flower (or a bouquet of flowers). I was taught that it represents a person, with arms outstretched. I do not think that any of these can be correct, because Egyptian gods are often pictured holding the ankh through the top loop, which they could not do if it were a mirror or a flower or a head. However, the hieroglyph was from earliest times used for "mirror," "bread," and "sandal-strap."[150]

To my mind, the ankh, if it represents any physical object, is most convincingly a key, or a rattle/sistrum. However, I remain unconvinced it is a picture of any physical object. No matter what the symbol originally represented, in witchcraft, it unquestionably means "life force." Today, in Anglophone iconography, the ankh is also used to represent pan-African solidarity by Black Americans, although this use is very rare in Africa.

The Amulet of the Open Hand

The nazar (or other eye emblems) is often found at the center of another type of amulet, one shaped like an open hand, made symmetric with an outward-curving pinkie finger and thumb. These amulets are called הָסְמַח ("hamsa") in Hebrew and ةسمخ ("khamsa") in Arabic; both words mean "five" and also refer to the hand.

Although the amulet of the open hand certainly predates Islam and Christianity, and likely also predates Judaism, these symbols are also sometimes

150 Viewed from above. Your ankle goes through the top part, and then the line goes between your toes.

referred to by more religious people as the "Hand of Miriam" (Moses's sister), "Hand of Mary" (Jesus's mother), or "Hand of Fatima" (Mohammed's wife). To me, these names strongly indicate that the talisman is associated with the Great Goddess, who is sister and mother and lover of us all. This is bolstered by the fact that similar open-hand designs frequently occur on ancient ritual objects sacred to Ishtar, Inanna, and Tanit, respectively Babylonian, Sumerian, and Carthaginian names for the Great Goddess.

In ancient Carthage (modern Tunisia), as well as in Jewish, Arab, and Berber houses around the world, a handprint was often painted on a door—usually in white on a red door or in red on a white door. These days, instead of being painted onto the door, the hand is most often hung as a metal ornament upon the door, either inside or out. Such amulets are nearly ubiquitous in Middle Eastern stores, with inexpensive versions made in steel and pot metal, and fancier versions in sterling silver or cobalt glass. Small bells are often attached to the ends of the fingers. Unlike the handprints, which usually occur fingers up, metal hamsa are usually hung with the fingers pointing down.

The hamsa, like most hand symbols, partakes strongly of the symbolism of the number five. It also represents all the things you might expect a hand to symbolize—it can reach, grab, or ward away. However, it is almost always used in the warding-away sense, such as the motion associated with the phrase "talk to the hand."

Ouroboros

The ouroboros, or snake swallowing its own tail, is an ancient symbol. Today, this symbol is often associated with immortality, but in ancient days, it was more often a symbol of the wheel of the year. Although snakes do sometimes eat their own tails (usually as a result of neurological damage from overheating), there is no reason to believe the symbol of the ouroboros as we know it is related to that phenomena—rather, it is probably derived from the way the constellation Draco circles the heavens. Today, our northern polestar is Polaris. However, because of slow movement of the Earth's axis relative to the backdrop of fixed stars (called the "precession of the equinoxes"), in the late

Neolithic, that "throne of heaven" was held by the star Alpha Draconis, which was closest to being a perfect northern polestar in 2750 BCE, when it was less than 0.17 degrees off of the pole.[151] Just as today the Great Bear circles Polaris over the course of the year, in those ancient times, the constellation Draco circled Alpha Draconis.

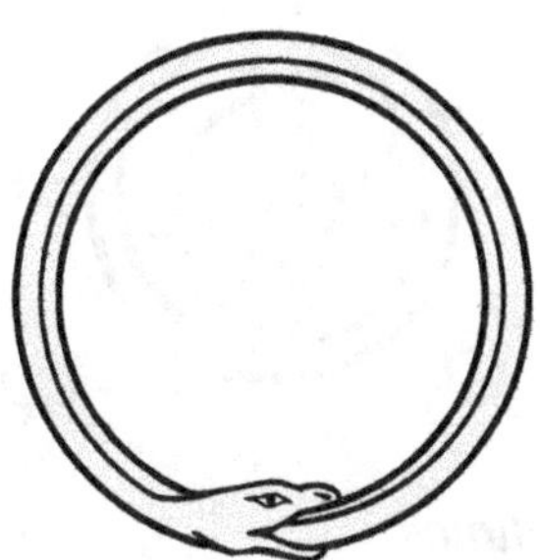

In Babylon, Alpha Draconis was called Tir-An-na, the "Life of Heaven." Semitic languages (both Hebrew and Arabic) name the star Thuban, some say because it means "subtle" in Hebrew, but this is more likely a corruption of the Arabic *raas al-tinnin* ("the serpent's head"). In Arabic astrological manuals, it was called "the god of this world... winding in his contortions round the pole of the world, as if to indicate his subtle influence in all worldly affairs."[152]

In ancient Greece, this star was associated with the Titan god Coeus / Koios (Κοῖος). Very little of his ancient myth or character remains (or, perhaps, ever existed). His name is usually translated "Question," although it derives from the word for "pebble." The word κοῖος can also mean "number" (probably by way of using pebbles as counters, as on an abacus). Some scholars[153] suggest that an early form of divination at Delphi involved pebbles,[154] and thus associate the god's name with Delphi. Whether that is how he came by his name or not, Koios is certainly related to the Delphic cult; he is the husband of the Titaness Phoebe and the father of the twin goddesses Leto and Asteria. Leto is the mother of Artemis and Apollo (the inspiration at Delphi), and Asteria

151 For comparison, Polaris is currently about 0.6 degrees from true north. Polaris will be its closest to true north in 2100, when it will be about 0.5 degrees off, and will then move slowly away.

152 Ethelbert William Bullinger, Witness of the Stars (1893).

153 For example, M. L. West, "Hesiod's Titans," *The Journal of Hellenic Studies* 105 (1985), 174–175.

154 For example, in "The Library of Apollodorus," we are told that Hermes traded a set of shepherd's pipes to Apollo for knowledge of pebble divination, as well as the caduceus wand. However (as is evident from the name), The Library is a paeon to Apollo, so it is unsurprising that it would claim Apollo invented such.

is a star goddess and the mother of Hekate, the Greek goddess of witchcraft, whom we will shortly discuss. Personally, I associate the ouroboros with the Milky Way, and with Asteria, particularly under the name Aktiophis ("ray serpent"), which we will discuss further in Chapter Five.

Hekate's Wheel and the Strophalos

Hekate's wheel (shown here) is a sort of pseudo-labyrinth. In ancient days, it was used as a decorative device, in particular on a collection of beaten gold "spangles" or very large sequins found at Mycenae, and now held in the National Archaeological Museum in Athens. There is no evidence that it was associated with Hekate in antiquity.

Starting around the 1970s, this symbol became associated with the *strophalos* (στροφαλος), a magic tool of Hekate's described in fragment 194 of the Chaldean Oracles. The word means "spinner," but no one knows for sure what the referent of that word is. Some say it is a drop spindle, and others, a spinning top. Personally, I believe it is a musical instrument similar to a bull-roarer, designed to induce trance, a theory which has begun to gain traction. Despite this modern conflation, in modern usage, the symbol is almost exclusively associated understood as a visual depiction of Hekate's strophalos.

Hekate

Hekate is a Greek Titaness (elder goddess) associated with liminality, doorways, magic, ghosts, crossroads, and the moon. Her origin is unclear. Some say she is from Anatolia (I am of this opinion), others Egypt or Sicily. The origin of her name is also unclear. If it is Greek (which I doubt), it might be related to the root ἑκάς, which means "far away," or ἑκών ("willing," "willful"). It might even mean something like "wished for" from the Old Persian 𐎣𐎠𐎶

(vašnā),[155] which sounds more like "Hekate" if you were to pronounce them both with a Turkish accent. Finally, the Egyptian word for magic, and the god thereof, is *Heka*. Although many linguists tell me the words *Heka* and *Hekate* are not related, I have trouble believing them.

Hekate is often pictured with torches, dogs, and keys, all of which are related to her role as a guardian of doorways, both literal and metaphoric. In ancient times, she is sometimes depicted as a single maiden, and at other times as triple-formed maiden,[156] or (less often) as a woman's body with three heads—one maiden, one dog, and one horse.[157] However, some modern witches imagine her as a crone, or as a maiden-mother-crone triple-form. This depiction is likely due to Shakespeare, who includes her as a character in *Macbeth*. While these modern depictions have no parallel in traditional sources, and I don't care for them, many people find profound meaning in them. Certainly, the gods are complex and multivariate. Hekate is a very minor character in Homer, but extolled quite extensively in Hesiod's *Theogony,* where there is a long section dedicated to her (lines 411–452) at the "inflection point" between descriptions of the Titans and Olympians. Hesiod, whose father was from the East, is generally credited with the popularization of Hekate's worship in Greece.

Getting to Know Hekate

If you do not yet know Hekate, please allow me to make an introduction! Read the following evocation out loud. It is my translation of her Orphic Hymn. You may need to repeat it many times until you feel it "catch her attention":

"Hekate Enodia,[158] Trioditis[159] most lovely,
I call to you now, oh saffron-robed lady.
You rule the heavens above and the black depths below.
You skate across waves and flow with the seafoam.
Sorcerous soul, you dance with the dead
And the deer and the dogs who delight in your tread.

---

155 This is the root of the name Vashti in Book of Esther. We will discuss more about the analogs between Hekate/Persephone/Vashti and Aphrodite/Ishtar/Esther in the next chapter.

156 As I mentioned earlier, it was Phidias, after whom the golden ratio is named, who introduced this triple-formed iconography to Athens.

157 In general, in both Greek and Egyptian art, a god having animal heads is a way to represent that they have both an animal and a human form.

158 "She of the Streets"

159 "Three-formed"

Persian One,[160] *Loner, irresistible Queen,*
You roar like a beast beneath the moon's gleam.
Unarmored, unconquered, chariot drawn by bulls,
Holding keys of the cosmos and heavenly rules.
Hierophant of the nymphs who haunt the high places,
You nurture children with charm and good graces.
We pray, hallowed maiden, please make our hearts light.
Goddess, indulge your initiates and visit our rite."

Hekate is the Queen of Witches and the goddess of magic. She is the goddess who guards gateways and who opens the gates of trance and travel. In this role, we call her as Propylaia, or "She Who Stands Before the Gates." Hekate is also mistress of the three-way (i.e., rural) crossroad, particularly at night. She protects all those who gather at crossroads or work corners—beggars, sex workers, drug dealers, street preachers, thieves, and witches. In this role, we will call upon her primarily by her name Enodia, or "She of the Roads," which you called in her hymn. She is also the guardian of mysteries, Kleidochus, or "Keyholder." Hekate can help open all locks, both those in the Other Place and also those within ourselves.

Read the following charm silently to yourself, and then, only if you agree to the implicit compact contained within, light some incense (frankincense is especially nice) and read it out loud. Do not make this compact lightly. If you're unsure, read the rest of the book before deciding.

"Hekate Propylaia,
Who Guards the Gates of the Three Worlds,
I stand before you as a supplicant,
I ask entry into your mystery—
Allow me to pass through the gates of initiation
and into your teaching.

I light incense before you.
I pay homage to you.
This I will do each dark moon,
for so long as we both so wish.

160 The name I've translated here, Persian, can also mean "Destructive One" or "Daughter of Perses."

Open the gates of my mind to know your truth.
Open the gates of my spirit to feel your presence.
Open the gates of my ears to hear your voice.
Open the gates of my eyes to see your vision.
Open the gates of my body,
that I may fly forth and return again.
Hekate Propylaia, open every gate to me,
and empower me to traverse them."

Sigils

Now that we've learned all kinds of "off-the-rack" magic symbols, let's learn how to make our own! There are many ways to do so, but the particular kind of custom-made magical symbols we're about to make are called sigils.[161] The word *sigil* derives from the Latin word for the kind of symbol we call a "seal." However, in modern Anglophone magic, a sigil is a kind magical symbol, made of smaller/simpler individual symbols, which encapsulates a complex meaning. Most typically, the smaller symbols are letters, and because I am a writer, that is what I will teach below. To learn to use other symbols in a more artistic style of sigil making, I strongly recommend *Sigil Witchery: A Witch's Guide to Crafting Magick Symbols* by Laura Tempest Zakroff.

There are many different methods for developing magical sigils, and most experienced magicians have their own "home brew" methods. The first I learned is the so-called kamea,[162] or magic square method, which I will teach you shortly. This method is common in both ancient and modern Hebrew magic, and was popularized among gentile European magicians in the sixteenth century by Agrippa in his *Three Books of Occult Philosophy*. Kamea seals rely on a kind of very ancient and cross-cultural math puzzle called a *magic square*. A magic square is a grid of numbers that, when added down the columns, across the rows, or along the diagonals, all produce the same result. For example:

Exercise: Magic Square

Fill in the digits from one to nine below to make a magic square. This isn't really a magical exercise at all, it's a math puzzle. Skip it if you're not into that. On the other hand, if you like this kind of puzzle, try your hand at a

161 The word *sigil* rhymes with "vigil," not "giggle."

162 The word *kamea* derives from the Hebrew word קמיע (qamea), which means "amulet." The is also the root of the English word "cameo."

bigger one. For example, arrange the numbers from one to twenty-five to make a five-by-five magic square.[163] In the next chapter, we'll discuss some of the larger magic squares, but for now, we'll work just with the three-by-three one.

One possible answer[164] is below...

How to Make a Kamea Sigil with a Magic Square

This explanation will be much clearer if you actually do the steps yourself in your magic journal as I explain them. For beginners, I recommend making all kamea sigils on the three-by-three square, but once you learn the bigger magic squares of all the planets in Chapter Five, you might want to experiment with using them.

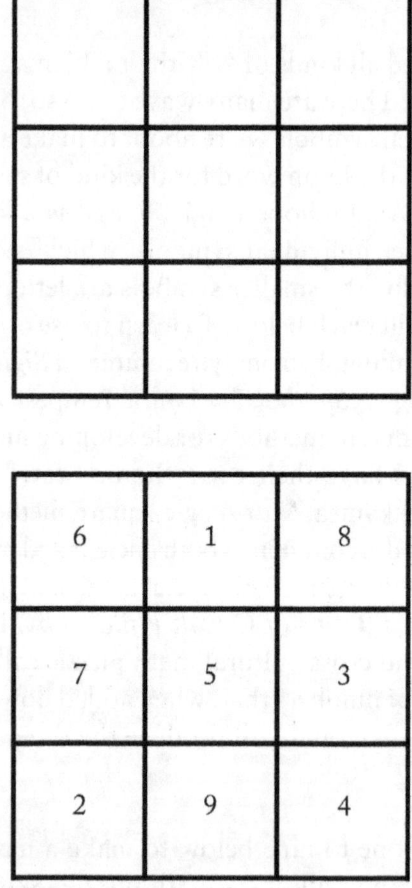

163 If you're a legit math nerd, try to find the "beastly magic square," a six-by-six magical square, filled in with the first thirty-six multiples of six, each row and column of which adds up to 666. (hint: What does a "normal" six-by-six square add up to?)

164 Fun fact: If you produced a square, examine it. You'll discover it's the same as mine, just reflected and/or rotated.

Steps:

1. First, we'll start by choosing what meaning we want to create a sigil to represent. Most often, this is a magical goal. For our example, I will enchant for "I will have safe and pleasant travel," because I'm on an airplane while I'm writing this.
2. If possible, reduce the number of words in your intent. I reduced to "safe pleasant travel."
3. Next, use the following table to encode your letters as numbers.

1	2	3	4	5	6	7	8	9
a	b	c	d	e	f	g	h	i
j	k	l	m	n	o	p	q	r
s	t	u	v	w	x	y	z	

"Safe pleasant travel" encodes as 1165 73511152 291453.

4. Next, trace that sequence of numbers onto the kamea (magic square), as shown in the images on the next page. There are many different ways to do this, and you will certainly invent many of your own. Personally, I tend to:
    - Make each word its own symbol, the results of which I sometimes use in sequence, and sometimes write overlapping each other.
    - I usually add a circle at the head and a cross at the tail of each word.
    - Sometimes, especially when there are a lot of words I want on top of each other, I use a different color for each word.
    - When I go through a number I wish to include without changing direction, I cross the line.
    - When the same number occurs twice in a row, I make a loop.
5. Next, clean up the images, add some decorative elements and talismanic symbols (here I've used the "all-seeing eye" at the top to watch over the traveler, as well as some moons, arrows, and dots that are mostly (but not entirely) just to make it look cool).

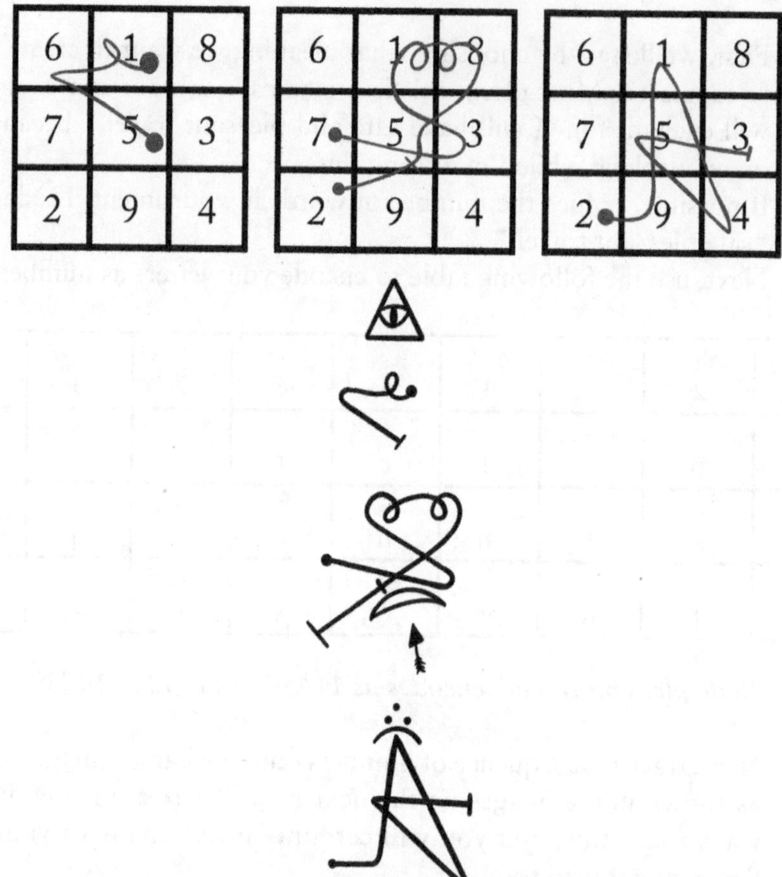

Sigils constructed in this way can be used for many purposes, but are generally used either as seals (that is, they are used to uniquely identify a spirit or "vibe") or as "batteries" in which power can be stored for later release. We'll talk about several of these methods on the next page. Of course, there are many other "home brew" ways to use them as well. Experiment and be sure to record your results, and share them with your learning circle.

The next method I would like to teach was popularized by Grant Morrisson, the incontestable king of the sigil, as well as one of the most significant bard-magicians of our time. If you are not familiar with his sigils, start with his graphic novel *The Invisibles Volume 1: Say You Want a Revolution,* the first of a series of stories about a cell of magical freedom fighters who make war on the forces of oppression. While the series was initially well received, it was soon in danger of cancellation. In the sixteenth issue, Morrison used the letters column to teach his style of sigil magic, and asked the readers to participate in a magical ritual with him to save the title. (It worked.)

Exercise: Morrison "Wankathon" Letter

Please read the letter here before proceeding:

Morrison, however, only popularized this method. To the best of my knowledge, he learned it from the work of Austin Osman Spare (1886–1956), an English witch and artist. Spare wrote about it in *The Book of Pleasure*. As he explains it, his sigil method has seven steps:

1. Determine true desire.
2. Write it a short sentence.
3. Combine the letters into a glyph.
4. Make it look magical. [Spare was a brilliant artist. Get arty about it!]
5. Enter magical time.
6. Launch. [If you've done the reading I assigned above, you'll already know what this means, but if you didn't, that's ok. I'll explain it shortly.]
7. Forget. [A. O. Spare provides no further details on this,[165] but I will discuss it a bit below.]

Shown is the example A.O. Spare provides in that book. Look carefully at each sigil, and you can see the individual letters within it.

Both the kamea and Spare methods we've discussed are beginner techniques. They're very reliable, and I use both of them in many circumstances. However, once you gain some fluency in them, you should start branching out into more sophisticated methods. Experiment with other alphabets and with calligraphy. Research Arabic figural calligraphy, where the words are manipulated into a sigilic form while retaining their readability. Turn a sigil into a character. Make a collection of personal sigils.

165 Spare was a much better artist than me, but I am a much better teacher than he was. His instructions leave something to be desired.

This my wish,

To obtain,

The strength of a Tiger,

Combined as one Sigil,

or

Using Sigils in Magic

In summary, the process of creating a sigil is as follows:

1. Carefully craft your intent. As with most magic, this is the most important (and usually the hardest) step. If you're having trouble making good wishes, review Chapter One.
2. Next, sigilize your intent using kamea method, Spare/Morrison method, or any other method.
3. Once you've done that, it's time to "launch" the sigil. Sigil launching is a multivariate process of charging and releasing. We'll discuss it as separate stages done sequentially, although in practice, the charge and release are generally braided together.

Once your sigil is made, it's time for the real magic qua magic. This begins with attaining a no-mind trance (or, really, any kind of magical space/time/consciousness). Morrisson recommends the refractory period after orgasm for this, which I do not find especially effective,[166] but if my target demographic for teaching sigil magic was young men who buy comics,[167] that's what I'd teach too.

Any of the trance methods (i.e., magical space/time/consciousnesses) we've covered so far will work for sigil launching, as will almost any other one. One of the best parts about sigil magic, and one of the reasons it's so often taught as an introductory magical technique, is that you only need to be able to maintain the trance state for a very short period of time to get good results. For me, the most reliable way to attain a "no-mind" trance is vipassana ("insight") meditation.

Once you attain trance, pour all your power into the sigil. The sort of color magic we learned in Chapter One is a great way to do this. Fill the sigil up like a battery, until it's full to bursting with power. You can do this over several sessions if you can't generate enough power on one go. You can also, as Morrisson did, distribute this across many magicians by publishing your sigil and asking others to empower it (or getting others to empower it without their knowledge, for example by weaving it into a piece of art that can capture a lot of attention). Is this whole book a sigil? Yes, it certainly is.

Perhaps because of Morrison's wankathon letter (although he doesn't say this), a perception has arisen that it is the psychic force of the orgasm which empowers the sigil. That's not really what's going on here, although that can also be an excellent method, especially with sexual partner(s) who are also co-magicians. In Morrison's method, as he explains it, the orgasm mostly just clears your mind. As a general practice, don't cum directly on your sigils,[168] it "clogs up" the magic with too much material link to you, and makes it difficult to target other people/forces/places/events.

Once the sigil is fully charged, enter trance again, and experience its full power, present in the physical drawing of the sigil. As rapidly as you can, explode the gathered force out of the sigil and into the "ether." The most common method of doing this is to burn the sigil, but there are lots of other

166 Possibly because male and female refractory periods aren't all that similar, and probably just because humans are all different from each other, and some personal variation is to be expected among all people.

167 I am not suggesting that only young men read comics. I am a woman, and I adored *The Invisibles,* which I first read as it was coming out, in my late teens and early twenties, and reread a few months ago (in my late forties).

168 I mean, I guess you can if you want, but that is not what Spare, Morrison, or I are recommending.

ways. For example, I sometimes write sigils on balloons, blow them up to change them, and then pop them.

After you have released your sigil, try to completely forget about it. Clinging to it, and continually reviewing/analyzing it in your head will prevent it from properly launching.[169] This is not unique to sigils, but applies to all kinds of magic.

Instead of destruction-releasing (like burning) sigils, you can also (as I said above) slow-release them by allowing them to continually "feed" off attention, subtly imprinting their intent into everyone who sees them. This is the sort of sigil magic you see most often in advertising. Every logo is a sigil.

Symbols for Divination

A slightly more sophisticated (that is, less introductory) way to deploy symbols in magic is to use them for divination, or fortune telling, which I define as "the art of making reliably good guesses." In fact, understood broadly, most divination methods rely on the interpretation of symbols. We'll dive very deep into this in the next chapter.

169 Google "chaos magic lust for results" if you would like to read more about this.

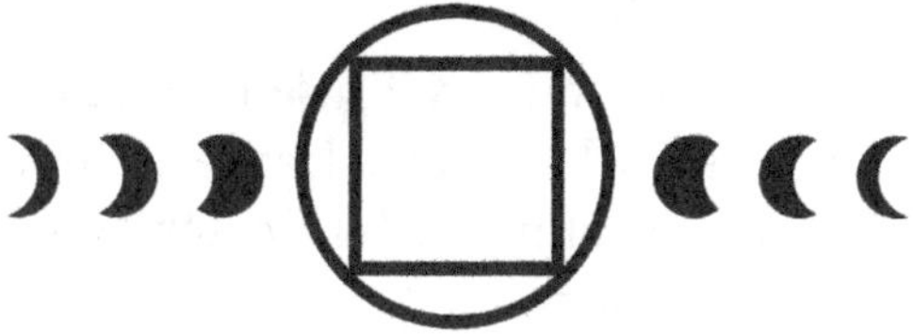

Chapter Four:

Divination

Perhaps more than any other topic in this book, this is the one where I expect the widest range of different levels of experience. Some readers have never done any divination at all, and some are professional diviners. No matter how much experience you have, I encourage you to try to approach this chapter with an open mind; the childlike trance you learned in the first chapter might help you get past preconceptions. Especially if you are an expert in multiple divinatory methods, I strongly recommend using a method (or multiple methods) with which you have very little experience as you work through this chapter.

Skill at divination is the ability to reliably make uncannily good guesses. Divination is an art of coming to Know things and (to a lesser extent) the art of communicating things Known to others. What distinguishes divination from other forms of knowing is that it is *inspired.* That is to say, it occurs by the action of a (non-normal) spirit inside us; when we are inspired, we are literally in-spirit-ed. Some part of this is a mystical/magical talent for spirit communication, which cannot really be taught until you've developed more facility for magic (which, if you do all the exercises, you should have by the end of Chapter Nine). However, even without specialized teaching, it will improve with practice.

However, in addition to the part that is a magic talent, a great deal of divination is about asking precise questions, paying careful attention with an open but discerning mind, and then rationally analyzing and pattern recognizing. Getting good at guessing without talking to spirits requires a lot of practice, and it also requires feedback from strangers.

Fortune Telling

While the most common questions we'll use divination for are about the present, I'd like to first discuss what I consider the archetypal form of divination—"fortune telling," or predicting the future. Obviously, future predicting (whether by divination, extrapolation, algorithm, or any other mechanism) is not an exact science. Mostly, this is because not everything is predetermined. Volition—that is, exertion of free will—changes the future.

That is to say, the future evolves in complex, chaotic, and self-referential ways. What follows is a quite technical explanation of how I think of that process. However, it's ok if you have trouble following it. Generally, I do not think this level of cosmological theory is especially useful for magicians. If you're not into that kind of complicated mathematical/metaphysical masturbation, then there's no real reason to dwell on it. Feel free to skip the next two paragraphs. When I was a mathematician, "What shapes can different kinds of weird space/time universes be?" was my specialty. If you're a nerd, like me, I think you'll be into this.

Here I am, in the moment-place-event in which I am typing this. Thus, I shall call this moment-event-place "Here." Many, many paths through space-time ("timelines") go through Here, but if we consider all possible timelines, it's clear that most of them do not. Only certain, very specific, arrangements of moment-events ("timelines") lead through Here. For example, in most timelines, I don't even exist, much less do I exist as a person writing this book for you.

All the timelines that pass through Here share certain features, but they differ in many details. These are all the possible pasts. Similarly, from here, many timelines spread out. These are all the possible futures. By carefully opening ourselves to them, and listening, we can hear what echoes across most of them. However, discerning the fine details that distinguish one timeline from another is not really possible while anchored to a specific moment-event-place, because our only access to other timeline is by "listening" to an "average" across the whole "cone" of "timelines" that spread out from Here. You can remove your consciousness from fixed space-time and learn other things, but that knowledge is very hard to carry back to Here/Now. With that said, I now return you to your regularly scheduled non-mathematical witchcraft.

All humans can divine. Like art or mathematics, it is an innate human capacity. However, like art or mathematics, divination comes more easily to some people than to others. There are lots of things you can do to help unlock your natural talent. We'll discuss many of them when we look more closely at trance in Chapter Eleven.

As you begin to carefully experiment, and record your results, you'll probably discover that you're a lot more talented than you might think you are. Don't let it spook you. The natural human reaction to the uncanny is dread, but lean in through the fear to the delight and wonder. That's what you're here for. I encourage you to practice divination every day. To begin with, try out the following system—among the simplest, cleanest, and most powerful divinatory systems, and perhaps the best known one. I'm reasonably confident you already know how to do it. It's called "flipping a coin."

Flipping a coin provides answers in binary. You can interpret them as "yes/no," but you can also flip several times in a row to provide more complex answers such as directions through a forest (as in the following exercise) or I Ching hexagrams (which we discussed in the previous chapter), or anything else you can answer in binary.[170] If you especially like flipping coins for divination, I encourage you to acquire and enchant a coin especially for this purpose. One nice choice would be a 2019 $1 "New Jersey / Lightbulb" coin which you have filled up with orange magic.

Exercise: Penny Adventure

This game works best walking in the city, but it can also be played driving out in the country. Unless you are in an especially magic-dense wilderness, it will take a *long time* (days, perhaps) to provide answers if walking in nature. It can be played alone or collaboratively in groups; it is non-competitive (although certainly you could develop a competitive version, which I imagine would be a sort of scavenger hunt). If driving, you'll need two people—one driver and one navigator/diviner. Don't trance and drive![171] This game isn't great in the suburbs; you'll probably end up going around in circles. A full game, when played as instructed, takes about an hour, although you can play for longer if you want.

1. Enter magical space/time/consciousness, and then begin traveling.

---

170 One insight at the foundation of modern computer science is that, if you get clever about how you word your questions, you can turn almost anything into binary, although it becomes rather tiresome to do so by flipping coins. Instead, in the modern world, we usually use "Turing machines," or "computers," which are sophisticated engines for doing binary math. That is to say, they flip coins very quickly.

171 Seriously. By this point, you've probably caught on that I'm not an especially cautious magician. I fully expect you to burn your fingers a few times with moderately dangerous magic. Driving while entranced is mortally dangerous, to you and others around you. It is criminally irresponsible. Don't do it.

2. When you get to a crossroads, ask, "What way lies adventure?" and flip a coin[172] twice.
3. If both results are heads, turn right. If both are tails, turn left. If mixed results, go straight.
4. If it is a three-way crossroad (i.e., a T-intersection), just flip the coin once.
5. Pay very careful attention to the landscape around you, until you find an omen calling you to adventure. It should be something strikingly unusual, something that repeats, or something else that feels like an omen.
6. Follow it to have an adventure.
7. If at any point you lose track of the omen, return to coin flipping.
8. You win the game when you are either led back home or when you've had a satisfactory adventure. Quitting before either of those things happens is losing (but you can put the game on pause and return to win it later).

Once you've played Penny Adventure at least once simply to find an adventure, play it to provide wisdom. This time, ask, "Please lead me to a sign about ____________." Play until you Know the answer. This will often result in you being led to a place of great beauty, where you should sit and reflect until the answer comes. If you are having trouble paying careful attention and keeping your mind focused on the game, I recommend narrating your quest out loud while adventuring, describing the things you pass like a tour guide.

Seven Methods of Divination

There are many methods to learn how to Know. I recommend developing at least some skill with all of the following methods:

1. Flip a Coin (you already know this)
1. Cartomancy (you'll learn this later in this chapter)
2. Telling Omens (later in this chapter)
3. Automatic Writing (later in this chapter)
4. Incubating Dreams (Chapter Ten)
5. Scrying (Chapter Thirteen)
6. Oracular Adorcism (Chapters Thirteen)

172 Despite the game's name, any kind of coin will work. I especially like a Mercury dime.

However, before we move on to specifics, we'll discuss the step-by-step process of actually doing divination. As I said in the prologue, I encourage you to casually read this whole chapter through first, and then reread it piece by piece over time, performing the exercises. This is especially important for this chapter, particularly if you have very little experience with divination.

All types of divination rely on some kind of "buffering" between you and Divine Madness. I have arranged the types in order from most to least buffered. I suggest you slowly shed layers of buffering protections as you become more skilled. My list of methods also proceeds, somewhat, from easier to more difficult. I do not mean in terms of how hard they are to learn, but rather how taxing they are on the diviner. Remember, however, that this is an introductory book on witchcraft, not a course in divination; while we'll touch on all these topics, this is the only chapter that focuses exclusively on divination.

The following exercise can be used to help to augment your natural talents for divination, psychism, and mediumship. If you are already strongly psychic, to such a degree that you find it difficult to navigate, *do not* ask for more skill in that arena. Instead, think carefully about what you do want, and ask for that. Read the whole ritual before attempting it.

Guest Teacher(s): The Circle of Sister Sibyls

The spirit-teachers I work with most often for divination are the Circle of Sister Sibyls, a sorority of dead human seers, mediums, oracle-speakers, priests, and prophets. Among the more famous members are Sarah (née Sarai), the sibyl of Mamre;[173] Hildegard von Bingen, the sibyl of the Rhine; Sarah (sometimes called Sarah Tzvi, after her husband), the sibyl of Livorno;[174] Cassandra, the sibyl of Troy; and several (maybe all?) of the Pythian sibyls of Delphi, whom I'll discuss shortly. There are many, many other members; these are just some of my main "mentors" from the Circle. Despite the name, not all members are female.

173 Whom I mentioned in the invocation of Arbatel.

174 And Podolia and Amsterdam and Jerusalem and Cairo. She moved around a lot.

The Circle has their own oracle,[175] inspired by Great Drakaina[176] (Δράκαινα), a chthonic serpent/dragon spirit in the court of the Great Mother. Drakaina is a shapeshifter, but I believe her "essential" form to be serpentine. To me, she most often appears briefly in the form of a giant black dragon, which usually quickly shifts down into a dark-skinned woman in an iridescent black-scaled evening gown. Her hair is mostly black, but with glowing flame highlights. Most often, she wears a very matte gray hijab or hooded cloak made of spiderwebs and smoke that smells like mugwort and bay leaves and star anise and sometimes lots of other things. I encourage you to invite or visit Drakaina if that is in your skill set, but she is not the easiest spirit to get in to see without an introduction. If you don't feel up to that, that's totally ok! In this chapter, our teacher will be an ambassador-egregore from the Circle, Pythia.

Pythia, of course, is not a proper name, but rather a title which was held by a number of women who served as oracle at Delphi in life. Πυθώ (Pytho) is the ancient name for Delphi, most likely derived from the Greek πύθειν (pythein), which means "to rot" or "to smell rotten." In ancient days, a foul-smelling vapor arose from the earth at Delphi, explained legendarily as the stench of the great dragon/serpent rotting below, who was named Πύθων (Python, the root of our English word). This vapor was said by some to be the foundation of the priestess's oracular trance. Likely because the underground aquifer has been diverted by human construction, the vapor no longer arises.

Pythia is not a single human, but rather an egregore spirit participated in by all those who become Pythia while they live, giving up their name and their family and their essential individuality, becoming slowly infused with the essence of Pythia, who lives forever among the ancestors. The vapors of Python were poison; they carried up the Python Voice, but each time they were breathed, they carried a tiny piece of the priestess down to live among the dead. A dangerous vocation.

Pythia is a master translator; in addition to the Python Voice, she understands the voice of the wind and the rain, and the voice that hisses in the flames. She speaks the languages of the birds and trees, and all the tongues of Babel. In my experience, she is relatively perfunctory and businesslike, without too much personality of her own. To me, she most often appears as a tall woman with

175 *Oracle* can be a very tricky word. An oracle is a prophecy, spoken by a medium who is possessed by a spirit, but an oracle is also both the possessed medium and the spirit doing the possessing, as well as the location where it is done. Oracles are spoken by oracles in the Voice which arises from the oracle.

176 Drakaina is not a proper name; it's a title that means "She-Dragon." It's used for a wide variety of goddesses, including this one.

olive skin and dark hair in a black pantsuit, often carrying a clipboard.[177] She's not a real person; she's an artificial construct. I think of her kind of like an artificially intelligent librarian who answers questions. I suspect she's really just a human-formed interface to Drakaina. If you are already skilled at spirit contact, you might also try reaching out to some of the Sisters. If you're not, that's ok.

The Seer's Trance

This is the oracular trance the Circle of Sisters teaches:

1. Clarify the topic you wish to Know until you have a properly formed question.
2. Sit very erect, ideally with the bottoms of your feet touching each other. Pull your feet in as close to your body as possible. Place your hands, resting palm up, on your thighs.[178] I often touch my thumb to my middle finger. A trick I learned from Jason Miller: touch the tip of your tongue to the roof of your mouth. I don't know why, but this really helps clarify the connection. I think it "completes" some kind of "circuit" in the body.
3. Close your eyes, and take several deep breaths, calming yourself.
4. You may wish to perform the Rainbow Star if you feel unbalanced.
5. Descend via the Granny Trance.
6. Usually, I encourage you to speak from the heart, in your own words. Not here. This is an exact passcode. Say out loud: "*Blessed oracle of the Circle of Sister Sibyls, I am [NAME] the oracle of [PLACE]. In the name of Great Drakaina I ask: help me speak Truth concerning ____________________.*" *For example, I might say: "I am Sara, the oracle of Witch House,"* but I could also say "the oracle of Hawkins

177 I don't know what's on the clipboard. She's never let me see it.

178 This is the posture I was taught by Pythia, but feel free to experiment with other postures. My body is almost certainly a radically different shape than yours. I am five feet tall, weigh around three hundred pounds, and am very double jointed. You will possibly need a different posture. All bodies are different! I expect full lotus would be a good option, but my legs are too short and my belly too big for me to be in that position, so I don't know. Feel in your body the right posture for you. It should keep your spine vertical and open up your root and your throat in particular. If it hurts, you're doing it wrong. Experiment to find what works best for you. If in doubt, just sit straight up in a chair with your feet flat on the floor and your hands on your knees.

Ave" or "the oracle of North Braddock" or "an oracle of the Eastern Woodland" or "an oracle of America" (which I usually reserve for political forecasting). Oracles are rooted in places. If you are not rooted (for example, if you are traveling or have recently moved), then you can say "oracle of the crossroads." I was an oracle of the crossroads for many, many years before Witch House, and expect to be one again soon

7. When you are ready, begin to breathe in slowly through your nose, and exhale through your mouth. You may feel pressure building in your sinuses. That is a good sign. Do not swallow, which will release the pressure.
8. Continue to breathe, imagining your head slowly expanding, like a balloon. This may be slightly uncomfortable, but shouldn't hurt.
9. When you feel "fully inflated," hiss the air out like a snake until you have no more air.
10. Begin breathing in through your nose again, but now start to roll your eyes in lemniscates, up on the outsides, and down on the inside. When you are fully inflated, hiss your way down again.
11. Once more, inflate through your nose. Continue making eye lemniscates. Feel two serpents twining up your spine, from bottom to top, one winding around the vertebrae in each direction. When they reach your head, and all three of you are fully inflated, hiss with all three heads together.
12. Open your eyes, open your mouth, and start divining out loud.
13. With this method, it is important to speak the divination out loud (to "speak Truth concerning ______"). Do not say other things while speaking Truth. Do not interpret or explain. Just speak Truth. I recommend recording yourself. If you completely remember everything you said, you're doing it wrong.
14. When you are ready, say thank you, and then make your goodbyes.
15. Breathe hard and fast for a bit to clear your head.
16. Return to normal space/time/consciousness.
17. Stand up. Move your body. Cackle like a witch.

Essential Skills for Divination

There are three underlying skills involved in divination: organizing ideas into words, careful attention, and pattern recognition. As I'll describe it below, divination has four phases, but the first and last phases use the same skill:

1. Articulate and accurate encoding of (often complicated, emotional, and messy) desire to Know into a clear, well-formed question (or series of questions)
2. Careful, attentive, open-minded, and impartial observation
3. Pattern recognition and analysis
4. Articulate an accurate communication of (often complicated, emotional, and messy) messages as answers to the questioner (which, in divination, is often called by the more old-fashioned word *querent*)

To simplify, we can call these phases:

1. Ask
2. Listen
3. Interpret
4. Answer

In my opinion, the most important way to become better at divination is to understand that these four phases are best kept separate, because they each require a distinct mental state, none of which are your everyday frame of mind. We'll discuss each phase individually and then put them together. At least in my experience, these phases remain the same in (almost) all methods of divination.

How to Divine

Before we proceed, a few warnings and caveats.

The first: Divination can be slightly addictive for some people; it punches the same buttons as gambling. Here are some signs that you (or whomever you're reading for) might need to be cut off:

1. Asking questions you already know the answer to.
2. Asking questions you don't want to know the answer to.
3. Asking the same questions over and over, hoping for a "do-over."
4. Asking questions and then not paying attention to the answers.
5. Asking questions to treat anxiety, rather than to inform decisions.

We're all guilty of doing these things sometimes. You don't need to cut them out completely, but be cautious about these behaviors. This kind of divination is like junk food; ok as a "sometimes treat," but neither healthy nor wise as a regular behavior.

Second: It is *much, much* harder to divine about your own life than it is to divine about other people's lives. It is particularly hard to get clean reads on matters in your own life in which you are heavily emotionally invested. Not just that, but you will improve much, much faster if you divine for other people, because you will get to see a much wider variety of situations, and you will be able to get results about the accuracy of your divination with less entanglement. There's no "control group" if you only ever read about yourself.

Step One: Ask (How to Frame Questions)

When I teach students with experience in divination—even those with many, many years of experience—I find the place they most often have the most room to improve is in the first step, framing the question. The purpose of Divination is to answer questions. And yet, I often find that people are very reluctant to actually ask questions. Instead, they want to describe a situation and then "divine on it." This almost never provides actionable intelligence, because it gives very little context in which to interpret the answer.

The first step in framing your question is to clearly describe the situation. For most situations, the ultimate purpose of your divination is to gather information to help you make a decision. So, the first thing you need to do is figure out what intelligence you'll need. One technique to help you think this through is the so-called Johari window, a method popular among intelligence professionals:

1. First, make a list of everything relevant to the topic that you confidently know. These are called "known knowns."
2. Next, make a list of specific questions you know you need answers to. These are your "known unknowns." Research, and try to answer as many of these questions as you can before moving on to divination.
3. Next, think about what you sort of feel and intuit about the situation, even if you can't really explain how or why. These are the "unknown knows" (including your biases). Divination needs to be segregated from these biases. Do your best to see these as clearly as you can, but, of course, the whole point of "unknown knowns" is that it's hard.
4. Finally, try to think about the parts of the situation you don't really have any handle on at all. Obviously, you will fail at this, but flail around for a while, changing your viewpoint to try to find blind spots. These are the "unknown unknowns." The goal isn't to know these things. It's to feel for their boundary, so as to get a sense of the shape of the thing you are trying to know. For the most part, defining those boundaries is where divination is most useful.

Begin by divining on your "known unknowns." Ask specific, concrete questions. One way to know that you've formed a good question is to make yourself list of possible answers, to be sure that you know how the divination system you are using could provide that answer. For example, "If the coin is heads up, that means I should take the job. Tails means I shouldn't." If you can't do this, you either need to clarify your question or choose a new method. The following exercise will help you practice.

Exercise: Stacking the Deck

In this exercise, I have provided both questions and possible answers. Translate each of these possible answers into the divination method of your choice. Although the questions are largely in the first person, assume you are reading for someone else if the situation is not relevant to you. I have done the first one with both flip a coin and tarot as an example.[179] You can use any method(s) you like. Obviously, it is impossible to uniquely and precisely translate with such a limited vocabulary; there are many possible translations for each one:

1. Question: Is my husband cheating on me?
    a) Yes. He has been shtupping his dark-haired ex for months now.
        i) Heads.
        ii) Three of Swords. Lovers. Queen of Swords.
    b) Yes. He is sleeping with his boss. The relationship is not entirely consensual.
        i) Heads.
        ii) Devil. Three of Swords. Empress.
    c) Not currently, but he slept with a prostitute while drunk on that business trip to Las Vegas.
        i) Tails.
        ii) Lovers reversed. Seven of Cups. Six of Pentacles.
    d) No, but he feels your constant suspicion, resents it, and is considering leaving because of it.
        i) Tails.
        ii) Nine of Swords. Moon. Four of Wands, reversed.
2. Will I get a promotion at work this year?
    a) Yes, and it will be great.
    b) Yes, but it will be a lot of extra work and will not come with a raise.

179 Examine the differences between the flip a coin answers and tarot. Even if you don't know tarot at all, you should be able to tell that tarot is giving more complicated answers.

c) No, but you should negotiate for a raise anyway.
d) No one will be promoted; the company is in trouble.
e) No, you will be passed over because your boss is racist.

3. What can I do to find love this year?
    a) Dress up and go out more.
    b) Heal old trauma first; you're a mess.
    c) Court your fair-haired neighbor.
    d) Look into getting back with an ex.
    e) You are unlikely to find a romantic partner this year.
4. What is causing my fatigue and hair loss?
    a) Stress.
    b) Hormone imbalance.
    c) Poisoning (includes food allergies).
    d) You are in mortal danger. See a doctor immediately, and keep seeing doctors until you get a solution.
5. What should I be watching for today?
    a) A lucrative business opportunity will be offered by a fat, light-skinned man in a blue suit.
    b) You are "penciled in" for a car accident. Wear your seatbelt, pay attention, and be careful!
    c) You will meet a brilliant, charming, and beautiful dark-skinned woman on the 61A bus. You'll get to marry her if you play your cards right.

Bonus: Go back and invent at least one more possible answer for each of those questions, and then translate those too.

Framing Questions for Divination

There are essentially two types of questions: questions of fact (objective questions) and questions of opinion (subjective questions). "Is my husband cheating on me?" is a question of fact.[180] "Should I take the apartment on 53rd Street?" is a question of opinion, and so you need to clarify who you are asking. If you

180 Although not a very precise one without clarifying what exactly qualifies as "cheating." My observation has been that with "normal" Christian wedding vows (like "love, honor, and cherish… forsaking all others"), almost everyone is in breach of oath almost all the time. Our culture teaches us to be very lax about oaths, but that's a very, very bad habit for a magician to be in. Don't make vows you won't keep, and don't be tricked into keeping vows you didn't make.

ask your favored ancestor, maybe she'll say yes, because it is so near to your mother's house, and by the way, you should call your mother more. If you ask Aphrodite, she might say no, you should take the one on 34th, because the neighbor is hot and available. If you ask Archangel Rafael, he might tell you to take the one on 5th because the heat does not work, and the suffering will help you become more enlightened and compassionate.

Step One: Ask

In general, I advocate first asking objective questions and then asking subjective questions, sometimes to a variety of allies. Here are some simple fact-questions I recommend. For the most part, each question can be answered with a single tarot card, rune, or other "word" in most sophisticated divination systems:

* "What is the nature of ___________?"
* "What are the causes of __________?"
* "How does ________ feel about ______?"
* "What is _____ planning to do about _________?"
* "What will happen tomorrow?"
* "What will happen if I _____? What if I don't? What should I do instead?"

Step Two: Listen (Pay Careful Attention)

As I mentioned above, there are three skills to divination: clarity of communication (asking/answering), mediumship (listening),[181] and pattern recognition (interpreting). For most people, the place where you will see the most immediate improvements is in tightening up your communication skills. Mediumship is a more difficult skill to improve, but (like all human activities) you can always get better at it. The most important part of listening is to *not* attempt to process, interpret, or analyze, because your confirmation biases will ruin the clarity. Simply receive and record the input.

In my opinion, one great way to improve your mediumship is to regularly assume the krokopeplos. Another great way to improve listening is with regular practice of meditation, so you become familiar with what your own brain sounds like and can distinguish that from an external source. In this context, I am *not* recommending meditation as part of your divination practice. Here, meditation is not intended to function as trance induction, but rather as a spiritual exercise that has the side effect of improving the clarity of your

181 Many people would probably call this seeing, but I'm not very visually oriented.

listening. For this purpose, I recommend a kind of mediation called vipassana, or "insight," meditation. Teaching this kind of sophisticated mediation practice is outside the scope of this book, but the exercise below has some quickie beginner instructions.

Exercise: Meditate

Sit still, with your spine straight. Quiet your mind. Pay attention to your breathing. If you notice that you've stopped paying attention, start again. That's mediation. I recommend you meditate for ten minutes every day this week. In my opinion, every day for the rest of your life would be better. If you are having trouble, here are several pieces of advice for beginners:

Stop filling every available minute with sensory stimulation. Next time you are on the toilet, do not take out your phone. Just sit there in silence and let your brain chatter about whatever it likes. Listen to yourself. Same with the next time you are stuck in traffic: turn off the radio, and just listen to yourself. Allow yourself to be bored. This is *not* meditation, but if the only quiet time in your life is when you're meditating, you will never manage to quiet your mind, because it has stuff to say to you, and it won't stop until you've listened. If you're having trouble focusing during these listening times, narrate your thoughts to yourself out loud.

Instead of setting an alarm, I like to use a sound that will turn off after the allotted time. Something gentle, like rain. This is soft enough that it won't jar you out of meditation if you go over time, but when you wonder "Have I done this long enough yet?" if it's still playing, you know the answer is no. I adore this website full of sounds:

Pretend you are an incorporeal spirit, inhabiting a human body for the first time, and eager to describe the experience to your discarnate friends. Pay very careful attention to breathing. What does it feel like? How are you doing it? What would it be like to forget to breathe?

If you have a minor pain or itch, instead of trying to ignore it, lean in and really feel it. How would you describe it to someone who has never had a body? I find that, with careful attention, the sensation sometimes "melts" away. If you are in real pain, if your body is signaling you that you are about to do damage, stop and change positions.

Step Three: Understand

The final skill required for divination is pattern recognition. There are many ways to improve this skill. We'll start with ways to improve your pattern recognition in general, and then I'll provide some advice specific to divination.

Unquestionably, the best way to improve your pattern recognition skills is to learn more theoretical mathematics, which is the art of pattern recognition, manipulation, and extension. I know that's not necessarily what people want to hear, but for millennia, mathematics was the gold standard of education for magicians and diviners. Plato says of mathematics that "They who know how to properly define and divide are as gods." In addition to steeply improving your pattern recognition, learning mathematics also makes you smarter. There is no other activity that has been shown to be nearly as effective for improving neuroplasticity in adults; it outperforms both music and language learning (which are both also good).

For people who enjoy math and are comfortable with it, I recommend either *The Higher Arithmetic* by H. Davenport or *Transition to Higher Mathematics* by Dumas and McCarthy. If you're not yet comfortable with the basics, I'd recommend *The Art of Problem-Solving, Vol. 1* (or *Vol. 2*) by Lehoczky and Rusczyk, which is designed for children but also great for adults. All of these books are serious texts for people who want to do some real work to see real improvement in their pattern recognition and problem-solving skills. They're not easy, but they're worth it. However, not everyone wants to put in that much work. That's ok! Here are some other, easier ways to improve pattern recognition:

* Play the game Set.[182]
* Keep a detailed journal—track weather, mood, health, and other factors. Review your notes for patterns.
* Learn as much as you can about a variety of subjects, particularly the natural sciences.
* Learn to guess the artist (or period) of a painting (or a musician from a piece of music) you've never seen before from seeing enough of their other paintings. Think about how you're doing it. Explain it to yourself in complete sentences. Hassle artist and musician friends

182 https://smart-games.org/en/set/

and make them explain how they do it. What characteristics are they using to make the identification?

* Develop precise "habits of mind." Do not accept sloppy thinking in yourself. When speaking, say exactly what you mean. When others speak, ask questions until you are confident you understand what they have said. Do not let go of a thought until you fully understand it. However, recall that I am recommending this as an exercise in pattern recognition. Doing this all the time will make you seem like an asshole. Sometimes, it's important to let people speak what's on their mind without repeatedly interrupting them to make them explain themselves. Choosing to accept others as they are, instead of forcing them to be as we want them to be is the essence of compassion.
* Refuse to acknowledge omens that do not repeat. Part of learning to analyze patterns is having the confidence to accept that not everything is a pattern. Demand that the spirits communicate clearly.
* *Always* be guessing. Predict tomorrow's weather. Try to predict TV shows as you watch them. Guess what people are going to say before they say it. Guess what a date's parents are like before you ask them about it. Make political forecasts. Gamble.[183] You don't have to announce your guesses,[184] but keep track of them in your notes. More importantly...
* Ruthlessly correct yourself. *Always* be looking for evidence that you are wrong. When you find out you've been wrong...
    * Publicly admit it and make a retraction (technically this step isn't so much about getting better at pattern recognition as it is about not being a dick)
    * Record in your notes that you were wrong, with details about how and why.
    * Make careful analysis of how you were wrong. Don't yet focus on why you were wrong, but how: What particulars were you wrong about? Was it an error of scale? An error of type? Did you confuse one person for another? Etc., etc.
    * Investigate the causality of what happened. Now that you know what happened, review what caused it. Which of its causal precedents did you know about? Which should you have known about? At what point should you have been able

183 "Enjoy responsibly."

184 I am told that this behavior is obnoxious and inappropriate.

to predict it? Next time a similar situation arises, what will alert you that it is a similar situation?

* Finally, figure out why you were wrong. Did you not read the signs properly? Did you miss them entirely? Did you fail to analyze them? Was this a freak event that no one reasonably could have predicted?
* The world is beautiful and strange and very, very chaotically emergent. You'll never be able to predict everything. Broadly, the easiest things to predict, in my experience, are:

* Large-scale simple natural processes, like the sunrise or the weather
    * The behavior of people you know well, singly or in groups
    * The behavior of unintelligent and uncreative strangers (or near strangers)
    * The behavior or very large (i.e., ten thousand or more) groups of people
    * The dynamics of systems driven by a single, powerful force

Step Four: Answer the Question(s)

The final step in divination is to clearly articulate the answer in complete, coherent sentences. You need to provide a specific answer to the question that was asked. When I receive readings from other people, this is the step I am usually disappointed by. You can start your answer by explaining the meanings of the cards (or etc.), but that is not sufficient. You must explain what those cards mean in the context of the question that was asked. Not the topic that was asked about, not the situation being investigated, but the specific question that was asked. Don't hem and haw. Don't hedge your bets. Answer the question, clearly and precisely. It's much better to be wrong than to be vague. You can learn to get better from being wrong. Being vague is at best cowardly and at worst manipulative, verging into fraudulent.

In general, I think this is among the reasons people find it harder to read for themselves than for other people. The need to communicate to another person forces you to actually give answers in words, and not in vague feelings, which is hard. When reading for themselves, many people don't bother to be take the time to move from vague feeling to actual, precise answers, and that's why their divinations aren't very good. Write (or speak, but you ought to keep a record) a specific answer in complete sentences.

What Is Sortilege?

Sortilege is a name for the broad category of divinatory techniques that involve choosing from a finite number of options. Flipping a coin, rolling dice, tarot (and other kinds of cartomancy), and reading runes or lots are all types of sortilege. The word itself comes from the Latin *sors* "fate" + *legere* "choose." In older contexts, it can sometimes mean any kind of witchcraft or sorcery, but in modern usage, it nearly always means some kind of casting lots.

Before we move on to learning specific methods of sortilege, let's talk a little bit about the pros and cons of sortilege when compared to other, more free-form methods of coming to Know.

The biggest benefit, in my opinion, is that a sortilege tool can bear some of the "cost" of the magic. Not only do sortilege tools provide a bit of a "buffer" between the reader and the querent's messy psyche, they are also physically easier on the diviner than methods like mediumship, where the diviner's body is the only bridge between the physical and the Other. Being that liminal is taxing and not entirely healthy for the body. This is not a big deal for people who only divine once or twice a week, but if, once you've had more practice, you choose to divine for clients or otherwise routinely mediate that gap for hours at a time, the exhaustion can become a very real factor.

Another big benefit of sortilege is that it is very socially acceptable in our culture. I often joke with other card readers that the biggest reason we use cards is that it makes it less creepy for the querent. Finally, perhaps the biggest benefit of sortilege is that, because of their limited vocabulary, sortilege answers can be easier to learn to interpret than more free-form methods.

The downside of sortilege is that, while it's easy to get started with sortilege, getting good at it can be hard. There can be a lot of "book learning" to plow through, especially with more complicated sortilege methods, like runes or tarot. Flip a coin, which we've already discussed, is the simplest sort of sortilege. Next, we'll talk about cartomancy, which is my preferred sophisticated method of sortilege.

Cartomancy

Tarot cards are my preferred method of divination in almost all circumstances. While I do not have space in this book to present a complete course on the tarot, I will do my best to give you a bit of an introduction. If you'd like a "quick-start" tarot guide, I've provided one on YouTube here:

To follow along with this section, you'll need a tarot deck, either paper or digital. The deck I recommend for beginners is the Smith-Rider-Waite tarot. For a paper edition, I particularly like the Smith-Waite Centennial Edition from US Games. For digital, I recommend the app from The Fool's Dog.[185]

A Very Brief History of Tarot

What we today call tarot cards developed out of playing cards, which entered Europe from China in the fourteenth century. Shortly thereafter, the first tarot decks were developed in Italy. They were (and still are) used primarily for gaming, and only much later for fortune telling. The Visconti-Sforza deck, one of the oldest surviving, emerged around the 1450s. The Marseilles deck, one of the earliest types—and still the favorite of many professional diviners—was developed around 1650. The use of tarot for fortune telling began to be widespread only in the 1700s. In 1789, the Etteilla deck was published. It was the first tarot to include overtly occult symbols, such as the four elements, astrological associations, and ancient Egyptian themes.

In 1909, the Rider-Waite-Smith (RWS) deck was published. It is named after three people. The "Rider" part of the name is for the publisher, William Rider and Son (now a division of Penguin Random House). Arthur Edward Waite, who wrote the accompanying guidebook, was a prominent occultist of the time. Until recently, one would often hear this deck called simply the

185 Full disclosure: I am the managing partner and Chief Education Officer (CEO) of The Fool's Dog.

"Rider-Waite" deck, erasing the contributions of perhaps the most important collaborator, Pamela "Pixie" Coleman Smith, the artist. Smith was an illustrator, artist, writer, publisher, theatrical set[186] and costume designer, and magician. I wish I had the space to tell you more about her here, but I do not. I recommend looking her up. Because of this history, the deck can go by a lot of names; Smith-Rider-Waite is my preference. Smith-Waite is also popular. But the most common is Rider-Waite-Smith.

Structure of a Modern Tarot Deck

Since the publication of the RWS tarot deck at the turn of the last century, the format and structure of most modern English tarot decks has been very similar. Standard modern tarot decks have seventy-eight cards: a "minor arcana" of four fourteen-card suits, plus a "suit" of trumps sometimes called the "major arcana." We'll begin by discussing the minor arcana, which is quite similar to modern playing cards, and then move on to discussing the major arcana.

As in playing cards, there are four suits in a tarot deck. In English, the names of the suits sometimes vary. I have bolded the names used in the RWS deck:

* **Pentacles**, Coins, Disks, or Diamonds
* **Swords**, Blades, or Spades
* **Wands**, Staves, Batons, or Clubs
* **Cups**, Chalices, Vessels, or Hearts

These four suits are closely tied to the four elements, which we discussed in the previous chapter, along with the number four. My experience is that, when they come up in tarot readings, minor arcana cards are generally talking about:

* Pentacles = Earth = Money. Sometimes the querent's housing or physical health.
* Swords = Air = Ideas. In many readings, swords cards are about the querent's career.
* Wands = Fire = Morals. Many of my colleagues would, instead, say that wands cards are about passion. But I think they become clearer when viewed in the context of ethics.
* Cups = Water = Relationships and Feelings. Not just romantic ones. All interpersonal relationships.

186 Pro tip: When reading RWS, remember the illustrator was a set designer. Try lining up the horizons of the cards to establish foreground and background cards.

Court Cards

As I mentioned above, each tarot suit has four court cards. In the RWS, and most decks that take after it, these are named Page, Knight, Queen, and King. These court cards are very similar to those in playing cards, but with the Jack broken into two—Page and Knight. Each of these is associated with one of the elements: Kings are Fire, Queens are Water, Knights are Air, and Pages are Earth. Employing what we learned about the elements in Chapter Three allows us to make some guesses about what the court cards must mean.

* Page (Earth): Practical matters, money, physicality
* Knights (Air): Messages, communication, intellect
* Queens (Water): Social savvy, "soft power," nurturance
* Kings (Fire): Leadership, authority, power, ethics

In most readings, I find that court cards tend to represent specific people in the querent's life; they can normally be identified by their relationship to the querent. At other times, court cards represent facets of the querent's personality, or a situation that calls for them to act in the manner of the court card. The table below provides a simplified understanding of the sixteen court cards for beginners, focusing on relationships to the querent. Some tarot readers, but not usually me, read with court card "significators." That is, in advance, they will choose a card to represent the querent, and then read other court cards in relation. For example, if the Queen of Swords is chosen as the significator for the querent, then the King of Swords is almost certainly their spouse or partner.

	Cups	**Pentacles**	**Swords**	**Wands**
Page	Child	Employee	Student	Subordinate
Knight	Lover	Colleague	Messenger	Inspirer
Queen	Nurturer	Manager	Teacher	Collaborator
King	Protector	Boss	Judge	Priest

Writing Prompt

For each court card, choose a character from your favorite books, movies, and TV shows that you feel embodies the card. Write a single sentence for each card explaining your choices.

The court cards are archetypes, but real people are not so simple. All humans have aspects of every court card within them. Write a single sentence about each court card, explaining how you see each one in yourself. Repeat this prompt with another person you know well. If you're brave, do this with your learning circle or study buddy, and tell each other your answers.

Exercise: Significators and Court Cards

Separate the sixteen court cards from the rest of your deck, and use them to do a reading about two people. Below, I'll use the example of a heterosexual romantic couple, but this can easily be adapted for any kind of relationship, such as parent/child, employee/boss, etc. One of the people can be you, but you can also read about others.

* Clear your mind, center your attention, and focus on the relationship you hope to understand.
* In your journal, record the date and the names of the two people you'll be investigating.
* Say something like, "Dear tarot, please use six cards to help me understand:"
    * Who he hopes to be
    * How he sees himself
    * How she sees him
    * Who she hopes to be
    * How she sees herself
    * How he sees her
* For each statement, pull a single card, and place it face up. You may arrange the cards however you like, but I usually do it in two rows of three.
* In your journal, write at least two sentences about each card, in the context of the question.
* Try this exercise again, for the same relationship, but this time, after you pull each card, write down the result, and then shuffle it back into the deck. Compare the results. Pay special attention to where the two readings seem to be saying different things. Find a way to reconcile both.

Pips

I have neither the space nor the inclination to provide meanings for every tarot card here. Your deck should have come with a small booklet (often called a "little white book," or LWB) with meanings. If you have a digital app, it probably comes with several such books. However, as a down and dirty generalization, the basic meanings of the numbered cards can be approximated by combining the meaning of the number[187] with the meaning of the suit. For example, the Two of Cups is about two-ness (polarity) and cups-ness (feelings). That card is traditionally called "love" and is usually about romantic relationships. The Nine of Pentacles is about nine-ness (wishes) and earth-ness (money). That card is often called "gain," and it's about getting/having money.

The Major Arcana

What follows is intended only as the briefest overview of a very deep and rich topic. Check your LWB for more.

0. **Fool:** Risk-Taker. Trickster. Beginning. Naivete.
1. **Magician:** Skill. Manifestation. Creation.
2. **Priestess:** Intuition. Divination. Channel.
3. **Empress:** Fertility. Healing. Nurturance. Care.
4. **Emperor:** Responsibility. Leadership.
5. **Hierophant:** Priest. Teacher. Institutions.
6. **Lovers:** Romance. Sex. Partnership.
7. **Chariot:** Travel. Momentum. Moving Forward.
8. **Strength:** Passion. Courage. Integrity.
9. **Hermit:** Wisdom. Insight. Autonomy. Loneliness.
10. **Wheel:** Luck. Ups and Downs. "Reply Hazy."
11. **Justice:** Cause/Effect. Court. Ethics. Vengeance.
12. **Hanged Man:** Challenge. Initiation. Suffering.
13. **Death:** Dying. Endings. Transformation.
14. **Temperance:** Balance. Alchemy. Union of Opposites.
15. **Devil:** Bondage. Addiction. Spirit Communication.
16. **Tower:** Catastrophe. Collapse of Systems.
17. **Star:** Hope. Faith. Spirituality. Renewal.
18. **Moon:** Illusion. Psychism. Obscurity. Shadows.
19. **Sun:** Clarity. Success. Joy. Celebration.
20. **Final Judgment:** Completion. End of Cycle.
21. **World:** Accomplishment. Big Picture. Integration.

187 Which we discussed in the previous chapter.

Telling Omens

Omens are spontaneous occurrences that convey meaning; usually, they predict future happenings. However, it is important to understand that, in its essence, an omen is less about the actual event and more about the significance attached to it, and the declaration of that significance by the omen teller. That is, if an omen happens, but no one tells it, it really wasn't an omen after all.[188] In my opinion, telling omens—reading signs—is at the foundation of all divination. It is a difficult skill that takes many, many years to master. However, there's no better time to start learning to tell omens than right now!

The most important part of telling omens is learning to recognize them. Omens are unusual events. Therefore, in order to recognize them, you need to know what is and isn't usual in the particular environment you're observing. In order to do that, you need to be paying attention to what is going on around you all the time. *All. The. Time.*

There is a classic teaching story about the great prophet Moses, which tells that he had walked past the burning bush[189] every day for years, and simply never noticed, because he was always staring at the ground, thinking about his problems, or else he had his head up in the clouds, imagining the future, instead of keeping his eyes and his attention on what was going on around him in the actual moment he was in. We are all guilty of this sometimes, but there is nothing that will so improve your magical practice as paying attention to the world around you. Put down your phone. Take out your headphones. Be in the moment you are in, in the place where you are, and pay attention to everything that happens.

Only once you have built up enough observational experience to know what is normal can you begin to understand what is unusual enough to be considered an omen. For example, if I were to see two black snakes twined around each other in late May, I would not consider that an omen, because that is blacksnake mating season where I live, and so it is not so unusual to see them mating. However, were I to see it in October, or if one of the snakes was black and the other white, I probably would consider it an omen (probably

---

188 Remember, ignoring omens doesn't prevent them from coming true. An omen is the prediction, not the thing being predicted.

189 If you are not familiar with the story of Moses and the Burning Bush, I encourage you to go read it now. It's in the third chapter of the book of Shemot (which Christians call "Exodus").

an epiphany of Hermes)[190] because that would be very unusual in the environment where I live. Sadly, climate change has greatly destabilized a lot of weather and wildlife patterns, making it even harder than it used to be to say something is truly "unseasonable."

It is hard to know what does and doesn't count as an omen, but that is not as big of a problem as you might imagine. Omens that are genuine communications from the spirit world will repeat until you acknowledge them. Indeed, my experience, and the experience of most magicians I know, is that omens repeat, louder and louder, with more and more outlandish unusualness, so often that we have a phrase for it: "getting hit by the clue-by-four." For beginners, I strongly advise you to refuse to acknowledge any omen that doesn't repeat at least three times.

In addition to watching for spontaneous omens, you can also provoke them by "asking for a sign." The following exercise is one way to do that.

Exercise: Sorting for an Omen

Here's an exercise to help you practice reading omens by using sortilege. It takes about fifteen minutes in the morning and another fifteen minutes at night. You'll get much faster at it with practice, but do this long-form to build your skill. The slower and deeper you go, the more the exercise will work.

1. Decide on a spirit to ask for advice. Spirits of revelation or illumination are good choices.
2. Quiet your mind, and prepare to listen.
3. Ask: "What omen should I watch for today?"
4. Perform whatever divination method you are practicing. Record the results.
5. Try not start trying to interpret the results until you have completed the divination method and recorded the results. For example, in the case of tarot, do not start interpreting until all the cards are out.[191]
6. Spend at least eight minutes taking notes and trying to understand it. Describe it in great detail. Ruminate on it. Make up stories about it.

---

190 Partly because entwined snakes are a very common symbol of Hermes (such as on the caduceus), but also because I have a long and deep relationship with Hermes, so him providing a sign of his presence isn't outside the bounds of reason.

191 I know that, in movies, they usually do it card by card. It's because it builds tension slowly, which is more dramatic, and makes for a better performance. For that same reason, professional diviners sometimes do it. But divination qua divination is much harder that way. I'm not saying you can't read that way if you want, but it's a less useful exercise for beginners.

Try and imagine all the possible things that were trying to be said in the encoded answer you were given.

7. Spend the day alert to the omen you were told to watch for.
8. As you are preparing to sleep, review your day. Did you find the omen? What was it? Did you understand the omen? Even if you didn't, just finding it alerted you to pay attention to what was happening at that time.
9. If you saw the omen, but failed to correctly interpret it, reinterpret it now with the benefit of hindsight. What was it trying to tell you? How will you know that next time?
10. If you didn't find the omen today, review your day and try to identify it now. If you can't, try to reverse engineer it by looking at what you should have been alerted to. What did you miss today that you should have noticed? What led up to that should have alerted you? Take copious notes about your day. Do you see the omen now?
11. If you still can't identify the omen, revisit your notes in a week, and try it again with the benefit of hindsight. Now do you see it?

Greater Ritual: Automatic Writing

Much of the time, when we're divining, we're not really looking for factual information, but rather for advice. In these cases, it's important to know who we're asking. You (and the querent) need to choose someone to ask before beginning. In general, I do not advise divination with spirits with whom you do not already have an established relationship. One method for asking for advice is a technique called automatic writing. This is a type of mediated oracular adorcism. That is to say, it is a gentle type of trance possession. Since you are writing, instead of seeking visions or even auditory communication, the spirit is forced to speak in words, and to go slowly enough for you to follow. In my experience, other types of possessory vision quest tend to flick so fast they are hard to keep track of, especially when you are first learning.

I developed the following method when I was a freshman in college, originally inspired by Austin Osmond Spare's essay "Automatic Drawing." This is not exactly how I did it then, nor exactly how I do it now—this is the method I believe is easiest for most beginners.

Although you can use any kind of writing instrument, physical or digital, for automatic writing, I find it easiest to use a felt-tip pen and unlined paper. The biggest problem with typing automatic writing is that it is difficult to switch alphabets or draw pictures, which are both things I frequently do while automatic writing. Make sure to have *lots* of paper on hand. I write very big with lots of white space when I do this, and there's nothing more frustrating than running out of paper. Review the writing immediately afterward, and add notes to clarify, as needed. I transcribe mine onto the computer. That helps me process it, and also store it for later analysis. I like to keep mine in Google Docs, where they are keyword searchable, and easy to cross-link.

You will need:

* Incense or oil associated with the spirit you want to contact
* A pen
* Paper (at least 20 pages)

Steps:

1. Start by "setting the mood." Pick some incense or oil that's associated with the spirit with whom you want to make contact. Listen to some thematically appropriate music. Print out a picture of the spirit and stare at it. Say a prayer, declaim a hymn, or sing a song.
2. Enter magical space, time, and consciousness by any method. As with all things, don't force it. If anything feels injurious or sickening, stop, banish, and rest.
3. Once you're feeling relaxed and "in the zone," begin writing out an evocation script. An evocation is a kind of a preliminary prayer or conjuration that lists the names and qualities of the spirit you're looking for. I write them spontaneously, but they follow a general format that goes something like the following example, which is a prayer to open communication with the angel Arbatel, angel of revelation, angel of the east, who is the spirit with whom I first developed this technique. The script below is presented simply as an example—you should write your own:

   "El Elyon, Adonai HaOlam, Immediate and Eternal, Instantaneous and Timeless, Emptiness Beyond Darkness, Light Without Limit, Father of Heaven and Earth, Mother of the Ten Thousand Things, Mystery of Mysteries, Door to All Wonders, make open the way. Open my eyes that I might see, open my ears that I might hear, open my mouth that I might proclaim your Glory. Send Arbatel to me, that we might freely converse.

I call you Arbatel, angel of revelation, angel of the east. I call to you, Arbatel, inspiration of my heart. Come to me, attend to me, speak with me, move my pen, and answer my questions. I am Sarai, daughter of the house of Jacob, inheritor of the line of David, blood kin to Solomon the magician king. With the voice of my ancestors, I call out to you, with the hands of the patriarchs and matriarchs of my tribe, I reach out to you. In the name of Sarah who was Sarai, and the line of sibyl Saras, I call you forth, blah, blah, blah, blah…"

4. Do not stop writing. Do not pause. Do not think. If your pen stops moving, start over.
5. After a little while of this (about a page's worth, usually), you should begin to feel inspired to write things. Often, especially for beginners, that will be a list of words, like Freudian free association. As before, do not stop writing. In my practice, I find that they tend to phonetically circle around a "key word" (often a "magic name" or "mantra" type phrase), and once I find that, the words just start to flow. You should be able to feel it when the connection "clicks in"; it is usually quite sudden. When I was new to it, the first part of what the spirit had to say was usually an effusive outpouring of love for me, and happiness that I was finally listening to them.
6. Once you have established contact, try to write both ends of the conversation—whatever the spirit has to say and also any questions you want to ask. Sometimes the spirit breaks into drawings, math, or not-English, or sometimes nonsense words. If it's nonsense for more than a line or two, remind it that it has to speak in clear and intelligible English, or you're going to hang up. If you get stuck in the middle or lose the connection, go back to free-associating words.
7. After a while, you'll run out of things to say. At that point, say thank you and good bye. Before breaking the connection, ask for some "speed dial" method.
8. When you're done, wash your hands, and face and put some water on the top of your head. Take a break and live in the mundane world for a while before transcribing and analyzing.

A full session of automatic writing should take at least half an hour, and no more than an hour. Choose a spirit, and attempt to make contact and write automatically. If you are having difficulty establishing contact, here are several things that can help:

* *Regular* practice with automatic writing. At least once a week.
* *Much* deeper trance. If you can safely drive, you're not nearly deep enough. If you can safely walk in a city, you're not deep enough. Over time, you'll learn to do it in less deep trance, but that may take a lot of practice. The trance should be deep enough that, like with dreams, the experience rapidly fades when you return to normal consciousness. If you are having issues, try to reframe your problem from a difficulty hearing spirits to a difficulty remembering what you are told.
* Specialized training in "shamanism" and trance work. I think this is better learned in person, but if you'd like a book, the one my teacher recommends is *Shamanic Journeying: A Beginner's Guide* by Sandra Ingerman.
* Work with spirits to get better at working with spirits. We'll discuss this further in Chapter Eleven.

Chapter Five:

Sun and Moon

As we discussed briefly while discussing the number seven, the Greek word *planetes* (πλανήτης) means "wandered" and is the origin of our English word *planet*. Historically, a planet was any celestial body that moved through the same path as the sun through the sky.[192] There are seven such planets: Sun, Moon, Mercury, Venus, Mars, Jupiter, and Saturn. In modern Anglophone witchcraft, the word is still typically used in this old-fashioned way, and that is the sense in which I will use it in this book. In this chapter, we'll discuss the two luminary planets, Sun and Moon. In Chapter Six, we'll discuss the other five planets.

Sun

The Sun is the center of our solar system, the axis around which the planets turn. Sun stands at the border between the inner, more personal planets (Moon, Mercury, and Venus) and the outer/civic ones (Mars, Jupiter, and Saturn). Similarly, the Sun works at those places where our secret inner selves meet the communal outer world—our identity. The Sun is the source[193] of almost all energy on Earth. Sunlight illuminates, warms, and heals, but it also disinfects, bakes, and burns.

Sun is our most essential guide to time. Sun sets, it is evening. Sun rises, and it is morning. Sun orders our days and our lives. For most people, the day is for doing and the night is for being. But for witches, typically the opposite is

192 This path is called the *ecliptic.*

193 Obviously, this is an oversimplification.

true. The witching hour is for some midnight, for some three in the morning. For others, it is the natural howling of the spirits that tells us it is night. And yet, for all, the witching hour is in the deepest night. In general, most witching should be done at night, unless there is a reason to do it by day. Magic for marketing, dating, or otherwise attracting attention is a notable example, as is divination, which is about clear sight. Broadly, if the magic wants to be seen, do it under the light of day. If it's better hidden, that's magic best done under the cover of night. For solar magic in particular, most of it should be done under daylight, although other conditions might move it elsewhere. One notable exception is magic concerning invisibility, which (for hopefully obvious reasons) is best done in the dark. However, magical timing is a deep and complex art. To learn more about it, I recommend Ivo Dominguez's *Practical Astrology for Witches and Pagans: Using the Planets and the Stars for Effective Spellwork, Rituals, and Magickal Work.*

Glowing with Borrowed Glory

Among the many magical domains in the purview of the sun is all magic related to vision, appearance, and shine. One of the most traditional powers of the witch is to put a special glimmer in our eyes. When malicious jealousy flows like a curse from the eyes of a witch, we call it the evil eye. But there is also a blessing eye, and it is the gift of the sun to witches. Although modern Anglophone witchcraft (including, sometimes, this book) leans much more heavily into the association of witches with the moon, rather than the sun, that is not a universal myth. In ancient Greece, witches—including the immortal witch Circe—were understood to be daughters and initiates of the Sun. The blessing eye pours the healing, vivifying light of the sun through your eyes. In addition to conferring blessings and healing, it also captures attention. In English, I most often hear it described as "angel eyes," but it is not as commonly discussed as the evil eye. It is a sad fact that many of us live in a culture of loud and rampant cursing, while blessing goes so frequently unnoticed and unspoken.

The magic of "blessing eyes" is simple to describe, but not always so easy to do. You assume the form of a solar god and stop holding back the witchfire that is always burning inside of you. However, "assuming the godform" is a relatively sophisticated technique, which you will not learn until Chapter Twelve. Conveniently, I'm about to teach you a beginner's version, called Glowing with Borrowed Glory. Although, here, I'm teaching it specifically in the context of solar spirits, you can try it with any spirit you trust. To Glow with Borrowed Glory, you first don a costume of the spirit whose glory you want to glow with. Then, you sincerely wish for their assistance, preferably by name and out loud. Unless a very dramatic negative sign occurs immediately after praying, assume you have their permission. Make believe you are that spirit until you make yourself believe. Next, perform the Greater Ritual of the Rainbow Star, and then "dial in" to yellow. Glow yellow. Make believe you are that spirit until you can make others believe. When you're done, instead of allowing the solar radiance to dissipate, infuse it into your costume. In this way, the costume will become more and more powerful every time you work with it. Do not wear your costume in too casual of a circumstance—it is a powerful piece of your spirit, not a party dress.

Exercise: Make a Solar Costume (a.k.a. Cloak of the Sun)

Costumes and masks are among the most ancient and cross-cultural of magical tools. Unsurprisingly, costumes are used in magic—just as they are in other circumstances—to blur the lines of identity. Although in the example below, I will talk specifically about cosplaying Sun, but a similar method can be applied to any planet, or, really, any spirit you trust. By making and wearing the Cloak of the Sun, we make manifest our inner solar power as a sort of glowing aura of solarity. Conveniently, as earth is solar powered, all earthlings have a glowing aura of solarity already. The costume just helps it shine.

1. Make, assemble, acquire, or (minimally) imagine a solar costume for yourself. If you're not going to make a costume, at least find a special piece of jewelry you can wear when you're being Sun. But know that Sun, who is somewhat vain and fashion conscious, is disappointed in you.
2. There are no rules about this costume—it should be something that makes you feel like the Sun. However, I have a few practical suggestions about magic costuming:
    * The goal is not to look like the Sun. The goal is to look like a human avatar of the Sun.
    * Look at a wide variety of traditional iconography of solar gods, angels, and other spirits from around the world until you find inspiration. I've listed a few here to get you started.
    * Be a solar spirit no one else can be. Magical costuming is about creating a new image of yourself, not hiding under the image of someone else.
    * Be creative and joyful. Play like a kid playing dress-up. Have fun in the Sun.
    * Make something comfortable and easy to wear over layers for warmth. It's hard to be Sun when you're cold, and sometimes magic is outside in the cold.

* Make something comfortable and not too hot. Most solar work is outside in the Sun. If you're sun-sensitive, be sure your costume includes a hat.

Spirits of the Sun

Spirits of the Sun are too numerous to list, so I'll just choose a few of my favorites to give you a feel for that variety. See if you can get a sense for what solar spirits, in general, are like. As you read, pay attention to how a culture's sun gods are often informed by their weather. In northern Europe, where it is cold, the Sun is all-beneficent, and rites surrounding solar gods tend to be invocational. On the other hand, desert sun gods are more wrathful, and their rites are often aimed at propitiation to quell the sun's more destructive power.

* **Helios** (Ἥλιος) is the Greek god of the sun. Like his sisters[194] Selene (Moon) and Eos (Dawn), Helios is the child of the titaness Euryphaessa, the goddess of heavenly bodies, by Hyperion, the Uppermost God. Hyperion and Helios were often syncretized and are sometimes difficult to disambiguate. Although sun worship appears to have been widespread in prehistoric Greece, Helios did not have a widespread cult in classical times. His worship was centered on the island of Rhodes, where he was an important tutelary deity. There, his statue, the Colossus, was one of the Wonders of the World. He rose once more to glory in late antiquity, partly owing to his conflation with the Roman Sol. He is most often depicted as a young and beautiful man wearing a golden crown and driving the chariot of the sun. Helios is an important figure in the Greek Magical Papyri, where he is one of the Great Powers, the source of all life. Later in this chapter, we'll take a look at PGM[195] IV:1596–1715, "a consecration for all purposes, Spell to Helios."
* **Sekhmet**, whose name means "Powerful One," is an Egyptian lion goddess who is both warrior and healer. She is an emanation or daughter of Ra (the Sun). She is most often depicted as a woman with the head of a lion, wearing the solar disk as a crown. She was most often understood as the goddess of the Sun's wrath. It is said that her breath formed the desert, and caused disease and famine. Like Apollo, and

194 Helios and Selene are sometimes, but not always, understood as twins, like Artemis and Apollo, with whom they are often syncretized.

195 PGM is short for *Papyri Graecae Magicae,* which is Latin for "Greek Magical Papyri" and refers to a specific collection of Egyptian magical texts from late antiquity, written in Greek.

many other solar plague deities, Sekhmet's temples were renowned centers of healing—whatever causes plague can also cure it.

* **Shemesh** (also called Shapash), a Canaanite solar goddess, is the daughter of El and Asherah. She is called The Torch of the Gods or The Divine Illuminator. She is a messenger and psychopomp, and is in some ways to Hekate Dadophoros (Torchbearer). She is, like many solar gods, an all-seeing eye[196] whose sunbeams witness everything that transpires on earth. In one story, she descends to the Underworld with her sister,[197] Anat, to rescue Baal (Anat's husband). While there, Anat cried a river of tears, which Shemesh lapped up, becoming drunk on them. She flies into a fury, unleashing drought and killing heat on the earth.[198] Among her favorite offerings are sparkling wine and garlands of bay leaves.
* **Auriel** (לֵאיִרוּא) is an angelic regent of the sun whose name means "Light of El." Most scholars agree that the traditions of most of the named angels entered Judaism during the Babylonian captivity, and this is almost certainly the case for Auriel. Auriel is usually identified as male, but is also sometimes depicted as female. They are a cherub (a winged lion with a human head), although in the modern day, they are almost always depicted in human or winged-human form. In iconography, they often carry a book or scroll, representing their gifts of illumination, enlightenment, and wisdom. With a fiery sword, they guard the northern gate of Paradise. Auriel is a great lover of humans, and can be called to testify on our behalf in the Heavenly Court. It was they who warned Noah of the impending flood. They (and their underlings) were the Passover angel(s), who brought death to the Egyptians, while preserving those Hebrews who painted their doors with lamb's blood. Sunday is their day, and one of their favorite offerings is poetry.
* **Superman**, as I mentioned when we discussed the red/blue color combination, is unquestionably a solar spirit. In addition to his color scheme, he fights for Truth and Justice—unquestionably solar virtues—protects the weak, defends the innocent, and also has magic powers granted to him by the power of our yellow sun. If you remain skeptical about the fact that Superman is a solar spirit, I encourage you to read the graphic novel *All Star Superman*, by Grant Morrison, the same magician whose letter about sigils you read in the previous chapter.

---

196 In much of the ancient world, vision was understood to be caused by some sort of beam shooting out of the eyes. This is called the "extramission theory" of vision.

197 It is unclear if this sisterhood is literal or not.

198 Compare this with the myth of Sekhmet's fury.

The Magical Key of Helios, Which Opens Every Door, Inspired by PGM XIII:1–343
This conjuration, which is based on the ancient Greek Magical Papyrus called "The Eighth Book of Moses," calls on Helios to open the four quarters of the cosmos and to cause any locks to crumble into pieces. It is effective at opening roads to almost any kind of goal, but is especially good for opening doors to healing, wealth, and fame.

Trigger Warning: Sex magic ahead with Helios ahead.

In what follows, "NAME" is your personal solar name, which you may or may not yet have. If you have worked with the Sun long enough to have been given a "secret" name for the sun, then use that. If you do not have this, choose the name of any solar god with whom you have a relationship. If you have never worked with our Sun before, but want to try it anyway, go ahead! All living creatures on earth, including you, have an intimate relationship with Sol. Say whatever name for Sol bubbles to your lips at the moment of invocation. Feel free to modify what follows however you like, and please report back your results!

You will need:

* A fancy brass key on a ribbon.
* Solar incense (frankincense is fine, or you can use the recipe that follows).
* Charcoal.
* A place to burn things.
* A short, squat candle, preferably beeswax. The shape is important. You're going to have to balance it, lit, on your head for about twenty-five minutes. Large tea lights are good.
* An idol or ikon in the shape of the Colossus of Rhodes, large enough to fit a key between its legs. You can print the image given here and use that, or use another that calls to you.
* Olive oil.
* Clean, fresh living water (that is, water from a natural source, such as rain or spring water); not moon water (because this is a solar rite).
* A vagina. Don't have one? Imagine that you do, however seems best to you. Don't want to imagine that? This ritual probably isn't for you, but feel free to devise your own based on this.

Solar Incense Recipe:

* 5 parts frankincense resin
* 2 parts amber resin
* 1 part dried orange peel
* 2 parts cinnamon chips
* 1 part local honey

To create the incense, simply crush the ingredients into small chunks or a fine powder, mix them together, and put them on incense charcoal.

The ritual is best timed to peak near solar noon[199] on a bright, sunny day. A Sunday would be especially good. Arrange the space in advance. Depending on how long it takes you to "catch the vibe," the ritual takes around half an hour to peak.

Steps:

1. Clean and arrange a small table altar sacred to Helios, with the picture faceup on a plate. Ideally, this work should be done outside, in direct sunlight, but for reasons that will become obvious as you continue reading, you'll want to work somewhere with some privacy, which might make outdoors impractical. If you have to be indoors, try to face south.
2. Make a substantial offering to your choice of solar charities.
3. Wash the key carefully, and get it slippery with olive oil. It's going partway inside your body.
4. Wash your hands, face, and genitals. Work naked, or wear a dress or robe without underpants (you're going to have to touch your genitals later in this ritual).
5. Cover your hair. This is an unusual request in Greek magic, but Helios specifically demanded it, possibly to keep us from getting hot wax in our hair.
6. Begin by entering magical space, time, and consciousness according to your usual method.
7. Recite the Orphic Hymn to Helios on page 157.
8. Light the candle, saying something like "*I conjure you, fire, daimon of holy love, the invisible and manifold, the one and everywhere, to*

199 I.e., halfway between sunrise and sunset, when the sun is directly overhead.

reside in this candle at this time, shining and not dying out, by the command of [NAME]."

9. Yell aloud: "*Helios Axabyxrōm AAA ĒĒĒ ŌŌŌ I I I AAA OOO Tsavaot YHVH-IAŌ Zagreus the god Arat Adonai Basim IAŌ.*"
10. Make the following noises: "*TAK TAK TAK POP POP POP HISSSSSSSSSSSSSSSSS*"
11. Pour honey over the idol, and then pour the olive oil over it.
12. Light the incense, and say something like: "*I am she of the two cherubim, at the middle of the cosmos, between Heaven and Earth, light and darkness, night and day, rivers and sea. Appear to me, archangel of G-d, set in authority under the Holy ONE. I call in the name of [NAME].*"
13. Yell aloud: "*Helios Axabyxrōm AAA ĒĒĒ ŌŌŌ I I I AAA OOO Tsavaot YHVH-IAŌ Zagreus the god Arat Adonai Basim IAŌ.*"
14. Clap three times, and then whistle, howl, or sing a long, shrill note. If you can ululate, that would be ideal.
15. Take the key in your hands and say the following, passing it through the fire and the smoke, then quenching it in the water. "*I call on you alone, the only one in the cosmos who gives orders to both gods and men, who changes yourself into holy things, and brings existence out of the nonexistent and nonexistence from existent things, holy Thoth, tongue of Ra. I conjure you, spirit coming into air: By the power of the eternal god, enter, inspire, empower, and awaken this key and let it partake of your essence, for I act with the power of Thoth, the tongue of Ra, the holy god.*"
16. At least three times, gently tap the key against the penis of Helios. Don't worry; he's into it! The goal is to pull the power of Helios out through his penis and into your key.
17. Stand with your legs spread, balancing the candle on your head. Hold the key between your hands as if you are praying. If you can do so while balancing the candle, sway your hips in circles, but it's ok to hold still.
18. Glow with the Borrowed Glory of Helios of Rhodes.
19. Feel the heat of the Sun on your head. Feel the candle there, a tiny sun shining up to meet it. Feel the sunlight descend through your head and infuse into you. Begin pushing sunlight into the key between your hands.
20. Chant to Helios as seems right to you. I recommend beginning with: "*Helios Axabyxrōm AAA ĒĒĒ ŌŌŌ I I I AAA OOO Tsavaot YHVH-IAŌ Zagreus the god Arat Adonai Basim IAŌ*" and then chanting

your sacred NAME, and then try to just speak in tongues[200]. Continue for at least ten minutes in this way, pushing yellow/solar energy into the key the whole time.

21. Eventually, you should feel it begin to overflow the key and explode back into your body. Try to hold still—there's a candle on your head. If you require healing, at this time, you can divert some of the solar energy into the relevant part of your body, perhaps while making a spontaneous chant that makes wordplay with *heal* and *Helios*.
22. If you are not hot for Helios by now, you are probably doing it wrong. Repeat steps 18–22.
23. Take the candle off your head, and put it on the table, where you are looking at it.
24. Uncover your head.
25. Pass the key through your legs from back to front, tapping your own genitals at least three times on the way. Pass from your right hand behind you to your left in front.
26. Say aloud:
    "Open, open, four quarters of the cosmos, for the lord of the inhabited world comes forth. Archangels, decans, angels: Rejoice! For the Aion of Aion herself, the only and transcendent, invisible, goes through this place. Open, I say to you, Door! Hear my words, Bar! Fall into pieces, Lock! By the name AIA Ainrychat, cast upon the Earth, for the Lord Who Contains All Things, the Storm-Sender, Controller of the Abyss, Master of Fire says OPEN! Open, for Achebykrome commands you!"
27. Say aloud:
    "Helios Axabyxrōm AAA ĒĒĒ ŌŌŌ I I I AAA OOO Tsavaot YHVH-IAŌ Zagreus the god Arat Adonai Basim IAŌ." Repeat it for a total of eight times.
28. "Tap that key" some more while you…
29. Commune with Helios. Have any loving intercourse you like. Be attentive to any pet names you are called during this exchange. That is the name by which the Sun itself addressed you, a name with great power. Don't forget to ask him whatever you want to know about how to use the key.
30. Now, says the papyrus, *"The god will talk with you as with a fellow god."*
31. Ideally, orgasm.

---

200 I know this sounds like ridiculous nonsense only a magician would say, but I'm literally not allowed to tell you how to say this aloud any more than I already did. Trust your witch-tongue.

32. Return to normal space, time, and consciousness.
33. Let the key air-dry, but don't wash it. Once it's dry, store it respectfully, perhaps wrapped in a white or gold cloth, perhaps with an idol of Helios. When needed, you can also wear it on a cord around your neck. You can also put it on a keyring with other magic keys.[201]
34. Drink some water. You're very thirsty, but you might not realize it until you start drinking. Take a nap, and attend to your dreams.

Orphic Hymn #8, for Helios

Hear me, blessed one, eternal all-seeing eye,
Gold gleaming light, Titan Most High,
You are self-made and tireless, of beautiful form:
On the right side, you give birth to the morn,
While with your left hand you pour out the night,
Compounding the hours, endless alchemy of light.
Your four fleet-footed horses gambol and play,
High spirited coursers leading light of new day.
Whizzing blissful and swiftly, fiery charioteer,
Whirl like a bullroarer on your endless road round the year!
Draw forth cosmic harmony, good guide of the good,
Scorch the wrongdoers, who act in falsehood.
You give the signal, and good deeds are done,
You measure the seasons with revolutions you run.
Multiformed and evergreen, eternally undefiled,
Lightbringer, life-giver, cosmocrat, all-fruitful Paian.
You are immortal Zeus, and undying Father Time,
Truth-doing, all-shining, round-running cosmic eye.
You measure seasons, making sense, giving signs,
When the sun sets, and when you rise up and shine.
Flow-loving cosmic king beaming righteous light,
Truth-guarding all-protector, radiant knight,
Whip-whistling horse rider, life-loving charioteer:
Attend to our prayer, and to your mystics, draw near.

201 As we move through the other planets, think about how you might modify this spell for other planetary gods.

Moon

From the position of an earthbound observer, the most striking qualities of the moon are its light and cycle. Like all luminous beings, the moon is associated with illumination in both literal and metaphorical senses. Lunar spirits are often associated with wisdom or knowledge. This is particularly true in cultures with an indigenous alphabet, because of the relation of Moon to counting and writing. While this association, of Moon and insight/wisdom, is very common cross-culturally, it is not an absolute.

Although it is simply not true that all women's cycles align with the moon,[202] there is a relationship between the Moon's cycle and the menstrual cycle. Because of this association, lunar gods often have close ties to female fertility and the women's mysteries. In our culture, the moon is almost always explicitly gendered as female. However, that association is not as cross-cultural as you might expect.

Lunar magic, generally, is about the unseen and the unconscious. To my mind, the archetypal lunar magic is dream incubation, which we'll learn in Chapter Ten. Dream incubation is the practice of inducing a specific dream before going to sleep. It was extremely common in ancient Greece—and all over the ancient world. For example, tablet 4 of the *Epic of Gilgamesh* includes Gilgamesh seeking a dream, and Genesis 46:1–7 describes Jakob's famous incubation of his "ladder."

The easiest way to time magic by the moon is to do magic intended to increase something when the moon waxes and magic intended to decrease things when it wanes. The full moon and dark moon are liminal gateways. The full moon is excellent for visionary work, and the dark moon, for initiations. The magic in this book, for the most part, skews heavily lunar. In fact, you've already met quite a few lunar spirits, so I shall introduce only one more.

Golden Crowned Phoebe

One of my favorite Titans to work with—and one of the spirits I most recommend conjuring as a beginner—is Phoebe, whose name, Φοίβη, means "Shining One." She is the daughter of Gaia and Ouranos, and inherits from both. Although she is associated with the moon, particularly in later writings, this elder Phoebe is not the goddess of the moon. When, rarely, she is associated with a heavenly body, it is Venus. However, Latin writers, when they speak of Phoebe, are

202 And, of course, there are many women who do not menstruate, as well as non-women who do.

referring to Diana. Greeks sometimes used Phoebe as a title of Selene, or of Phoebe's granddaughters, Hekate and Artemis, much as Apollo is called Phoebus. She is, in some traditions, one of the inspirations of Delphi, having inherited it from her sister, Themis, and passing it to her grandson, Apollon. This myth of how Apollon came to Delphi is very different from the tale of his violent conquest of Python; like many of the stories told from the Titanic viewpoint, it paints a picture of harmony between the chthonic and celestial gods very different from the contentious gender war present in much classical Mycenaean myth.

There is some reason to believe that Dione is another name or title for Phoebe; the Homeric Hymn to Apollon of Delphi says (trans. by Evelyn-White): "Leto was racked nine days and nine nights with pangs beyond wont. And there were with her all the chiefest of the goddesses, Dione [Phoebe] and Rhea and Ikhnaie [Theia] and Themis and loud-moaning Amphitrite [Tethys] and the other deathless goddesses." In this guise, Phoebe Dione was the inspiration at Dodona, another chthonic oracle. There, her priestesses were called *Peleiades*, or "Doves," highlighting her relationship to the planet Venus.

As with many ancient goddesses, Phoebe is often given the appellation "cow eyed." If you do not understand why, I encourage you to look at some pictures of a cow's eyes. Aren't they beautiful?

Much like the English words *enlightenment* and *brilliance*, Phoebe's name bespeaks both literal and metaphoric shining. Far before I ever began working with Phoebe, the word "shine" had taken on a colloquial meaning in the circle of magicians with whom I work. We say that a person or object is "shiny" to indicate that it has the aura of a magic about it. A magician's "shine" is that ineffable quality somewhere between wisdom, charisma, and genius that comes over you when you're "filled up with the spirit." To me, then, it was very natural when I came to know that the goddess who inspired such shining was Phoebe, the goddess of the light of the mind.

These days, Phoebe is most famed for her grandchildren: Hekate, Artemis, and Apollo, all of whom express her light in various ways. With her husband, Koios, Phoebe bore two daughters, whom I believe to be twins, Asteria and Leto. Asteria, Hekate's mother, was the goddess of night prophecy. Leto, the mother of Artemis and Apollo (sometimes called Phoebe and Phoebus), is the more famous sister, and the goddess of day prophecy. I call her most often as Phoebe Chrysostephanos (Phoebe Golden Crowned). She is a magnificent goddess in her own right, and one I recommend building a relationship with. She is particularly helpful for work involving psychism, dreams, prophecy, intuition, and magical inspiration.

Invocation of Phoebe for Prophecy

"I call upon you who have all forms and many names,
Double-horned goddess, Moon, brilliant night-flame.
Phoebe, purple robed, golden crowned, aflame with scintillation,
You weave together night and day, with golden braids of filiation.
Your true form is a mystery, known only by the One Who Makes,
Who created the world entire, including your twenty-eight shapes.
Your forms complete every figure, they taught us how to count.
You breathe out full flourishing life on every creature's account.
You grow from obscurity into light, brilliant light from tiny spark.
Then withdraw your brilliance, giving space once more to the dark.
Radiant enlightener, fountainhead of prophecy, who inspired oracles of old,
Come, Chrysostephanos, and crown your priestess in shining gold."

Exercise: Pushing the Envelope

Choose a spirit associated with revelation and/or communication. Here, I use the example of Golden Crowned Phoebe, but any type of lunar or solar spirit is a great choice. Someone with whom you already have a connection is better than someone new.

1. When you've chosen which spirit you're going to work with, choose a color you associate with them. White, gold, yellow, purple, and silver are the most obvious choices, but you may have a different inspiration.
2. Get a candle that color, and write the spirit's name on it with a permanent marker.
3. Fill a pretty glass with water.
4. Decorate the space in a way that feels appropriate—not just visually, but also with music, scents, etc.
5. Make an opening oration to the spirit, something like this:

   "Golden Crowned Phoebe, Brilliant Grandmother, Shining One, goddess of prophecy, goddess of intellect. Holy Mind, Beloved Queen of Thought, Oracular Intellect, Shining Eye That Pierces Every Veil, bring me Clarity. Lend me the strength to see what lies ahead, lend me the strength to face it. Beloved Phoebe, Shining One, lend me your eyes to see and your ears to hear. Lend me your wisdom and your clarity, your foresight and your brilliance. Help me shine, shine, shine!

   Phoebe, Shining One, eldest of your name, mother of Asteria, mother of Leto, grandmother of Apollo, grandmother of Artemis, grandmother of Hekate, wellspring of prophecy, wellspring of mediumship, bless me now! Come to me, work with me, empower me. Open my eyes that I might see your Brilliance and open my ears that I might hear your Ringing Voice. Help me to perceive, and help me to remember all that I perceive. I kindle flame for you, Shining One! I burn incense for you! I have poured water for you, but I want to do more! I want to pour out libations in your name! I want to bake you cakes and sing hymns to you, and make grand and public gestures in your name, but I cannot without your word. Speak to me now! Appear to me now! Whatever reasonable thing you ask of me in the next five minutes, if I hear your request, I will honor it as well as I am able."

6. Wait five minutes, but not a second more. If you hear something, then it worked! Give everything that was asked and more! If not, then proceed like this:

   "Blessed Grandmother, I am sorry, Shining One, I cannot yet hear you. I beg you to empower me to continue improving in my mediumship, so that soon I will hear your voice, and be able to honor you with offerings. I will call again tomorrow [or next week, or whenever you intend to repeat it]. Thank you for your help. If there is more you would like to communicate to me, please visit me tonight in my dreams."

Now, this is important: *do not* make *any* offerings other than fire, water, and incense until you hear a sufficiently clear communication that you are convinced it was genuine. Ideally, make very elaborate offerings to other spirits within sight of the candle for your mediumship teacher. Look over at her candle and say aloud, "I'm sorry I can't give you offerings like this, but I can't hear what you want." Most people should get results in a few weeks.

Trance: Opening the Crown

This energetic practice is good for all sorts of trance work, but it is especially designed as preparation for drawing down the moon. For most people, it will be easiest when you are ovulating and/or when the moon is full. Try Glowing with the Borrowed Glory of Phoebe if you're having trouble.

1. Feel the weight of your body standing on the floor, solid and heavy like a tree trunk from the hips down.
2. Take a moment to breathe deeply, from the top of your head down to the bottoms of your feet. Feel your focus follow the energy up and

down. Do this several times.

3. Breathe some "surprise" breaths to remind the body to use the entirety of the lungs. Take a fast, deep, gasping inhalation, *"Ah!"* as if you have just been shocked.
4. Make several "surprise" breaths, as deep as you can.
5. On the last one, let the air out slowly, really emptying your lungs, hissing like a snake or a deflating balloon until you are out of breath. Do that three times.
6. Now, make a "woo" sound that, like a ghost or a siren, will go all the way to the top of your vocal range, and then down as low as you can. Rather than listening to the sound you are making, focus on the feeling of where the sound concentrates in your body when high and low. Feel it move up and down inside you. Do this three times. If you are a singer, you will have to break yourself from always breathing from the diaphragm. It's not important that you put a ton of power behind the breath/sound. It's important that you be moving the power from the right place.
7. Use the breath and the voice to open, remove blockages, and intensify the movement of energy in your body. Make each sound in the following table. You may want to make a particular sound several times if it feels "stuck." Focus on opening the energy rather than on the sound of your voice; the voice is only delivering and shaping the energy. You should be able to feel it "click" when you've gotten it right.
8. As you make each toning noise, imagine the energy intensifying in brightness and color, spinning, and growing. An imagining I use for this is to imagine each as a ball of fire in its own color that suddenly flares up into a full flame. The colored fires blend into and overlap each other. Others imagine flowers unfolding their petals or simple rotating spheres. It doesn't really matter. All of these are poor metaphors for what is actually happening. With your imagination, rise through your body in each location, until you rise up through your head and out the top.

Area of Body	Color	Sound
Base of Spine / Buttocks	Red	Uhhhhhhh
Womb	Orange	Ooooooooo
Belly	Yellow	Ohhhhhhh
Heart	Green	Ahhhhhhh
Neck	Sky Blue	Iiiiiiiiii (like "eye")
Forehead	Indigo	Ayyyyyyyy
Crown	Purple	Eeeeeeeeee
Moon	White	Eeeeeeeeee
Center of the Universe	Rainbow Shimmering	Eeeeeeeeeee

We'll learn much more about these energy centers in your body in Chapter Seven, "Circles and Centers."

Before drawing down the moon, we'll also need to make a protective amulet for use in that work. You can use any kind you like, but one great option follows.

Lunar Phylactery

This very simple charm to produce a lunar phylactery[203] is expanded from PGM VII:317–318. The complete text there reads: "*Another phylactery to the moon.* 'Αχθιωφιφ 'Ερεσχιγαλ Νεβουτοσουαληθ σαθωθ σαβαωθ σαβρωθ *plus whatever you wish.*"

The "barbarous names"[204] written in Greek above are:

203 A *phylactery* is a type of amulet where the primary "motive force" is written magic words or Names of Power.

204 This is a technical phrase in Greek magic, which literally means "foreign words" but contextually means Names of Power.

* **'Αχθιωφιφ:** Aktiophiph, which I understand to be an alternate spelling[205] of the name Aktiophis, which some say is untranslatable, but I understand to be from *akti-ophis*, or "ray serpent," which I take to be a reference to the Milky Way. Personally, I associate this name very closely with Hekate's mother, the star goddess Asteria, but that is a somewhat fringe opinion.
* **'Ερεσχιγαλ:** Ereshkigal is an ancient Mesopotamian name for the Queen of the Underworld. Her name is often translated as "Great Lady Below," but actually it means more like "Lady of the Great Below." In the Greek Magical Papyri, she is often syncretized with Hekate, although in some ways, she is more like Persephone or even Gaia.[206] She is the elder sister[207] of Inanna/Ishtar, the Queen of Heaven and Earth associated with the planet Venus. Ereshkigal has no surviving ancient iconography, but has often appeared to me as a winged, bird-headed skeleton in a black robe. Ereshkigal is a fascinating and complex goddess close to my heart. I encourage you to learn more about her.
* **Νεβουτοσουαληθ:** Neboutosoualeth is a less straightforward name. It appears frequently in the PGM, usually along with either Aktiophis and Ereshkigal, often with both. Most often, this triple name is applied to the Selene / Hekate / Persephone / Artemis goddess whom I generally call "Queen of Witches," but occasionally she is also called Aphrodite or Eros.
* **σαθωθ σαβαωθ σαβρωθ:** Sathoth, Sabaoth, Sabroth, which, to me, all appear to be variant spellings of צְבָאות (Tzavot), which means "army" or "host." Biblically, it is generally glossed as "Hosts of Angels" or "army of Heaven" or "Lord of the armies of Israel." It is also related to the Thracian god Sabazios. The two names may or may not be etymologically linked, but they were deeply syncretized by late antiquity (when the PGM were written).

Before the full moon, prepare:

* A locket or scroll case.
* A printout of the image included here on heavy linen paper, sized to fit inside your case. You can also draw it by hand, but I do not notice

205 The notion that there is a single correct way to spell a word is a *very* recent invention in the history of literacy, and is still mostly just classist nonsense.

206 It's actually *really* weird that she even appears in the PGM. She is the only ancient Mesopotamian deity in there.

207 Or sometimes the twin sister, or sometimes the maternal aunt.

a difference in potency from doing so for this particular spell.

* A headscarf.
* Three matching candles[208] and a way to light them.
* An incense of resin, mugwort,[209] and honey, and a way to burn it. You could add some marijuana if you wanted. Because you are going to huff it, *do not* use artificial incense, or anything in which you cannot identify *all* the ingredients.

As written, the spell assumes specific anatomy. If you don't have that, just imagine that you do. Shapeshifting is a key skill for magicians, which you'll learn more about in Chapter Twelve.

Full moon night:
If possible, cast outside, under the moon. If necessary, you can stealth cast outside. If you cannot be outside, imagine that you are. Whenever you're ready:

1. Use the bathroom before beginning. Expelling energy through your genitals (which you'll do at the end of this spell) can lead to some "leakage" otherwise.
2. Tuck the phylactery (not yet in its case) into your underpants. If you're bleeding, that's fine, but arrange it so the paper won't get bloody. If you wanted to also tuck in a remote vibrator, that might be a good

208 I especially like rolled beeswax candles for this spell, but any candles are fine.
209 Or any other Artemisia. Tarragon will work, and will lend the work a slightly draconic air.

idea (you'll see why).

3. If possible, select a location where you can see the moon when looking up. Sitting directly on the ground is good for this spell, but on a blanket or low stool is also fine.
4. Arrange the three candles in a triangle around you, with the incense in front of you, so you are huffing it.
5. Light the candles and incense.
6. Drape your headscarf so you're huffing incense.
7. Enter magical space/time/consciousness.
8. Connect to the moon, high above your head, and feel the moonlight descend through your spine and into your womb.
9. Slowly beat on your belly like a drum. Experiment until you find a rhythm that feels right. For me, this spell likes a three-beat, like a mid-tempo waltz. Feel the power within you ripple.
10. Say something like: "*Luminous goddess, pregnant with wonder, I call you by your many names: Aktiophis, Ereshkigal, Neboutosoualeth: Tzevaot, Tzevaot, Tzevaot!*"
11. Repeat the names. Hum, chant, or vocalize, feeling the words rumble in your belly.
12. Rock back and forth. Keep drumming, but slowly pick up the pace.
13. When the energy crescendos, expel the energy forcefully through your vagina and into the phylactery. If you can orgasm, that would be ideal, but it is not required.
14. Lie back and stare up at the moon, communing[210] for a while. You may receive messages during this time.
15. When you're done, fish out the scroll, and put it in its case. Fumigate the case with some incense smoke, if desired. You could also add a pinch of the incense ("plus whatever you wish") to the case.
16. Go to sleep without grounding or centering after the ritual for instructive dreams.

Drawing Down the Moon

This is, by a wide margin, the most sophisticated magic I've yet taught you. In fact, you might not yet be quite ready for it. I encourage you to read it now, but if it feels daunting, come back to it once you've finished the whole book.

---

210 co-Mooning!

Drawing down the moon[211] is a broad category of adorcistic[212] rites in which a priestess[213] becomes possessed with the spirit of the Moon. Today, the ritual is most often used in a group setting, where one person draws down the moon to speak prophecy for an audience; there are many, many variations of the rite. In its modern form, the ritual was developed in the early days of Wicca, based on several classical sources, including the (possibly spurious) illustrated vase pictured and a fourth century Latin work of epic poetry, by Claudian,[214] in which Megaira, a Fury whose name means "the jealous," is pretending to be an old man, and speaking to Rufinus, an early Christian theologian:

"Despise not an old man's feeble limbs: I have the gift of magic and the fire of prophecy is within me. I have learned the incantations wherewith Thessalian witches pull down the bright moon, I know the meaning of the wise Egyptians' runes, the art whereby the Chaldeans impose their will upon the subject gods, the various saps that flow within trees and the power of deadly herbs; all those that grow on Caucasus rich in poisonous plants, or, to man's bane, clothe the crags of Scythia; herbs such as cruel Medea gathered and curious Circe."

211 There is a related "Drawing Up the Moon" category of rituals, which you can see an example of in PGM IV:2241–2358.

212 *Adorcism* is the opposite of *exorcism,* intentionally drawing a spirit into a person, usually for the purpose of prophecy.

213 I'll consistently use *priestess* and *she,* but anyone of any gender and any sex can do these practices.

214 An amazing pagan poet, priest, and political polemicist, whom Augustine called an "adversary of the name of Christ."

The version below is vaguely based on the version I learned from my first teacher, when I was young, but it is my own creation, cobbled together from many sources:

1. Before beginning, acquire or prepare some kind of protective talisman. The lunar phylactery you learned is a great option. The Bear charm you will make in Chapter Ten is also an excellent choice. Such a talisman need only be made once, and can be used in all lunar trance work.
2. It is best to abstain from sex, violence, drugs, meat, and emotional intensity for thirty-six hours prior to drawing down the moon. While not strictly necessary, this will make the channeling clearer and easier on the body.
3. This rite is done under a full moon, or a day or two before or after. You can also do similar rituals at other times, but they will have a different character.
4. Usually, this ritual is worked (often for an audience) with two witches: a medium and an anchor. For simplicity of pronouns, I'll be describing a female medium and a male anchor. You can substitute a tree for the anchor person if you can't get a partner. You can also do it without an anchor, but I don't recommend that for beginners. In my method, the medium and anchor sit back-to-back. If there is an audience, the anchor should face them. The anchor's job is to protect the medium, who is very open and psychically vulnerable. The "danger" isn't maliciousness (the protective talisman is for that), it's just the normal sort of psychic effluvium that will knock a person out of trance.
5. The anchor roots down into the earth. The medium enters a deep trance.
6. A preliminary invocation of a/the moon goddess is made, usually by both medium and anchor. For this, I tend to work with Phoebe Chrysostephanos, whom we discussed previously.
7. The medium opens her crown and arises out of her body, up, up, up to the heavens, and then falls back down, catching the moon on her way down, and pulling it down, down, down into her head.[215] That is, from your position at the center of the universe, simply let go of your focus, and let yourself fall back into your body. But don't let go too much; be alert. As you go past the Moon, grab it, and drag it back down with you, a pillar of moonlight connecting the physical moon in

215 As I understand it, to swallow the moon, you pull it the whole way down into your womb, while the anchor ejaculates into you. I have never performed this rite (as, personally, I am *deeply, deeply* opposed to conceiving).

the sky with the energetic moon, now located in your head. This might feel instead like you have grown very tall, with your head in the sky. If so, reassert your will until you pull the moon down into your physical head. This is difficult, and will likely take practice if you're new to it. You should expect to be lightheaded and "fuzzy." If you don't feel weird, you're doing it wrong. It's hard to describe what it feels like to have the moon in your head, but you'll recognize it when it happens.

8. The medium opens herself to allow the Great Goddess of the Moon to speak through her.
9. The anchor asks (usually predetermined) questions and records the answers. Sometimes, especially for beginner mediums, he may need to remind her of the need to speak out loud.
10. The anchor should pay attention to the medium, who may not be able to monitor her own safety. When she's flagging, he should wrap it up.
11. Ideally both, but sometimes just the anchor, should say thank you, make some final offerings, and give license to depart.
12. The effect of this rite can linger for several days for the medium, although this is very different from person to person. Don't be surprised by fatigue, headaches, menstrual cramps, powerful dreams, emotional swings, and changes in menstrual cycle.[216] If symptoms are extreme or last more than a few days, seek expert advice.

Opening the Mouth

Do this part *only* if necessary. If you're stuck on step 8, and the medium isn't speaking, the anchor should check in with the medium to see if she is ready to speak. Avoid calling her by her human name, as this will often bring her back to herself, and the goal is to talk to the moon, not the medium. If she does not respond, the anchor can stand up, walk to face her, remove her veil, put his hands on her shoulders, and say something like the following spell (from the Egyptian[217] Book of the Dead). However, usually, with an experienced medium, this will not be necessary. If she needed this, he should remain sitting facing

216 I often spot or even heavily bleed the night after I draw down the moon, despite being on hormonal birth control that usually completely suppresses my menstrual cycle. Personally, I understand this to be among my body's ways of cleaning out residual junk. It sometimes happens after other kinds of magic as well, but not as frequently.

217 Why the mix of cultures? It's because the anchor partner with whom I initially developed this rite is largely Egyptian in his focus, whereas I like Greek and Jewish stuff, mostly. But we're both equal-opportunity magicians. As always, you can write your own words or choose another spell. Psalm 51 would work well.

her, looking over her head at the audience, until the connection is strong, and she is speaking clearly.

"You mouth is opened by Ptah,
Your mouth's bonds are loosed by the god of this place.
Thoth has come fully equipped with spells,
He looses the bonds of Seth from your mouth.
Atum has given me my hands,
They are placed as guardians over you.
You mouth is given to you,
You mouth is opened by Ptah,
With that chisel of sacred metal
With which he opened the mouth of the gods.
You are Sekhmet-Wadjet who dwells in the west of heaven,
You are Sahyt among the souls of On."

Chapter Six:

The Other Five Planets

As I mentioned before, in this chapter, we'll be discussing the five non-luminary classical planets, Mercury, Venus, Mars, Jupiter, and Saturn. We'll be discussing them in the traditional "Chaldean order," arranged by the speed of their apparent movement in the sky, from slowest to fastest.

A Quick-Start Guide to the Magic of the Seven Classical Planets

♄

Saturn is the planet of boundaries, measured/linear time, harvest, control, and all other kinds of limitations. By extension, it is also associated with death, binding, sleep, and darkness. Its color is black and its metal is lead. Saturn's symbol is the sickle, and its day is (logically) Saturday. Some people are afraid of Saturnine magic, but I love it.

♃

Jupiter is in some ways the opposite of Saturn. Whereas Saturn is most often worked with to direct power inward, Jupiter is all about expansion. This is the planet of growth, kingship, grace (divine gifts), health, and material success. By extension, it is often associated with money, business, and command. Its color is blue and its metal is tin. Jupiter's day is Thursday, which in English is named after Thor, the Norse god of thunder. Some say its symbol is an eagle, and others that it is a lightning bolt or staff. I believe it to be a lightning bolt.

If you examine some ancient Greek paintings of Zeus hurling lightning bolts, you'll see the resemblance between that style of lightning bolt iconography[218] and our modern Jupiter sign.

Mars is the planet of war, conflict, justice, and lust. By extension, it is also associated with victory, competition, impregnation, and other acts of strength or virility. Its color is red, its metal is iron, and its day is Tuesday (which has its English name from Tyr, a Norse warrior god). Its symbol is the spear.

The Sun is the power of radiance, healing, vision, and the source of life-sustaining energy. By extension, it is also associated with ego, charisma, peace, and youth. Its color is yellow (or gold), its metal is gold, and its day, unsurprisingly, is Sunday.

♀

Venus is the planet of procreation, beauty, love, friendship, green growing things, and luxury. By extension, she is also associated with fertility, emotion, glamour, social skills, and status. Her color is emerald green and her metal, copper, which was mined on her sacred island of Cyprus. Her day is Friday, which in English is named for the Norse goddess Freya. Venus's symbol is typically described as a mirror.

☿

Mercury is the planet of the intellect, swiftness, athletics, games, and the marketplace. By extension, it is also associated with the information age, trickery, merchants (which are named for Mercury), and literacy/education. Mercury's color is orange, and its traditional metal is, unsurprisingly, mercury, a.k.a. quicksilver.[219] These days, many magicians associate Mercury with aluminum. Mercury's day is Wednesday, which derives its English name from the Germanic/Norse deity Wodan, Wotan, or Odin. Mercury's symbol is the caduceus wand.

218 Which looks a lot like a Tibetan dorje.

219 Although how you're supposed to carve a pentacle in liquid mercury, I've never understood.

☽

The Moon is the planet of the night, the subconscious, intuition, female hormone cycle, and changeability. By extension, it is understood to be in alignment with femininity, luxury, dreams, all types of trance work, and most types of magic. Its colors are purple, gray, and silver; its metal is silver; and its day is the appropriately named Monday. This information is summarized in the following table.

Planets, Days, Colors, Metals, and their Virtues

Planet	Day	Color	Metal	Powers
Saturn	Saturday	Black	Lead	Boundaries, Death, Harvest
Jupiter	Thursday	Blue	Tin	Kingship, Money, Expansion
Mars	Tuesday	Red	Iron	Conflict, Courage, Strength
Sun	Sunday	Yellow	Gold	Health, Ego, Grace, Vision
Venus	Friday	Green	Copper	Emotions, Intersubjectivity
Mercury	Wednesday	Orange	Mercury	Intellect, Patten, Words
Moon	Monday	Purple	Silver	Subconscious, Change, Lust

In a moment, we'll learn several types of planetary magic. First, however, let's talk a little bit more about timing magic with the planets. If you are an experienced astrologer, you should already know much more sophisticated ways to do this. However, one simple way to begin timing magic, in addition to the day/night distinction and lunar cycle timing we've already discussed, is to do your magic on the day of the planet most relevant to the task at hand. For example, enchanting to do well on a math test should be done on a Wednesday. A slightly more sophisticated method is to combine the planetary days with the so-called *planetary hours*.

Just like the word *planet* retains its old-fashioned meaning in magic, so too does the word *hour*. While in modern scientific language, *hour* means "sixty minutes,"[220] traditionally, an "hour of day" was 1/12 of the time from sunrise to sunset, and an hour of night was 1/12 of the time from sunset to sunrise. That means that, in the northern hemisphere, day hours are longer in the summer and shorter in the winter. For example, I am writing this on Monday, May 26, in Pittsburgh, and it is around 7:30 p.m. This morning, the sun rose at 5:55 a.m., and it will set shortly, at 8:40 p.m. That is a total of 885 minutes of daylight. Dividing that by twelve gives us seventy-three minutes and forty-five seconds per hour for each hour. The first hour (which begins at dawn) of any day is the hour of the planet's day. So, for example, today is Monday, so dawn hour is Moon's. Thereafter, they run through the Chaldean order "top down," as in the following chart. Similarly, we can calculate the hours of night. Tomorrow, the sun will come up at 5:54 a.m. From 8:40 p.m. to 5:54 a.m. is 554 minutes. Dividing by twelve gives us night hours, which are just over forty-six minutes in length. The planets keep going in the same order after sunset, as you can see in the following table.

220 Technically, I think it's actually 3,600 atomic seconds.

Pittsburgh, Monday, May 27, 2025					
Hours of the Day			**Hours of the Night**		
Start	**Planet**	**End**	**Start**	**Planet**	**End**
5:55	Moon	7:08	20:40	Venus	21:26
7:08	Saturn	8:22	21:26	Mercury	22:12
8:22	Jupiter	9:36	22:12	Moon	22:58
9:36	Mars	10:50	22:58	Saturn	23:45
10:50	Sun	12:03	23:45	Jupiter	0:31
12:03	Venus	13:17	0:31	Mars	1:17
13:17	Mercury	14:31	1:17	Sun	2:03
14:31	Moon	15:45	2:03	Venus	2:50
15:45	Saturn	16:58	2:50	Mercury	3:36
16:58	Jupiter	18:12	3:36	Moon	4:22
18:12	Mars	19:26	4:22	Saturn	5:08
19:26	Sun	20:40	5:08	Jupiter	5:55

However, in modern practice, most people do not calculate their own planetary hours, but use an automatic calculator for them. This is my favorite:

For beginners, it is generally best to match the day and hour, and to keep the work inside the hour. So, for our "ace a math test" spell example, we'd be looking for a daytime hour of Mercury on a Wednesday, and you'd want to both start and stop inside that same hour.[221] However, once you get some more practice, you can mix them. So, for example, if a non-beginner was specifically concerned with their memory and focused/disciplined study for the math test, we'd still want a Wednesday, because math tests are essentially mercurial, but we might choose a Saturn hour because of its association with discipline.

For the rest of the chapter, we'll talk a little more about each planet and learn a different type of planetary magic for each one. The choice of which magical style I matched to each planet was informed more by pedagogy than planetary associations. They're just examples.

Mercury

Mercury is the smallest and innermost planet of our solar system. It moves very quickly, completing a circuit around the sun every eighty-eight days. Because it is so fleet, it is often syncretized with travel gods (such as the Roman Mercury, the Greek Hermes, and the Babylonian Nabu); however, it has been syncretized with many other gods as well. For example, in ancient Greece, the planet Mercury was often understood as two different bodies, one appearing by morning and sacred to Apollo, and another in the evening, sacred to Hermes.

In prehistoric times, most people never traveled very far. Among those that did were messengers, storytellers, translators, and traders, and so all of these activities fall naturally into the sphere of Mercury. Additionally, all activities done "by one's wits" belong to Mercury. This includes literacy, mathematics, fast-talk, gambling, con art, sleight of hand, sorcery, spirit-speaking, spirit-travel, and all types of navigating, both literal and metaphoric.

---

221 You can get all set up before the hour starts, but don't actually start the magic until you're in the hour.

As I mentioned in the quick-start, Mercury's day is Wednesday.[222] Mercury does not have a single clear color attribution[223] but bright orange, eggplant purple, all neon colors, and rainbow opalescence are all sometimes associated with this planet. Mercury's metal is (unsurprisingly) mercury, or quicksilver. Some of Mercury's special sacred numbers are 8, 23, 64, 88, and 260; others include 10^{100} (called a "googol"[224]), $\aleph_0$ (the number of counting numbers there are), and the golden ratio ($\frac{1+\sqrt{5}}{2}$). In truth, however, *all* numbers, and the very concept of number itself, are sacred to Mercury.

Mercury magic generally involves communication and/or complex interconnected maps of paths (which can be literal roads, but can also be more metaphorical paths, such as social networks). Almost all the symbol magic we talked about in Chapter Three was mercurial in nature.

In Chapter Three, we very briefly discussed the kamea. Now, I'd like to talk a little more about them and the system they are most closely associated with, that of Agrippa's *Three Books of Occult Philosophy*. It's unclear where the kamea and their modern magical use were first developed, but my instinct is that it was in China or India around 300 BCE. They appear to have entered Europe by way of Al-Andalus (modern Spain), and were widespread among European Jewry by the late 1200s. Their spread among Christians was slower.[225] They were known in Christian Italy in the early fourteenth century, and throughout Christian Europe by the end of the fifteenth. The form they are most often used in today is primarily due to Agrippa's teaching of them in Chapter 22 of Book II of *De Occulta Philosophia*.

---

222 In English, Wednesday is named for Wotan, but in Romance languages, the association with Mercury is very clear. For example, in Spanish, it's miércoles.

223 One of many dangers of quick-starts and tables is that they make things seem much more systematized than nature actually is.

224 Google, the search engine, is named after the number. It is a very big number, on the order of the number of grains of sand on Earth times the number of elementary particles in the universe.

225 Mostly because, at the time, many European Jews read Arabic, and almost no Christians could.

In that chapter, Agrippa clearly associated each planet with a specific magic square, as shown:

Venus = 175

22	47	16	41	10	35	4
5	23	48	17	42	11	29
30	6	24	49	18	36	12
13	31	7	25	43	19	37
38	14	32	1	26	44	20
21	39	8	33	2	27	45
46	15	40	9	34	3	28

Mercury = 260

8	58	59	5	4	62	63	1
49	15	14	52	53	11	10	56
41	23	22	44	45	19	18	48
32	34	35	29	28	38	39	25
40	26	27	37	36	30	31	33
17	47	46	20	21	43	42	24
9	55	54	12	13	51	50	16
64	2	3	61	60	6	7	57

Luna = 369

37	78	29	70	21	62	13	54	5
6	38	79	30	71	22	63	14	46
47	7	39	80	31	72	23	55	15
16	48	8	40	81	32	64	24	56
57	17	49	9	41	73	33	65	25
26	58	18	50	1	42	74	34	66
67	27	59	10	51	2	43	75	35
36	68	19	60	11	52	3	44	76
77	28	69	20	61	12	53	4	45

Saturn = 15

4	9	2
3	5	7
8	1	6

Jupiter = 34

4	14	15	1
9	7	6	12
5	11	10	8
16	2	3	13

Mars = 65

11	24	7	20	3
4	12	25	8	16
17	5	13	21	9
10	18	1	14	22
23	6	19	2	15

Sol = 111

6	32	3	34	35	1
7	11	27	28	8	30
19	14	16	15	23	24
18	20	22	21	17	13
25	29	10	9	26	12
36	5	33	4	2	31

Exercise: Seal of Mercury

Along with each kamea, Agrippa also produced a seal for each planet. He says that the seals are symmetrical symbols that pass through every number in the square, but that is not actually true of several of the seals he gives.[226] A method by which the seals are produced for kamea of even sizes is known, but that method does not work for the odd ones. I'll show you how it works with Mercury.

1. Begin with the kamea.

Mercury = 260

8	58	59	5	4	62	63	1
49	15	14	52	53	11	10	56
41	23	22	44	45	19	18	48
32	34	35	29	28	38	39	25
40	26	27	37	36	30	31	33
17	47	46	20	21	43	42	24
9	55	54	12	13	51	50	16
64	2	3	61	60	6	7	57

226 Venus and Mars fail spectacularly, and Saturn also, but less so.

2. Next, number the squares, starting with one in the top right corner, as such:

8	7	6	5	4	3	2	1
16	15	14	3	12	11	10	9
24	23	22	21	20	19	18	17
32	31	30	29	28	27	26	25
40	39	38	37	36	35	34	33
48	47	46	45	44	43	42	41
56	55	54	53	52	51	50	49
64	63	62	61	60	59	58	57

3. Now, if the number in the kamea is the same as the ordering number, mark that square.

8	58	59	5	4	62	63	1
49	15	14	52	53	11	10	56
41	23	22	44	45	19	18	48
32	34	35	29	28	38	39	25
40	26	27	37	36	30	31	33
17	47	46	20	21	43	42	24
9	55	54	12	13	51	50	16
64	2	3	61	60	6	7	57

4. Connect the marked squares using straight lines.

8	58	59	5	4	62	63	1
49	15	14	52	53	11	10	56
41	23	22	44	45	19	18	48
32	34	35	29	28	38	39	25
40	26	27	37	36	30	31	33
17	47	46	20	21	43	42	24
9	55	54	12	13	51	50	16
64	2	3	61	60	6	7	57

5. Next, do the same for the unmarked squares.

8	58	59	5	4	62	63	1
49	15	14	52	53	11	10	56
41	23	22	44	45	19	18	48
32	34	35	29	28	38	39	25
40	26	27	37	36	30	31	33
17	47	46	20	21	43	42	24
9	55	54	12	13	51	50	16
64	2	3	61	60	6	7	57

6. Now, make it pretty, and you have Agrippa's seal of Mercury. This method works for the Mercury, Jupiter, and Solar squares, but not for Venus, Mars, Moon, and Saturn.

If you'd like an additional exercise, you can use this method to generate the seals of Jupiter and the Sun.

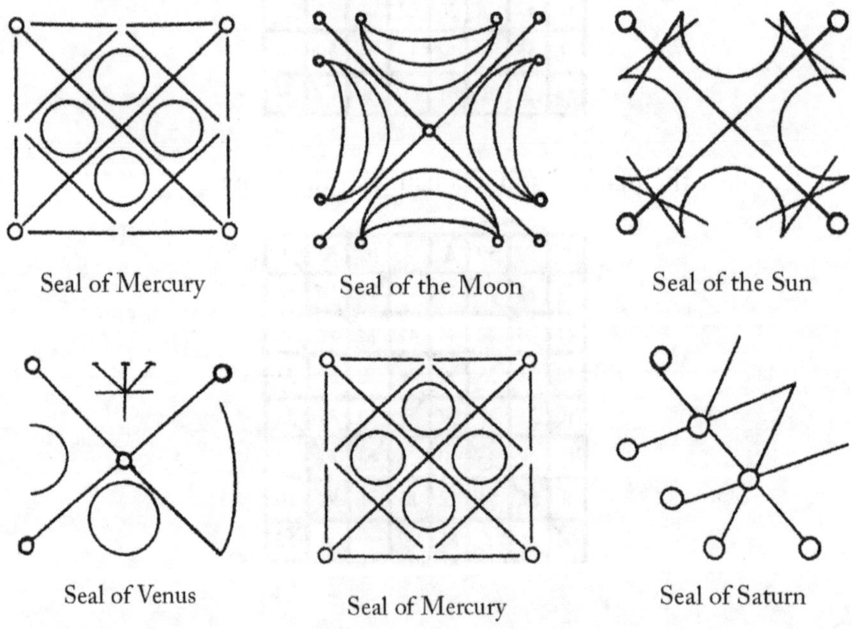

Seal of Mercury   Seal of the Moon   Seal of the Sun

Seal of Venus   Seal of Mercury   Seal of Saturn

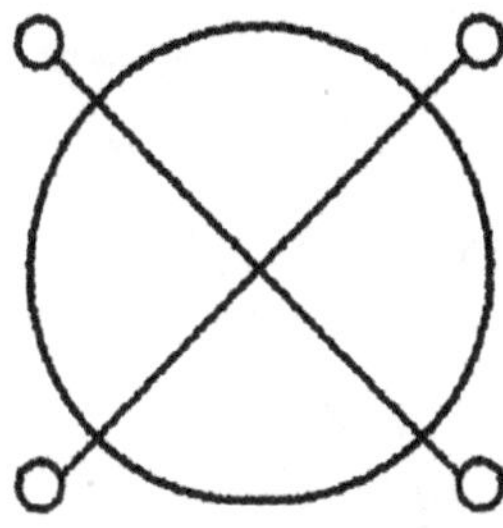

Seal of Jupiter

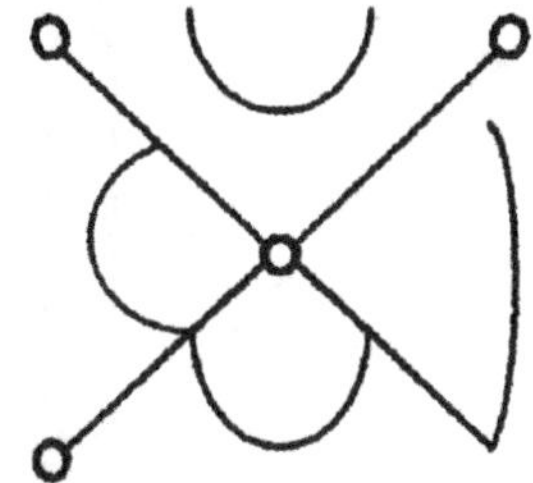

Seal of Mars

These seals can be used in any of the ways we discussed in Chapter Three. Most often, they are used as a sort of portal through which the planetary powers can be evoked. At its most simple, you can draw the seal on a mirror with a magic marker and stare through it until your vision goes wavery and a spirit replaces your reflection. *However*, these spirits are not entirely beneficent. This kind of conjuration can be difficult to control, and I do not recommend this practice to beginners. If you already have some experience with dark mirror conjuration, feel free to experiment responsibly. If you do not currently have that experience, I recommend waiting until after Chapter Thirteen.

In addition to using the kamea to generate the seals, Agrippa also uses them to generate seals for spirits and intelligences of each planet. He does this by a very similar method to the one you learned in Chapter Three, except in Hebrew. If anyone reads Hebrew and wants to learn the method, you can google "AIQ BKR Nine Chambers." That method gives the following seals:

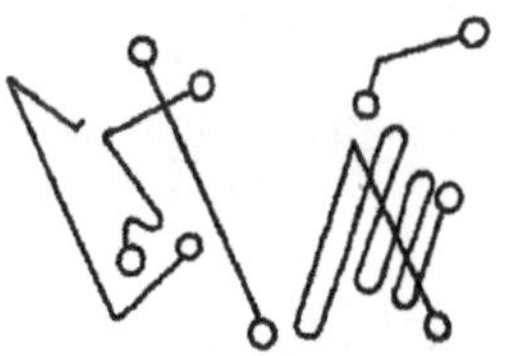

Sigil of the Intelligence of the Moon

Sigil of the Spirit of the Moon

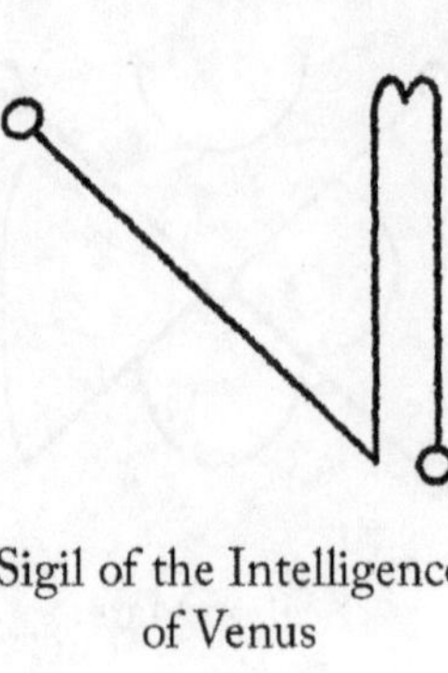

Sigil of the Intelligence of Venus

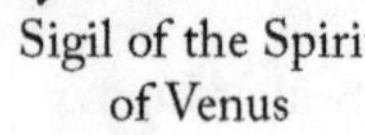

Sigil of the Spirit of Venus

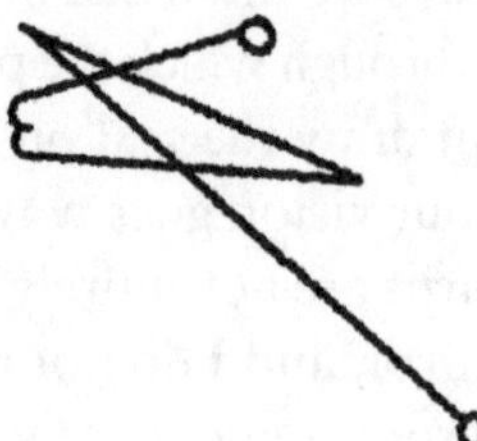

Sigil of the Intelligence of Mercury

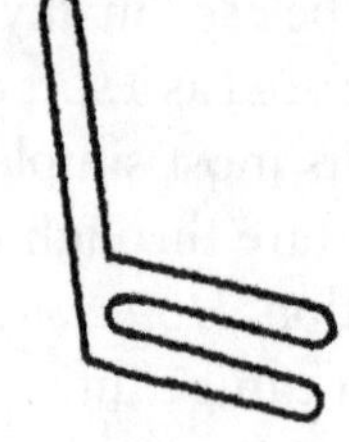

Sigil of the Spirit of Mercury

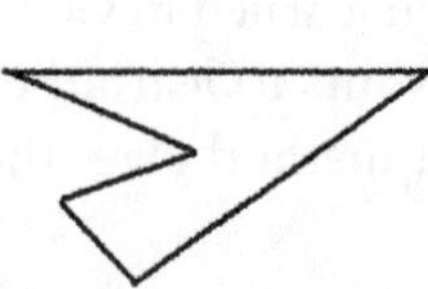

Sigil of the Intelligence of Mars

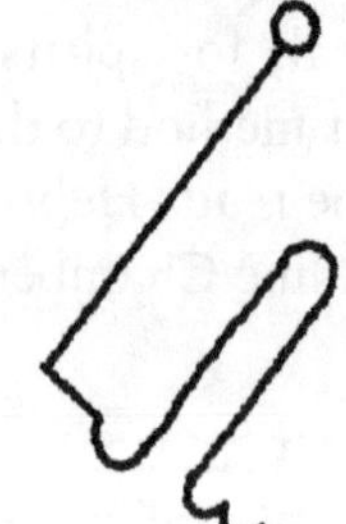

Sigil of the Spirit of Mars

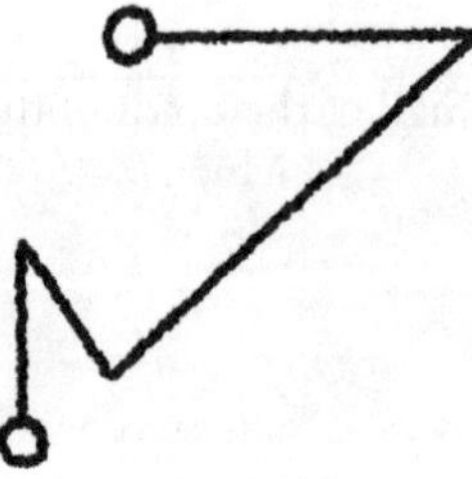

Sigil of the Intelligence of the Sun

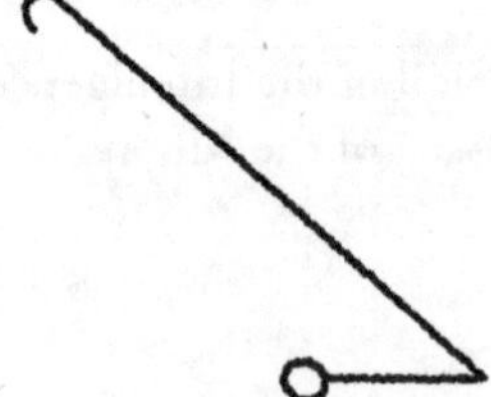

Sigil of the Spirit of the Sun

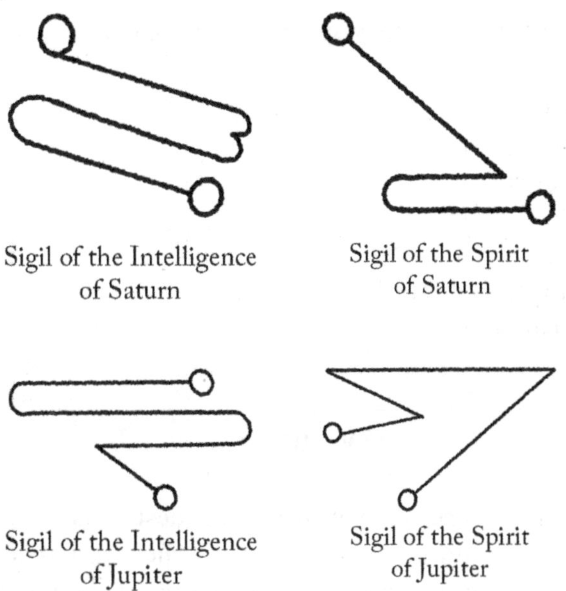

Sigil of the Intelligence of Saturn

Sigil of the Spirit of Saturn

Sigil of the Intelligence of Jupiter

Sigil of the Spirit of Jupiter

The planetary intelligences are broadly beneficent personalities and can be invoked to help control the planetary spirits, which are more wild and less anthropomorphic. Some people contextualize the intelligences as angelic and the spirits as demonic, but I don't think that's an accurate or helpful way to understand it. I think it is better to think of the spirits as the raw planetary energy and the intelligences as the planet's appointed ambassadors[227] to humans.

One traditional set of names for the planetary intelligences are:

* **Moon:** Malkah be-Tarshishim ve-ad Ruachoth Shechalim
* **Mercury:** Tiriel
* **Venus:** Hagiel
* **Sun:** Nakhiel
* **Mars:** Graphiel
* **Jupiter:** Iophiel
* **Saturn:** Agiel

227 To me, they actually feel a bit unnatural, more like AI than like people.

And the names of the planetary spirits are as follows:

* **Saturn:** Zazel
* **Jupiter:** Hismael
* **Mars:** Barzabel
* **Sun:** Sorath
* **Venus:** Kedemel
* **Mercury:** Taphthartharath
* **Moon:** Chasmodai

Venus

Venus's sphere is the sphere of love in its broadest sense. Venus controls all the forces that unite humans one with the other: romance and family, community and communion. Venus's magic is one of the most widely and practically applicable. Anytime you want someone to like you, whether a boss or a neighbor, a mother-in-law or a lover, the spirits of the sphere of Venus are the ones you want on your side. If you need help navigating complicated social situations, Venus, the Wile-Weaver, the Charming One, is who you need to win to your cause. All social interconnection between human beings is of the sphere of Venus.

But Venus is even more than that—she is the generative force that brings forth life from life, the Great Green Goddess. The oldest known use of the name "Venus" is in the context of the ancient pre-Romah Latin festival of Vinalia Rustica, the celebration of the ripening of the vines and gardens, celebrated in late August. That festival was originally dedicated to Venus Obsequens, Venus the Gracious and Giving. As Latin cultures became Roman ones, the festival was given to Jupiter. Similarly, our cultural understanding of Venus has also been given over to the Patriarch. Venus, as we know her today, is much reduced and deformed.[228]

Venus is the goddess who taught us to garden, who taught us the relationship between seed and plant. Venus is the goddess who taught us men's role in causing pregnancy—the relationship between seed and child. Venus is the goddess of fecundity: the fertile vigor of the garden and the orchard, the field, the livestock, the mother, the community. Venus is the overflowing Greenness of

228 As are many or most of the planets and gods of our ancestors.

Life, the essential "life-ness" of the soul, called *viriditas*. Says Saint Hildegard of Bingen: "*There is a power that has been since all eternity and that force and potentiality is green!*"

Because she orbits between us and the Sun, Venus cannot always be seen from Earth. She often disappears on one horizon and reappears on the other. For this reason, many cultures speak of her as two distinct entities: the Evening Star[229] and the Morning Star.[230] However, by the time writing had become widespread in Mesopotamia, and we have sufficient records to judge, those are known to be the same object. There, she was known by many names: Inanna, Ninsi'anna, the Bright Lady, the Shining One of Heaven, She of Red Skies, the Holy Queen of Heaven and Earth. Most Western cultures, including our own, inherit at least part of their understanding of Venus from this tradition, and it is well worth your time to learn her myths and names. Of them, my favorite is the "Nin Me Šara," or "Exaltation of the Goddess," one of the most ancient human sacred texts. Written in the twenty-third century BCE by Enheduana, high priestess of Ur and daughter of King Sargon of Akkad, Nin Me Šara positions Ishtar as a powerful and politically important goddess of both love and war.

The symbol of the planet Venus, which has become the symbol for femaleness, is usually understood as a hand mirror. In the ancient world, mirrors were often made of copper (Venus's metal). Most ancient Greek copper came from Cyprus, the island of Aphrodite, a Greek goddess associated with Venus. However, the symbol is also linked to the "rod and ring" symbol of Mesopotamian kingship, very often held by depictions of Inanna and other Mesopotamian Venus goddesses. In Egypt, this same sign was called the "shen ring" and represented eternal protection. It may also be related to the so-called "knot of Isis," also called the *tyet*, which is thought by many to represent a tampon. Others think it may represent a sistrum[231] or a necklace.

In Hermetic systems, Venus's number is seven, and her day is Friday.[232] She is associated with lions, doves, wolves, and peacocks. As mentioned before, her metal is copper, her color sea-green, and her gem is the emerald. The angel most often associated with Venus is Anael (לאינה), whose name means "Joy of El." Their name is sometimes also spelled "Haniel."

229 *Vesper* in Latin

230 *Lucifer* in Latin

231 A kind of a rattle with jingles, like on a tambourine.

232 In English, the day is named after the Norse goddess Freya, whom the Romans equated to Venus.

Another method of planetary work is that of the *Arbatel De Magia Veterum* (*Arbatel: Magic of the Ancients*), a renaissance grimoire[233] sometimes falsely attributed to Agrippa (whose work we just learned). People disagree about the meaning of the word "Arbatel." I understand it to be a proper name of a specific angel, Arbatel, angel of the east, angel of revelation,[234] with whom I have a close and complicated relationship. His Hebrew name means something like "Four god" or "Fourness of El" or "The Divine Four-principle." The author is unknown, but the text was almost certainly first published in Switzerland in the late 1500s. Unlike many other grimoires of the period (including the Keys of Solomon), it does not claim ancient origins.

The text claims that the work consists of nine books, although only the first, called *Isogogue*, exists. There is no evidence that the other books were lost; they appear to never have been written. According to the table of contents, those books (were intended to) contain nine kinds of magic. The English names below were fixed by Robert Turner, who translated the Arbatel from the Latin is 1655.

1. "The first is called *Isagoge,* or, A Book of the Institutions of Magick which in fourty and nine Aphorisms comprehendeth, the most general Precepts of the whole Art."
2. Microcosmical Magick, self-knowledge and knowledge of the personal "genius."
3. Olympick Magick, which I'll say more about shortly.
4. Hesiodiacal and Homerical Magick, which teaches how to work with cacodaemones (Greek for "bad spirits"). [This is how it is in the 1655 Robert Turner English translation, however, the Latin edition says "calodaemons" or "good spirits".]
5. Romane or Sibylline Magick, which is about talking to spirits. The text says that this is also called "the art of the Druids."
6. Pythagorical Magick, which is basically academic magic, for learning from spirits.
7. Magick of the *Apollonius*, which is similar to Sibylline Magick, but more celestial in nature
8. Hermetical or Ægyptiacal Magick, which "produces gods of all kinds"
9. The final kind is that which "depends on God," which is called Prophetical Magick or Divine Magic.

---

233 A *grimoire* is a type of spell book, most usually applied to books of Christian ceremonial spirit conjuration from the late medieval and early Renaissance periods.

234 That whole thing is his name; it's not really a name and a description.

The *Arbatel* was the first complete grimoire I had access to (I was sixteen or seventeen the first time I read it), and this list was *very* powerfully inspirational to me. Until I reviewed it just now, I didn't realize just how much I had considered it a "checklist" to guide my magical learning. In the intervening thirty years, I think I can fairly say that I have learned and routinely practice all of these types of magic except perhaps the seventh.

As I mentioned, only the first book, the *Isogogue*, is known. It consists of forty-nine aphorisms, most of which are just sensible advice for any spiritual person. For example, aphorism two says, "Live to thy self, and the Muses: avoid the friendship of the Multitude: be thou covetous of time, beneficial to all men. Use thy Gifts, be vigilant in thy Calling; and let the Word of God never depart from thy mouth."

Exercise: Arbatel Reading

Read the *Isogogue*. If you don't read the whole thing, at least read the Third Septenary, that is, aphorisms fifteen to twenty-one, which discuss the Olympick spirits. It's only three pages long.

To the best of my knowledge, these Olympick spirits are not known from any earlier sources, and I have no reason to doubt the author's claim that they were introduced to him in personal spirit communication. I will talk about Hagith, the spirit of Venus, as an example.

The text tells us that Hagith governs Venereal (Venus-y) things. It says that if we wear his character (pictured), he will make us very fair and adorn us with beauty. He converts copper into gold in a moment, and gold into copper.[235] He gives spirits that faithfully serve those to whom they are attached. He has four thousand legions of spirits, with a seasonal king appointed over each thousand.

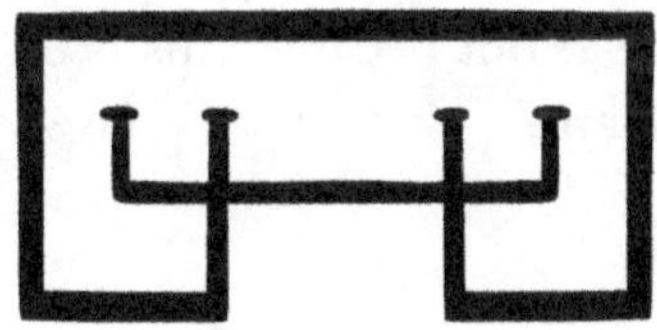

Although not everyone agrees, I believe the name Hagith to be closely related to חַגִּית (Haggith), a minor biblical character whose name means "festive." Very little is said about her in Torah, except that she is a wife of King David and the

235 I have had no success with this sort of literal metal transformation. I also tried working with him to metaphorically convert pennies to wealth, and got some results, but not strong ones. However, the "make me pretty" part works quite easily for me (perhaps because I have a lot of room to improve in that area!).

mother of Adonijah. Since Adonijah's name among Christians is sometimes given as Adonais, it's hard not to suspect he shares at least some sympathy with Adonis, the fosterling/lover of Venus. So, this associates Hagith with the mother of Adonis (the myrrh tree).

Exercise: Hagith Amulet

Using all the skills you've learned so far, make a Venus/Hagith amulet to make yourself appear more beautiful. The amulet can be in any form you like. If you are not comfortable designing your own amulet, I encourage you to rework Chapter Three and then return to this exercise.

* What color will yours be? Why?
* What kinds of plants and other materials will you employ for this work? Why? How?
    * If you're making a paper talisman, you can soak it in oils to add the plant elements, for example.
* Is there a sympathetic/playing with props element in this work?
* What symbols will you use in addition to the seal of Hagith?

Once you've decided what you want your amulet to look like and gathered your materials, think about the framing ritual. Do you want to make it in mundane space/time/consciousness and then charge it in ritual, or do the whole thing in ritual?[236] What powers will you call? How will you use the materials?

To begin, try adapting the following ritual.

Ritual: Amulet Consecration

This ritual is best performed on a Friday, in a daytime hour of Venus. A waxing moon would be best, but because this is daytime (visible) work, the moon timing is less important.

You will need:

* A green candle
* 7 red roses
* A bowl of water

236 Generally, this will be decided by how much time you can reasonably be in ritual space/time/consciousness without being interrupted or distracted.

* Incense that seems Venus-y to you (rose is nice)
* The amulet you designed in the previous exercise

Steps:

1. Arrange the space, and decorate it for Venus.
2. Take a shower (or a bath) and dress up nice for Venus. Wear perfume. Be fancy. Consider wearing green or white.
3. Once the proper planetary hour has begun, enter magical space/time/consciousness.
4. Begin your green imagining. Once you are all full of green, shoot the greenness upward toward the planet Venus.
5. Chant the Orphic Hymn to Aphrodite (my translation follows this exercise), or any other Venus-y chant that speaks to you. Portions of "Song of Songs" could be good. Repeat the chant until you "catch the vibe" and feel a Venereal presence descend on you.
6. Pray out loud. You can use the all-purpose Christian prayer in the Arbatel or write your own specific to this work. I said something like: "*Great Goddess, Venus, Shining Star: I wish to learn your Arts. However, they are occluded and polluted by the culture I live in. I fear I will never learn them without your help! I beg you to teach me! Send me an ambassador spirit, who can teach me in your name. Give me the skill and talent to learn, that I may easily understand, and discover the infinite treasures of your wisdom. Give me grace to know how to use my new power. All this I pray in your holy name, known only to the magicians, which is Neferiri.*"
7. Light the candle and the incense. Say something like: "*Hagith, ambassador of the sphere of Venus, I offer you the light and heat of this flame, the depths and coolness of this water, the sensual delight of the incense. I make you a gift of these roses. In the name of Great Venus, and by my own name, [NAME], I ask, please empower this talisman, bearing your sacred seal, so that [what you want].*"
8. Commune with the spirit for a while if you want, getting to know each other. But let them go before the "hour" is up, saying something like: "*I give thanks to Great Venus, in whose Holy Name you came, and to you, Hagith. As you came in peace, so depart in peace, and return again when I shall call you. Peace be between us. Good bye.*"

Orphic Hymn to Aphrodite

Aphrodite, Ourania, ever sought after,
Seaborn mother goddess, bright lover of laughter,
You delight through the night in revels and raves,
Rousing lovers to couple like you rose from the waves:
Glistening wet wile-weaver, mother of need,
All that awakens begins as your seed.
Genetrix of the universe, eternal all-queen,
You rule over all worlds, those seen and unseen—
The bright shining heavens, and the ever-fruitful earth
And the depths of the seas—to all you give birth.
You sit beside Bacchus, loud-shouting god of wine,
You rejoice in abundance, cheer, and good times.
You yoke people together, lover to lover,
Bringing forth love's variety, Erotes' mother.
Seductress, joy-bringer, kind-hearted Persuasion,
You coax forth our pleasures hidden within,
And lead us by hand to our lovers' beds,
Where you whisper sweet nothings in our anxious heads.
With everyone watching, or in deep-secret tryst
Your hair all disheveled, your lips all raw-kissed,
You are empress and goddess, bearing queen's rods.
Honored guest at the weddings of all of the gods.
Desirable one, she-wolf, bringing longing and heirs,
O life giver, love gifter, attend to our prayers:
Your philters fill us with lust-frenzied greed
Locking lovers together in unquenchable need.
Come, daughter of Cyprus, and lend us your charms,
For all living creatures get lost in your arms.
We behold you, great goddess, splendid of countenance,
Whether lounging in heaven, or on high Olympus,
Or on Syrian throne, redolent of frankincense,
Richly adorned or unveiled of pretense,
Or roaming around in your iridescent chariot,
Or flanked by your priests on the river of Egypt,
Or in your swan-driven carriage upon the wide sea,
Delighting sea-creatures as they dance in your breeze.
You bring joy to the nymphs of the earth and the forest,
And those who leap lightly in sea-foamy chorus.
You are seated in Cyprus, O Queen most divine,

where your blessings are spoken by maidens most fine.
They sing for you, blest one, and immortal Adonis,
He the grain god, and you the great goddess.
We summon you now with fine words and pure souls
Hear our words, drink our wine, and smoke of our bowls.

Mars

Mars, the Red Planet, is red because its surface is laden with iron oxide (rust). Of all the planets in our solar system, it is in many ways the one most like Earth. In English, the planet is named after the Roman god of war, as are words like "martial" and "military." Mars's month in March,[237] his day is Tuesday,[238] his color is red, and his symbol is the spear and shield. He is associated with wolves and bears, as well as cattle, horses, woodpeckers, and most red birds.

Mars's energy is virile, powerful, and direct. Mars helps you defend yourself and prove yourself. All ambition is his. Mars is that fortune which favors the bold. This planet is associated with all things martial and manly. Mars is the "masculine principle" and represents physical strength, mental discipline, and spiritual courage. Some people argue that it is wrong to associate these traits with the male gender, and in many ways I agree. However, Mars's associations with war, bravery, and strength are all culturally extrapolated from his association with men. Mars's role as the god/planet of war is not his primary attribute; his maleness is. Mars *is* Big Dick Energy.

He begins life as an agricultural god, who defends the boundary between tilth and wild. In our culture, Mars is a planet of war, bravery, etc., but he is also much, much more than that. Just as patriarchy distorts our view of Venus, turning the Great Green Goddess into a bimbo, patriarchy distorts our view of Mars, making the Great Red God into a brute. Further complicating matters is that much of the revilement of Mars in our culture is inherited from classical Athens, where Ares (the Greek equivalent of Mars) was associated with their enemy, Sparta. Almost every story you've ever heard about Ares (or Mars) is at least partly Athenian political propaganda. Carefully examine your own biases in regard to Mars (and everything else!).

Mars magic can help steel you for battle and also help you find calm in the center of chaos. It can be employed to improve confidence before an interview

237 The month of March is named for Mars, but the verb *to march* (walking in time like a soldier) is not. The word is more closely related to Mercury's name, by way of words meaning "boundary."
238 In English and other Germanic languages, Tuesday is named after the god Tyr.

and provides strong and reliable protection. Mars's help is also excellent to attract male/butch sex partners, or to ramp up your own sexiness as a man.[239] Mars's martiality is protective and community minded; he fights to protect his home and his family, his tribe and land. Mars guards the boundaries of the fields; preventing wild nature from creeping back in. Mars is also good for justice work.

For a quick spot of martial protection, repeat "Mars, Māvors,[240] macte esto"[241] under your breath, and imagine an iron fence surrounding you. Do not continue until you are successfully imagining that. On top of the fence, imagine shadow soldiers in gleaming armor, wearing red cloaks that flutter behind them like Superman's. How many are there? Above them, the dragon of your red imagining is flying. The dancers leap, cavorting, from fence post to fence post, pounding their spears on their gleaming shields, dancing their warrior dance. Do you hear the clash of iron and brass? Experiment with imagining them going both clockwise and counterclockwise.

Spell: Mars's Fiery Wall of Protection

You will need:

* An iron nail
* A beeswax or red candle, and something to burn it
* Black pepper
* Myrrh
* Cinnamon
* Rock salt

Steps:

1. Create an incense by crushing the black pepper, myrrh, cinnamon, and rock salt, and blending them together.
2. Using an iron nail, carve the following into a beeswax (or red) candle: "*Mars servabit*" which means "Mars will protect!"

---

239 I have no experience working with Mars for lesbian or other "no boys allowed!" love/sex magic, but I'm sure you can make it work if you want. That being said, Mars probably wouldn't be my first go-to in that instance, unless the goal is to help someone feel more masculine. For sapphic magic, I usually default to the Moon.

240 This is, as I understand it, an old, pre-Latin, Italian name for Mars, although this is not an entirely settled topic among experts.

241 "Mars, Māvors, honored is" Remember that *v* makes a *w* sound in Latin and proto-Latinate languages, so *Māvors* sounds like "may-wars."

3. Enter into magical space/time/consciousness.
4. Burn the candle, along with the incense of black pepper, myrrh, cinnamon, and rock salt, while walking a circle clockwise around your home.
5. As you walk, sing/chant a description of all the things you would like to be protected against, and how Mars will defeat them. Be specific and graphic.

Spell: Cross of Iron Talisman

This talisman allows you to store stamina and fortitude for later use. This general category of magic is generally understood as "battle magic"—something you prep/train in advance to be able to deploy on the fly.

Part One: Creating

Begin by finding two long, thin pieces of iron. I usually use antique iron nails, but anything from needles to railroad spikes to iron pipes will work. Broadly, the larger the pieces you use, the harder the talisman will be to charge (and carry around), but the more charge it will hold. You'll also need a length of red cord, of a size proportionate to the iron rods. For nails, I use embroidery floss. You'll need quite a lot of cord. You may wish to use a special magical blade to cut it, if you have one, but that's not necessary. I just use scissors. These talismans are best made during hours of Mars, on Tuesdays, and when Mars is well positioned. In particular, these are good when Mars is in Virgo. Avoid charging them when Mars is retrograde.

You will need:

* Two long, thin pieces of iron, such as large nails or railroad spikes
* Red cord
* A magical blade or scissors
* A clean, sharp razor blade

Steps:

1. Begin by cleaning and preparing yourself, and setting your mind to the task at hand, which is creating a talisman to store physical stamina and mental fortitude. You may wish to dress in all red.
2. Begin to call forth the martial parts of yourself. Stoke the fire in your belly that sparks as rage and stokes as discipline. Drums might help.
3. Tap the iron rods together until you find a pleasing rhythm.

4. Begin to chant: *"Mars Māvors, macte esto!"* which literally means "Mars, Māvors is honored," but figuratively means more like "Bravo Mars!"
5. When you feel the energy is about to crescendo, stop tapping and start wrapping the cord around the rods to tie them into a cross shape while you whisper the chant.
6. When the rods are secure, knot them together. Leave long tails so the talisman can be hung around your neck.
7. Using the razor blade, cut a *small* nick in the center of your non-dominant palm, and press the tied portion of the iron cross into the wound, getting it bloody.
8. Set the talisman aside while you clean and bandage the cut appropriately.
9. Wrap the cross and put it away, or hang it from a hook, until you are ready to begin the charging phase. It's better not to do them back-to-back; give the cross a little time to "firm up" before moving on.

Part Two: Charging

This phase can (and should) be repeated whenever you like. It's especially good during the times listed previously, but generally, more often is better than less often.

1. Begin by preparing yourself, entering into martial space/time/consciousness.
2. Hang the iron cross around your neck, so that it hangs between your collar bones and your sternum. If you happen to have gymnast rings you can hang from, you can try to hang in the iron cross posture, but that is not practical for most people. Instead, choose hand weights of an appropriate weight for you, and hold them with your arms out at full extension.
3. Do this as long as you can, chanting, *"Mars Māvors, macte esto!"*
4. When your arms begin to tremble and burn, keep them extended and repeat the chant at least five more times.
5. Then slowly bring your hands into your chest, and transfer the energy into the talisman.
6. Rest for a while (this can mean a minute, but it can also mean a week) and then repeat. Every time you repeat this, you store up more power in the talisman (and you get stronger in the normal way, too!).

To release the stamina when needed, press the iron cross into your non-dominant palm until it hurts and say, "*Mars Māvors, macte meum!*" which means "*Mars Māvors, honor is mine!*"

Jupiter

Jupiter is the largest of the (non-solar) planets—more than twice as large as all the others put together. I have frequently heard people say that it is almost large enough to have become a second sun, but that is not the case. Jupiter is less than 1/1000 the size of our Sun, and about 1/75 the size of the smallest stars. That being said, Jupiter is thermally radiant, and slowly shrinking. His surface is covered in roiling clouds and storms the size of continents. Astrologically, this planet is called the Greater Beneficent and the bringer of miracles. Its power is broadly expansive; it grows fields and bank accounts, kingdoms and influence. Jupiter can help you be a better father, leader, or judge, and he can help win those people to your side.

The planet Jupiter takes his English name from the Roman god Iupiter, who is one of a coterie of closely related gods with names evolved from Indo-European *Dyēu-pəter ("Sky Father" or "God the Father"). Zeus Pater, for example, is his Greek incarnation. This god is complicated and multifaceted; he is the god of leadership and fatherhood, but also of empire and patriarchy. He is the god of kings, the king of gods, and wields a lightning bolt as his scepter and weapon. He is associated with eagles, bulls, oak trees, thunder, lightning, and mountains. One easy token of Jupiter is the old style of quarter, with George Washington (our American Father-King) on one side and his eagle on the other. Jupiter's color is usually the light, bright blue of the sky, and sometimes also imperial purple.

In essence, Jupiter is the god of unchecked expansion. His is a complicated power because we live in an overculture where unchecked expansion is literally ruining the world. Jupiter (Eu-pater) is the True Father, the Patriarch at the core of Patriarchy. I, and probably you as well, have a deeply conflicted relationship with Jupiter.[242]

In fact, I never had much use for Jupiter at all until I was a teacher, and even more so when I became an administrator. Never before had I really been set in power over other people, and certainly not in such a completely nonconsensual way. Students are compelled to be in school by the authority (and, ultimately, the violence) of the State, a fact that I thought I understood as a student, but had to really wrestle with as a teacher. When I had power, it was Jupiter who taught me how to use it for good. Jupiter is the god of empire, but he is a divinely good, just, and wise king, and he can teach you to be as well.

242 A perhaps less kind way to say that would be: "I have some daddy issues." And another would be "Patriarchy has damaged me (and you too!)."

Although the angels associated with the planets are not entirely fixed, the angel most often associated with Jupiter is Tzadkiel,[243] (לאיקדצ) the angel of tzedekah. The root word קדצ is both the Hebrew name for the planet Jupiter and also a verb meaning "to be just" or "to be righteous." In colloquial English, I think the best translation is "do good" or "do right by."

Warning: Preaching Ahead

Tzedakah (הקדצ) is usually translated as "mercy" or "charity"—however, almost no one thinks those are good translations. The Lubavitcher Rebbe, for example, said:

"'Charity' commonly means alms, gratuitous benefactions for the poor. The giver of charity is a benevolent person, giving when he need not. He does not owe the poor anything, but gives because of his generosity. 'Tzedakah' has a completely opposite meaning. Instead of connoting benevolence, it is the idea of justice—that it is only right and just that one gives tzedakah."[244]

On this point, I agree with him. However, even more so than "justice," I like to think of tzedakah more broadly as "right action," or "action in accord with Creation." As a devotee of the Divine Krokopeplos, I believe that there are five basic components of right action. Take from this what you will:

1. **Respect for Creation.** The world we live in is a beautiful, magical, wonderful place. Whether humans are intended to be the stewards of the world or not is a matter of endless theological debate; however, whether we are intended to do so or not, we *do* exercise unprecedented control over our environment, both personally and collectively, and that de facto makes us her stewards. As my father, of blessed memory, would say, *"Don't shit where you eat."*
2. **Generosity and non-covetousness.** *Give freely and without expectation of reward.* Everyone has things they do not need (time, money, space, etc.), and everyone has needs they cannot meet themselves. Similarly, try not to take more than you need. We all have an inner pack rat—a desperate, gluttonous hoarder who whispers that there is never enough, that we could lose everything at any moment. Don't be that guy.

---

243 People without Hebrew literacy also spell this name Zadkiel or even Sachiel.

244 Likkutei Sichos, Vol. II, pp. 409–411

3. **Careful speech.** Like the evil eye, the evil tongue—speech born out of malice or jealousy—has a real, lasting, negative impact on the speaker, the listener, and the subject. For the magician, more so than anyone else, having a "good tongue" is important. A sorceress is only as good as her word. If you expect the things you speak into being to be true, you need to *watch your fucking mouth.*
4. **Compassion.** It's easy to imagine that compassion is about being nice to everyone all the time, but that isn't so. Compassion, like mercy, is about the knowledge that *you do not deserve to be loved,* and neither does anyone else. Love, and life, are things so powerful, so amazing, that no person could possibly ever deserve them. No one can earn them. You have no right to exist; the world would probably be better off if you (and I, and people in general) weren't here at all. And yet, we do exist. Because love. Because compassion. Because grace. The sun shines on all of us, warm and generative, making no judgments or discernments between us. Divine Compassion (grace) is just that: the warmth of the sun on the murderer's face. And that's what compassion is too: shining on others, regardless of whether they deserve it or not. I strongly recommend a practice called metta meditation. It will make you happier.
5. **Community-mindedness.** It's easy, especially the way we live now, to sequester ourselves, so that we only think of "me and mine." So many of us live, essentially, alone, either by ourselves or with only our immediate family. Tzedakah calls on us to understand our behaviors in terms of others—to prioritize the community (both our immediate community and our global community) and not just ourselves, not just our family, not just our friends and neighbors. At its root, tzedakah about understanding that our personal experience is very different from other people's, that other people's needs are different from our own, and yet all those people, no matter how different, *are* kith and kin. To only care about your immediate community (your family, your neighborhood, your religion, your tribe, your race) is just as hateful, spiteful, and selfish as to value only yourself. *We're all in this together.*

In any case, as I was saying, Tzadkiel (sometimes written "Sachiel" by non-Hebrew-literate magicians) is the angel of right action and of the sphere of Jupiter. Legendarily, Tzadkiel is the angel that held back Abraham's hand when Isaac lay bound. He is sometimes called the "angel of the Violet Flame." In the *Heptameron*, an early renaissance grimoire attributed to Peter de Abano, he is given the seals shown here. The *Heptameron* presents a complete system for the conjuration of the planetary angels, including a relatively straightforward Solomonic ritual, but is distinguished by instructions for the construction of elaborate circles of magical names—which vary according to the hour, day, and season—provided in several pages of tables. While I enjoy that sort of thing for its pure nerd value, I simply don't think all that foofaraw is necessary for most beginner magic. Here is a simpler method for invoking the presence of an angel via automatic writing (as you learned in Chapter Four). In the example below, we'll be conjuring Tzadkiel, but this same method can be used with any planetary angel, such as those listed in the following table. The assignment of angels to planets is not fully standardized; you may see other tables in other sources.

Moon	Sariel	שריאל	Prince of El
Mercury	Raphael	רפאל	Healing of El
Venus	Anael (Haniel)	חניאל	Grace of El
Sun	Michael	מיכאל	Who Is Like El
Mars	Gabriel	גבריאל	Man(liness) of El
Jupiter	Tzadkiel (Sachiel)	צדקיאל	Right(eousness) of El
Saturn	Qaspiel (Cassiel)	קצפיאל	Wrath of El

Conjuring an Angel

Make sure you are clear of mind and clean of body. It would be best to fast from meat, intoxicants, sex, rage, and handling dead bodies for three days prior to angelic conjuration, but one day will probably do for this. Confess any guilt or shame that is weighing on your spirit, and absolve yourself of it. Dress in white or in the planetary color, and perfume and decorate yourself.

You will need:

* A white candle
* A glass of clean, cold water
* 20 or more pages of clean white paper
* A pen (in black ink or the angel's corresponding color)

Steps:

1. Decorate the space for the angel, using appropriate colors, incense, etc.
2. Place before you a single white candle; a glass of clean, cold water; a good supply (at least twenty pages) of clean white paper; and a black ink pen. You may also use ink of the appropriate color for the angel being summoned.
3. Enter magical space/time/consciousness by any method. Prayer is especially appropriate for angelic invocation.
4. Take the pen in your hand, poised over the paper, and recite (something like) the following in your best magician voice:

   "*O, you glorious and benevolent angel, Tzadkiel, Tzadkiel, Tzadkiel, angel of the violet flame, angel of the sphere of Jupiter, I invoke you, adjure you, and call you forth to visible apparition in and through the great prevalent and divine Name of the Most High G-d, El Chai, El Shaddai, who is Elohim ve'Daath, and by the ineffable and efficacious virtues and powers thereof, whereby you are governed and called forth, it being absolutely necessary, and ordained, appointed, and decreed, and by the obeisance you have made, I do most earnestly entreat and powerfully command you, O you benign angel Tzadkiel, angel of the sphere of Jupiter, come to me now.*

   I command you, Tzadkiel, to move and appear to me visibly in this mirror here before me. In and through this same mirror, transmit your ray to my sight, and your voice to my ears, that I might hear you and plainly see you. Move my hand that I might see your writing, and transmit to me your revelation and your sign. Include me in your mysteries, that I might be the instrument of the Most High. I earnestly adjure you, O benevolent and amicable angel, Tzadkiel, in the most excellent Name of G-d, Adonai Elohim, I am the servant of the Name, and by the Name I conjure you; show yourself firmly to me, and let me partake of your wisdom. Tzadkiel, Tzadkiel, Tzadkiel, I invoke you now. Tzadkiel, Tzadkiel, Tzadkiel, I invoke you now...."

5. Continue to repeat the invocation until the spirit makes its presence known. If you don't feel anything, start writing the invocation while you read it, and don't stop writing. Feel free to modify the exact phrasing to better suit your own style; the worst thing that will happen is nothing.

Saturn

Although some people appear to be afraid of it, I adore Saturn. It is the furthest planet visible, unaided, to humans—the boundary of our visible world. It is the liminal avant-garde between the known and the not-yet-known. Saturn, as his name suggests, is fully satiated. Saturn is death, but also liberation. Saturn breaks chains. Saturn's color is black, and his day is, unsurprisingly, Saturday.

Saturdays are the Great Sabbath, the Temple of Saturn built not in space, but in time.[245] On Saturdays, in the sphere of Saturn, with the Saturnian spirits, Creation is complete, and we pause to reflect, before we once again kindle our inner fire and begin Creating again. Think carefully about what you devote your Saturdays to; those things will be both what limits you and also the boundaries that keep you whole. You are encouraged to remember Saturday and keep it holy (advice broadly applicable to all days, but often more logistically feasible on Saturdays).[246]

Saturn is a useful magical ally in any work that involves limiting or containing. In English, the planet Saturn is named after the Roman god Saturn, the King of the Golden Age and master of the sickle, which he uses both to bring in the grain and to castrate his abusive father. He is a god of agriculture, "civilization," good order, the social contract, and old age. In syncretic late antiquity, the god of Israel was understood to be a face of Saturn, as was the god of Carthage. Saturn's is the age before Eu-Paters's, the mythic age before Patriarchy.

Saturn-dread, white supremacy, and antisemitism are tightly wound together in Anglophone culture. This makes Saturn an especially good magical ally for containing and restricting these powers and some (but not all) forms of fascism.

There are many spirits of the sphere of Saturn; as I mentioned, the god of Israel has a home here, as do (of course) Saturn and Kronos. Most gods

---

245 I strongly recommend to all magicians, Jewish or not, a famous essay called "Shabbat as a Sanctuary in Time" by Abraham Joshua Heschel, one of the most important teachers of Jewish mysticism of the twentieth century.

246 While *sabbath* is generally understood religiously in our culture, traditionally, it also carries the meaning of "general strike." To my mind, the very essence of the holy sabbath is labor solidarity: "If we all refuse to work on Saturday, the boss can't make any of us work."

associated with liminality and boundaries partake of the sphere of Saturn. Most spirits depicted with sickles, or other tools of grain harvest, tend to be Saturnian. Psychopomps (spirits that guide the newly dead) generally partake in either Saturn and Mercury.

We've spoken a lot about entering into magical space/time/consciousness, but now I'd like to teach you a ritual for formally exiting it. The ritual below is called הַבְדָּלָה (havdalah), a word that means simply "separation." It is most often used to gently end and seal a household's observance of the sabbath, but it is also used among Jewish folk magicians to gently end and seal many types of mystical and magical rites.

Your use of this ritual to gently end and seal contact with the divine is not culturally appropriative unless you pretend to be Jewish while not being Jewish. Shabbat, unlike some other Jewish observances, is not a closed practice[247]. You partake of the Sabbath whether you are Jewish or not, whether you follow her rules or not, whether you celebrate her joys or not, whether you even notice it is Shabbat or not. It's Saturday whether you want it to be or not, so you might as well try to find the joy in it. One way to do that is to remember the Sabbath, and keep it holy. That is to say, if we all refuse to work on Saturdays, they can't make any of us work on Saturdays.

Drawing Down Other Celestial Spirits

Using basically the same method we learned for drawing down the moon, you can also draw down any of the other planets. However, I don't recommend this for beginners. The moon is far easier to draw down than the other planets. Partly, this is because it is closest to us, both physically and psychically, but I think it's mostly because the moon is particularly potent in our subconscious, and is, by nature, a shape changer. I recommend practicing with the moon until you are very comfortable with it before attempting to draw down other planetary forces. Channeling can be exhausting and confusing; the danger is in wearing yourself out to the point where you lose control, and can't regain it. This is not a problem if you have a co-magician there who is not possessed and can guide you back if you "get lost." I have quite a lot of channeling practice, and am not especially prone to trance-fatigue, but I only rarely channel supra-lunar planetary spirits without a co-magician.

247 To grossly oversimplify, in modern diasporic Judaism, practices directly related to Jewish ancestry, Jewish tribal identity, and Jewish history are closed to non-Jews, while those related to seasonal or astronomical events are not.

Chapter Seven:

Circles and Centers

This chapter is a little more theory heavy than some others, especially in the first half. I beg your indulgence. I spent many years as a professional geometer; I have a lot of deep mystic shit to say about circles. I promise that, by the end, we will get back to practical sorcery. As Oppenheimer says, "There's nothing more practical than a good theory."

Guest Lecturer: Hypatia of Alexandria

Hypatia (circa 370–415 CE) was a renowned teacher at the Great Mouseion[248] of Alexandria. Today, we would characterize what she taught primarily as Neoplatonic metaphysics, geometry, and astronomy, but she would have thought of herself primarily as a teacher of Platonic philosophy. Like many prominent philosophers, she also served as an adviser to people of power, including Orestes, the Roman governor of Egypt. Although she was a pagan, she was not especially religious. She never married, nor had children. Publicly,

248 This word, Μουσεῖον, means simply "place of the Muses" or "place of inspiration." It is the root of our word "museum." The great Library of Alexandria was one part of the Mouseion complex, which also included schools, temples, and concert halls, and was famed for its anatomical models. It did not include a significant collection of visual art (although other Museums did). Around one thousand scholars lived in the Mouseion of Alexandria, along with their families and households. Hypatia most likely grew up in the Mouseion; her father was its headmaster.

she had a reputation for entirely eschewing the romantic company of men, but it is unclear if she was celibate, asexual, lesbian, or simply discreet.

Although none of her original writing on mathematics survives, her commentaries on others' works plainly show that she was among the most gifted mathematicians of her age. Her annotated edition of Euclid's *Elements* (sometimes falsely attributed to her father) was the de facto standard textbook of geometry from the time she wrote it until the early 1800s. She appears to have specialized in epicycles—the movement of circles whose centers are also moving in a circle, like amusement park tilt-a-whirls. This kind of geometry is especially important to calculating the movements of celestial bodies—moons orbiting around planets orbiting around suns.

In life, Hypatia's metaphysics focused on the idea of the Divine Unity, the Intellect, and the Soul, which she understood as concentric. First, at the center of all things, there is the one, the singularity within which all things come into Being. This is deeply connected, but not exactly identical, to what I call the Sacred Center, which we will discuss in detail below. From that central One emanates the Intellect, the world of Platonic forms or ideas, whom we might today call "spirits." Thence emanates the Soul and the world of instantiation, what we might today call "bodies" or "reality." She saw the purpose of life to be unity with the all-encompassing Oneness of the divine, and she understood careful observation and contemplation of reality as the best mechanism for achieving that unification.

By the age of forty-five, Hypatia was among the most well-respected scholars of the Great Mouseion. Students came from all over the empire to study with her. High-ranking priests and government officials sought her council; her teachings and philosophy carried great moral weight throughout Egypt. Of course, she was not without her detractors, chief among them "saint" Cyril of Alexandria.

In 415 CE, Cyril whipped up a mob of Christians who brutally and publicly kidnapped, tortured, and murdered Hypatia on the stairs of the church. Although the mob was motivated by Christo-supremacy, Cyril's aims were almost certainly political; he wished to separate Orestes (the governor) from her influence, so that he could more easily control the governor.

Since her death, Hypatia has become known as a martyr for paganism, philosophy, and more broadly, for rational open-minded inquiry, and particularly for women's intellectual liberation. Although the Great Library at Alexandria burned before she was born, in the long centuries since, her murder and its destruction are often rhetorically conflated, and she is often considered the "last librarian of Alexandria," martyred trying to save ancient wisdom from Christian conquest. In modern (nineteenth to twenty-first century) hagiography, she is often held up as the ideal of the chaste and bookish martyr, dedicated to the ideals of reason over all other things. Although, in contemporary depictions,[249] she is often portrayed as young and beautiful at the time of her martyrdom, she was probably well into middle age by that time, and there is no evidence to suggest she was especially beautiful, even in her youth. As with almost all heroines, our culture implies that beauty is the only road to power for women, but history teaches us that (as with men) real power is most often intelligence backed with education, connections, and charisma. As with all Mighty Dead, Hypatia the saint isn't really the same as Hypatia the historical figure; they continue to grow and adapt and flourish. That's what it means to "live forever among the heroes." Living things are not static.

Writing Prompt: What Is a Circle?

* Define *circle*. Be as precise and technical as possible. (Ask Hypatia if you're stuck!)
    * Hint: When I say *circle*, I mean the boundary only. If I wanted to also talk about the interior of the circle, I'd call it a *disk*.
* Next, define *circle* as expansively, metaphorically, and poetically as you can.
* Reconcile your two definitions.

Although there are many correct ways to define a circle, all correct definitions come down to the fact that a circle is a collection of all points equidistant from a central location. This is true in a very precise way of two-dimensional geometric circles, and also metaphorically, as in a "circle" of friends (or a circle of witches!) who, instead of being centered on a leader, are centered on a common purpose. Here are some facts about circles that should be self-evident, although you might not have considered their application to magic before.

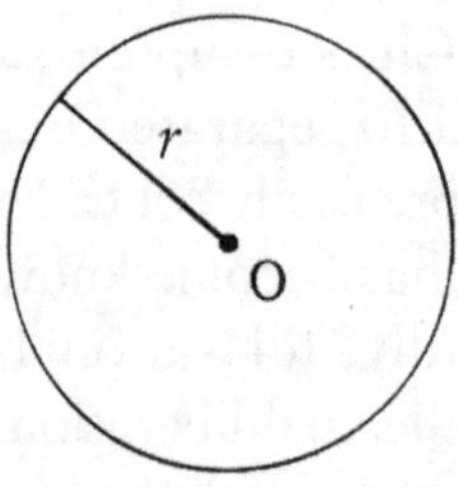

249 For example, there is a movie about her called *Agora* that I highly recommend, in which she is played by Rachael Weisz. Although it is not at all accurate as history, it is an excellent hagiography and also a beautiful film.

1. Of all shapes, a circle (or sphere, in 3D) encloses the most area (volume) inside a given perimeter (surface area). That is why bubbles are spherical. That is to say: in general, the easiest (i.e., lowest effort) way to contain something is in a circle. In a magical sense, this informs the fact that the easiest portals to open are circular.
2. Given three points not on a line, there is exactly one circle which passes through all three. If those three points don't move, the circle can't move. As a general (but not universal) rule, you need at least three competent magicians to anchor a big group ritual.
3. Circles are wholly defined by their size (radius) and their location (center). Other than those things, all circles are identical. If you want to "match" two pieces, the easiest shapes to "match" are circles. For this reason, it is very easy to sympathetically link any magic circle to any other magic circle.

How Are Circles Used in Witchcraft?

While everyone has their own magical style and practices, circles are used in three broad categories of ways: By focusing on their center, as we did above, we can use them as *anchors*. By focusing on their size, we can use them as *boundaries*. By making sure to do both at once, we use them as *portals*.

The Sacred Center

Magically, the most basic of ways to interact with a circle is to be at the center of it. This operation is often called "centering," "anchoring," or "grounding." Most people use those three words more or less interchangeably. Centering is most typically used as preparation to consolidate power and influence at the beginning of a ritual, and/or as a "cool down" at the end of out-of-body work. There are many, many types of centering rituals. The Greater Ritual of the Rainbow Star you learned in Chapter One is a basic centering ritual. If you haven't practiced it since then, go back and relearn it. The Lesser (Banishing) Ritual of the Pentagram (which Professor YouTube will happily teach you) is another (complicated) example of a centering ritual. I'll teach another later in this chapter. All of these rituals share a common purpose: they relocate the magician to the center of the world.

The Center of the World

Before proceeding, a brief shout-out to my friend Jake Rabinowitz, whose work on the Sacred Center in "Face of God" (a study of the survival of Canaanite mythology in the writings of the Hebrew prophets) has deeply informed my thinking about the Sacred Center.

The Sacred Center of the World is an important concept in many cultures. In Greek, it is called'Ομφαλός (Omphalos), which means "navel" or "hub," and is sometimes also a euphemism for the vagina or womb. Many sites in the ancient Levantine world were understood as the omphalos. This plurality of centers is something I'll touch on in more detail shortly. In Greece, the most famous was the Omphalos of Delphi, where Zeus's eagles met.[250] To this day, the exact site is marked by a sacred stone (also called the omphalos). Delphi (and the rest of Mt. Parnassus) is one of a large category of Sacred Centers I call the *Holy Mountain*, from which wisdom is dispersed. Mt. Sinai is another such example, as is Jabal al-Nour, the Holy Mountain of Mecca. Although Delphi is not a tourist attraction, Jerusalem's Temple Mount and Athens's Acropolis are examples of Sacred Centers that strongly retain their political and rhetorical power in the modern world.

Another great Sacred Center of ancient Greece was the Holy Island of Delos, which lies at the center of a ring of islands today called the Cyclades. Among other claims to fame, Delos is notable as the place where Leto gave birth to Artemis and Apollo. It is very closely associated with Asteria, the mother of Hekate and sister of Leto. Delos's history as a Sacred Center is very, very old—far, far older than the religion of the Olympians in Greece. In fact, the cult of Delos was often in conflict with that of Delphi. In the fifth and sixth centuries, several "purifications" of the island were made under instruction from the Oracle at Delphi. In the most famous of these, the sacred tombs were defiled, and the island's dead were separated among several islands. It was decreed that no one could be buried on the island, and no one might give birth there. Shortly thereafter, all inhabitants were "relocated." While a few communities have arisen on Delos since, none have lasted long. Today, the island has an official population of fourteen; the entire island is a World Heritage Site administered by the Greek Ministry of Culture. Tourists may visit, but not spend the night.

Delos is one of a large category of Sacred Centers I call the *Holy Island*. They are distinguished from Holy Mountains primarily by being more remote and having very clear boundaries. The power of the Holy Mountain rolls down into all the surrounding land, but the Holy Island keeps its secrets. Because they usually have unobstructed views of the whole sky, Holy Islands tend to

250 If you don't know this myth, look it up.

be important centers of astronomical and astrological learning. At Delos, you can see this in the connection with Asteria, the goddess of night prophecy. Another prominent example is the Hawai'ian Holy Island of Kaho'olawe. Glastonbury, in England, is a particularly interesting example, because it began as a Holy Island but is today a Holy Mountain.

Another kind of Sacred Center is the *Sacred Garden,* or "Cradle of Civilization." Geographically, these occur most often at river confluences and deltas. Mythologically, the Garden of Eden, with her four rivers, is undoubtedly the most famous of Sacred Confluences. In the ancient Mediterranean, the most famous of these was Hypatia's home of Alexandria (where the Nile meets the Mediterranean), but Khartoum (while the Blue Nile and White Nile meet) and Qurna (where the Tigris and Euphrates meet) are other important examples. The Sacred Garden, by nature of its lush natural resources and convenient shipping routes, is the type of Sacred Center most likely to exert material power in our world. Note that while Delos is entirely uninhabited, and Delphi is a relatively small tourist town, Alexandria is an economic powerhouse with a population of 5.3 million. Sacred Gardens very rarely fall. Personally, I resonate most strongly with Sacred Garden as a Sacred Center, particularly because I live less than ten miles away from the Sacred Confluence where the Allegheny and Monongahela rivers meet to form Father Ohio.

All regions have their own Sacred Centers. Every city or region has a Sacred Center. For example, the Sacred Center of Philadelphia (where I used to live) is marked by the statue of Ben Franklin above city hall. Although I have never lived there, I suspect the National Mall is the Sacred Center of Washington, DC. In some places (like Pittsburgh), the regional Sacred Center is very obvious, because it is big and geological. In other places, it can be more subtle, and harder to determine, especially if human architecture has buried the natural focus. For clues, look at geographic features, traffic patterns, monumental statues, and iconic architecture. Talk to old people who have lived there all their lives.

Less developed regions like forests and cemeteries also have Sacred Centers, although they are sometimes more difficult to identify. Homes have Sacred Centers, which we usually call "heart of the home." Historically, the hearth was the heart of every home, but in many homes today, the kitchen table fills that role.

Exercise: Sacred Centers

Here's an exercise to explore some of your specific centers.

1. Where is the center of your home? Be as precise as possible. If you're not sure where yours is, here are some questions to ask yourself:

   a) Where is the actual geometric center of your home's ground floor?
   b) If you were going to leave a note for another resident, where would you leave it?
   c) Where do (should) you leave offerings to your house spirits?
   d) At parties, where do people congregate?
   e) As an example, mine is not just "in the kitchen," it's at the eastern corner of my counter peninsula.
2. If you have a yard, where is its center? It's likely to be the biggest tree.
   a) For example, I have two yards, which have only been one property since I moved in seven years ago. They each have their own center. My backyard's center is an old black walnut tree. The side yard, which was, until recently, an abandoned, burned-out shell of a house, now has a herm at its center.
3. Where is the center of your region, town, or neighborhood? Be as precise as possible.
   a) As I mentioned, the center of the greater Pittsburgh area is the fountain at Point State Park. If you are local, I *strongly* recommend you collect and drink water from it. Both legendarily and historically, its waters are that of our secret and sacred fourth river, a.k.a. the Wisconsin Glacial Flow aquifer. However, these days, it's just regular City of Pittsburgh tap water. The "sacred" center of Braddock (my immediate neighborhood) is inside the blast furnace of the Edgar Thomson Steel Mill.
4. If possible, spend some time in these places, feeling their centrality.
5. What "shape" of center resonates most with you?
6. When you imagine the center of the world, what sort of geography does it have?
   a) Draw a map.

Working at the Center of the World

Obviously, the easiest way to magically operate from the center of the world is to relocate your body to a Sacred Center. However, this is rarely practical. In anchoring/centering rituals, we recontextualize our frame of reference so that the center of the universe is located wherever we are. I promise I'm going to teach you another centering ritual soon. However, Hypatia has something to say about the notion of the Sacred Center as a concept:

You are usually taught that, in ancient days, people thought that the Earth was at the center of the universe. And that later, we discovered this was in error, and learned that actually the Earth goes around the sun. This is simply not true.

Writing Prompt

* Sometimes, very young children believe people on the other side of the planet are upside down. Formulate a clear and compelling explanation as to why that isn't true. What determines what "down" means? What does it mean to be "upside down"?

There is no center. The path the Earth traces, relative to the center of the sun, is a simple shape (almost but not exactly circular). The path the sun makes in space relative to the Earth is also a simple shape (almost but not exactly circular). The paths the other planets trace, relative to the center of the Earth, are much more complicated than those they trace relative to the center of the sun. And yet: *There. Is. No. Center.*

Our most basic understanding of the "Sacred Center" is along a line. From the "Center," you can go down, or you can go up. There is Here, and the Things Above the Here (the "Heavens"), and the Things Below the Here (the "Underworld").

However, we don't live on a line, but on a (mostly) spherical planet. On Earth, "down" means "toward the center of the Earth." You can always feel in your body where the center of the Earth is, because gravity is pulling you toward it.[251] By understanding the Earth as a sphere that we live on the outside of, we know that "the center of the world" isn't actually in "the world" we live in.

As humans made the move to heliocentrism (the idea that Sun is the center of everything), our understanding of the Sacred Center radically changed. It wasn't just really far away; it was a thing we couldn't feel in our bodies. By day, the Sacred Center was visible, but by night, it disappeared. This is a big difference. You can feel where the Sun is, but you can also avoid feeling it.

The sacred power that keeps the Earth in motion around the Sun is the same power that pulls us to the heart of the Earth. And yet, when we talk about the power the Earth exerts on us, it is so obvious as to be undeniable. The Sun exerts far more gravitational pull than the Earth does. The effects of the Sun's gravity are everywhere; they make possible every moment of your existence. And yet, that pull is so subtle that you forget about it until you stop

251 If you are ever "lost" in the spirit world, try to feel gravity's pull on your body and let it guide you home.

to think. The Sun is reassuringly "real"; it shines on every point on earth. You can see it in the sky and feel its warmth kiss your skin. It will burn you if you remain too long in its glare, and staring directly at it will make you go blind. But the sun is not the center of the universe. *There is no center.*

That's not because the Sun orbits around the Galactic Center (although it does). It's not because our galaxy is also slowly dancing through the void (although it is). It's not even because the universe is simultaneously expanding from every single point (although that is also true).

It's because the very notion of a "center" is *absurd*. There is no such thing as a center. People were mistaken when they believed the Earth was the center of the universe. They were still mistaken when they made the Sun the center of the universe. They are still mistaken when they worship the Creator of All That Is as the center of the universe. They are even mistaken when they look for the center of the universe by going inside of themselves. *The whole notion of centricity is made up bullshit,* and it's important for magicians to get over it.

When we center magically, we begin by abiding in the understanding that there is no true center. This is not a mystic metaphor. It is a mathematical truth. Every place in the universe partakes, equally, in the universal *One,* which is the only true center, at once all-pervasive and completely transcendent. Remember that where you are at this very moment is the center of the universe.

Exercise: Bodily Center

In the following exercises, I will assume that you have two legs, which are more or less the same length, and two arms, also about the same length as each other. If that is not the case, you might want to work with a movement teacher (such as a yoga instructor, dance master, or martial arts sifu) to help you adapt these exercises to your own body.

1. Determine the Sacred Center of your body, which is related to, but not identical to, your center of mass. For most people, their center is somewhere around the sacral chakra,[252] but all bodies are different,[253] and the location of your center will change as you take different positions. For example, lifting your arms straight up and fully inflating your lungs moves your center up. At times, your center is even outside your body entirely, although these positions are generally difficult to maintain.

252 Close to where your spine meets your pelvis.

253 For example, because I have a very large belly, my center of mass is substantially in front of my spine.

2. Watch some dancers, and pay attention to how their center of mass moves as they do. If you can, do a pirouette. Throw your arms and legs around while you spin, and feel your center of mass move.
3. Watch some gymnasts, and pay attention to how they are sometimes flipping around a center external to their body. If you can, do a cartwheel. What is the center of that movement?
4. Walk in a circle like a Bagua master. Keep yourself aligned to the center, outside of yourself. Think about what it means for a fighter to always keep their opponent at the center of every motion, turning and wrapping around them.

Exercise: Rooting

The goal of this exercise is to stand in such a way that you cannot be knocked over. This feeling is called "being rooted." It is a good practice before embodied magic or after out-of-body magic.

1. Stand up. Put your feet about hip width apart, with your toes pointing forward.
2. Be sure your weight is spread evenly across your feet—not just across both feet, but also spread to both the front and heel of each foot. Be sure your knees are not locked, but they needn't be bent.[254] Move your feet around until you feel very stable.
3. Now, very slowly, shift all your weight onto the front of your left foot. Feel how that changes your relationship with the ground.
4. Now, shift your weight to the heel of your left foot.
5. Next, shift to the front of your right foot, and then the back.
6. Now, back to the left front. In this way, you should be making very slow lemniscates (∞) with your weight, without moving your feet, and with only minimal movement in your hips. Go as slowly as you can, and focus on how your connection to the ground changes as you move your weight.
7. When you feel very sure, smooth, and solid in the movement, come back to a balanced position for a while. Does it feel any different than it did before?
8. Next, reverse the movement and make lemniscates in the other direction. Does one direction feel different from the other?
9. Once you've gotten the hang of how this movement feels in your body,

254 As a more advanced exercise, do it with your knees bent.

do it again, this time imagining pillars of strength running down both of your legs, out the arches of your feet, and into the center of the earth, the Womb of Being, while you do it.

10. Wiggle your toes a little, digging into the ground for maximum purchase. Feel those pillars holding you up while you shift your weight. Feel their connection to the earth.

Lesser Ritual: Pore Breathing

Pore breathing is a magical act. It is not literally breathing through your skin. In pore breathing, we draw magical energy (such as the color energy you've already worked with) in and out of your skin. It is most often used to absorb energy from the environment preparatory to spending that energy elsewhere. It is easiest to pore breathe naturally occurring energies. Sunlight and moonlight are easy energies for beginners to start with. After that, move on to some other natural energies, like colors or elemental powers (Air, Earth, Water, Fire), but once you get the hang of those, you can also pore breathe more abstract concepts like "creativity."

1. Before beginning, stretch your arms, shoulders, and neck, paying careful attention to where you hold tension.
2. In a clear and alert state of mine (*not* in trance), sit or stand with your spine straight and vertical. Breathe slowly and deeply. Pay attention to the feeling inside.
3. Hold your hands out in front of you like you're holding a big beach ball. Try to keep the circle of your arms parallel with the floor at shoulder height. If your arms get so tired they start to shake, you can put them down to rest. Attend to your breathing until you are calm and focused.
4. Begin to stretch your fingers slightly on each inhale, and relax them back inward slightly on each inhale.
5. Begin to flex your joints outward on each inhale, as if the ball is getting slightly bigger, and pull them slightly in on each exhale.
6. Practice that for around nine full breaths. Feel vital life force entering into your body (through your lungs) with each breath, diffusing into every cell. Feel the death-energy waste leave your body on every exhale. Know, as you do so, that your waste nourishes the plants, just as their exhalations give you life. The air you are breathing connects you to every other living thing on earth.
7. Next, allow your "you-ness" to expand slightly outside of your skin as you breathe in, and contract slightly within your skin as you exhale. Feel the energy cross in and out of your skin. You might get goose-

bumps on your arms; that's a good sign that it's working, but it doesn't happen to everyone. Some people get tingles, pins and needles, or even little electrical shocks. If this happens, attend to where on your body they are; they are sometimes a sign of an issue in that area. It is possible you will have some kind of strange pseudo-emotional response. As best as you are able, simply observe whatever is happening without trying to analyze it. However, if it hurts (not just soreness, but pain), you're doing it wrong, and you should stop. This should be a gentle and natural process.

8. Next, focus on drawing vital force in through the pores of your skin on each inhale inflating you like a balloon, and feel it soaking deep into your bones as you exhale. It helps to breathe very slowly.
9. Once you feel like it's working, stick with it for a little while, until you feel "full." The final step is to exhale the energy with a magical intention on the way out. Breathe in, through your pores, a type of energy relevant to the intention at hand, and then hold that breath for a moment, and "imprint" your intention. Next, slowly exhale from your lungs and your pores simultaneously, radiating the intent like a glowing saint.

Circulation of the Body of Light

Once you've gotten the hang of pore breathing, it's time to progress toward "circulating the body of light," which is just a pretentious, magician-esque way to say "moving energy through your body." There are natural "cycles" or "circuits" in the body through which our vital energy (a.k.a. chi, a.k.a. prana) moves. For the purposes of the magic in this book, the three most important such circuits are pictured in the images below.

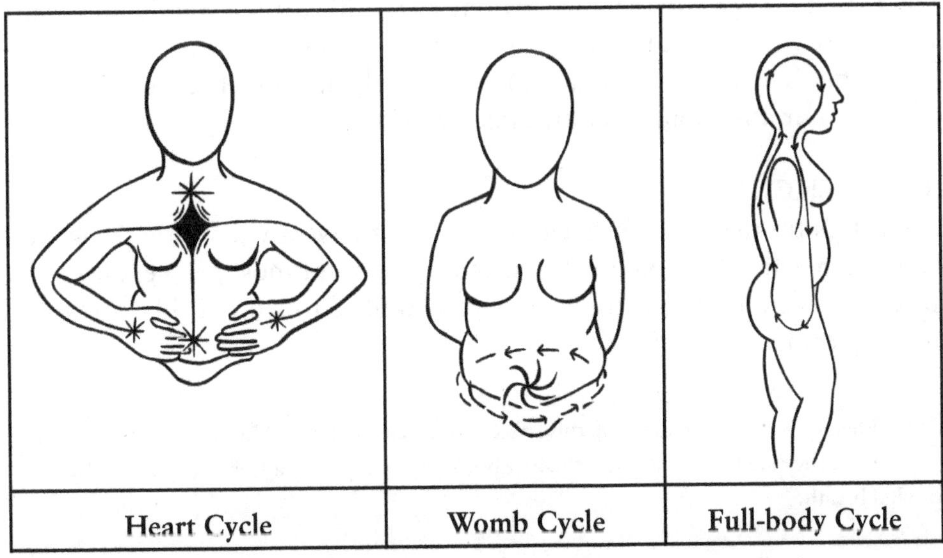

Heart Cycle	Womb Cycle	Full-body Cycle

The Heart Cycle

We'll begin with the heart cycle, partly because we already activated it in the pore-breathing exercise above.

1. Begin by rooting.
2. When you feel sufficiently rooted, move your arms around, stretching your shoulders, elbows, wrists, and fingers. Get the blood pumping through them.
3. When they feel alive, put your arms out, at shoulder height, as if you are hugging a tree. Your palms should be facing your breasts, with your fingers not quite touching.
4. Begin to imagine energy moving through your body in a circle, passing about halfway between your throat and your sternum, then continuing through your right shoulder, down your right arm, through your right middle finger, into your left middle finger, up your left arm, through your left shoulder, and back across your chest.
5. If the energy "gets stuck" at any point, or you notice a pain, try to slowly ease into that spot, gently warming and loosening it.
6. Practice at different speeds, both slow and fast, and in both directions. Try to make the flow as smooth and effortless as possible. In truth, energy is always moving through this circuit in both directions—focus on feeling for it as much as directing it.

If you can't feel the energy moving, that's totally ok. Energy follows attention, so just move your attention along the circuit, and the energy will follow, whether you can feel it or not. Spend some time thinking about what you expect energy moving in your body to feel like. What if it doesn't really feel like that? Simply attend to your body and notice what it does feel like, even if that's nothing. If you don't feel it, simply imagine that you can, while moving your attention smoothly along the circuit.

The Womb Cycle

Next, let's try the womb[255] cycle. If you don't have a womb, that's ok, you can just imagine that you do! The womb cycle is, for most people, the easiest place to generate energy in your body, as well as to store it (like a battery) for magical use.

---

255 When cisgender men describe this space, it is often so "cloaked in mystery" that it is hard to tell what they are talking about—the first book on the topic I read referred to it as the "oven of vital breath."

1. Begin by rooting.
2. When you feel sufficiently rooted, move your arms and legs around, stretching your shoulders, elbows, wrists, and fingers. Get the blood pumping through them.
3. Imagine a magical cauldron behind your belly button, where vital essence collects, grows, and—under the right conditions—matures into a whole new person. That space is the center of the womb circuit, which orbits your hips.
4. Just as with the heart circuit exercise, smoothly and slowly move your attention (and thus your vital energy) along the loop.
5. At first, you may want to circle your hips, like a hula hooper, to get the feeling, but also practice doing this while holding completely still. If the energy "gets stuck" at any point, or you notice a pain, try to slowly ease into that spot, gently warming and loosening it.
6. Practice at different speeds, both slow and fast, and in both directions. Try to make the flow as smooth and effortless as possible. In truth, energy is always moving through this circuit in both directions—focus on feeling for it as much as directing it.

The Full-body Cycle

Movement along the full-body cycle is what most people mean when they say "circulate the body of light." This circuit runs up the spine, across the top of the head, through the spot on your skull that was soft when you were a baby, down the nose, down the throat, down the chest, and between the legs, as pictured.

1. Begin by rooting.
2. When you feel sufficiently rooted, move your arms and legs around, stretching your shoulders, elbows, wrists, and fingers. Get the blood pumping through them.
3. Practice moving your attention/energy through the circuit. Our modern Western lifestyle is not very good for this energy circuit, so it might take a lot of practice to get it to flow smoothly and effortlessly.
4. As with the other cycles, practice going both directions (down the back and up the front, and vice versa). Most people will find that one direction comes more easily than the other, but practice both directions until they are clear, smooth, and effortless.

Greater Ritual: Plugging In

In normal life, we usually understand our existence to be made up of three dimensions (and thus six directions): up/down, east/west, and north/south. Basic anchoring rituals, like the Greater Ritual of the Rainbow Star or the Lesser Ritual of the Pentagram, begin with you centering yourself relative to the six sacred directions. That is, you can remain grounded along the same vertical axis while reorienting your sense of direction from external dimensions (east, west, north, south) to internal dimensions (front, back, left, right). However, you can actually center yourself relative to any set of coordinates, geometric or otherwise.

For example, in this rite, you'll orient yourself at the center of many sets of dimensions. There's a lot of complicated visualization/energy manipulation in this ritual, which can take some time to perfect. At least, it took me a long time to get the trick of it. That's ok! This is one of those "fake it until you make it" kind of things. You'll feel it when it clicks in. I promise that you'll feel the connections "pop" when they're right.

At first, you're mostly just faking it, secretly wondering if there's something wrong with you that you can't do it "for real." Then, you kind of get into faking it, twitching muscles and breathing hard and whatnot, but you still suspect that you're "doing it wrong," because you don't really *feel* it. Then, there's a little mini-quake. You definitely felt something! "Wait...was that it? This shit is overrated." Then, all of a sudden, out of nowhere, it washes over you, all at once, and you're plugged in. That's what everyone was talking about! You can feel the connection.

In this ritual, we're invoking various powers. There are two basic ways to think about this: The first is that these powers are always present inside of you, and you're just tuning into them, making mental connections to them, getting "in the zone." The second method is to think of them as external powers that you're making contact with. There's a great deal of debate in the magical community about which is "right," which I don't really want to get into. Personally, I think that, in order to really make it work, you have to do both. In this chapter, I'm talking about it as if they're external, because the language is less complicated that way.

We're going to connect to fifteen powers/dimensions in this ritual, but you can add or remove them to suit your particular needs. By the end of this ritual, you'll be a World Tree[256] uniting all the powers. This ritual is longer

256 We'll talk more about the World Tree in Chapter Eleven.

and more complicated than many you've learned. It might feel overwhelming if you haven't been doing the exercises up to this point. If you're having trouble remembering the steps as you do them, I recommend making an audio recording of yourself slowly reading the instructions out loud. However, you should wean yourself off using the recording as soon as you can.

1. Start by *rooting*, using a method like the one in Exercise: Rooting on page 211.
2. Next, begin *centering in your heart*. Seriously, your heart needs to be the center of the motherfucking universe. To do this, start by making a fist with your left hand and putting it over your heart. Remain centered in your heart for the rest of the ritual (or, ideally, for the rest of your life).
3. Put your right hand on top of that fist, and press your fist into your chest, hard enough that it hurts your chest a little bit.[257]
4. Breathe in, concentrating your essence down, down, down into your heart. Feel the whole universe contracting down, down, down into your heart.
5. Eventually, when the pressure is at its limit, feel everything explode out, Big Bang style. Grow larger and larger, more and more diffuse, colder and slower.
6. Way, way out, at the outer circumference of the universe—past the black, past the cold, past the depths—the light of Ein Soph Aur (or whatever you call the Light Beyond the Darkness) shines. Hypatia called it μονάς (monas), or "singularity." Feel it radiating into the world, moment by moment creating it, the subtle, warm heartbeat of the cosmic background radiation (metaphor!).
7. Stretch up, up, up, becoming so large you fill the universe, becoming coextensive with all that is. Feel the Light Beyond Light filling you, warming you.
8. Shrink back down to your regular size, but maintain a shining cord of light connecting you to the outer edges, through the darkness, to the Light Beyond. The cord should "plug in" at the top of your head.
9. Feel the crystalline song of the stars descending through you, down your spine, passing through your heart (the center of the universe), and continuing down along your spine.
10. You might feel as though the flow is getting "stuck" at certain points. If that happens, try to imagine it like warm water, softly melting through

257 I learned this pushing trick from Jason Miller; it's very effective.

the obstruction, and it should flow past. If it's really, seriously *stuck* and won't move, you're probably going to need some help from some kind of energy manipulator. I've had excellent results with acupuncture, but Reiki is another good choice.

11. This energy should naturally collect and pool in your center. If you can't feel it settling, try very subtly tensing and releasing your abdominal muscles rhythmically, from top to bottom, in a ripple. Leave a reserve of energy there; we're going to use it to connect to all the other powers.
12. Let the energy sink the whole way down through your spine, exiting through your anus and sinking into the earth. Deep, deep down, through the earth and the rock, deeper and deeper, at the center of the world below, is the Heart of the World, the power of life and evolution and decay and renewal.
13. Feel all your tension and worry, all your filth and impurity and "sin" sink off of you, washed down into the earth, where it will decay and renew, being made clean again. Keep a cord/pipe running down into the *Heart of the World*, plugged into your anus. (Ha ha, she said "plugged into your anus.")
14. Turn your attention again to the pool of energy in your center. Send it down your *right leg*, sinking roots into the earth. Connect to your *maternal ancestors* (as literally or metaphorically as you want). Feel the love of your mother, and her mother, and hers, and Mother-love in general. Feel the unbroken flow of connection, mother to grandmother, back through time to All-Mother Eve (or whatever you want to call the First Human Mother).
15. Through her, connect to any goddess (or god) that descends and returns. And from Her into the Heart of the World. This is *not* the "universal brotherhood of man" kind of ancestry. It's your *personal* tribal ancestors. This is the pillar of order, of tribe, of safety. This is the pillar of love. We'll plug into universal human ancestry next.
16. Return to the pool in your center, and send roots down your *left leg,* tracing along your *paternal ancestry.* This time, we are going back further. Run back through your paternal ancestors (literal or not), paying special attention to any magicians. Keep going back, back, back to the Paleolithic era, the first emergence of people like us.
17. Find a magician there. Connect through them to Pan (or any other spirit of wild places), and from there, back to the Heart of the World. For me, this involves tracing back evolution though animals, back, back, back to the first single cell where life sparked. This is the pillar of chaos, of wild, of nature. The pillar of power.

18. Return to the pool of energy at your center. Reach out with your *left hand,* and grasp the hands of your *past*[258] *incarnations*. Feel how they've made you who you are. Remember what you learned when you were them. Pull this power back into your center, and let it pool there.
19. Reach out with your *right hand*, and lean into the waiting hands of your *future incarnations*. Feel how you've grown, how much stronger and wiser and more whole you are. Pull this power back into your center, and allow it to pool there, intermingling with all the other powers.
20. Expanding from your center, feel the great cross that unites you with the four sacred directions: left, right, front, and back. These directions are centered in you. As you turn, so do they.
21. For any other powers you choose to work with, connect them similarly with energetic umbilical (omphalic) cords plugged into your center. Pay attention to where on your body different powers connect.
22. When you are fully plugged in, relax completely, and hang on the cords for a moment, feeling them support you, knowing that you can trust them.
23. Slowly retract all the cords into yourself, and then retract your entire self down to a glowing ember at your center. Explode back out, bringing the universe into being. Repeat as needed.
24. Practice this ritual every day for a week, and then once a week until you can do it in ten minutes or less.

Circles as Boundaries

As we discussed before, a circle *is* the boundary in space between things which are "inside," because they are "near" to the center, and "outside," which is "far." In our everyday life, those categories *near* and *far*, or *here* and *elsewhere*, have no clear boundary. However, in magical circumstances, sometimes we want to be able to work separately in two different spaces without things mixing together. Sometimes, this is because we need a "clean room" in which to work delicate magics. Sometimes, it's because we're working dangerous magic, and we want to keep it behind a blast wall, just in case it blows up. Sometimes, it's because something scary is in the world, and we want to be safe from it. Sometimes, this is because we would like to summon someone or

258 They don't exactly go "in order," so *past* and *future* are not as clear-cut as they seem here. Don't worry about it too much.

something who needs a different "natural habitat" than we do. Sometimes, it's because we want to work in two worlds at once, without those works interacting.

No matter why you want to create a boundary, circles are almost always the easiest boundary to form. This is because they are natural boundaries between those places that are *near* and those that are *far,* with no other restrictions. On a more practical level, magical boundaries with corners tend to produce little energy vortices that are difficult to "keep clean," just like the corners of a room are where dust builds up.

In this section, we're going to focus on circles to keep things in. We'll work more with circles to keep things out in Chapter Eight, on protection.

How to Cast a Circle

So, now that we know why we might want a circle, let's talk about how to create one. Creating and enforcing a magical boundary is broadly called *casting a circle.* However, what most people imagine when they hear that phrase is actually an elaborate centering rite followed by a brief circle casting. Here, I'll present the simplest possible form of circle casting, which is casting a circle with yourself at the center. In general, it is easiest to cast a circle from the inside, even if you later step out, but it is also possible to cast them from the outside. If you're casting a small (tabletop) circle, "stand" with your index finger on your dominant hand, and center in your fingertip.

Exercise: Balloon Breathing

This exercise is intended to teach you how to expand and contract your energy body, which you'll need to be able to do for step three of casting a circle. You know how, when you first blow up a balloon, you stretch it out a couple of times first? This exercise stretches out your *energy body* (or whatever you call it) in preparation for expansion. In addition to being a good exercise, it's also very good for when you feel tired or dejected as a quick energizer.

1. Get comfortable and close your eyes. I do this sitting down, because I sometimes get a little dizzy when I do it, but you can stand up. While you can do this lying down, for most people, it's easier with the spine vertical.
2. Take a deep breath in, making your spine very straight. Feel your whole body fill up like a balloon; your stomach should be very round.
3. Breathe in and in and in until you're entirely full of air. You'll be amazed how much more air your lungs will hold than you usually put in them.
4. Hold the air in for just a moment more than is comfortable, and then exhale.

5. Exhale as much as you can, deflating your whole body like a balloon. Your shoulders should relax and your head might drop a little.
6. Keep your lungs empty for just a moment, and then repeat.
7. Once you've gotten a slow, steady rhythm, imagine that not just your belly, but your entire body filling up, getting bigger and bigger with every inhale, and smaller and smaller with every exhale. The goal is to shrink to a single point (like a black hole) on each exhale and to become infinite (bigger than the universe) on each inhale, but it's ok to just get "very small" and "very big."
8. Once you've gotten the hang of that (which takes quite a while)...
   * With each full-hold, rename yourself "Infinity."
   * And each time you empty-hold, rename yourself "Nothingness."
9. Whenever you're done, start taking smaller, more usual breaths, and return slowly to your regular size by naming yourself with your regular name as you breathe.

Exercise: Casting a Circle

Step One: Choose a Center

Decide where the center of your circle will be, and anchor there. It's better to not have walls or furniture or anything else intersect your circle, but if it's unavoidable, you can do it. It's just harder.

Step Two: Choose a Size

In general, you'll either want a small circle (around the size of a dinner plate) on a table for doing small work, like potions or talismans, or a circle big enough to move around in.[259] The size of the circle you'll want depends on what you're doing and where you're doing it, and on the shape of your particular body. It doesn't really matter how big you decide on, but it is important that you make a clear, firm decision about how big of a circle you are casting. Something is only a circle if the distance from every point on the boundary to the center is exactly the same the whole way around. Your circle does, in fact, want to be as close to circular as you can make it. It's best to take your

259 For most people, the minimum comfortable size for a circle is about as big (in diameter) as you are tall, and it's unusual to want a circle much more than twice as big as you are tall unless there will be a second person in there with you. For group circles, you usually want a circle a foot or two bigger than the one produced by everyone holding hands. That is to say, in a circle where everyone is holding hands, it should be difficult to leave the circle without your neighbors' consent.

time to cast a good circle, although I'll teach you a trick at the end to help correct for sloppy circle casting.

Particularly when you are first learning, it is *much* easier to cast a circle with a visible boundary, such as chalk or cornmeal, already in place before you begin casting. For public rituals, I like to "draw" circles with red rope, which I enchant for this purpose, and keep rolled up in a skein.[260] If you can't draw, can you set some crystals (or whatever) up at points around the edge to help anchor it? Even dropping a few coins around the circumference can make it much easier. If you cannot physically mark the boundaries of your circle, carefully trace the boundary with your eyes, and decide on some landmarks to help you remember exactly where it should be. In rooms where I often cast circles, I have strategically placed art on the walls to serve as anchors, but for beginners, larger, denser, three-dimensional anchors will help more.

Step Three: Tzimtzum

Tzimtzum (צמצום) is a Hebrew word that means something like "contraction" or "in-rushing" or "condensation." In Kabbalah, it refers to the first act of the Creator, when Xe withdrew partially into Xirself to create a void into which Creation could emanate. That's exactly what we're going to do in this step.

To start, stand in the center of the circle. Unless the work you are going to do with the circle is directional, it doesn't matter what direction you face. If you are in a room with only one door, you should probably start (and end) facing the door, all other things being equal.

Next, contract your sense of self into a dense, glowing ball in your center (which should also be the center of the circle—if it's not, move). Smaller, smaller, smaller! Shrink down to a single point (but it's ok if you can't get that small).

Then, reinforce the hard boundary between "inside" and "outside" that is your skin. For most people, it is easiest to use your hands to "paint" this second skin on from top to bottom, but whatever works for you is fine. If you haven't done this sort of thing before, it might take some practice to be able to maintain your concentration on being deep inside your body, but still controlling your body like a puppeteer. Just imagine it as hard as you can. You'll get the knack of it.

While remaining small, travel around inside your body, lightly bouncing up against your skin—the boundary between "you" and "other." If you feel

260 A circle *d* feet across requires about d+1 yards of string, which leaves plenty of string to tie the ends together if desired. (Because there are three feet in a yard, and pi is slightly more than three.)

yourself losing control, come back to the center and breathe until you're back to being a small ball. When you're very confident you know where the edges of you are, come back to the center, take a deep breath in, remind yourself that you are the place of the world, but the world is not your place, and....

Step Four: Expand

Do not explode. In a controlled way, expand your ball outward, completely filling your body, and pushing on that inside/outside boundary a bit. This may be slightly uncomfortable, and you may want to let go and be usual-shaped again. Don't. Stay a glowing liquid, filling your body and slightly puffing it out. Take a bit to steady yourself here. Feel the boundary you set on your skin before. Take a deep breath in, and....

Step Five: Expand More

Exhale again, pushing outward, expanding the "skin" you created before into a bubble surrounding you, just like blowing up a balloon. If you focus on pushing out from the center, it will naturally form a rough sphere, or sometimes an oblate spheroid. Once it is more or less spherical, and far enough away from you that your hands can't reach the edges, start to spin it, like a pizza, getting bigger. It might flatten out or it might not. Either is ok, as long as both your head and feet are still inside.

In general, circles intended to keep things in should be drawn clockwise and circles intended to keep things out should be counterclockwise, but these rules are *very* variable. In some circumstances, you'll want to stack circles with opposite orientations inside each other, but (because the opposing circles tend to fight each other) this requires some skill and practice. Keep spinning and expanding until you meet your preestablished boundary circle. Take a deep breath and....

Step Six: Reinforce

Take some time to anchor the boundary, so it will remain after you stop paying attention to it. That is to say, make sure the boundary has an existence external to you. If you are having difficulty with this, go back to Chapter One and repeat the color imaginings until you can externalize them. This is exactly the same skill as that. One easy way to maintain the boundary is to hand it off to a spirit ally. Some people use four allies, one at each cardinal "corner," but I find that unnecessarily complicated except in group work. Carefully withdraw back into the center of the circle, and make sure the bubble holds. For a stronger barrier, repeat the whole process several times. Once you're good at it, this whole process should take three breaths.

Step Seven: Do Whatever in the Circle

In general, we open circles for the purpose of creating a vessel to hold other magical work. Whatever that magical work is, do it. If you're just practicing circle building, just take a few deep breaths, relax for a bit, and then move on to step eight.

Step Eight: Release

Circles need to come back down at the end of a ritual. Depending on what you've done in the circle, you might want to contract the whole circle back into you. If you want the energy that's been inside the circle to come back into you, do this. Often, however, we use a circle as a cauldron to hold and shape magic that we want to direct into the world. This type of operation is often called "raising a cone of power," especially when done in a group.

For beginner magic, at the end of the working, there are probably two options to take a circle down. If the "target" of the work was inside the circle, you can just pop the circle, and allow the energy to drain out on its own. If the target is outside, carefully drill a small hole in the circle, which you can use like a nozzle to direct the power inside the circle toward a specific target at high pressure.

What Happens If I Cross the Boundary?

This is probably the most common question I get, and I understand why. Movies make it seem like if you accidentally step over a circle, a demon will grab you and eat you. This is highly unlikely. The most common thing that will happen, with a properly made circle, is that you will feel it "catch" a little, and the circle may leak after that. This isn't usually a problem for beginner magic, but it is a sloppy habit that will cause trouble in more sophisticated work. However, if your circle is not properly reinforced, it can pop like a bubble, and you'll have to start over.

Once you get better at casting circles, you can either "cut a door" to enter and exit (this is what I was taught to do, and my general recommendation for beginners) or you can learn how to "attune" a circle to your "frequency" so it becomes semipermeable, letting you through, but nothing else (this is what I do now).

Chapter Eight:

Cleansing and Protection

You are now more than halfway through this book. Up until this point, we've mostly been learning individual skills in witchcraft. From this point on, we'll be combining those skills into more sophisticated witchery, culminating in the dark mirror conjuration of Chapter Thirteen. In this chapter, we'll discuss a variety of types of magical cleansing and protection, which we'll need before we move into more sophisticated (and thus more messy/dangerous when they go wrong) magics.

In my experience, almost all beginner magicians banish too much and employ too much protection, and it greatly impedes their magical learning curve. Many people wrap themselves in layers and layers of magical protection, even in the absence of any kind of specific threat. In my circle, we call that "wearing plate mail to a picnic," and all it does is make you look like easy prey—a lunkhead who barely knows how to throw a punch but is still spoiling for a fight. People who are confident in their own power do not go around draped in protection.

We live in a dumpster-fire culture of rampant cursing. I can almost guarantee you've been cursed at least once in the last month. Every breath of air you take is swarming with germs, but most of them aren't a problem for most people. Similarly, for most people with healthy spiritual psyches, most of those curses are just background noise. Just as the best protection from disease is an intact skin and a healthy immune system, the best magic protection is to address your psychic trauma, clean and cover any open wounds, and live in right relationship with the world around you.

However, just like our physical health requires basic sanitation, similarly, our spiritual health also greatly benefits from regular prophylactic cleansing.

I recommend "casting off" (a simple cleaning process you will learn in a moment) and regular salt baths, instructions for which I will provide below. For most people, once a month is a good frequency. People in the public eye should try for once each week. People who attract a lot of negative attention, or who work in miasmically dense environments (like psych wards or prisons, for example), should bathe with salt every day.

Of course, there are times when more aggressive protections are called for. When in dangerous circumstances, your best bet is a single simple layer of protection. The *most* important kind of magical protection is simply to keep your wits about you and be prepared to react when something actually does happen. When something weird happens, don't be complacent, but also don't freak out.

Exercise: Casting Off

This exercise is best done while showering, but it can also be done without that. If you are in the shower, wash first, then cast off, then do a final wash. However, if you feel something psychically "stick" to you, do this as soon as possible, ideally while washing your hands and rinsing out your mouth. Do it again in the shower/bath before sleeping. Some people like to sing or pray while they cast off, which is nice, but not necessary.

1. Make clear in your mind why you are doing this.
2. Enter magical space/time/consciousness.
3. Anchor/center.
4. Wash your hands, ideally scrubbing them with a little salt.
5. Next, put your hands on top of your head (you can also do this part with a hair brush), and slowly run them through your hair, and all over your head and face. Rinse your mouth and spit the water out.
6. While you do so, review anything that doesn't feel like you.
7. Whenever you find something, grab hold of it and gently remove it. If that doesn't quite make sense, that's ok. You can pretend it's a metaphor until it does!
8. Continue scanning your whole body with your hands. It's better to scan from top to bottom, paying special attention to the back of your neck and your wrists, genitals, and ankles.
9. If at any point your hands start to feel hot, tingly, or itchy, wash them again and start over at the top of your head.
10. After you've made your first scan, review your day from beginning to end. Were there any times when you felt someone's ill will toward

you? Any other times when it felt like something punched you in the gut, psychically/emotionally?

11. Carefully investigate those times, and try to determine where the impact "stuck" in your body. Double-check those areas, and remove anything you find there.
12. Do one more physical scan, top to bottom, and then you're done.
13. This whole process shouldn't take more than eight minutes. If you are concerned you need more, you might follow this with a salt bath (or shower), in which I will instruct you next.

Lesser Ritual: Salt Bath

These instructions are for a bath, but you can also do this in the shower. You can do this ritual with any kind of salt, including plain table salt. However, my friend, student, and co-magician Avril Korman of Beautiful Freak Cosmetics makes a "Witch's Purification Salt" we designed to go with this ritual. It is black and scented with lemongrass, frankincense, and thyme. You can order it at the URL below. Personally, I like sandalwood soap for this, but any soap is fine. https://beautiful-freak-cosmetics.myshopify.com/collections/xtras-urban-witch

1. Begin by awakening the salt, but do not yet pour it in. You can use these exact words if your salt is black, but it is also better to speak your own words directly from your heart. If your salt is not black, you'll obviously need to modify them:

"Black salt, witch's salt, volcano salt,
awaken to your life and your purpose,
You are the velvet darkness and the moonless night,
Undriven by reckless desire,
Undriven by worry, by fear, by grief,
Undriven by others' urgency,
Black salt of the moonless night, I call you now to my aid."

2. Next, run a hot bath (or shower). Get naked, get in, and then awaken the water by saying something like:

"Water of the deepest seas, awaken to your life and your purpose,
You are the water of mystery, the water of the Ancient of Days,
Untainted by the work-a-day world,
Untainted by worry, by fear, by grief,

Untainted by the harm humans do to one another,
Water of the deepest seas, I call you now to my aid."

3. If you're taking a bath, now is the time to add the salt. If you're in the shower, you'll use it as a scrub a bit later on.
4. Wash yourself, and then cast off, using the instructions from the previous exercise.
5. When you're ready, think about everything you're trying to get rid of—emotional, psychic, spiritual, or otherwise. Speak aloud your surety that you are rid of it. Some generic words are provided, as an example:

"By water and salt am I made clean.
My guilt is washed away.
My worry is washed away.
My fear is washed away.
My grief is washed away.
I am newborn, clean and pure.
My inner vitality brings light to the darkness.
My inner light brings vitality to the deep."

6. If in the bath, try to get your whole body under the water three times. If in the shower, use the salt scrub top to bottom.
7. Soak as long as you like, and then rinse. Get out, drain the water, and exit the room without looking back.

Protection

The one kind of protection I think is universally useful is threshold protection—a barrier that delineates your space (such as your home) from public space, which I'll discuss a little more in the section titled "Threshold Protections." First, I want to talk about why I think prophylactic banishing is a very, very, very bad practice, and what I recommend instead.

Natural spaces, healthy spaces—including healthy human bodies—have dense and flourishing spirit ecosystems. I firmly believe that cultivating a healthy, harmonious, flourishing spirit ecosystem is more or less the same as cultivating a biological one. The ecosystem requires certain things in order to thrive. In the same way that overuse of antibiotics can throw off your whole microbiome, too much banishing can throw off your spirit ecology. As always, turn to visible nature to provide a model for invisible nature.

Energy, "elements," predators, prey, and decomposers are all important parts of a complete spirit ecosystem. In a small, semi-closed, newish ecosystem (like an apartment or house), the magician has to supply most of those things, at least in the beginning. For the most part, the older, larger, and less densely populated a space is, the healthier its spirit ecosystem is likely to be.

In a biological ecosystem, energy enters primarily in the form of sunlight, and that's one way it enters a spiritual ecosystem too. However, most of the "spiritual" energy in a human home is generated by the people (biologically). Music is another great way to add energy, as is fire, light, etc. While I don't understand the exact way it works, and I don't think anyone else does either, there's clearly some relationship between the "energy" that spirits need and actual "physics class" energy. Anyone who's noticed how fast batteries drain or tea goes cold in the presence of active spirit evocation knows that.

The "matter" that a spiritual ecosystem needs is by far the most confusing for me. I don't really understand why spirits want physical food, but it's clear they do. In my experience, it's the "caloric" aspect of food offerings spirits really crave. Fat, sugar, alcohol...maybe spirits are just really into the citric acid cycle? In my experience, while different spirits have their favorites, you can't really go wrong with an offering of grain covered in oil and honey. No wonder IHOPs are always haunted!

Kinds of Spirits in a Magical Ecosystem

I believe most healthy, well-functioning spirit ecosystems include spirits of all of these types:

* **Shining ones**, radiating energy in from the cosmos. I think other people would mostly call these gods, angels, saints, and celestials.
* **Wandering ones**, who circulate the energy, stirring it, creating currents and eddies, "cross-pollinating" things. These are the (non-solar, non-saturnine) planetary spirits, egregores, smaller gods, fairies, elementals, djinn, that kind of stuff.
* **Rooted spirits**, like ancestors and land spirits, help to hold everything together the way ground-cover plants prevent erosion.
* **Humans and other embodied creatures** are a kind of slow-wandering rooted spirit, and we play an important role, tending, creating, curating, and moving things around.
* **Hungry spirits**, like ghosts and shadows and demons. These guys have a bad rep, but they keep things circulating, and keep egregoric spirits

(including humans!) from getting too "puffed up." Like anything else, it's not ok to let them get out of balance.

* **Death spirits**, cool and cold and clear and sharp, cut strings. I mostly work with Ereshkigal, who tells me that, before she was the Queen of the Dead, she was Flint, the first knife.
* **Chthonic spirits**, who make their home within the earth, in the moist dark places, are the decomposers. Baphomet is great for this; I get the feeling that's really their whole schtick—they complete the cycle of life. These recycle all the "goo" and spiritual waste. Mushroom spirits are also good at this.

Now, there are also specific roles you need in an artificial spirit ecosystem (artificial systems can eventually "naturalize," but it takes years and years, possibly generations.) Some of the most important kinds to think about are:

* **Producer**, which is probably you. Because artificial spirit ecologies are very spirit dense compared to "natural" places, the system isn't anywhere near being energy self-sufficient. Someone/something has to consistently add energy. The easiest way to do that is with regular offerings of light, sound, food, and attention.
* **Distributor**, because you probably aren't going to make offerings to each spirit by name. If you can do that, there aren't enough spirits![261] You need to charge a spirit to take your offerings and distribute them to each individual spirit, giving to each what it needs/wants/likes. I use "The Wet Egg" for this (see the following section). Other great choices are any god whose mythology includes the phrase "knows the name of every god," like Hermes or Isis.
* **Doorman**, which is a spirit to regulate who comes in and out. Not a "Guardian," but just a spirit who knows who is coming and who is going. Threshold gods like Hekate are great choices here.
* **Bouncer**, or someone who can run off anyone who needs to get gone. Mine is dragon-formed.

261 Disclaimer: Many people, including some of my teachers, strongly disagree with this sentence. Lots of people like their home to be clean and Zen-like in its spiritual simplicity. YMMV.

Lesser Ritual: The Wet Egg

For me, an important moral precept—perhaps one of the most important—is that of *hospitality*. When someone comes to my home in need, I feel that it's incumbent on me to feed them. Pretty much the only thing that can excuse me of my host-responsibility is if they violate the laws of hospitality as they apply to a guest (for example, by attacking me or mine). When I was a kid, my parents never would have let a guest (announced or not) leave without offering them food and drink. I'm the same, including with spirits. Unless a spirit is actively and intentionally threatening, they're welcome in my home. For me, that extends even to spirits who aren't friendly or helpful. If they're hungry, I feed them. I only banish when I absolutely have to. All that being said, I'm not suggesting that you ought to be bound by the same moral precepts as me. However, if you'd like to try it out...

Here's How I Do It

On a raw egg, preferably white, I write "Please distribute our offerings to All" with a permanent marker (sometimes, if the marker tip is too big, I just write "For All"). I put the egg on a small plate and surround it with coins, beads, candies, spices, a tiny metal goat,[262] some crystals, and whatever else seems right at the time. I pour some rum, oil, and honey over it. Whenever any offering is made in the house (and whenever else I feel like I should), the egg gets wet (with liquor or oil) first. Every few months, when the egg is light or the plate is sticky or gross, I throw out the egg, wash off all the nonperishables, scatter down some candy and spices, and pour more rum/honey/oil over it.

My egg plate lives in my kitchen. I say hello to it when I come home and goodbye when I leave. *"Hello egg! I had such a shitty day today. I'm so glad to be home. Drink with me!"* or *"Hello egg! Today was great. Drinks are on me!"* or whatever feels right.

Exercise: IAO Shield

Sometimes you need an extra layer of protection *right now*. The Greater Ritual of the Rainbow Star is one good option, and you should be very fast at it by now if you've been practicing. But let's pretend that you haven't been. Here's an even simpler choice.

---

262 It's a token from a game called "Tiger and Goat," which I bought at a thrift store a long time ago. It was missing some bits, but I use the tokens for magic, so it worked out great.

* Draw your energy into your center.
* Stoke it, and then explode piercing blue energy while singing *"EEEEEEEEEEEEEE"* as long as you can hold it. You should try to feel the energy radiating out of your head.
* Take a deep breath, and radiate yellow, while singing *"AHHHHHH-HHHHHHHH"* from your chest.
* Take another deep breath, and stoke as much red energy as you can. Explode out a wall of red energy while singing *"OHHHHHHHHHHH!"*
* Repeat the sounds *"EEEEE AHHHHH OHHHHH, IAO, IAO, IAO"* several times, fast but still radiating the colors.
* Yell it one final time and radiate all three colors at once.

If that still feels too complicated in the moment, you can try this ultra simple version: Stoke white energy, and fill a bubble around yourself with it, while repeating, *"I stand in a circle of light that nothing may cross."*

This is simple and fast, but not very robust. The instant you take your attention off it, it will collapse. That is the value of practicing more sophisticated things like the Greater Ritual of the Rainbow Star; with practice, you build a memory for them not just in yourself but in the universe. There is an echo of them already there, just waiting for you to fill it back in. Spells such as the Rainbow Star have enough structure to them that they can retain their shape without you for at least a little while, while IAO Shield doesn't really.

Threshold Protections

The door (or doors) of a home is the main portal that connects your home to the outside world. It is your first line of defense to keep unwanted things at bay, and also the most natural place to enchant for drawing things in. It's hard to imagine, but it's very likely that, for most of human existence on earth, we lived without doors. The mists of prehistory are hard to pierce, but it appears that humanity's first doorways were closed off by leather curtains. A proper door—a solid panel that swings on hinges—is a relatively sophisticated piece of engineering.

We do know that, by the time of the earliest Egyptian tombs, doors were commonplace. They are depicted in the tomb drawings in both literal and metaphoric forms, as gateways to the Next World. Although doors have many purposes, including noise and light control, their primary functions are to control the access of humans and other living creatures to a space, creating a boundary between one space and another. These functions give rise to their magical potential: Doors are guardians on the boundary between your home and the outside world (and, to a lesser extent, guardians between one room and another). Doors are portals to another place. We'll mostly be talking about that first use, as guardians, in this chapter, because the construction of portals is a more advanced magical technique that beginners are unlikely to get much success with. If you'd like to try constructing your own portals, I recommend turning to fairy stories for instruction, and experimenting with mirrors as well as doors.

Throughout this section, I'll be referring to your "front door." Many homes have only one door to not-home—if this is the case, then that one is assuredly the "front" door, whether it opens into nature or into a public hallway. If you have multiple doors, the "front" is the one that appears to be the main entrance from outside, even if that is not the one most commonly used. For most purposes, everything we'll talk about here can be worked on any door, but there are a few rules that distinguish a front door from others. Perhaps most important is the old wives' tale (and, really, who is more witchy than old wives?) that you must always leave a home by the same door that you entered, lest you lose a piece of your soul within. In a similar vein, it is said that the first time you enter your own home, you ought to do so by the front door. This is especially true for new brides. Corpses must leave by the front door; to carry a corpse through a back door invites death to visit the home again. Finally, as we discussed in the previous chapter, remember that slamming doors angers house spirits; it's very bad luck!

To my mind, the most important sort of threshold magic is based in mindful animism. Every time you exit your home, bid it farewell, and ask the door to protect what lies within. Each time you enter, greet your home, and thank the door for its protection. In addition to being mindful as you cross the threshold, there are many other enchantments you can lay on it for protection, to draw luck, and to create a happy, welcoming, and harmonious home. In the pages that follow are some of my favorites.

The Gods of Doors

In Rome, many different gods of doorways were worshipped: Janus of the door, Cardea of the hinge, Limentinus of the threshold. However, to me, the most important god of doors is Hekate Propylaia, the Magician Who Stands Before the Gate. Hekate is the goddess of (among many other things, including magic) all liminal (boundary) places and times. I'll talk more about her special role in protecting doorways at the end of the chapter.

Janus, after whom the month of January is named, is often depicted as having two heads, one facing "in" and one "out" (of the doorway). Janus was a very important god in Rome, although he had no priesthood of his own. By extension, from doors, Janus became the god of all transitions, of beginnings and endings. Every public ceremony in Rome opened with an invocation of Janus. Like Saturn, Janus is a god of time as well as limitations, and there is reason to believe that in archaic Roman religion (before the empire), Janus was among the most important of all the gods.

Ritual: Blessing of Cardea

Some witches of my circle have a special devotion to Cardea, a lesser-known Roman goddess. She is Janus's wife and the goddess of hinges. In ancient Rome, the blessing on a home was yearly renewed with a ritual invocation of Cardea. Traditionally, this blessing was done only by women, but of course, your mileage may vary.

You will need:

* Water, in which you have soaked purifying herbs (such as verbena or pine)
* A clean cloth
* A branch of mulberry or hawthorn
* Olive oil or wolf's fat
* Three leaves of mulberry

Steps:

1. Begin by washing down your door with clear water in which you have soaked purifying herbs, such as verbena or pine, or you can use any all-purpose magical wash, such as a commercial van-van floor wash. For this ritual, the washing should be done with a particular motion, explained in the next two steps, from inside the home.
2. Hold the two ends of your cloth together, one in each hand, and place them on the bottom left corner of the doorframe.
3. Stretch your right hand out as far as the cloth will permit, and then bring your left hand to meet it.
4. Continue your way around the whole door, as if you are measuring it in cloth-lengths.
5. Once the whole doorframe has been purified, marking the boundaries of the portal into your home, use a branch of mulberry or hawthorn to lightly coat the hinges in olive oil or wolf's fat.
6. Next, three leaves of mulberry ought to be placed on the doorsill.
7. Finally, asperse (magically sprinkle) the door itself with pure clean

water, while reciting a prayer. As in all things, it is best to pray in your own words directly from your heart, but if you would like a formula to inspire you, you might say something like "*Cardea, Lady of the Hinges, care-taker of all who dwell within, wield your white thorn to protect us! Beloved of Janus, you have been given power over every doorway; you alone decide who enters and who cannot. Be faithful to us, Cardea, as we are faithful to you!*"

In addition to this blessing, you can call Cardea's favor to your door by hanging a sprig of hawthorn, her sacred plant, above the door. This hawthorn can be wrapped in red string for extra protection. For even more extra oomph, take two sticks of hawthorn, and tie them together in a cross with red string. Above the cross, hang a chaplet of thirteen hawthorn fruits.

Washing Your Doors

Whether or not you use Cardea's rite, the first thing you'll want to do, as you begin enchanting your home, is to wash the front door, in order to really "lay claim" to the place. When washing your door, you should work from the top down, and from the inside out, effectively sweeping all negative energies and unwholesome gunk right out the door. If you have a porch or sidewalk, you may want to sweep away from the house when you are done. This cleansing should be repeated every year in the early spring.

Door Protections

In addition to the options we've already discussed, like the Eye Against Evil and Hand Against Evil, there are many other ways to magically protect a door. Several of my favorites follow.

The Red Door

In many cultures around the world, it is traditional to paint doors red. In China, it is considered especially lucky to do the painting during the Lunar New Year's festivities in early February. In Ireland, a red door is thought to ward off the hangry dead and other malicious spirits. Many Jews believe that a red door symbolizes the blood of the Passover lamb, which wards off the angel of death. Christians have a similar belief that a red door calls on the power of Christ's protective blood. In colonial America, a red door was a sign of welcome, and red doors were used as an indication of "safe houses" on the Underground Railroad. Popular legend even has it that Albert Einstein painted his door red because he was so absent-minded, he often forgot which house was his. For all these reasons, now that I own my own home, I painted my doors with high-gloss red. I like to mix a few drops of dragonfire protection oil into the red paint. I also like to paint white crosses on my doors as a ward. You can read more about that shortly as well.

Dragonfire Protection Oil

The powder involved in this recipe can be stored for use, or added to a carrier oil, as we'll do here, which keeps longer. You can also add whole materia (magical materials) to the bottle. For this recipe, I like iron nails, whole blackthorns, and mirror shards. As in most recipes, you can make substitutions if needed.

You will need:

- Dragon's blood resin
- Cinnamon
- Black pepper
- Hot chili peppers
- Frankincense
- Ginger
- Sandalwood
- Dirt from the grave of a just warrior
- Ashes from a lightning-struck tree
- A dead wasp
- Carrier Oil

Steps:

1. The easiest way to make any enchanted oil is to start with a base oil—in this case, dragon's blood resin, which you'll place in an appropriately sized container.
2. Grind all the other materials very fine (I use an electric coffee grinder) until they are powdered (try not to breathe in the powder).
3. Add all the powdered ingredients to the oil.
4. Stir thirteen times, while thanking the ingredients for their help, and praying for protection. For this, a prayer to Saint Michael is a good choice or the Orphic Hymn to the Kouretes, but, as always, your own spirit-inspired words are best. If you prefer, you can pray directly to the ingredients as you add them.
5. Allow the oil to simmer at very low heat (a crockpot on "warm" is

ideal) for several hours. Do not strain the oil, but allow the "sludge" to sit at the bottom of the bottle. The oil will get stronger and stronger over time.

Another use for this oil is to awaken a small (or large) statue of a dragon as a guardian over your home. A small plastic toy works fine. Give it two names—a secret one that only you know and a use-name that is okay for others to know. Rub the oil into the statue, speaking to the dragon by both their names, and thanking them for guarding over your home. Place the dragon near your front door, looking out. Greet them by name and speak to them when you pass through the door, and encourage others (especially kids) to do so as well. Once a month, pour a little more oil over them, leave a small present (like a cookie), and always remember to say thank you.

White Cross Door Protection

After you paint your door red, you might want to add more protections. When I moved into my neighborhood, many of my neighbors were scared of me because I am a witch. As is so often the case, fear morphed into rage, and so I felt I needed a little extra protection. I painted white crosses on each corner of my red door, and more surrounding the doorknob and deadbolt (see picture). Things have settled down, and we're neighborly now, but my door crosses remain.

The first step in this spell is to prepare a magical protection and purification powder made from powdered eggshells. Similar preparations are often called *cascarilla* (which just means "shells") in Latin American traditions. Save your eggshells as you use the eggs (they won't smell, because the tiny bit of egg on the inside of the shell dries out before it can spoil), so you can later grind them into a fine powder. It can be made into a sort of chalk by adding some baking soda and water to form a dough, and allowing that to harden. But, for most purposes, I like the powder better.

You will need:

* Eggshells (powered)
* White paint
* Salt
* Paintbrush
* Kitchen sponge
* Permanent marker
* Scissors

* A cross-shaped stamp (optional)

Steps:

1. Grind your eggshells into a fine powder.
2. Mix some eggshell powder and some salt into your white paint. I use plain acrylic craft paint, but my front door is under a porch and behind a glass storm door. If yours is exposed to the weather, you'll probably want exterior paint. The exact amount of powder and salt to paint isn't very important. Use enough to infuse all the paint, but not so much it makes the paint thick.
3. To apply the paint, you'll want to make a stamp of an equal-armed cross. (You can also paint the crosses freehand, but the paint is difficult to control with the cascarilla and salt in it.)
4. On a kitchen sponge (the kind that stays soft when dry), draw a cross with a permanent marker.
5. Cut the shape out of the sponge with scissors. I particularly wanted a "primitive" look, so I didn't bother with doing too careful a job with the stamp. You could, obviously, make a much better stamp, or even use a professionally made one, if you wanted, but I like the way mine came out, looking homemade and extra witchy.
6. Stamp crosses onto each corner of the door, and anywhere else you'd like them.

The Witch's Broom

Imagine a witch. What is she holding?

The broom is perhaps the most classic tool of the witch. Yet these days, it is one of the ones least talked about. That's a shame, because it's an important and powerful aid to any witch. Traditionally, the witch's broom (or besom)[263] is made from a plant called "Scotch broom";[264] however, they can be made of anything and still work. American brooms are often made of broom corn, which is not related to maize corn; it is a kind of sorghum grass. The witch's broom is usually propped next to the front door, with the bristles pointed up, as a sentinel to protect the home.[265] It should be used for regular sweeping as

263 This is just an old-timey word for a broom. Historically, *broom* was the plant from which broom straws are made, and *besoms* were the tool themselves.

264 This plant is highly invasive in the American West.

265 Many modern Instagram witches say the bristles must be up because otherwise the luck will run out. Witchy old ladies know that resting a broom on its bristles bends the bristles out of shape.

well as for sweeping "energy" and spirits. For the most part, our ancestors did not own single-purpose tools, and I generally advise against doing so. Knives want to cut. Cauldrons want to bubble. Brooms want to sweep. Let them!

Any broom can be used for magic, but in what follows, you'll ideally want a natural bristle broom with a wooden handle. Some say that brooms ought to be made from ash wood, but I think any kind of wood is fine. Although I have several fancy, decorative witching brooms that have been given to me as gifts, the broom I actually use for magic is an O'Cedar "corn warehouse broom" in black. They cost around twenty dollars, and you can get one at most hardware stores. It is an excellent broom that holds its shape and doesn't shed bristles. In my experience, fancy witch brooms generally fail at being proper brooms, shedding bristles and making more mess than they clean. They are, however, of great interest to my youngest visitors, who love to ride on them.

The first step in enchanting your broom is choosing a name for it. The name of your broom should be kept a secret, known only to those who live in the home. Write the broom's name on the handle with a permanent marker. If you're extra (like me), carve the name of the broom into the handle, putting a tiny drop of your blood over the name. You may want to use an easy-to-carve magical alphabet for the name, such as runes or ogham, which you can learn online. While carving, silently meditate on why you chose the name you did. What qualities will your broom have? What work will it do? What are its strengths? What is its personality like?

The next step is to anoint the broom with oil while speaking its name to it, just like you learned to do with a poppet in Chapter Two. The most important part of this process is to love the object as a friend and ally. If the handle is sealed, you might want to sand it down first, so that it can absorb oil. Any magical oil below is a fine choice for this, but ideally, you'll want to use a flying ointment. Traditionally, flying ointments are made from entheogenic plants and used to induce ecstatic trance. Apocryphally, these ointments were applied to the mucous membrane of the vagina, often with a broomstick. Our witchy grandmas sure knew how to party! Unless you are a competent herbalist, it's better not to experiment too much with flying ointments, which can be quite dangerous.

After you've oiled and awakened your broom, stand or hang it bristle-end up[266] near your front door. When you leave your house, pick up your broom and hold it before you, facing the door. Say (something like), *"[BROOM-NAME], beloved broom, protect this house while I am gone, looking after all who live*

266 I was taught that storing brooms bristle end down lets the luck run out. However, it is also bad for the bristles to stand a broom on them.

here. No stranger, no ill wish, no illness, injury, or danger of any sort may enter. If they do, blast them! [when you say this, point the broom outward like a wand]. So says the one who awakened you, [MAGICIAN-NAME]!" Knock the handle on the door three times, then put the broom back, bristles up, and be on your way. Remember to greet the broom and say thank you when you return.

Okeanos

Beyond the planet Saturn (and also beyond Pluto, and also beyond our whirling galaxy's tutu fringe), but still part of Saturn's celestial sphere, is Okeanos, the great "river" that encircles "the world." He is, in some accounts, the eldest Titan, and in others the youngest of Protogonoi.[267] In his youth, he was in the waters of the Mediterranean, the cold depths of which the peoples of the Aegean islands could not yet safely navigate. In time, Poseidon conquered the Mediterranean, and Okeanos retreated to the Atlantic, always protecting his children, a boundary for them to push against. Time passed, and humans learned more, and sailed all the oceans. Okeanos retreated again, teasing, tantalizing, fleeing for the fun of being chased, but always waving, always swelling up, the source of thirst and refreshment both. Today, Okeanos dwells at the bottom of the sea and the deep reaches of space, and in all the other boundaries, physical and imaginal, that humans push against. Wherever there is an avant-garde, Okeanos is there, quarry and hunt-leader both. There is no end, and no beginning. There is only the known and the unknown, and Okeanos's delicious cutting edge between them.

Okeanos's River of Protection Spell

Sometimes, there are people who are bad for us. Sometimes, it's their fault; they're malicious, evil, and want to do us harm. Sometimes, it's less intentional; they're broken and full of poison, which is just leaking out onto us. However, no matter the reason, there are times when you just want to keep a person away from you. You don't necessarily want to hurt them, but they need to keep the fuck away, physically as well as energetically/spiritually/psychologically. This magic is designed to create a sort of "bubble of protection" that keeps them and their shit away from you and yours. It's important to include your home

267 The "first born" gods of ancient Greece, traditionally including Xaos (Chaos/Chasm/Space), Gaia (Earth/Matter), and Eros (Love/Gravity), and sometimes others.

and "affiliates" in the mix here, too, because otherwise, there is some danger that badness aimed at you might splash off onto someone else.

The way I've constructed this particular spell, anything headed your way is deflected into the nearest body of running water, there to be washed out to sea. It's effective against most kinds of malicious magic, but particularly proof against stuff that arises from "hot" emotions like anger. There is almost no risk of damage to the person who you are protecting yourself against, and also little risk of "blowback" onto others in your vicinity; the work is grounded into the groundwater and eventually washed out to the sea. This work is not recommended for people who live in the desert.

The work centers on Okeanos, one of the oldest gods of Greece. Ὠκεανός is the primeval water god of Greece. Hekate tells me he is her father,[268] although few classical sources concur with this. Unquestionably, he is the father, with his sister Tethys, of the Okeanides and the Nymphs, genii locurum goddesses who guard over sacred pools and springs. In the *Iliad*, Hera seems to think of Okeanos and Tethys as her foster parents: "To the ends of the generous earth on a visit to Oceanus, whence the gods have risen, and Tethys our mother who brought me up kindly in their own house."

In this charm, we call on Okeanos to create a circle of watery protection around you, a circle of running water that the "restrained" party cannot cross. Any energy they send your way (intentionally or not) falls into the boundary river and is washed out to the sea, where it diffuses (and de-fuses) into the depths. The spell is worked with the ikon of Okeanos drawn by Brian Charles, which I have included here, from my book *Orphic Hymns Grimoire.*

You will need:

* A pen with black ink
* Colored markers or pencils
* A printout of the Okeanos ikon
* A small bowl of saltwater (ocean water is great, but tap water with table salt in it is also ok)
* A white candle (a tea light is fine)

Steps:

268 Parentage among the gods, who are incorporeal, is generally at least partly metaphoric.

1. Enter magical space/time/consciousness.
2. Preform the Rainbow Star or any other balancing ritual.
3. Using the pen, write your name on the chest of the Okeanos ikon, as though you are held in Okeanos's arms. Encircling you are the ouroboros snake of protection and Okeanos' river, which is the root of all water on earth.
4. Outside the circle, write the name or description of whomever or whatever is threatening you. They cannot cross the ring of water. Any spellwork or energy they send your way is trapped by the water, diverted into the groundwater, and thence washed out to sea.
5. Read Okeanos's hymn (my translation is given right after this spell) aloud.
6. Color the ikon while speaking to him, asking him to protect you.
7. Place the candle on top of your name, within Okeanos's arms.
8. Dip your fingers in the saltwater, and trace along the circle of the ouroboros snake, beginning at his head and proceeding clockwise. Be sure to get the whole circle wet, which may require wetting your fingers several times.
9. Once you've got the whole circle wet, wet your fingers one last time, and make at least three complete circuits without picking your finger up, while saying aloud:

   "Okeanos, sea snake that encircles the world, encircle me, my home, my family, and my livelihood in your mighty waters, protect and defend me from all attack. Any incursion by those that threaten me, send it away. Sink it to the deepest depths, let it diffuse into the water and lose all of its power. If my enemy comes by, turn them away. If they ill wish, let the wish be diverted into the waters. If they curse, let the curse be drowned at the bottom of the sea. Turn them, and all their works, away, away, away! They cannot cross your encircling boundary; they cannot cross your running waters. Any ill wish, any energy at all, if it comes from my enemy, turn it aside, and give it to the waters.

   Let your daughters, the Silver Maidens of the Springs and Rivers, dewdrop clad, with hair of seafoam splash, let them ensnare it in their spider-silk shawl, let them sink the tangled mess into the waters below, its fires all are gone out. Let it pass through the ground and be grounded, let it rish and rush, burble and bubble down through the streams, rubbed clean and smooth and safe, like sea glass; all its sharpness gone, transformed into a thing of beauty. Let it wash out into the waters and be gone. Let it come to rest at the bottom of the sea, cold and beautiful, a glittering magical treasure that can do no one any harm. There let it rest until it is found, and let it be a blessing on the finder.

Okeanos, Lord of the Great Waters Below, Lord of the Great Waters Above, Great Water Who Encircles the World, encircle me in a river of protection, and keep me safe and whole and strong."

This spell is also great to work with children. Begin by telling them the following story about Okeanos. Next, have them write their name in the center of the chest, and their "enemies" outside, as usual. (You can write it for them if they are too young to write.) Then, have them color in the picture while talking to Okeanos about their problems and asking him to help them feel safe.

Orphic Hymn LVIII, for Okeanos

Imperishable ocean, to you we now call,
Eternal Okeanos, undying Father of All.
Gods and humans both arise from your infinite flow
And all things Above begin deep Below.
You encircle the earth with great heaving surges
Eternal blue depths where every river converges.
Wellspring of water nymphs, source of the sea,
Birth waters of the Earth, awesome and holy,
Hear us, blessed one, sumptuous divine purifier,
And rain down on our planet all we require.
Your watershed reaches the ends of the earth,
Your encircling boundary is death and rebirth,
Great Father Ocean, grant your initiate's pleas:
Gift your favor forever, as vast as your seas.

Four Protection Charms of Hekate Ereshkigal against Fear

Brimo as an epithet of Hekate Ereshkigal appears in a fragmentary katabasis (Underworld descent) ritual in the PGM (LXX:4–25). It presents four separate charms, all of which fall under the general category of being "against fear." The first two are incantations against attack to be used as protection when traveling the Underworld. The third is less clear, but appears to be a "password" to be used in three different circumstances: First, one uses it at a crossroads to gain entry into the Underworld. Second, it can be said at bedtime to incubate a dream. Finally, it can be used to ward off death. The fourth and final incantation can be used as a curse, to cause sleeplessness and worry, or to ward off such a curse. The text of the ritual fragment appears below in italics:

[Four Charms] of Hekate Ereshkigal, Against Fear of Punishment

The "punishment" in the title is punishment in the Underworld, both after death and also while traveling in the Underworld while yet living, the distinctive skill of the mage. This is an especially potent charm for those who have been trained since childhood to fear the Underworld.

First Charm, to deflect fearsome spirits:

If it comes forth, say to it: "I am Ereshkigal, the one holding her thumbs, and not even one evil can befall."

It is not clear from the text who/what is expected to come forth. Some scholars believe that what might "come forth" is Hekate herself, and others, that it is a sort of Underworld demon. I, however, understand this to be an all-purpose banishment/protection spell for use against any kind of malefic being, particularly effective against the so-called Dweller on the Threshold and other fear-based apparitions.

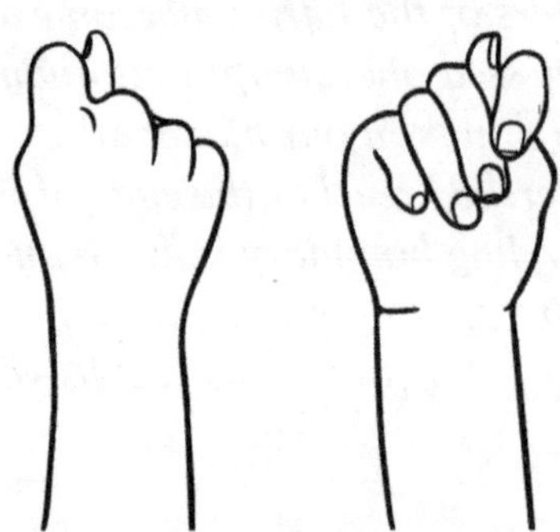

"Holding the thumbs" is a magical gesture of protection mentioned several times in the PGM. I make it by balling my hands into fists, with my thumb protruding between the index and middle fingers. This gesture has been used since ancient times to mean something more or less like "fuck off" in a variety of Eastern European cultures, from Italy[269] to Ukraine. Charms in this shape were quite common in ancient Rome, and continue to be so across the

269 Where it is called the *fica* in *mano,* or "fig hand."

Eastern Mediterranean. I understand this charm to basically say, in modern English: "I am Ereshkigal, who tells every evil spirit to fuck right off."

Second Charm, to protect against attack, if the first one didn't work:

> *If, however, it comes close to you, take hold of your right heel and recite the following: "Ereshkigal, Virgin, Bitch, Serpent, Wreath, Key, Herald's Wand, Golden Sandal of the Lady of Tartarus." And you will avert [them].*

Personally, I cannot hold my right heel and remain standing. I hold the pose at left instead. I understand this charm to be an exhortation to "cosplay" the goddess Hekate Ereshkigal by shapechanging to wield all of her sacred symbols that follow. This same list of symbols appears in a hymn to Hekate, found in PGM IV:2241 ("Document to the Waning Moon"). In this spell, the list is used as a mnemonic to call to mind the full form of the goddess.

Third Charm, to enter the Underworld, or to incubate a dream, or to avoid death:

[Say aloud:]

> *"Askei kataskei eron oreon ior mega semnyer bayi phobantia semne, phobantia semne, phobantia semne. I have been initiated, and I descended into the (underground) chamber of the Dactyls, and I saw the other things down below, Virgin, bitch, and all the rest."*

Say it at (the) crossroad, and turn around and flee, because it is at those places that she appears.

Saying it late at night, about what you wish, it will be revealed in your sleep.

If you are led away to death, say it while scattering seeds of sesame, and it will save you.

There's a lot to unpack here. The "askei kataskei..." formula is a common one, sometimes known as the *Ephesian Grammata* ("words from Ephesus") or the Orphic Formula. So common was it that the phrase *askei kataskei* came to be slang for "magic" in Greece, just like the English phrase "hocus pocus." Here, it probably functions as a sort of "password" that verifies the speaker's status as an initiate of the mysteries. No one knows for sure what the Ephesian words mean. Many scholars claim they are nonsense words, but I do not think that is so. I think they are from a lost protolanguage retained in this cult context. I have been taught that the first two words are *askei* (from ἄσκιον), meaning literally "without a shadow" or metaphorically "empty threat" and *kataskei* (from κατάσκιον) meaning "shadowed" (as something under an overhang). The rest of the words' meaning, you will have to win for yourself, as an Underworld initiate of Hekate Brimo.

The Dactyls[270] were a group of (often ten) mythic magician-priests of the Great Mother. They taught metalworking, mathematics, writing, and magic to the new gods and, later, to humans.

The initiatory descent into the underground chamber is one you should have now undertaken many times, starting with the Grany Trance in Chapter Two. If you have never done so before, ask Hekate to show you the way to the chamber of the Dactyls, and there show you the sacred signs.

Fourth Charm, a Curse, and a Counter Curse:

[Say aloud:]

"Phorba phorba Brimo azziebya."

Take bran of first quality and sandalwood and vinegar of the sharpest sort and mold a cake and write the name of NN upon it, and inscribe it in such a way that you speak over it, into the light, the name of Hecate, and this: *"Take away his sleep from this NN,"* and he will be sleepless and worried. Against fear and to dissolve [a spell] speak through two knives loud-sounding this spell; but against evil animals it does not work compellingly.

Phorba (φορβα) appears several times in the PGM, almost always in relation to Hekate. It may be a secret name of Hekate, but it is unclear what it means. It may be related to φορβ-ειά, which means "halter." It can refer both to the halter that ties a horse to a manger, and also to a small leather band that was part of musical pipes, acting as a "stop" to prevent them from playing too loudly. If so, then the name relates clearly to the operation at hand, which is to halter or stifle someone, making them sleepless and worried, or to ward off such a curse.

Brimo (Βριμώ) is usually translated as "angry" or "scary." It derives from the word βρέμω (bremo), which is Thracian, and was imported to Attica by way of Thessaly. βρέμω means to "roar like a wild animal," but it can also mean to "roar like a bonfire." In addition to the use of Brimo as a

270 Their name means "the fingers."

name of Hekate, the epithet was also frequently applied to both Persephone and Dionysus, and occasionally to Kybele (Cybele) and Ares. Hekate Brimo's largest cult center, however, was at Pherae (Φεραί) in southeastern Thessaly. Nearby is the sacred Lake Boebeis, where Hekate Brimo "laid her virgin body at Mercurius's [Hermes's] side." A much later scholiast relates that Hermes attempted, at Lake Boebeis, to rape Hekate, who let out a bloodcurdling scream that frightened him off, earning her the name Brimo. However, I do not think that is so. There is nothing in the original text to suggest that. I believe Hekate Brimo and Hermes were lovers. It's an important coupling, because it's neither a marriage nor a rape. It's two "confirmed bachelor" deities coming together as lovers, for one encounter, initiating each other, without violence or hierarchy. I think it's an entirely different kind of a scream.

Chapter Nine:

Malefica and Curse Breaking

We live in a culture of ubiquitous cursing. I can almost guarantee you've been cursed at least once in the last month. We curse in traffic. We curse when we read the news. We curse ourselves, our loved ones, our livelihoods, and our homes with false oaths, sloppy magic, and indiscriminate intimacy with monsters. In this chapter, you'll learn to curse when need arises, and (perhaps more importantly) you'll learn how curses work so that you can learn to diagnose and unweave them.

For the most part, however, curse diagnostics and breaking are *not* beginner skills. What you'll learn in this chapter isn't witch doctoring, it's witch first aid. If, when reading this chapter, you suspect you have been seriously cursed, you should begin prophylaxis, but in the case of a serious curse, you will likely have to seek help from a trained expert. Generally, it is much easier to break curses from the outside.

Many beginner witches worry that their curses will rebound on them as some sort of moral retribution from the universe. That's nonsense. Curses do not rebound back because of any cosmic ethical system. They rebound because of sloppy casting. In fact, all spellwork is prone to splashing when it's messy; the effect is simply more noticeable and less desirable with malefica. Splashing doesn't just cause unwanted issues; it also drains power out of your spell. Be precise and cast cleanly. If you have not been practicing thus far, this isn't the chapter to start with.

A final note before we dive in: The exercises in this book are things I think will help you learn, but they're entirely optional. However, in this chapter, there are no exercises, because cursing isn't really a thing you should practice without meaning it.

Malefica and Curse Breaking

What Is Malefica?

Malefica is "bad" magic which is intended to cause harm, what some people (with a less sophisticated understanding of color magic) might call "black magic." In this chapter, you'll notice that, for the most part, I use the terms "malefica," "cursing," and "banework" interchangeably. So, what makes some magic malefic and other magic not? I'm not going to define that for you. It's really one of those "I know it when I do it" type situations.

Magical Ethics

Like everything else important, magical ethics are complicated, messy, and deeply personal. Broadly, I do not think magic comes with its own set of ethics. If something would be wrong to do without magic, it's just as wrong to do with magic. For example, I consider coercive "love" spells unethical for the exact same reasons I consider date-rape drugs unethical. If you find yourself in need of some ethical guidance, I'd recommend starting with that offered by Hillel the Elder: "What is hateful to yourself, do not do to a comrade."

If you would like an in-depth discussion of magical ethics, my comrade and coven-brother Dr. Matthew Valentine, a professor of ethics at Duquesne University, has prepared an optional lecture for you, which you can watch on YouTube at the link:

I have distilled much of the common wisdom about cursing I have learned over the decades into the following seven aphorisms, which should be considered as generic advice for beginners, rather than immutable rules.

1. **People in glass houses oughtn't throw stones.** Be sure you're well rooted and in right relationship with most other people (human and otherwise) before cursing. Having guilt or shame weighing on your heart is the most common cause of splash back when cursing.

2. **Choose your target(s) carefully,** name them precisely, and link to them as tightly as possible. Do not try to curse large groups of people or abstract forces. Such curses are not impossible, but they are complicated, messy, and not for beginners.
3. **Curses are a dish best served cold.** Don't curse in the first flush of anger. Wait until you've calmed down enough to take a rational look at the situation.
4. **Curse like a lawyer, not like a sailor.** While you are in a cool, rational state, write a script and stick to it once you are working the magic. Do not extemporize curses. This is *not* an "it's the thought that counts" situation.[271] Be sure you are saying exactly what you mean, not more and not less. After you write a curse, check it carefully for loopholes. Sleep, and then check it again.
5. **There are forces lying in wait for your invitation to do harm,** and those forces are just as happy to hurt you as someone else. Be careful not to accidentally invoke spirits of blind rage, hate, or vengeance. They will fuck you up.
6. **Cleanliness is next to godliness.** Immediately after cursing, dispose of any materials, ideally in a metal dumpster, and carefully wash your hands. Cast off, and ideally take a salt bath, before going to sleep.
7. **The Moon, when waning, is good for bane-ing. Mercury Retrograde is the sly curser's aid. Mars direct, the Just protect.**

Prosecutory Cursing

In my opinion, the best kind of curses for beginners to cast are those curses which function by bringing the target's bad behavior to the attention of relevant divinity, and sending that spirit to torment them. I call these "prosecutory" curses. Because these curses are often written, we have many ancient examples of them. They have many names and forms, depending on their culture of origin, but they all function basically the same way.

1. Explain what wrong has been done to you.
2. If known, name the perpetrator. If not, describe them. One common formula in historic examples is something like "*...whosever has done*

271 In truth, I am skeptical that there are such situations.

this thing, whether man or woman, whether slave or free, whether Pagan or Christian..."

3. Ask the god to punish them.

What follows is a general template upon which you can construct your own prosecutory curses. If you're not comfortable doing that and need step-by-step instructions, you're not ready to be casting curses. Go back to Chapter One and practice writing your own spells first.

1. Calm down. If you are still too traumatized to control your emotions, you should not be cursing. You can get someone else to do it for you, or wait until you are ok.
2. If you are partially culpable for the crime you are cursing in response to, seek absolution before cursing.
3. Choose a single divine ally to work with. This should be someone with whom you have an established relationship. If you'd like to call more than one (not recommended), assign one as "project manager."
4. Prepare a protective talisman of some type for yourself.
5. Begin by creating sacred space/time/consciousness in your usual fashion.
6. Light a fire. An outside fire is better, but a tea light in the sink is also ok. As always, use appropriate safety precautions.
7. Call a divine ally(s). Use names and titles related to the work. For example, if you are cursing a business, you might call "Mercury, Meddler in the Marketplace..."
8. Pour libations. Since this is an established ally, you should know what they like, but wine, eggs, honey, and oil are almost universally appreciated.
9. Describe the injustice you are seeking to avenge. Be clear, specific, and graphic, but do not get emotional, and do not suggest punishment. Simply describe the situation; stick to giving the facts.
10. Raise energy however you desire. Sex, singing, dance, pain, tai chi, etc. As the power peaks...
11. In your most magical voice...
12. Read your petition aloud.
13. Burn the petition. Scatter the ashes, either on the wind or into water. Ideally, scatter them in natural running water, but either the wind or down the drain is fine. Down the toilet is good for many types of curses.
14. Thank your allies, the fire, and any other forces you called on.
15. Exit sacred space/time/consciousness in your usual fashion.

16. Wash your hands and face.
17. If you are having trouble coming back, sprinkle some salt on your head and then take a shower.
18. Ground fully into your body, including drinking water and eating something, even if it's just a small snack.
19. If you have nightmares the night after cursing, pursue additional cleansing and protection.

An Example of a Prosecutory Curse

This curse, presented solely as an example, calls upon Lilith to curse Daesh (a.k.a. ISIS).

Lilith, Lamashtu, Night Monster, Lilith, Lamashtu,
Screech Owl, Lilith, Lamashtu, Howling Desert Wind: We cry out to you.
Your desert is being defiled. Daesh, the trampler, Daesh, the bigot, Daesh tracks filth across your holy places.
Lilith, Lamashtu, Fury of Woman. Lilith, Lamashtu, Scorned One.
Lilith, Lamashtu, Demon Queen: We cry out to you. Your women are being defiled. Daesh, the rapist, Daesh, the enslaver, Daesh tracks filth across your holy bosom.
Lilith, Lamashtu, Flail of Fire. Lilith, Lamashtu, Silent Death by Night.
Lilith, Lamashtu, Blackest Scourge: We cry out to you. You are being defiled. Daesh, the cowardly worm, Daesh, the excrement of dogs, Daesh tracks filth everywhere they go.
Howling Wind, Warlike Daughter of Night, Fiercest of the Sisters,
Lilith, Lamashtu, we summon you! Avenger of Women, Enemy of the Sons of Oppression, Lilith, Lamashtu, we summon you!
Demon Queen, Poison-Wife, Queen of Darkness, Lilith, Lamashtu:
Wipe Daesh from the earth!
With fire and wind and scouring sand, flail the flesh from their bones!
Empower their enemies, give strength to those whom they seek to destroy!
Lilith, Lamashtu, Flint-Bladed Knife of the Night,
Only their blood will make you clean again,
Only their deaths will bring back balance.
Only their utter destruction will right the scales.
Kill them, O Lilith Lamashtu! Kill the defiler. Kill the rapist!
Scourge them, O Lilith Lamashtu! Scourge the enslaver!
Scourge the oppressor!

Pour out their blood on the sands, O Lilith Lamashtu!
Let it trickle into your dark places.
Crush their skulls with your stones, O Lilith Lamashtu!
Let their brains sink into the sands.
Scatter their organs to the scavengers, O Lilith Lamashtu!
Let vultures and jackals feast on them.
Scour their bones with sand and wind, O Lilith Lamashtu!
Let their corpses be forgotten.
Lilith Lamashtu, Demon Queen, Screeching Owl,
Howling Desert Wind, erase them and all they have wrought.
Lilith Lamashtu, Ancient One, Nameless One, Oldest Power of Darkness,
Eat their souls, pale and powerless, whining ghosts,
that they may never know peace!
Eat their souls, that they may never be born again.
Eat their souls and be sated. Eat their souls and be avenged.
Eat their souls and return to your Underworld home.

Nemesis and the Furies

Our guest lecturer in this chapter is Nemesis (Νέμεσις), a Greek goddess of reparations. She is a sister of Tyche (Latin: Fortuna), the goddess of fortune. When blind luck is too blind, Nemesis sees with wide-open eyes. When things are out of balance, she balances the scales. Her name derives from a word for "fair distribution"; Nemesis is the righteous anger that unfairness engenders, and she is also the just retribution that punishes it. She is often described as the goddess who punishes ὕβρις (hubris).

Although ὕβρις is the origin of the English word *hubris*, they don't mean exactly the same thing. In English, *hubris* implies excessive pride, but the ancient Greek concept of ὕβρις was different. Aristotle[272] defined it this way, saying ὕβρις:

> "*...consists in causing injury or annoyance whereby the sufferer is disgraced, not to obtain any other advantage for oneself besides the performance of the act, but for one's own pleasure; for retaliation is not [ὕβρις], but punishment. The cause of the pleasure felt by those who [enact ὕβρις] is the idea that, in ill-treating others, they are more fully showing superiority. That is*

272 *Rhetoric 2:2*

why the young and the wealthy are given to [ὕβρις]; for they think that, in committing them, they are showing their superiority. Dishonor is characteristic of [ὕβρις]; and one who dishonors another slights him; for that which is worthless has no value, either as good or evil."[273]

In English, I think the best translation for that is "bullying."

When she is understood as the goddess that punishes bullying, Nemesis is restored as a glorious and powerful goddess of the people. That her name, in our speech, has come to mean "enemy" is a byproduct of how deeply ὕβρις is wound into our culture. So much of our popular entertainment glorifies shaming people for personal gratification; this is the very definition of ὕβρις. We have been trained to believe that Nemesis is our enemy, but she is the goddess who upholds equity and punishes bullying. Don't forget who the real bullies are. On the next two pages, you'll find my translation of the Orphic Hymn to Nemesis, as well as her ikon, from *Orphic Hymns Grimoire*.

Orphic Hymn LXI: Nemesis

I cry out to Nemesis: goddess, all-seeing queen,
Who sees into the hearts of all mortal beings.
Eternal one, exceedingly venerable, holy, august,
Delighting in Dike, ally of the just,
Shapechanging shifter, quixotic, dynamic,
Chaotic, confusing, perhaps even erratic,

273 Aristotle, *Aristotle in 23 Volumes, Vol. 22,* translated by J. H. Freese (Harvard University Press; William Heinemann Ltd., 1926).

Your word's ever changing and under discussion—
A long, winding road, but arcing toward justice,
For you hear every care in the hearts of mankind,
And the fear of you weighs on each mortal mind,
The overproud psyche, and the promiscuous liar,
Can try to escape you, but finds no safe harbor.
You see all, you hear all, you judge every lie,
Justice dwells in your heart, O daemon most high,
Come, blessèd one, mystic friend of the wise,
Give good intent wings, cut down hateful lies.
Replace unhallowed thoughts and contemptuous feeling;
Stop the fickle, flip-flopping wheeling and dealing.
Blessèd goddess of fairness, please heed our cry,
And to your task, mighty Nemesis, now fleetly fly.

Lesser Ritual: Renunciation

This ritual need only be done once, unless you are in the habit of casting a lot of ill-advised curses. Make it special. Read all the directions before beginning. The different phases should be done on different days.

Make a list of every curse you remember having cast in the past and why you cast it. Make note of any you wish to remain active. If you can't even remember why you cast a curse, you should let it go, which is what we'll be doing in this spell. It's ok if you can't remember everything. The goal is to make a specific list of curses that you don't want to renounce. I recommend you always err on the side of liberation.

Once you've completed your "keep them cursed" list, gather some supplies.

You will need:

* Paper—brown paper bags are a traditional choice.
* Colored pencils or another way to draw a picture.
* A lighter or matches.
* A large, fireproof cauldron, bowl, or pot,[274] preferably with a fireproof lid.
* A lot of salt, preferably sea salt.

274 I use a cast iron Dutch oven as my "cauldron." It is probably my most-used magical tool.

* At least a cup of living water; that is, water collected directly from a natural source, such as a lake, river, ocean, or rain. For this particular spell, water collected during a heavy thunderstorm or ocean water would be ideal, but any water, including purchased spring water, will work.
* Two hours of uninterrupted time. The spell can be done in two phases up to a week apart, but it's easier to do it all in one go.

Phase One

Set a timer for eight minutes. During that time, meditate on the nature of enslavement and coercion, including how and why they're bad for everyone involved. Feel the weight of your actions, in this lifetime and all others, and how they oppress and enslave others. If you can't summon up some regret about how you, in this lifetime and others, have ever oppressed and enslaved others, I encourage you to do some reading on economics and then try again. When you can feel your guilt upon you, take about half an hour and draw an image representing that regret. You can draw whatever you choose.[275] Do your best to capture your feeling in the picture. When you are done, make a donation to a cause that feels appropriate. It should be enough to hurt, but not so much that it makes you unable to care for yourself and your family.

On a piece of scrap paper, draft an oration (magical speech). This work can be emotional. It's critical that you have a script to stick to. Your speech should hit all the key points below, but it's *important* to do this in your own words, speaking Truth directly from your heart.

1. State your full name, and explain, in your own words, your intent (which is to release curses that you have cast).
2. Individually reinforce the curses on the people you want to stay cursed, by name, saying something like "*[NAME], my curse is still upon you. You are not released. I curse you to ____ because ____.*"
3. Something like: "*Every other curse which I have cast, in this or any other lifetime, I release. All others whom I have enslaved, in this life or any other, I set free. I regret my actions.*"
4. Something like "*I give this sacrifice in token of my regret, in lieu of restitution, which I cannot make.*"
5. "*This I do sincerely and completely, of my own free will, and without expectation of reward.*"

275 I (badly) drew a person in chains.

6. When you're happy with your oration, copy it onto the back of your drawing in your best handwriting. Sleep at least once before moving on to phase two.

Phase Two

This phase is best done outside, in daylight. Put about an inch of salt in the bottom of your cauldron. Open magical space, time, and consciousness. Meditate on your guilt until it arises like a lump in your throat. When you feel as though you have to scream, read your script out loud, and then set it on fire. Scream if you still need to. Drop the paper into the cauldron. Be sure it burns completely, down to the ashes. If possible, cry onto the ashes. When the ashes have cooled, scoop them up into your hands, along with some salt, and massage that into the top of your head. Save the salt, and take it inside with you.

When you're ready, take a hot shower, scrub yourself down, from head to toes, with the ashy salt. Take a salt bath before you go to sleep.

Diagnosing Curses

While different types of curses present differently, there are certain signs that are common across most types of curses. The first is nightmares. These are *so* common that I am extremely hesitant to ever diagnose cursing in their absence. Nightmares that involve being bound can be especially indicative of cursing, in my experience. However, most nightmares are not a symptom of a curse. Other symptoms—not quite as ubiquitous as nightmares, but still common—include unusual headaches, sudden and unexpected mood changes, bad luck, repeated unusual electronics glitches, and (especially for competent magicians with proper threshold wards) unexplained damage to the threshold of your home (broken doors, loose porch tiles, etc.). Mirrors or photos of ancestors and beloved dead that spontaneously fall off the wall and break are also a classic sign of curse activity.

As I've mentioned, most curse diagnostics and curse breaking are outside the scope of a beginner book. However, I will introduce some common curses and offer some first aid recommendations.

Common Curses

In my experience, there are certain types of very common curses in our culture, so be on particular lookout for these. Note that these are examples that I've seen in my practice. They may or may not match up with what you experience. This list isn't intended to be in any type of order.

The Evil Eye and the Wicked Tongue

As we briefly discussed in Chapter Three, the evil eye is a type of curse fueled by jealousy. Belief in the evil eye is present in many cultures worldwide, but it is especially prevalent in the eastern Mediterranean, the Near and Middle East, and the Indian subcontinent. Although less familiar to gentile Americans, the related belief in the "wicked tongue" (called ערה ןושל or *lashon hara* in Hebrew) operates primarily the same way, although it is cast via jealous talk, rather than jealous glances. In fact, the phrase *lashon hara* can also mean "malicious gossip" among less superstitious Jews. The two curses function similarly and can be cast, diagnosed, treated, and prevented in similar ways.

Casting the Evil Eye

When you intend to cast a curse, the evil eye is not an especially good method. It's difficult to control and target, and almost always involves some amount of splash back. It's not by chance that people who routinely evil eye others tend to be deeply bitter, miserable, and unlucky people themselves, and most are also prone to "mystery" diseases.

1. Be looking at your target, directly in their eyes.
2. You can also mediate this curse through live video or even a poppet, but it's harder.
3. Enter magical space/time/consciousness.
4. Build energy in your womb loop.
5. Stoke the hate, jealousy, and rage within you.
6. Swallow it into your belly.
7. Pretend the energy you built in your womb loop is a fire and your hate, jealousy, and rage are boiling in a cauldron above it.
8. Boil it, under pressure, until it explodes up and out your eyes.
9. Feel the energy shoot, like hooks, out of your eyes.
10. Attach the hooks into the pupils of the target's eyes, and yank, hard.
11. Detach the hooks from yourself.

12. Walk away.
13. Get clean.
14. Confess your wrongdoing.

Curing the Evil Eye

Generally, I recommend that the first step in most curse breaking should be diagnosis, but the truth of the matter is that it is almost unthinkable that there exist humans who haven't been the victim of the evil eye or the wicked tongue. We live in a culture of ubiquitous cursing. The symptoms of the evil eye are difficult to distinguish from other types of cursing, but generally include nightmares, excessive clumsiness, and sudden, unexplained drama with friends and family. Eye issues, such as unexplained itchiness or blurry vision, are particularly common.

In general, I find it's not really worth it to try to figure out who evil eye'd you and why, but if you're being repeatedly cursed, it might be worthwhile. In Greek folk magic, cloves are used both for diagnosing and treating the evil eye. To diagnose, seven cloves are burned over a candle flame, one at a time. If they burn silently, all is well. The more popping there is, the worse the curse. Some people say you can also name a specific name before burning a clove, and see which person's clove pops to determine the guilty party. Personally, I do not fully trust that method.

The salt bath you learned in the previous chapter will clear out most minor/accidental curses; this is just a slightly souped-up version specifically for curing evil eye. I recommend it about once a month, unless you are someone who gets cursed a lot,[276] in which case you might want to do it weekly. Full moons and Saturdays would be good for this bath, but really, any time is fine.

Note: This bath does not smell especially good. Use a muslin tea bag to avoid making a mess in the bathtub. If you do not have a tub, you have my sympathies. You can make this up as a salt scrub to use in the shower instead. The proportions are quite flexible.

You will need:

* 4 parts garlic peels
* 1 part thyme
* 1 part cloves
* Salt (a lot of salt)

---

276 Some examples of people who get cursed a lot: very pretty people, debt collectors, mental health professionals, etc.

Steps:

1. Combine the garlic, thyme, and cloves together in a muslin tea bag, and add them to the bath water.
2. Stir the salt into the bath, making sure it dissolves.
3. Carefully wash yourself from top to bottom, paying careful attention to your head, face, hands, genitals, and feet.
4. As you wash, be very cognizant of your intention to remove all curses and crossed conditions.
5. If you would like words to say, here are two options:

Option 1:

"Holy Virgin, Queen of Heaven,
Mother of God, Mother of All,
take me under your sky-blue cloak,
and protect me from all evil.
Avert, avert, avert!"

Option 2:

"Thea Euryphaessa, Queen of Heaven,
Holy Wide Shining One,
Mother of the Dawn, and the Moon,
and the ever-unconquered Sun,
Yours is the eternal Aithre; yours the clear blue sky,
Yours is the vision of prophecy, yours the all-seeing eye.
Shine your light upon this bath.
Send evil away, along with wrath!
Avert, avert, avert!"

Oath-Breaker Curses

Our culture does not have a healthy relationship to oaths; we do not take them seriously enough. For most people, the most highly ritualized oaths we swear are marriage vows. Indeed, I don't even like to attend weddings, because I know I'll be asked to witness an oath—usually one I think is unwise.[277] Breaking

277 In almost all cases, I think marriage—an antiquated patriarchal rite designed to transfer ownership of a woman from her father to her new husband—is a bad idea.

those vows has magical consequences. The most common symptom of an oath-breaker's curse is anxiety, and the next is repeated betrayal by friends and loved ones. Joint pain or rashes, particularly in the wrists and ankles, are also common. A sudden inability to keep plants alive is another common symptom, but is not always present, and is difficult to diagnose in people who didn't have a green thumb to start with.

To "cast" an oath-breaker curse, you're really just prosecuting a contract the target already swore to. Use the prosecutory method you learned earlier in this chapter, appealing to whatever spirit(s) sealed the original oath.

The Begging Bowl, Chastity Belt, or Ball and Chain

Similarly to the chains of silence, which we will discuss shortly, these curses also appear on the spirit body, and are quite common in witches, magicians, and other spiritual people. They are three separate curses, but they very often present together.

* The begging bowl, which is usually chained between bound hands, is a poverty curse. It manifests most often as repeated financial self-sabotage, and sometimes also bad financial luck. It sometimes also causes wrist and finger pain that shoots up the arms.
* The chastity belt, which is the variant I most commonly encounter, causes a lot of weird sex hangups, and sometimes fertility issues, unexplained rashes (especially on the back), and atypical hair loss.
* The ball and chain are usually attached to the left foot and can cause issues in the ankles and knees, as well as an almost compulsive need to caretake others. It can also exacerbate breathing issues. It is very often entangled in other traumas caused by childhood abuse by authority figures, which can be more difficult to cure.

I am almost 100% confident that these curses occur because of repeated past lifetimes swearing to "poverty, chastity, and obedience." Once diagnosed, they are very easy to cure by ritually renouncing the oath, which can be done using the Nullification of Oaths ritual that follows, or another renunciation ritual. However, the victim will still have to break the habits they've developed as coping mechanisms.

Nullification of Oaths: Fuck It All and Fucking No Regrets

The ritual is loosely based on two Jewish rituals, the first called *Tashlich* and the second *Hatarat Nedarim*. The ritual requires four people (even if only one person is annulling; they need three witnesses). I see no reason the witnesses need to be physically present; I think video conference will suffice, but in person is more fun. At the end of the rite, each participant is freed from any and all ritual vows or oaths she has made. This includes but is not limited to vows made to oneself, vows made to other people, and vows made to nonhuman beings. If there are vows you do not want to nullify, write a white list before beginning and be sure to keep them in mind during the performance. Before beginning, each person should privately develop a sigil to represent what they wish to renounce.

For best results, it's best to have at least four humans old enough to understand what is going on, a natural body of water, and a patch of dirt for this ritual. Each person should have a green apple, a red magic marker, and a piece of matzoh, ideally stale and left over from Passover. If you can't assemble all of those things, just make do with what you have. It's important to pick a bright day when it is pleasant to be outside. It's better to skip this ritual or modify it to be indoors than to do it in unpleasant weather. As written, there's a leader, but that's just for logistics. Anyone can read any part. Feel free to adapt the language to suit.

Leader: *"In your hands, you hold the Bread of Affliction. It was the Bread of Slavery in the House of Bondage, and it is now the Bread of Obligation. With your sign of red, it becomes all oaths, all sin, all regret. Whatsoever oath you renounce, whatsoever sin you regret, whatsoever it is you cast off, write it on the Bread of Obligation."*

Everyone should draw their sigil on the oh with the red marker. Wait until everyone is done writing before moving on.

Leader: *"Inheritor of a Living World, we call you into Supernal Beauty. Break your bonds, and feed the waters of liberation! Like the tree that sheds its leaves, let go of those things that can no longer nourish you. Like the serpent that sheds its skin, wriggle free from anything that holds you back. As you throw these things into the living water, know that you pledge nothing, are bound by nothing, are bathed in Nothing, awash in the Wild Dark. Repeat after me! I pledge nothing. I am bound by nothing. I am bathed in Nothing. As I say it, so do I become."*

Participants should break their matzoh, throw the pieces into the water, and say: *"I pledge nothing. I am bound by nothing. I am bathed in Nothing. As I say it, so do I become."*

When everyone is done, hand out the apples. No one should have an apple while anyone else (including the leader) still has matzoh.

Leader: *"In your hands, you hold the Fruit of Life. It was the Fruit of Paradise in days gone by, and it is now the Fruit of Hope. With its seeds, it becomes all resolutions, all goals, all hopes. Whatsoever resolution you make, whatsoever goal you pledge yourself to, whatsoever hope you cherish, whisper it to your apple as you eat."*

Wait until everyone has eaten their apple. Each person should eat their whole apple down to the core, which should be put aside for later in the ritual. If you cannot eat apples, choose another fruit.

Leader: *"Wanderer in the Wild Darkness, you have stepped into the Boundless Light. Plant your seeds. Like the tree that aches for the sky, your hope grows strong. Like the rain that lusts for the silent earth, your goals are met in joy. Light without Limit pierces the veil, and you are enlightened. Take the Boundless Light and hang stars of wonder in the Dark."*

Leader: *"May everything be permitted to you; may everything be forgiven you; may everything be allowed you. Repeat after me: Everything is permitted. Everything is forgiven. Everything is allowed to me!"*

All: *"Everything is permitted. Everything is forgiven. Everything is allowed to me! Selah and Amen."*

Everyone should plant their seeds. In my circle, we often plant them all together, and then plant an apple seedling on top of them. When everyone is done, join hands, spin, and laugh until dizzy and exhausted. Spinning and laughing is not optional! It's what seals the work. Making merry afterward is encouraged, but not strictly required.

The Chains of Silence

I see this curse most often in older women,[278] but it is common in all demographics. To me, this affliction appears as chains, or sometimes barbed wire, wound around the person's throat. It is sometimes accompanied by thyroid problems or other throat or neck issues. I believe that it is related to being silenced as a child—typically, being prevented from talking about traumatic experiences.

I will first describe how I diagnose and treat it in someone else, and then how you might treat it at home, if you suspect you may have this issue. I have never done this work on myself, but I would imagine it is harder to do on yourself than someone else (as most curse breaking is). This work may be too advanced for beginners, but you can't really hurt anything by trying. The worst thing that will happen is nothing. If it doesn't make sense, come back to it after you've finished the book. The skills you will learn in the final chapters will help.

How to Diagnose Chains of Silence (or Similar Curses)

For this exercise, you'll need to work with an ally with whom you have a relationship. Asclepius is excellent for this work, although I usually work with Merlin, who has given me a sort of tricorder/dowsing rod for when we do this work. You might ask for a similar diagnostic tool. It is extremely important to work with a trusted long-term ally for this, and to do a lot of grounding first, to be sure that you're not projecting your own issues onto other people.

1. First, enter into the Underworld (as, for example, in the Granny Trance), and contact an ally you work with for diagnosis.
2. Examine the soul-body. While not relevant to this particular affliction, always be sure to check the feet and ankles. I often find bindings there. To me, this affliction presents as chains or barbed wire wound around the neck, but I do not know if it will appear that way to you or not. Examine the area. Most often, the chains have grown into the flesh in a very unwholesome way, like they would into a tree. Sometimes, they can be almost completely covered.
3. Examine the chains to see if they are attached at any other points. Sometimes, there is some involvement in/near the heart chakra as well. If there is, you may need a more complicated healing than what follows.
4. Once you have examined the area, call Our Lady of Sorrows. This is

278 Older women are strongly overrepresented among my clientele.

not a spirit I usually work with, but she taught me this technique, and so I work it with her. If you are strongly opposed to working with her, I imagine you could work out a similar technique with another goddess who weeps over her child, perhaps Demeter of Eleusis.

5. When she has come, ask her to tell you about the chains, what caused them, and how they can be removed. In general, I would not share this information with a patient.

As I said mentioned, in my experience, these chains are a curse laid on little girls, most often by their mothers, when they are not permitted to speak about something bad (often sexual abuse) that has happened to them. Generally, when performing this work for other people, it's better not to describe what you see to them in too much detail, as it can be very triggering. Just explain that you see a curse related to them being silenced, and you would like to remove it.

How to Ameliorate

Before you begin the work, explain to the patient that you will be working on unbinding their throat and unsilencing their voice, and that they may feel pressure on their neck while you work. Make sure they know to tell you if it becomes too much and they want to stop or take a break. Tell them that the most common feeling they will have is a "lump in the throat," such as accompanies grief, and that they may experience unpleasant memories. Advise them that the best thing they can do is to try to observe in a detached manner. It is very tempting to reach out and try to grab at these memories: "Oh no! My grief! I need that!" Advise them to avoid that as much as possible. However, make sure they know that they can stop you at any time, and that if they ever feel like they want you to stop, even if they can't talk, they should gesture or tap you. Many people will not feel anything.

1. When everyone is ready, return to the Other Place and ask Mary (or whomever) to cry on the chains. This will transform them into rose vines (with thorns).
2. Begin to unwind the rose vines very slowly and carefully. Try not to tear the surrounding area, but some tearing is inevitable if they are really overgrown. You might not be able to unwind all of it in one session.
3. When you and/or the patient have had enough, use a magical knife to cut the vines.
4. Take the part that you have removed to a disposal location, such as a naga pool, volcano, or abyss. *Do not* leave it lying around, because it can slither like a snake and reattach (or attach to you).

5. Return to the patient, and call Hygeia (or another healing deity who carries a cup). Have her wash the wounds from her healing cup.
6. Then apply yellow energy (mine is in salve form) to promote healing. Oftentimes, the patient's power animal will appear and lick the wounds clean.
7. "Bandage" the wound with white energy, which I think of as cloth dressings. Sometimes, Theotokos offers her veil for this purpose.

If necessary, repeat the procedure at a later date, but allow time for healing in between. (I would say at least a month.) Tell the client that they might expect dreams related to this, but to report if they are having nightmares or if they develop any throat-related illnesses.

How to Cure Chains of Silence on Yourself

If you have experience with the sort of work outlined above, I think you could use a very similar procedure on yourself. You may wish to call all the allies at the beginning, and instruct them all before beginning. However, if you do not feel you are up to that (which I wouldn't have been as recently as five years ago), then I think you can probably do this:

1. Begin by journaling about the silencing that you think caused the affliction. Get out as much of it as you can.
2. When you're done, burn the paper.
3. Prepare a salt bath, as salty as you can get it (if you do not have a bath, you can just wash your neck with saltwater).
4. Light a candle, and get in the bath.
5. While bathing, recite a prayer to Our Lady of Sorrows (googling "Our Lady of Sorrows novena" produced several nice results, all of which are too Christian for me, but maybe you'll like them).
6. Repeat this process each day for nine days, ideally while the moon wanes.
7. Close with the hymn to Hygeia, which follows.

I would imagine you would probably need to repeat the entire process three times (i.e., do the novena for nine days ending on the dark moon, and then do that again for the next two months). If you do this work yourself, please report back to me on how it goes.

Orphic Hymn to Hygeia

Ever-blossoming Queen of All,
Many-blessed All-Mother, Hygeia, I call.
You banish all injury, affliction, and illness
And cause every home to blossom in bliss.
Every craft lusts after your ordering hands,
Reaching out, ever gentle, you plumb the dry lands,
Saving those souls that Hades would destroy,
And filling up every house with the fullness of joy.
You're hated by Hades, who plunders the souls of the living.
Eternally thriving, your prayers are life-giving,
Without your holy magic, your guiding spells,
Humans lives drift, bobbing like corks on the swells,
In the absence of you, Plouton's gifts lose their sweetness,
And human old age brings only hardship and weakness.
For you alone hold such power over peasant and king.
Multi-mysterious Goddess, your praises we sing,
Defend us from sickness and all leaden pain,
Let us bask in your light and rejoice in your reign.

Chapter Ten:

Oneiromancy

Guest Teacher: Pasithea the Trance Goddess

Pasithea (Πασιθέα), whose name means "All Vision,"[279] is the youngest[280] of the Graces,[281] a daughter of Aphrodite[282] by Dionysus, and the mother of Morpheus (god of dreams). She is a goddess of trance and is related to the ancient Minoan Poppy Goddess. Known only from surviving statuary, the Poppy Goddess of Crete is found in many sanctuary spaces, both public

279 It can also be translated as "acquired goddess," or even, perhaps to stretch it a bit, as "entheogen."

280 Some say she is the eldest.

281 Some say she is a Nereid (a kind of mermaid-like daughter of the sea).

282 Some say Hera is her mother.

and royal. Very little is known with any certainty about the Poppy Goddess, but she appears to have some ties to the Mistresses of Eleusis,[283] Demeter and Persephone. Poppies are an ancient symbol of the Eleusinian mysteries. When I visited in February of 2015, many people, including the concierge in my hotel and the taxi driver who took me there, told me that spring came early to Eleusis, by way of the sacred cave through which Persephone reenters the world after her time in the Great Below. That was my experience: in February, Athens was chilly and gray with nothing in bloom, but the fields of Eleusis were covered in blood-red poppies.

There is also not much about Pasithea in classical literature, save for a story where Hera sells her to Hypnos for a favor and one in Nonnus's *Dionysiaca* wherein, during a weaving contest between Aphrodite and Athena, Pasithea spins Aphrodite's wool. As we discussed in Chapter Two,[284] spinning is deeply associated with trance in almost all cultures; like many types of monotonous "women's work," the activity itself induces a mild trance,[285] independent of any magical intent.

Pasithea is a goddess of all types of altered states of consciousness, ranging from relaxation and meditation to drug trance and hallucinatory states. Personally, I associate her most closely with the hypnagogic trance—the liminal state between wakefulness and sleep.

She would like to teach you a meditation for relaxing and opening yourself to dream and vision. In this meditation, you will imagine yourself to be in the bed she shares with Hypnos. This meditation is also good to help you sleep if you are having trouble.

Pasithea's Bed Imagining

It is easiest to do this meditation in your own bed, but it can be performed anywhere, especially once you are good at it. Your eyes should remain closed

283 Eleusis (modern Elefsina) is a sacred site in Greece, about twenty kilometers west of Athens. It was the ancient seat of the Eleusinian Mysteries and the central cult cite of Persephone and Demeter. The most profound spiritual experience I have ever had occurred in the Plutonion Cave in Eleusis.

284 If you have not yet mastered the Granny Trance from Chapter Two, now would be a good time to review that. If you have not been doing the exercises, you might find yourself struggling a little bit with this lesson. Some of these techniques take time and practice to master, and learning isn't always linear. It's ok to pick and choose the parts that appeal to you; however, many of the techniques in this chapter build upon those previous skills.

285 Personally, I find dish washing quite trance inducing.

while working this. Among the many virtues of this meditation is that, because it is entirely nonvisual, practicing it helps build your other inner senses. If visualizations begin to arise before your closed eyes, gently dismiss them, and return your attention to your other senses, and to Pasithea's bed.

Close your eyes, and connect to your breath. As you breathe in, know that the air you breathe in was exhaled by the trees and plants, and that your exhalations give them life. The air you are breathing connects you to every other living thing. All life shares in the cycle of respiration—the eternal breath of the earth. Feel the air around you. The air is cool and slightly damp, refreshing and comfortable. A slight breeze caresses you, carrying the scent of forest and river. It is dark, the velvet black surrounding you like a lover's embrace. No light can enter this cave; it is always and ever and always unseen, but deeply, deeply known.

You are snuggled into a soft bed. Feel the silken smoothness of the sheets, and the comforting weight of the soft linen covers. Stretch your body. Wiggle your toes. Take delight in your body. Smell the clean, bright, slightly floral scent that lingers on the bedclothes: jasmine and pine and an herb you can't quite identify, green and fresh and magical. Smell the flowers that twine around the bedposts and form a thick carpet around the bed: morning glories and hops, night blooming jasmine, poppies, marijuana, mugwort, and valerian. Smell the smoke of the fireplace, redolent with cherry and applewood. Hear the fire hiss and crackle. Listen to what it has to tell you. Perk up your ears to hear the water cascade at the cave's entrance, from whose fountainhead the lazy Lethe[286] burbles her distant lullaby, carrying every care away. Know that you are safe here. This is the bed of Pasithea and Hypnos, the goddess of trance and the god of sleep, and you are here as their honored guest, to partake in their blessed gifts.

Recall, this is an imagining, not a journey. You're just imagining being in Pasithea's bed. The experience is entirely subjective; it's literally all in your head. At the end of the lesson, we'll discuss how to start making the jump to the intersubjective Other Place where Pasithea's bed[287] actually is, but being comfortable with this exercise will help make the transition smoother. Obviously, you should not journey to Pasithea's bed (or anyone else's bed) without permission.

---

286 The river of forgetfulness, also called Ameles, or "unmindfulness."

287 I don't think this is Pasithea's actual bed that she actually sleeps in. She's not an embodied person who sleeps in a bed. Think of it more like her "landing pad" or "lobby."

Oneiromancy

What Are Dreams?

Dreams, the fantastical experiences we have when we sleep, are mysterious and not entirely understood. And yet, they are among the most natural of human activities. Evidence of human fascination with dreaming goes back as far as evidence can go. In the earliest collections of written stories, from Sumer, we have accounts of the dreams of gods and men. And yet, although dreams seem so quintessentially human, they are not exclusive to humans. Studies have observed signs of dreaming in every mammal studied, including monkeys, dogs, cats, rats, elephants, and shrews. There have also been signs of dreaming in birds and reptiles. Indeed, there is good reason to believe that all amniotes (what used to be called "higher vertebrates") dream.

Many theories have been proposed to explain what dreams are. I have roughly classified "explanations" of dreaming into the following categories:

* **Biological Processing:** Many theories suggest that dreams are simply a side effect of the brain's natural processes. Certainly, it is the case that not dreaming enough is very bad for you.
* **Memory Processing:** Some say dreams help with processing and organizing memories and experiences. This is evident when we have dreams that clearly recall events of the few days before.
* **Emotional Processing:** Other dreams help us manage our emotions by providing a consequence-free environment to "try out" things we're worried about in waking life.
* **Psychological Processing**: Many psychologists have proposed that dreams reflect our unconscious back to us.
* **Spiritual Processing:** In almost every culture, everyone knows that some dreams represent communication from spirits outside of ourselves.

I am generally of the opinion that all of the above explanations are partly true. However, since this is a book on witchcraft, we'll be focusing almost exclusively on dreams' role in spiritual processing and magic. We all know that dreaming is among our most powerful magical acts, but it's one that is under assault in our society. A culture that glorifies pervasive sleep deprivation has *stolen your dreams* from you. In the first part of this chapter, I'm going to talk about taking them back, which is a necessary first step to oneiromancy (dream magic).

Improving Sleep to Improve Dreaming

Almost everyone knows—and science backs this up—that a lot of us aren't getting enough quality sleep.[288] Most healthy adults need from seven to nine hours of sleep per night; fewer than 3% of adults can remain healthy if they are regularly getting less than six hours a night. Healthy young people need more, and healthy older adults need slightly less.

If you wake up refreshed and ready to tackle your day, you're likely getting enough sleep. However, if you dread your alarm or find yourself nodding off in the afternoons and evenings, you are almost certainly not. A wide variety of health concerns can be dramatically improved by proper sleep. Getting good sleep can improve memory, focus, mood, anxiety, metabolism, and energy, as well as reinvigorate a low sex drive. Chronic sleep deprivation increases risk of heart attack, diabetes, obesity, and stroke. Sleep is important, and long-term sleep deprivation is never a good idea. Almost all oneiromancy (dream magic) interferes with proper sleep. You should make sure you have at least two nights of good sleep in between oneiromantic experiments. This is particularly true for us older folks. Below are some charms to help with occasional sleep issues. If you routinely have trouble sleeping, you should see a doctor about it. Before we move on to dreaming, here are two quick and easy spells for better sleep, adapted from the Greek Magical Papyri for modern witches.

Bay Leaf Sleep Charm, Inspired by PGM CXXIII

1. Find a large, dry, unbroken bay leaf.[289]
2. On it, write[290] the magical characters shown here and the words θάρρος θάρρος ("courage, courage").
3. Place the bay leaf under your bed (or under your pillow), and you will find restful, healing sleep free from all nightmares.

288 All data in this section is from the 2014 National Sleep Foundation Study.

289 Generally, in Greek magic, bay leaves are associated with Apollo, and I would expect that is the case here as well.

290 I use a black fine-point Sharpie marker.

Charm Against Insomnia (Evil Sleep), Inspired by PDM[291] XIV:706–710

You will need:

* A jar
* Dried dates, diced small (enough to fill the jar)
* 11 whole cumin seeds
* 8 whole star anise
* 3 strings of saffron
* 1 whole nutmeg
* Whole cow's milk
* Blender
* A glass of warm wine or milk
* Ground marijuana (optional)
* Heavy cream (optional)
* Almond paste (optional)

Steps:

1. Pack a jar about 7/8 of the way full with dried dates, diced small.[292] Pack them in tightly; do not leave too much space in the jar. But remember to leave some room in the jar, so it doesn't shatter if it freezes during later steps.
2. Add eleven whole cumin seeds, eight whole star anise, three strings of saffron, and a whole nutmeg. Simply add these on top of the dates. Do not stir them in.
3. Fill the jar with just enough whole cow's milk to barely cover everything. While you pour, think about the cow who jumped over the moon, and the great cow-eyed Queen of Heaven. What if those are the same creature? Imagine the milk of creation streaming from her breasts, streaking across the sky in a stream of stars. That it be cow's milk is important both symbolically and chemically. If you're not into cow's milk, I would just skip this recipe entirely. For extra potency, simmer ground marijuana in heavy cream, and use that in place of some of the milk.

---

291 PDM are the Demotic Magical Papyri, which are like the PGM (Greek Magical Papyri) except they are in Demotic instead of Greek. Demotic is a late form of ancient Egyptian writing.

292 It's better to purchase whole dates and dice them yourself. Pre-diced dates are often coated in stuff like rice powder to keep them from sticking. While that's not a deal breaker for this, it's better not to introduce extra stuff without need.

4. Allow the jar to sit, refrigerated, for three nights, while the moon is full. If it is cold enough to keep milk from spoiling, you can leave it outside under the moon.
5. Remove the star anise and nutmeg, pour the entire jar into a blender, and blend until a smooth paste is formed.
6. Form the paste into small balls, about the diameter of a quarter. This is easier if you chill the paste first. If it is too thin, add a little almond paste.[293]
7. The balls can be stored for a week or two in the refrigerator, or frozen for long-term use.
8. Dissolve one ball into a glass of warm wine or milk and drink it at bedtime. It may not entirely dissolve—don't choke on it.

Icelandic Spells for Sleep

The Icelandic grimoire called the *Galdrabók*,[294] written in the late sixteenth century or early seventeenth century, gives several spells to ward off insomnia. The first, most simple one simply calls for the magician to write *"MILANT VA VITALOTF JEOBOA FEBAOTH"* on a scrap of paper and secret it into the nightcap or inside the pillowcase of the sleepless person. It strongly cautions that the target must not know, and my experience is that it is not very effective to use on yourself.

The next spell, however, I have used to good effect. On a piece of alder wood,[295] carve the following symbols, and place the wooden plaque beneath the bed. This piece of magic appears to be designed to put an enemy to sleep, but I have found it very efficacious for helping to put myself to sleep.

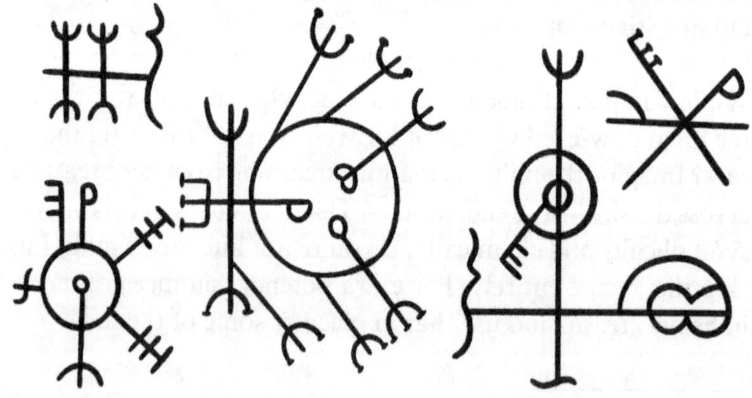

293 Most groceries will have this in the baking section, near the icing.

294 As translated by Stephen Flowers, who, I wish to warn you, is kind of a fascist.

295 I have never tried alder wood. It works perfectly well for me on paper.

Take Back Your Dreams

The first step in any kind of oneiromancy is learning to remember your dreams. Every night, before falling asleep, speak aloud (something like), "I will sleep well, dream powerfully, and awaken refreshed, remembering my dreams," and then drink a bit of water. When you awaken, immediately write down anything you can remember of your dream. After that, the first thing you should do, before getting out of bed, is take a sip of water. I have been told by many people that your mind doesn't like two such similar events being separated by blankness, and so it will try to fill in the gap by remembering more of your dreams. Honestly, I'm a little skeptical about that reasoning, but it seems to work![296]

On days when you can afford to sleep a little later, set an alarm for two hours before you have to be up. Wake up, write down any dreams you can remember, and move around for a little bit to make sure you're really awake (this is a good time for a bathroom break!). Then, go back to sleep. The dreams in that second sleep are likely to be much easier to remember. Practice until you can reliably remember your dreams, and then it's time to learn to incubate the dreams you want.

The Dream Altar

If you would like to get serious about your practice of oneiromancy, you'll want to set up a bedside altar for your dream work. On the altar, you should have a lamp with a red bulb, a journal, a pen,[297] and a carafe of water with a glass. You may also want an image of Selene, Hypnos, Morpheus, or another lunar or sleep/dream god/dess. The ikon of Hypnos, Pasithea, and Oneiros that opened the chapter is a good choice. Mine has a statue of the "sleeping goddess of Malta."

If your nightstand has drawers, it is perfectly acceptable to keep anything you like in them, but the top of the nightstand should be reserved for the dream altar, and things appropriate to sleep and dreams. As with any altar, your first step should be to clean it. After this, you may want to lay down an altar cloth

---

296 I rarely have trouble remembering dreams, so I am not 100% sure what works for others, but many people report success with this method.

297 I recommend attaching the pen to the journal with a long string. Remember, you'll be using this while you're mostly asleep, and nothing kills a dreamy mood like having to root around under your bed for the pen you dropped.

to "set the mood." If you are including a divine image on your altar, it should be the first thing placed on the altar (after an altar cloth). This is true not just for dream altars, but for any kind of altar. Divine images destined for altars, whether they are two or three dimensional, should always be awakened before being "seated" on an altar.

After you've placed the divine image (if you're using one), arrange the lamp, journal, pen, and water so that they are convenient to the bed. If you wish, you can also make your altar elsewhere in the room and keep only the necessities at your bedside. You may also keep other appropriate items on the altar. For example, my dream altar also contains a feather I collected from a dream incubation chamber at Epidaurus, a protective Bear charm, a large amethyst,[298] and several personal tokens.

Bear is a powerful ally for dreaming, especially for protection from nightmares. Every child who has ever turned to teddy in the middle of the night knows this to be true. The existence of a pan-European Neanderthal bear cult, remnants of which remain to this day—a hot topic of debate among scholars for generations—is a deeply inspiring idea for me. While I am unconvinced that there was a single unified but widespread cult, what is unquestionable is the existence of a great number of bear cults, all over the world, some of which exist to this day, and so I assume that there must have been some Paleolithic bear cults as well.

Ritual: Bear Charm

The spell below can be used to enchant a teddy bear as a protective guardian. If you prefer something more adult, it will work equally well with any kind of bear image or statue. Small, carved stone bears are easy to find. Personally, mine is made from the tanned head of an American black bear, but that's probably a little extra for normal people.

This spell is best worked under a full moon and is more fun with a partner. It's best out of doors, but inside is also ok. If inside, a basement or other underground space is preferable.

You will need:

* A teddy bear, bear image, or bear statue
* Drum recordings
* A bear-friendly snack that is also human-friendly (for example, blueberries)

---

298 I don't usually work with gemstones, but I am sometimes given them as gifts.

* A glass of water
* A piece of paper
* A writing utensil
* Mugwort (or another artemisia)
* Red ochre
* Bear fat, ghee, or coconut oil

Steps:

1. Before beginning the ritual itself, choose some magical-sounding drum recordings to play,[299] and prepare the bear-friendly snack and glass of water. (You'll need both your hands,[300] so you can't drum yourself.)
2. Copy out the invocation below nice and big, so you can read it in the dark while trancey.
3. Prepare a salve by warming the mugwort, red ochre, and bear fat (or ghee or coconut oil).[301] Allow the salve to sit and infuse overnight, and then warm it again and strain it.
4. Strip naked and use the salve to paint spirals, zigzags, and other Paleolithic-feeling designs all over your body.
5. Whenever you're ready to begin, start the drumbeat.
6. Assume your very best Paleolithic magician persona, and begin to sway with the music, hold your bear in both hands, and dance with wild abandon. When you feel the spirit come upon you, say something like:

"Bear, Bear, you who rule the heavens, the stars, and the entire world; you who make the axis turn, you who control the whole cosmos by only force and will, I appeal to you, imploring and supplicating that you bless this little bear, breathe into it with your breath. Awaken this little bear as a protector and guardian for [NAME], child of [NAME], that it may watch over them forever in your great name. Do this thing because I call upon you by all your holy names, at which your divinity rejoices, which you cannot ignore. BRIMO,[302]

299 You'll need about thirty minutes of drumming. You'll also need two hands for the ritual, so unless you have a partner, you can't drum for yourself in this one.

300 If you don't have two hands, I can help you adapt this (or any other) ritual for your own needs.

301 You can also add amanita mushrooms, if that's your kind of thing.

302 We discussed this name in the previous chapter.

Earth-Breaker, Queen of the Hunt, BAUBO[303]*... AMOR AMOR AMOR, IEA, shooter of deer AMAM AMAR APHROU, All-Queen, Wish Queen, AMAMA, well-bedded, Dardanian, all-seeing, night-running, man-attacker, man-subduer, man-summoner, man-conqueror, LICHRISSA PHAESSA, O ethereal one, O strong one, O lover of song and dance, protectress, spy, delight, delicate, protector, adamant, adamantine, O Damnameneia, BREXERIKANDARA, most high Taurian, unutterable, fire-bodied, light-giving, sharply armed. O Great Bear, lend me your powerful breath: ROOOOOOAAR!" [Don't say "roar." Roar like a bear.]*

7. Roar into the bear doll, image, or statue, and then go back to dancing with it. You may find yourself shapechanging into a bear. Do not be alarmed by this.
8. When the drumming ends, breathe into the little bear one last time.
9. Amble over to the snack and eat it, sharing the sensation with Bear,[304] and slowly return to yourself.
10. Drink the water, shake off the bear trance, return to your human form, and return to this time and place.
11. Remember to say thank you to Great Bear before you go to sleep. Expect to see bears in your dreams.

Dream Incubation

Incubating a dream simply means deciding in advance what you will dream about. It is an important first step to many other kinds of dream magic. Dream incubation has always been considered an important magical art in a wide variety of cultures. For example, in the great healing temples of ancient Greece, the Asclepia—priests of Asclepius, the god of healing—helped patients incubate dreams where the god appeared to them and taught them what they needed to do to be healed.

Dream incubation can be thought of as a kind of divination. In the dream world, you seek out information and solutions to problems. It's very simple.

---

303 Βαυβώ (Baubo) is the goddess of delight, who entertains Demeter, in her grief, with bawdy humor.

304 If you do not provide a better snack, there is a non-zero chance Bear will find some grubs and eat them with your mouth.

The first step is to decide what you'd like to dream about. The easiest kind of dream to practice with is finding a solution to a problem you are anxious about, or otherwise emotionally invested in. Erotic dreams can also be easy to incubate, for people for whom they are common.

Exercise: Dream Incubation

1. First, write a clear statement of the dream you'd like to incubate. Mine are usually several pages long, but I put words in order for a living. Do your best to be clear, specific, and detailed.
2. Find or make a symbol to represent the problem. It could be a picture of a person you're feuding with or an open book you're having trouble understanding, for example. You can also make a sigil. If you're not very good at visualizing (I'm not!), then you can use a keyword or short phrase instead, but most people do best with pictures.
3. Before falling asleep, turn the problem over and over in your head, trying to hold the image (or words, or whatever) in your head as far into sleep as you can. In several clinical studies, it's been found that just this is enough to incubate a dream for well more than half of subjects.
4. If you wish, make a short recording of yourself speaking your dream intention and keyword, and play it on repeat at a very low volume while you sleep. If you have trouble falling asleep because of the sound, try mixing it with some rain or ocean noises.

If this exercise doesn't work for you, you can try adding some magic to the mix, such as any of the dream incubation spells that follow. Once you've gotten good at incubating problem-solving dreams, try incubating other kinds, such as dreams of meeting a spirit, erotic dreams, or anything else you'd like.

A Dream Incubation for Revelation, Modified from PGM VII:664–685

You will need:

* A mat or blanket
* Ink, preferably myrrh

* A strip of linen
* An olive branch
* A pillow
* A black or silver permanent marker
* A white novena candle
* Matches or a lighter

Steps:

1. Place a mat or blanket on the floor to sleep on.[305]
2. Ideally with myrrh ink, write a brief summary of the question or concern you would like to dream a solution to on the strip of linen.[306]
3. Wrap the linen around an olive branch.
4. Put the branch to the left of your pillow.
5. Using a black or silver permanent marker, write the following on the glass jar of a white novena candle: "Οιοςενμιγαδων Οπθω Βαυβω νιοηρε κοδηρεθ δοςηρε ςυρε ςθροε ςανκιςτη δωδεκακαςτη κοδηρε ρινωτον κουμετανα ρουβιθα νουμιλα περφερον Απουωρηρ Αρουηρ."
6. Light the candle, and then speak the following words to the candle flame seven times:

"Hermes, lord of the inner world, precious tick-tock heartbeat,
Circle of Selene, shining sphere of light, butter rich and sweet,
Square of Reason, who invented all words and speech,
Mantle-garbed advocate, who hears all just pleas,
Who whirls on airy courses with golden-sandaled feet,
Holding spirit reins, driving through Underworld deeps.
Bearing the sun's bright lamp, singing with light and heat,
You give joy to those below the earth, who weep and gnash their teeth,
Those for whom Fates have spun a tapestry, complete.
You're well-known as the Witching One who sends to us our dreams,
And oracles, by night's deep dark and by day's all-brilliant gleam.
The pains of mortals you soothe away, and all our cares you heal,
Hither, oh blessed one, mighty son, no longer stay concealed.
The goddess who brings full mental powers, ever true and real,

305 I do this spell sleeping in my regular bed, and it works fine, but I'm generally a strong dreamer, so doing it doesn't take much for me. YMMV.

306 I use plain black ink on plain white printer paper, with no branch at all, and that works just fine for me.

By your beautiful form and graceful mind, I beg you to reveal,
The skill of true prophecy, the signs, and all the seals."

7. Go to sleep. The flickering of the candle on your closed eyelids will carry the spell into your dreams.

Another Dream Incubation Spell from the Greek Magical Papyri

You will need:

* A whole bay leaf
* A writing utensil
* A pillow with a pillowcase

Steps:

1. Before going to sleep, write the magic formula "AIAI AXENE IAO" on a whole bay leaf.
2. Place the bay leaf inside your pillowcase.
3. As you lie in bed drifting off to sleep, say: *"I call upon you, Sabaoth, Michael, Raphael, and you powerful archangel Gabriel. Do not simply pass me on your nightly journey, but let one of you enter here, and reveal to me concerning ____________________."*

Exercise: Seven Suggested Dreams to Incubate

1. A dream that reminds you of something you've forgotten.
2. A dream that answers a question.
3. A dream of a long-ago ancestor, to seek their wisdom.
4. A dream of a place you have dreamed before, but never been to in waking life, with the intention of discovering more about it.
5. A dream of a legendary magical teacher, with the intention of learning more witchcraft
6. A dream of the Great Library, where all the books that have ever been written, or ever will be written, are available. Ask the library to help you find your own book.
7. A dream of what will happen tomorrow.

Trance: Lucid Dreaming

Lucid dreams are those where, within the dream, you realize that you are dreaming, but continue to dream. This permits you some degree of control over the dream itself. The technique I learned is called WILD, or Wake Into Lucid Dreaming. To practice it:

1. Set an alarm for about four hours after you expect to fall asleep.
2. Go to sleep.
3. When the alarm goes off, get up and do something to ensure you are actually awake. (I usually switch wet laundry to the dryer.) Try to keep light to a minimum; do not use screens.
4. When you return to bed, snuggle down, and go back to sleep, while repeating (something like), *"My body is asleep, but my mind is awake."* If you wish, you can make a recording of yourself saying that and play it on repeat.
5. Lie still, breathe deeply, and act as though you are trying to convince someone watching that you are asleep. Watch the back of your eyelids. If you are prone to inner vision, you may begin to see things, but it's totally ok if you don't see anything. You may begin to hear sounds or voices, or to feel sensations of floating or buzzing or other weird things. These are all very normal signs that your body is falling asleep, but your mind is still awake. Don't let them startle you.
6. Eventually, you may find that you feel paralyzed, as if you couldn't move even if you wanted to. It might be frightening, but this is an excellent sign. Your body has fallen asleep.
7. Keep repeating your reminder, watching your eyelids, and pretending to be asleep. You may find yourself reliving memories or previous dream narratives. Try hard not to attach to them, but simply observe them and let them pass. Once this starts happening, you're ready to begin lucid dreaming.
8. If you are a strong visualizer, begin to visualize a dream scene around you. If you can't see things in your head, that's also ok. Just imagine that you can.
9. Once you've set the scene, imagine moving through it. Walk, run, dance, or even fly. Moving is the surest way to break contact with your sleeping body and fully inhabit your dream self.
10. From here on out, all you have to do is remember that you are dreaming. However, it takes some practice. The first few times, you may find yourself waking up with a start from the surprise and excitement of finding yourself lucid dreaming. That's ok. Just try again another night.

Other people have luck with another method called *reality testing*, although I have never had much luck with it. For this method, you'll need to train yourself into the habit of, several times a day, checking to see if you're dreaming or awake. There are many options for this, but I recommend counting your fingers. If you get ten (or however many you have IRL), then you're not dreaming. If your hands are weird, or you can't count, then you're dreaming (or on hallucinogens, which induce a very similar state). You need to do this so often in your waking life that you also do it in your dreams. When you reality test in your dreams, you may find yourself waking up from surprise. It might take many tries to get the hang of it. This is not magic; it is simply a "human trick" that all people can do. It just takes practice (and sufficient healthy sleep).

One word of warning: Like most of the things we've discussed in this chapter, lucid dreaming interferes with your natural sleep and dream processes. It's best not to do it two nights in a row. Be sure you are getting enough normal, natural, healthy sleep. More experienced magicians can combine lucid dreaming with dream incubation—incubate lucidity and then perform a ritual in the dream once you are lucid. Additionally, you can request spirits meet you in your dreams, and then become lucid to speak with them there. Personally, while I enjoy lucid dreaming for lots of things, I do not find it especially useful magically, partly because it is too difficult to control, and partly because it interrupts normal dreaming, which I do find useful. I prefer to receive messages in dreams and respond in my waking life.

Chapter Eleven:

Trance Journey

Among the most traditional of witch's skills is exiting the body to travel in the Other Place. This practice is known by a panoply of names: trance journey, witchflight, hedgewalking, shamanic journey, and many others. While not everyone agrees that these are all identical experiences, for the most part, the phrases can be used interchangeably in most conversations with other witches. For more detailed or sophisticated witches' "shop talk," always be sure to clarify to make sure everyone is on the same page.

No matter what we call it, witches and other magicians travel both to meet with the spirits on their own "home turf" and to perform magics too delicate or ephemeral for physical incarnation. While you should have done this several times by now, beginning with the Granny Trance in Chapter Two, in this chapter, we'll delve a bit deeper into trance journey practices and go a little further afield. We'll begin with a brief overview of the "geography" of the Other Place, and then discuss the central ally in my method of trance journey, the World Tree. You'll discover your own personal World Tree, then descend by World Tree into the Near Underworld. You can also climb the World Tree to explore the Middle World and Heavens, but that is outside the scope of this book, and not an entirely beginner practice.

Of everything in this book, I think this is probably the hardest to learn out of a book. I am naturally talented at witchflight, and had been a practicing witch for decades when I first learned this technique, and yet I do not think I ever would have learned it if I had not seen it done in person. If at all possible, try to find an in-person teacher for journeying. It is substantially easier to learn in person than from a book, because if you're in the room with someone else who is journeying, you can sort of "piggyback" on their "vibe" physically the first time, and once you have journeyed once, it is very easy to do it a second time. My godmother, from whom I received my advanced training, has since retired from teaching, but this is a website her teacher maintains, which is one place to start looking for a teacher: https://www.shamanicteachers.com/instructors/. I found my first shamanic teacher (not my godmother) on such a website many years ago. She and I were not philosophically a good match (I am too witchy for her), but I'm still glad to have taken the class. Even just one afternoon in a "journey circle" can help open up your practice.

Three Worlds Cosmology

A *cosmology* is a map of the universe, a big-picture explanation to questions like "What exists?" and "How does the world work?" For the most part, the cosmology I subscribe to is that of the Three (and a half) Worlds. This rough map of the universe is a sort of "average" across a wide variety of cultures from all over the earth. However, as I describe it here, it should not be understood as even attempting to create an actual map of the universe as it exists, but rather a very simplified set of paths for beginning travelers.

A Three Worlds map is generally centered on the viewer; that is to say, if there were a "you are here" arrow, it would be in the middle of the map. Here, where you now sit reading these words, is in the "Middle World," a realm populated mostly by the spirits of embodied living creatures, like animals and plants; spirits of embodied natural formations, like mountains or rivers; and unembodied spirits like...

* Genus genii, or species totems, like American Black Bear or Oak or even Rosaceae, a wonderful, magical spirit of a large family of flowering plants that includes roses, apples, strawberries, hawthorn, and many other witch-friendly plants.
* Genii locorum or spirits of places (singular is "genius loci").
* Some kinds of ghosts.

Recall that this map was invented by humans, for human needs, which is why it centers the world experienced by humans in typical states of consciousness. Thus, from Here, there are two basic directions to go. You can go up to the Upper World (or "Heavens") or down to the Underworld. The Upper World is often understood as a series of spheres surrounding the Earth. The first (lowest) Heaven is more or less the same as Here; it runs from the surface of the Earth up to the outer edges of the atmosphere. We live at the very bottom of the lowest Heaven, although we often think of ourselves as living "in" Earth. We do not. We are creatures of the lower sky. This region is sometimes called the *sublunary sphere* by fancy magicians.

Above this are the seven planetary spheres (Moon, Mercury, Venus, Sun, Mars, Jupiter, Saturn) and then the realm of the fixed stars. These are closely related, but not identical, to the celestial bodies for which they are named. Above the planetary spheres is the sphere of the fixed stars, and then a variety of far celestial realms. These are inhabited by many types of spirits, including angels, gods (although different gods live in different places), planetary and stellar spirits, and several other, stranger, things.

Finally, if you go down from Here, you come to the Underworld. There is a significant amount of cultural agreement about the denizens and geography of the Underworld, far more so than about the Heavens. I suspect this is because we live on a (nearly) spherical planet. When we go up from where we are, we can each get to a different place, but if you go far enough down from anywhere on Earth, we're all headed to the same place. That is the special nature of "down-ness." Here on our round planet, all "downs" go the same place, the center of the Earth, and then "further down" into the same Underworld. That is (I believe) why most people have much more similar experiences when traveling to the Underworld than in Upper World journeys.

Preparing for Trance Journeying

As I teach it, there are three "phases" in trance journeying. The first is *anchoring,* like the "Plugging In" ritual you learned in Chapter Seven. The next is the alignment of the spine with the *World Tree,* and the final one is the *descent* (also called *katabasis*, which is Greek for "go down"). Begin with phase one, and do not bother going on to phase two until you have mastered it (which, if you've been practicing as you read, you should already have done by the time you're in this chapter).

World Tree

Your most important ally in this chapter is your World Tree. Every person has a personal World Tree, a spirit closely related to your spine. I believe (and encourage you to consider as well) that all world trees (and all embodied trees)[307] are

307 And all vertebrates, and quite possibly everything else too.

avatars of the one Great World Tree, but that's more or less irrelevant to the work we're doing in this chapter. Your World Tree is not a physically embodied tree;[308] it is an ephemeral spirit. It can shapeshift to be different kinds of trees if it wants and will look different in different circumstances. This is particularly true in circumstances where you are working with a living tree ally, in which case your World Tree will almost certainly take on its form.

Do not try to conscript very young trees or saplings as world trees. They are not strong or wise enough yet, and you will damage them. You can raise up a tree to be a World Tree, but it takes a long time.[309] Like people, trees grow up slowly. In general, it is best to work with trees that are substantially older and bigger than you are.

If you already work with a particular World Tree, feel free to use that one and skip the rest of this section. If not, we will find one for you now. The goal is to discover a tree whose roots are in the Underworld and whose leaves are in the Heavens. There is probably a hollow opening of some sort, which will function like a door. If you have a good visual imagination, you may be picturing it clearly already. If so, flip through some pictures of tree species until you can name it, and skip the rest of this section if you wish.

If you're not sure, we'll walk through some steps to help you discover it. As soon as you can clearly imagine your tree, you can skip ahead to anchoring. As we discussed right at the beginning of this book, some people's imaginations aren't visual, and that is not a problem. You can imagine your tree by name instead of picture. However, discovering a tree's name is harder, so try to manage a picture if you can. Alternatively, you may use a "public" World Tree, such as Yggdrasil or Ashera, until you find your own. If you choose to do this, go research the public tree very well before moving on to part two. However, it is better to find your own, which the following exercises are designed to help you do.

Writing Prompt: World Tree

Answer the following questions. Answer as quickly as you can. Try not to think about the answers before responding. Don't decide. Don't determine. Just guess. (Some of these questions may or may not apply to you.) Note that, unless I specify otherwise, when I say "tree," I mean a specific living tree, not a species of tree.

* What is the tallest native tree where you live?

---

308 Technically, it is physically embodied in your spine, but I mean it's not a tree.

309 I think you can, anyhow. My beta test (which is a weeping willow) is only about ten years old, and I've only been raising her for seven years. Thus far, it is going very well, but she is only barely big enough to journey with, and only because I am carrying most of the load for her.

* What is the biggest, oldest tree near you?
* Did you have a tree house as a kid? (It's ok if it was imaginary.) What species of tree was it?
* When you were a child, which tree was your friend?
* Is there a particular tree under which you pour out offerings? What kind of tree is it?
* What kind(s) of trees grow on land you tend?
* Imagine the white rabbit from *Alice in Wonderland*. Imagine following him as he ducks into the roots of a tree. What kind of tree is it?
* Imagine Winnie the Pooh's Three Acre Wood. Remember how each character lives in a treehouse? Imagined living in the Wood. What kind of tree is your home in?
* Imagine shapeshifting into a tree. What kind of tree are you?
* Imagine the Great Tree whom all trees worship. What kind of tree is it?
* There is a "Wood Between the Worlds." Imagine you are there. What kind of trees predominate near you?
* When your very first human incarnation died, what sort of tree grew on your grave?

Exercise: Drawing the World Tree

You will need:

* A timer
* A pen
* A blank piece of paper

Steps:

1. Set a timer for one minute.
2. Close your eyes and draw a picture of the World Tree.
3. When the timer goes off, stop.
4. Set a timer for one minute.
5. Close your eyes, and draw a leaf from the World Tree.
6. When the timer goes off, stop.
7. What kind of tree is it? Check Google for reference images.

Exercise: Wander the Woods

Go to the woods. Walk around for a while, until you cannot see anything but forest. Close your eyes, and spin around like a little kid, until you are very dizzy. Close your eyes, put your hands out in front of you, and walk until you run into a tree. Experiment with the tree as World Tree. Record your results.

Greater Ritual: Witchflight

Phase One: Anchor

For beginners, I recommend learning to journey while seated or lying down in a fixed location. With practice, you should learn to journey while walking, or even on fast-moving transit, like an airplane, but that can be quite disorienting for a beginner. In addition to keeping your body physically anchored to a specific place, you should spiritually anchor/center as well. To anchor before a trance journey, I recommend either the "Plugging In" you learned in Chapter Seven, or something very like it. If you have not yet done that enough times to know how to do it without looking back, you are not yet ready to trance journey. Practice more.

Phase Two: Become the World Tree

If you are new to this kind of work, I encourage you to try this several times as I've explained it before making changes. Try making an audio recording of yourself reading instructions to yourself, but wean yourself off of that as soon as possible. Eventually, you should be able to do this completely unguided. Once you can, feel free to develop your own methods.

In terms of sound, a repetitive noise like a drum or rattle can be very useful in this work. I prefer to do it to the sound of bubbling water, but many people prefer a loud drumbeat instead, and that is how I learned. Personally, I recommend practicing outside, near running water. However, I appreciate that can be impractical for a variety of reasons. If you need to use artificial noise, be sure it is animated and random, such as the ones at https://mynoise.net. Personally, I find loud drums—especially recorded drums, which are always the same—quite distracting and much more difficult to journey to than ambient noise or even silence.[310] If you would like to experiment with a recorded drum beat, I recommend this one: https://schamanenstube.com/gratis/schamanentrommel-mp3-download.html

You'll be out of your body while trance journeying, so be sure to set up somewhere you would feel safe falling asleep (although you should not be asleep). Set out a journal, pen, and bottle of water. You'll want all of them when you come back. You may want a blanket if you get cold easily. There is no significant risk to this experiment; however, it can leave you feeling dazed or disconnected if you're not used to it. If you feel improperly grounded after the exercise, move around, drink water, go outside in the sunshine, eat something that will "stick to your ribs," or take a nap. You'll be fine when you wake up.

In my experience, journeying is easiest with your back against your tree, your spine straight and vertical (sitting or standing is fine). If that is not possible, make believe your back is against the tree.

Assuming the World Tree Form

Feel the bark behind you, warm from the sun. Feel the ground below you, cold and a little bit wet. Breathe deeply. Feel the air fill your lungs. Feel the life-giving oxygen permeating every cell in your body. Breathe out, expelling all stress, toxins, and waste. Breathe in and out, your breath a constant circle. Breathe in, remembering that the air you breathe in was breathed out by the trees, and that your exhalations give them life. Breathe, an eternal cycle of respiration linking every living thing on earth.

With each inhalation, feel the environment permeating your skin, as you become slightly diffuse. You may notice your sphere of sensory awareness getting very large, so that, for example, you can hear things that are very far away as if they were right next to you. Don't let that distract you. Keep your eyes closed, and continue breathing and becoming larger and larger and more diffuse. Feel yourself sinking into the tree behind you. Keep focusing on your breathing, slow and deep.

---

310 I feel duty bound to mention that my godmother and many other Anglophone "shamans" are of the opinion that my practice of journeying without a drum is dangerous, because there is no drumbeat to listen for to find the way back to the body. However, I have never had any trouble with it, and to the best of my knowledge, neither have any of the hundreds of people to whom I have taught this technique, both online and in person. In general, what unites those of us who travel without the drum is our general distaste for loud noises. I am also that person who is always asking people to turn their music down.

Feel yourself merging with the tree. Feel your leaves extending up to the heavens, drinking in delicious sunlight. Feel your roots sinking down into the earth, drinking in the cool, refreshing waters of the earth. Feel your rootedness, your connection to the chthonic biome. Feel how time slows down and expands in this form.

If you are not accustomed to shapechanging work, this will feel weird. It's an entirely uncanny thing we're doing, and it should give you the heebie-jeebies if you're doing it right. Try to not let it startle you out of trance and back into your body, but expect to have to repeat this exercise several times if you're not accustomed to this work. Feeling weird means you're doing it right. For the most part, beginners tend to have trouble holding this form, rather than trouble shaking it off, but if you are having difficulty returning to normal human consciousness, focus on the feel of your breathing. Take notes on what you experienced. The experience will fade quickly, like a dream.

Once you've practiced enough that you can hold tree form for at least ten minutes, move on to trying the descent phase.

Phase Three: Descend to the Womb of the Earth

Once you've gotten the hang of being a tree, we'll practice using this World Tree form to travel. Begin by anchoring, and then assuming the form of your World Tree.

Feel the sunshine beating down on your leaves. Feel the energy moving down, down, down into your roots. Feel your roots grow downward into the earth, winding around rocks, further and further into the cool, welcoming earth. Take note of anything you encounter as you go down. As in the Granny Trance, you should feel a distinct, physical sensation of downward movement. Keep going down, down, down until you run out of earth. You should find yourself in a hollow space, like a cave, womb, or room. Drop onto the ground if you're not already there. You may still be in tree form, or you might be back in human form. You may find yourself in some other shape; animals are common. It doesn't really matter. As with the previous exercise, you should expect this one to take a little practice if you've never done it before. If you've already mastered the Granny Trance, that should make this one easier to learn.

Examine the space you are in. There should be a sort of curtain of shimmering, which is often described as a waterfall in modern Anglophone witchcraft. In my opinion, it is actually more like a region of neurological white noise. If you can't see it, listen for it. Find the waterfall, but do not yet go through it. First, take some time to get to know this place. I call it "Womb of the Earth." Each person will have their own version of this "landing pad," but they are all actually the same intersubjective "place" being interpreted differently by different human brains. Explore the cave a little, and then come back up to the surface, the whole way back into your body. Take notes. Stand up, walk around, live your regular life. Go back down. Once you've been up and down a few times on different days (taking notes each time), move on to part four.

Phase Four: The Between Place

Anchor, Tree, Descend, and then, from the Womb of Being, go through the waterfall (or however the curtain appears to you). For many people, as you cross the curtain, there will be a very sudden sensation of the experience "clicking in" and sensations becoming much more vivid. There may be someone waiting for you on the opposite side of the curtain. If it seems threatening or scary, that's just your own fear manifesting. You are on a well-trod path. There's nothing dangerous here. Calm down, and breathe through it. Do not attempt to fight or banish the Dweller on the Threshold. If you are too afraid to go on, then go back, and try again later. Most people with experience in witchcraft will not encounter a fearsome Dweller.

Once you are through the curtain, you should come to an open and beautiful space—for most Anglophones, it presents as a meadow. You may explore the meadow, but be sure to note the way back to the cave. If you get lost, listen for the waterfall. While you explore, it is likely that an animal spirit will come to meet you. Greet it politely, and introduce yourself. If you hit it off, ask if it is willing to be your guide for this trip. As I mentioned before, you are in a sort of way station, which I call "the Between Place." Most of the spirits wandering around here are either tour guides or fellow travelers. If it says no, say thank you and ask if it has come for some other purpose. Be polite and friendly. Explore as long as you like.

While animal-formed guides are most common, spirits in the form of dead loved ones are also typical. If no guides appear, you may summon one. I recommend Hekate Torchbearer, but you can ask almost any spirit with whom you have a strong relationship to come and help. Make several journeys exploring the Between Place with your guide(s). Take copious notes.

Return to Your Body

When you're done, return to your body by the same path you traveled down. If you feel lost, try to first feel for the sensation of gravity on your body. Try to focus on your breathing. Even when you stopped paying attention, your body kept breathing, and no matter how far away you are, you'll be able to feel it if you pay attention. If you can't, hold your breath until you do (but that is a rather unpleasant way to return).

Explore

Once you've made several journeys to the Between Place, you're ready to start exploring. Remember while you do so that, once you leave the immediate area outside the Womb of Being, you are no longer in a safe intersubjective space, partly inside your own consciousness, but straying further out into nonsubjective space. As Gandalf says in *The Lord of the Rings*: "It's a dangerous business, Frodo, going out your door. You step onto the road, and if you don't keep your feet, there's no knowing where you might be swept off to."

It is important to be on your best behavior in this place. Many people, perhaps imagining that they are inside their own mind, behave in abominable ways in the Other Place, causing havoc and treating others as figments of their imagination. Such disrespect can be very dangerous. Remember: *All fairy tale rules apply*. If you are not sure what I mean by that, my first piece of advice is that you need to read more traditional folklore. Here are some basic guidelines, but recall that this is all advice for beginners:

* Don't galumph through the wild places like a heavy-footed human, leaving a swath of destruction in your wake.
* Don't eat the food. Don't make promises. Don't have sex. Don't accept gifts unless you can do so graciously and without incurring a debt.
* If you see someone in trouble, help them. "Someone" includes inanimate objects. Everything here is a person; nothing is an object solely for use.[311]
* Be polite, courteous, and respectful. "Please" and "thank you" and "I'm sorry" really are magic words.
* Stay on the path (unless you want to have an adventure).
* Keep your weapons peacebound, and don't wear plate mail to a picnic.[312] Some people have a way about them that clearly communicates that they are looking for trouble. Don't be that guy.
* Keep your wits about you. This is a weird place full of weird creatures doing weird stuff. When things get weird, don't be complacent, but also don't flip out.
* If you make a deal in the Other Place, expect to be cheated. Compacting is not a beginner practice, and not one I generally advise while entranced, even for more experienced witches.

---

311 As an animist, I believe this is a right and proper way to behave in our world as well.

312 To be more explicit: *Do not* travel with every ward in the world hung about you, bristling with psychic weapons and expecting attack from every corner. It is not just inhospitable but outright rude and hostile. This is not the Danger Room, and it is insulting to our hosts for you to so overtly imply you don't feel safe here.

Seven Suggested Journeys

Sacred Center

1. Revisit Chapter Seven and make a list of Sacred Centers you'd like to explore. Research them online, looking at lots of pictures and videos. Journey to them. Compare/contrast the experiences.

Watershed

2. When a drop of rain hits the ground at your feet, where does it go? As you begin to answer that question, you'll come to understand how the spirits of water move and live and flow where you are, and you'll learn to work with them. When you pour out offerings on the ground, it is this watershed that you are feeding. When you travel in water-form, it is along these paths that you can most easily swim.

   If you cannot similarly recount the path a raindrop takes from your home to be united with the ocean, I strongly recommend spending some a few hours with Google until you figure it out. Go and visit your streams and rivers; if you can, swim or boat in them. Once you have a firm intellectual grasp of the path, I strongly encourage you to journey in spirit as a drop of water along the path you have learned, and make contact with the spirits along the way. Feel yourself as part of a greater whole, and maintain that sense as long as you can, as the "whole" becomes larger and larger, until you feel yourself united with Great Okeanos.
3. Revisit the Frau Holle story in Chapter Two. Journey to her home by from the Womb of Being (instead of going down the well).

The Dwarves of the Four Pillars

4. The thirteenth century Norse poet, scholar, and lawspeaker Snorri Sturluson compiled three books of cultural teachings, called the *Prose Edda*. The first, called *Gylfaginning*, or *The Deception of Gylfi*, is the most complete surviving telling of Norse mythology. It is in this work the four dwarves of the pillars first appear, in a list of legendary dwarves. However, little is told of them there. In my experience, the four dwarves of the pillars are anthropomorphic ambassador spirits of the four Holy Mountains that uphold the sky, the pillars of the

earth. They are named Norðri (Northern), Suðri (Southern), Austri (Eastern), and Vestri (Western).

Journey to meet them while walking a clockwise circle, in nature, thumping the ground with a staff. Journeying while walking around requires a lot of practice. You can use this rhyme, which I've adapted (with her permission) from the Seiðhjallr group oracle rite, by Diana Paxson.

"Sunwise I walk the way of wonder
With sacred staff the worlds I sunder,
As I walk the spiral rounds,
With word and will I beat the bounds.
Norðri, Suðri, Austri, Vestri,
By beaten Earth I ask you bless me,
Dwarves who dwell as pillar sentries,
Open Earth-gate and grant me entry."

5. Visit the palace of the god of your choice. *Be respectful!*
6. Revisit the Pasithea imagining in Chapter Ten. Journey there. Do not journey directly to her bed (*so rude!*); instead, follow the river upstream from the Womb of Being and ask for permission to enter her cave. If you're having trouble finding it, smell for the flowers.
7. Ask a guide to take you to the Goblin Market. Before going, think about what you will trade (secrets are a good option). Take Hermes of the Marketplace with you. Barter for a magical item there. *Do not* make trades without Hermes's approval.

Chapter Twelve:

Shapeshifting

Warning

Shapechanging is the first dangerous magic we will attempt in this book. The danger is entirely psychological, but this can be difficult work for many people, and it can bring up a lot of residual body issues. Our culture's relationship with bodies is deeply, deeply fucked up, and we all have some of that in us. Take it slow, and do the exercises in order. In particular, you should master the "inward smile" and "lying with your eyes" before attempting any of the others. If you are prone to any kind of body dysmorphia or dysphoria, I strongly recommend reading the chapter carefully and contemplatively, thinking carefully about how these exercises will impact you before trying any of them. As a beginner, you are under no obligation to learn shapeshifting at all; however, it is a key skill for many types of more advanced magic, so if you continue in your studies, you'll probably want to come back to it eventually.

Exercise: Inward Smile

This is a much-simplified version of a more complex qi gong, which I encourage you to learn. I learned it from Master Mantak Chia, whose book *The Inner Smile: Increasing Chi through the Cultivation of Joy* I strongly recommend. The practice has a variety of physical, spiritual, and psychological health benefits. However, in this exercise, we're really just using it as preliminary aura manipulation practice.

1. Sit in front of a mirror. A full-length mirror is ideal, but you only have to see your face.
2. Relax your whole body and your whole being—every muscle, every thought.
3. Touch your tongue to the roof of your mouth. Leave it there.
4. Remember what it is like to be happy.
5. Arrange your face and body to convince an onlooker that you are serenely, divinely happy.
6. Feel it in your eyes and in your whole face.
7. Attempt to summon up that feeling within you.
8. Collect the happiness in your forehead, like a floating giddiness of bliss.
9. Allow it to seep out of your forehead, dripping down your face, and over your mouth, brightening your smile. Smile big, and radiate the sensation of smiling.
10. Turn the smile inward, and feel it trickle down your throat.
11. Feel it suffuse your heart, radiating pure bliss.
12. Inwardly, thank your heart for all its hard work.
13. Fill your lungs with bliss.
14. Feel the joy infuse, with your breath, into your blood, and from there to every organ, every cell, every particle of your body.
15. Observe what colors the bliss is in various parts of your body. Feel how it moves and changes and develops differently at every place in your body. Smile with your entire being.
16. When you are completely full of smile, connect down into the earth and up into the heavens (as you learned in previous chapters). Allow that energy to enter only as quickly as you can "color" it with smile energy.
17. Put your hands to your mouth, and take some of the smile energy into your hands. Paint your entire skin with it.
18. Push the colored field of happiness outward, extending it past your skin, into an aura of smile.
19. If your eyes are closed, open them, and examine your face. You should look beatifically happy.
20. Carefully memorize what it feels like, inside, to be in this state. Carefully memorize the physical sensation, look, and aura you are currently projecting.

Whenever you're ready, release the smile, but there's no need to force it back out. Smiling inside is very good for you!

Exercise: Lie with Your Eyes

Before you do this exercise, make sure you've already extensively experimented with the Inward Smile. The goal of this exercise is a convincing communication of sadness, while retaining your inner happiness. If you are not already an accomplished liar, this will take some practice. Shapeshifting is, in many ways, a type of advanced lying.[313]

1. Smile inwardly. Fill with divine joy.
2. Now, put a different emotion on your face. What sort of face would you make to convey that you are sad?
3. Make a sad face,[314] but maintain the aura of happiness.
4. If you'd like, take a video of yourself holding that face, and then examine it once you're back in your normal state. Being filled with beatific bliss is not the ideal brain state for careful analysis. Practice until you can convince people who know you that you are sad, while still being blissfully happy inside.
5. Now, pull the happy aura back inside your skin, and cover it with an *aura* of the fake emotion. The frown that your face is wearing? Collect the frown energy, like you did with the smile. Surround yourself with a bubble of sadness, but do not allow it to penetrate your skin by more than an inch or two. What colors is it? How does it arrange itself on your body? What does it smell like? What does it sound like? Is it hot or cold?
6. Relax your face, so it can transition through normal emotional states, but leave the frown painting up. Talk. Interact. If people ask "What's wrong?" you're doing it right.
7. Practice until you can do it quickly and fluently.
8. Try again, with rage instead of sorrow. Next, try fear.
9. Experiment with painting other, more subtle, and more complex emotions while maintaining your inner happiness.

Absolutely do not reverse this exercise and infuse your body with a negative emotion while faking a pleasant one. I should think this goes without saying, but intentionally suffusing your organs with despair, rage, or fear is not good for you!

313 In fact, quite a lot of magic is. Part of what a magician does is that she speaks things into being. Those things are false when you start speaking.

314 If you've never done any learning about the seven basic emotion-faces, I encourage you to do so.

Exercise: Fake Aura, a.k.a. Glamour

1. Choose a complex mental/emotional state you want to project, such as "charming, innocent, and very slightly pitiable" or "highly qualified, confident, slightly ostentatious, but not a dick."
2. Put your face into a shape that conveys such. If you need help, consider some training in acting.
3. As above, paint the outside of your body with that aura.
4. Fix the aura around you, and go about your normal life.
5. If you have an ethical way to do so, practice interacting with other people while doing this, and monitor their reactions. When you can convince even people who know you very well, you're doing it right.

Next, you need to learn to "copy-paste" an aura from someone else onto yourself *without* impacting your inner emotional state. Begin by mimicking someone else's facial and bodily expressions, and then paint it over yourself, as before. Usually, I recommend students go sit in a crowded place and just people-watch for a while, copy-pasting from different people and feeling what their "skin" is like. When people take a second to recognize you or start to ask if you've gotten a haircut because you look different, you're doing it right. When your dog barks at you like you're a stranger, you've mastered it.

Lesser Ritual: Assumption of the Godform

The phrase *assumption of the godform* arises from (or at least, was popularized by) the teachings of the Hermetic Order of the Golden Dawn, a late nineteenth-century British magical order that grew out of Freemasonry, whose members[315] included S. L. M. Mathers, William Wescott, A. E. Waite, Pixie Smith, Aleister Crowley, William Butler Yeats, Arthur Conan Doyle, Bram Stoker, Dion Fortune*, Israel Regardie*, Paul Foster Case*, and many other notables. It's unclear whether or not Gerald Gardner (the founder of modern Wicca) was ever a member, but he certainly moved in the same social circles. The Golden Dawn is an important building block of the modern Anglophone magical tradition. If you don't know much about it, I encourage you to read up. I first learned this technique from Israel Regardie's audio lessons, which are

315 Those with * were not technically members of the Golden Dawn, but one of its several closely allied splinter/inheritor groups.

now available on YouTube. The method I will present below is not identical to his, but it is very close.

Assuming the godform is a type of shapeshifting where you (as you might expect) assume the form of a god.[316] It is best done with gods with whom you have an existing relationship. I will be using the Hellenized (Greek-ified) avatar of the Egyptian scribal god Thoth, the divine patron of this book, as my example, because his was the first form I learned to assume, but you can use any god that has a very well-defined image. Egyptian gods work well, because they have quite specific and relatively consistent iconography. Once you've learned to assume the form of well-defined gods, you can move on to learning to assume less fixed godforms.

It takes some practice to master, both as a general practice, and for each particular form. That being said, the first godform you learn to assume will likely be the hardest. Picking up other forms is much like switching to a different car when you already know how to drive; it takes a little getting used to, but not that much. Assumption of the godform is well worth learning; once you can fully assume the form of a god, you can act in their name—one of the biggest keys to more advanced types of witchcraft and sorcery.

Phase One: Research

This phase is quite simple. Learn everything you can about the god you've chosen and their iconography. What follows is only a brief overview of Thoth; you should do your own research to supplement this. Thoth (Θώθ) is the Greek name for the god more Egyptians called something like Djehuty, which means "Ibis-man." He has two main forms: one is baboon-headed and the other, with whom we'll be working, wears the head of an African sacred ibis. He is a god of magic, literacy, science, literature, and wise judgment. Although the Greeks thought of him as an analog to Hermes, he is not traditionally related to the planet Mercury. Rather, in keeping with his role as someone who invented (along with his lover[317] Seshat, the goddess of measuring, recording, and writing) calendars, counting, and hieroglyphics, He is of the moon, and often wears a lunar crown.

Choose a particular image of the god to work with. Generally, it is best, when beginning, to choose a specific historic image. Unless you're very good at visualization, it's better to choose a simple one. Make sure you understand everything that's in the image. I chose the one at the right, which is from the

---

316 Sometimes, the phrase is also used to reference taking the form of other non-god spirits as well.

317 Or, sometimes, daughter.

1275 BCE Hunefer papyrus. In it, Thoth is recording the results of the weighing of the heart of the dead scribe Hunefer.

He is pictured, as he so often is, with the head of a sacred ibis. Note the similarity in shape of the ibis's beak to the moon. He is wearing a blue headscarf with gold trim. Because I understand animal-headedness to be an artistic convention intended to convey not a man with the head of an ibis, but a god who is human and ibis both, I am choosing to understand it to be a blue headdress in human form, and feathers in ibis form.

His shoulders are broad, and his waist slim.[318] He is wearing a simple linen *shendyt* (kilt) and sash, the common menswear of the day. His feet are bare. His hands are held stiffly in front of him, and he holds a reed pen and a slab. Because of the context of the image, I know that he is recording the fate of Hunefer. More broadly, the so-called Book of Thoth is a record of all things, something like the Book of Destiny in modern folklore.

If the god has an animal (or animal-headed) form, it's also really important to research that animal. This is particularly true in cases like Thoth's sacred ibis, which you may have never seen in "real life." I haven't, and (given the species' limited distribution) most of you probably haven't, either.[319] If possible, watch the animal in their natural habitat. If that's not possible, watch a video. Pay special attention to how the animal moves and sounds.

Phase Two: Construction of the Form

From memory, draw the image. It doesn't have to be a technically skillful drawing, but it has to include all the relevant features. If, like me, you have a weak visual imagination, you might need to practice a few times first. What are they holding? What are they wearing? How is their body positioned?

Now, close your eyes and carefully think about what it would feel like, physically feel like in your body, to be in that position. Where do you feel the air hit your skin? What texture is the clothing? Now, move onto the god's body. How is it different from yours? Do you need to get taller? Thinner? Sculpt the "auric body" you found in the "fake aura" exercise into the shape it needs to be. In my experience, it's easier to make them bigger than you, so that your entire body is inside theirs, rather than shrink yourself to fit inside them. For example, to make my (very fat) waist slim like Thoth's, I need to be ten or eleven feet tall.

Start with the human parts. No matter what shape of human you are, surely it is easier for you to imagine yourself as a broad-shouldered, slim-

318 This is the ancient Egyptian "ideal form" of a man.

319 The Australian white ibis, which has become a successful urban scavenger, is closely related but a slightly different species.

waisted Egyptian man in a kilt than it is to imagine your head is that of an ibis! Your inner body doesn't need to change much from the neck down. Thoth is mostly human-shaped. Your insides don't need to move around. If you need to change the shape of your genitalia to match Thoth's (male) parts, I recommend feeling for the rest of your human body first, and doing the genitals last (of the human-shaped parts). Remember to change your internal reproductive structures, not just the external ones.

Once you've imagined in great detail the human parts of the body, shift from your imagining-brain to your analysis-brain. Unless you're practiced at this, you'll probably drop the imagining when you do that. That's ok. You can pick it up again later.

What shape is the energy body of the god whose form you are assuming? This is not necessarily the same as that of the animal whose head they have. *Think* about how their mind works, how their third eye works, how their crown works. *Don't* imagine it yet; don't feel it yet. Stay in your analytic human mind and think about it, without imagining it. If you imagine it at this stage, you will not be properly open to the true form when it happens. Some amount of experimentation is needed. Because I have done this particular shift many, many times, I can tell you what it feels like for me, but most of the time, you'll have to figure it out for yourself by just trying it. For now, follow these instructions to imagine your energy structure. Energy follows attention; whether you can feel it or not, the energy in your body will follow where you imagine it to go, as long as you continue to focus your attention.

Thoth's energy body is more or less the same as yours up to the throat. What happens from there? Thoth "was born from the lips of Ra" and is the "voice of Ra," so we know his throat must be (one of) his most essential energy center(s). That is to say, when Thoth is at the center of the universe (a la the centering lesson), the exact center is not in his heart, as when we humans center, but in his throat. This is also the boundary where his human and ibis selves meet; this is the center of the transformation from manform to ibisform, and also from human-form to Thoth-form.

Begin by centering in your throat, which may be slightly uncomfortable and leave you a bit lightheaded. It may cause your breathing to become shallow. You might choke up a little, like a "frog in your throat," or feel strange emotions unrelated to anything. Breath through it and allow the sensations to pass.

For almost all humans, there are three strong energy centers in the head: one in the throat; one deep in the brain, behind the forehead (sometimes called the "third eye"); and the third in the top of the head, where the coronal suture meets to sagittal suture (often called the "crown"). This "crown" spot is where babies' heads are soft.

There are two slightly less strong centers at the back of the head. The first is at the back "peak" or "moon crown," where the lambdoidal suture meets to sagittal suture. The other is just under the base of the skull, where the neck meets the skull. This is sometimes called the "jade pillow." Carefully attend to each of them in your human-shaped head, opening them up. If they feel blocked or uncomfortable, try gently massaging them with your hands.

Next, let's figure out where those move to in Thoth-form. Thoth is a perceptive god of wisdom and of the moon. The crescent of his beak is the crescent of the moon. Thus, the beak must be connected to the moon crown center. Feel the energy rise from your throat and slope back through the jade pillow, into the moon crown at the back of your head. Activate the energy center back there, which you might not normally be aware of. Feel the energy curve forward though your brain (*not* over the top of your skull), through your third eye, through your forehead, and down your crescent moon beak. Feel the moon arc between the back point and the tip of your beak. Thoth's energy does not flow through the crown of your human head.

Phase Three: Invocation Script

Choose or write an invocation script for the god in question. As always, I am of the opinion that it is better to write your own than use someone else's.[320] I learned this particular godform assumption with Israel Regardie's "Invocation of Thoth," which you can read below and listen to online. You should either memorize the invocation or, minimally, familiarize yourself with it and listen to it while you work.

This is, in my opinion, not the best invocation script for Thoth. It makes several choices that I wouldn't make these days.[321] But this is the one I learned with, and it's as good as any other to start with. If you choose to get good at assuming the Thoth godform, you'll doubtless develop your own. Once you're familiar with a godform, you'll be able to assume it with just his name, or perhaps a short string of names.

320 But of course, I'm a writer, so surely that colors my experience.

321 Mostly because it is a culturally appropriative muddle that identifies Thoth with many almost unrelated gods from other cultures.

The Golden Dawn's Invocation of Thoth

Procol, oh procol este profani![322] *Balasti! Ompada!*[323]
In the name of the Mighty and Terrible One,
I proclaim that I have banished the shells unto their habitations![324]
I invoke Tahuti,[325] *the Lord of Wisdom and of Utterance;*
the god that cometh forth from the veil.
Oh thou, majesty of the godhead, wisdom-crowned Tahuti,
Lord of the gates of the universe. Thee, thee I invoke.
Oh, thou of the ibis head. Thee, thee I invoke.
Thou who wieldest the wand of double power.[326] *Thee, thee I invoke.*
Thou who bearest in thy left hand the Rose and Cross of Light and Life.[327]
Thee, thee I invoke.
Thou whose head is as an emerald, and thy nemyss[328]
as the night sky blue. Thee, thee I invoke.
Thou whose skin is a flaming orange[329]
as though it burned in a furnace. Thee, thee I invoke.
Behold, I am yesterday, today, and the brother of tomorrow.
I am born again and again.
Mine is the unseen force whereof the gods are sprung, which is as
life unto the dwellers in the Watchtowers of the Universe.
I am the charioteer of the East; Lord of the Past and the Future.
I see by my own inward light; Lord of Resurrection who cometh forth from
the dust, and my birth is from the house of death, Oh ye two divine hawks
upon your pinnacles who keep watch over the Universe.
Ye who company the Bier to the House of Rest, who pilot the ship of Ra,[330]
ever advancing onwards the heights of heaven. Lord of the shrine which
standeth in the center of the earth. Behold!

---

322 This is line 257 from Book 6 of the *Aeneid.* In context, a seer is banishing all profane beings from a portal for underworld descent she is opening for Aeneas with the aid of Hekate.

323 I do not know what "balasti ompada" means, and I'm not sure anyone else does either.

324 This is Hermetic Kabbalah talk for "I have set things in their proper order and cleaned up all the mess."

325 This is a (flawed) pronunciation of D'jewhty.

326 This is a Golden Dawn–specific tool that is half white and half black, but in my experience, it's better to think of it as the was scepter.

327 This is, again, a Golden Dawn symbol. However, better to just imagine the ankh.

328 Headdress of the type King Tut wears.

329 This is Hermetic Kabbalah. I have never seen Thoth be orange.

330 This is to say, Thoth navigates the ship that carries the sun across the sky.

He in me and I in him.
Mine is the radiance wherein Ptah floateth over the firmament.
I travel upon high.
I tread upon the firmament of Nu.
I raise a flashing flame with the lightening of mine eye,
ever rushing on in the splendor of the daily glorified Ra,
giving my life to the dwellers of earth.
If I say, "Come up upon the mountain!"
the celestial waters shall flow at my command.
For I am Ra incarnate, Kephra created in the flesh.
I am the idol of my father Tmu,[331] *Lord of the City of the Sun.*
The god who commands is in my mouth, the god of wisdom is in my heart,
my tongue is the sanctuary of truth and a god sitteth upon my lips.
My word is accomplished every day, and the desire of my heart realizes
itself as that of Ptah when he created his works.
I am eternal, therefore all things are as my designs.
Therefore, do thou come forth unto me from thine abode in the silence,
unutterable wisdom, all light and all power.
Thoth. Hermes. Mercury. Odin.
By whatever name I call thee thou art still nameless to eternity.
Come thou forth, I say, and aid and guard me in this work of art.
Thou star of the east that didst conduct the magi.
Thou art the same all present in Heaven and in Hell.
Thou that vibratest between the light and the darkness, rising, descending,
changing ever, yet ever the same
The sun is thy father; thy mother the moon. The wind hath borne thee in its
bosom and earth hath ever nourished the changeless god head of thy youth.
Come thou forth, I say, come thou forth, and make every spirit of the
firmament and of the ether, upon the earth and under the earth, on dry land
and in the water, of whirling air and of rushing fire, and every spell and
scourge of God, the Vast One, may be obedient unto me.

Phase Four: Preliminary Invocation

If you have not memorized the invocation, queue up a recording of it. You will need about half an hour of uninterrupted time for your first experiment, but it will get much faster with practice.[332]

331 Another name for Atum.

332 It should be almost instantaneous with several years of practice.

As much as possible, put your body in the position of the form you are assuming. Enter into magical space, time, and consciousness. Reconstruct the form around you. Make yourself into the appropriate shape of vessel for the god. Know what it feels like for your physical body to be their shape. Expand the central channel—a clean, clear channel from Underworld to upperworld, a pillar of undiluted white light. Feel yourself hollow out, making room for the god.

Begin the invocation script. Feel the god bubble up inside you. Release the energy channel you've been holding open and allow it to reshape itself into the required form. It may or may not be what you thought it would be.

Once you feel your energy body stabilize, take possession of it. This is not possession. The god is not filling you, with you on the outside. You are inside them, wearing them like a costume. Explore your new body. What does it feel like? What can it do? Most likely, you will find it difficult to hold the form for very long. You'll get better with practice. It just takes time.

Note: it is possible that, while doing this sort of exercise, you will feel spectral hands opening your skull at the sagittal suture. It feels weird, but this is actually desirable, and can be a powerful healing. Try not to freak out if this happens.

Phase Five: Shake it Off

As I mentioned, you'll most likely find it difficult to remain in the godform for any length of time. If you would like to release it at any time, simply shake your actual physical body around and concentrate on feeling it. Your energy body will slide back into human shape, using the architecture of your body to support it, as intended. If you are having difficulty "resetting," drink some water, eat something substantial, have an orgasm, and take a nap. You'll wake up right as rain.

Mask Magic

Another way to access a shape change is with an enchanted mask. Start by purchasing or making a mask of the form you'd like to assume. This is easiest near Halloween. In this, I'll be talking about animal masks and forms, but you can adapt this to other forms as well. For this example, I'll be working with Great Raccoon, the totem spirit of all raccoons, a clever and skillful spirit, with a fondness for pranks and tricks. Raccoon is also, unsurprisingly, excellent at mask magic, which is why I chose them for this example. Where I live, raccoons are ubiquitous, even here in the city. It was only when I began teaching Europeans that I realized raccoons are unknown there! If you don't know from raccoons, start with a different animal that you do know well.

To enchant a mask, begin by learning about the animal, its anatomy, and how it moves, and then learning to assume its shape in the Other Place. Once you have some facility with that, establish communication[333] with the ur-spirit of the animal, what I like to call the *genus genius*. Wear the mask while you do so. There is a recipe for the incense I recommend for raccoon (and most spirits of the Eastern Woodlands) on page 121 of my book *The Big Book of Magical Incense*, but you can use anything that feels foresty; pine resin would be a nice, and simple, choice. Once communication has been established, ask Great Raccoon to bless the mask as an instrument of communion between you and them.

Take the mask off, and bathe it in the incense (this is especially effective for porous masks, like the felt one above), all the while talking or singing to it. When you are done, put it back on, and feel the power it now holds. If you cannot feel it, continue bathing it in incense, while making raccoon noises.[334] Find the form of the animal and assume it, beginning by allowing the mask's essence to "sink into" your third eye, and then spread from there, almost like a liquid coating, enclosing your body. The use of a properly enchanted mask will help you "hold" the shapeshift even when you divert your attention elsewhere, making them *excellent* for ritual.

You can also make masks from the skulls, fur, feathers, or etc. of animals. When doing this, you'll generally find that you are connecting with the specific spirit of that specific animal, rather than (or perhaps in addition to) the genus genius of the category of animal. As always, I encourage you to source materials ethically and engage with them respectfully and responsibly. Making and using such magical masks can be, in my opinion, a great thing to do with furs or other materials you rescue from less respectful environments (for example, thrift stores, which is where I get my furs). For more on the magic and technical craft of making this type of mask, I recommend the book *Skin Spirits* by Lupa Greenwolf. She helped me make a mask that I personally use. I charged it using something very similar to the teddy bear consecration in Chapter Ten.

333 For example, via automatic writing.

334 If you don't know what raccoons sound like, ask YouTube. You will not be disappointed; they are very expressive animals.

CHAPTER THIRTEEN:

Dark Mirror Conjuration

When I was first learning magic as a teenager, dark mirror conjuration was the thing that really made me feel like a real witch, for whom magic was really, really real. For this and many other reasons, I love this technique very much; I hope you do too! I first learned this technique from Poke Runyon in his famous video lesson *The Magick of Solomon Documentary*, which came out in 1996, the year I graduated from high school. You can find it online.

In its earliest forms, his course/book was structured by asking himself, "What do I need to teach them, before I can teach dark mirror conjuration?" In this chapter, we'll start to put together pieces you've already learned into more complicated magics. At several points, you'll be advised to review previous chapters. More so than in other chapters, here, we'll be focusing on a single specific technique—dark mirror conjuration. Read the entire chapter before doing any conjuration.

What Is Dark Mirror Conjuration?

Dark mirror conjuration is a technique for communication with a spirit by conjuring it into a mirror in a mostly dark space, with just a bit of reflective light. The goal is to create a portal in a mirror that permits your reflection to shapechange into that of the spirit you are conjuring. For the most part, the point of dark mirror conjuration is to open a conversation, often to broker some kind of deal (called a compact). I learned to conjure in a regular silver mirror, but many prefer a darker surface. Traditionally, this technique is often done with a large, polished black stone. For example, the famous Elizabethan magician John Dee used a polished obsidian "shew stone" that Cortez looted from Latin America, which is today held by the British Museum, pictured.

Many people today make their own black mirrors by painting one side of a piece of glass matte black, and then scrying on the other side. Bowls of ink or red wine are also common, as are moonlit lakes and pools.

Different tools have different advantages and disadvantages. In my opinion, the ideal tool for dark mirror scrying is a powered-down LCD screen.[335] They're an ideal mix of reflective and matte, they're black, they have an excellent "depth" to them, and they're nearly ubiquitous in our culture. Generally, people are accustomed to seeing others stare at cellphones with a faraway, glazed-over look in their eyes, so LCD screens are great for "stealth" scrying. Throughout this chapter, I'm going to use the word "mirror" to mean "any reflective surface," including regular mirrors, black mirrors, nonoperational LCD screens, bowls of water, puddles, crystal balls, paperweights, and what have you, and everything in this chapter will work with any of those options.

Exercise: Opening Your Eyes

This exercise isn't magic at all. It's just a preparatory exercise. The goal of this exercise is to enter into an "open-eyed focus," which is the state you want your eyes to be in while scrying. There's no magic or mysticism to it; it's a physiological trick all humans (with undamaged eyes and optic nerves) can do. It just takes practice. You will probably want to practice the eye movements a few times, until you can slide into the "open focus" state with some ease. This should not take more than three or four practice sessions. To begin, we're going to learn some physical skills for the technique.

You will need:

* Some candles
* A dark room at night
* A dirty window through which you can see faraway things (if it's raining and there are water droplets on the window, that's even better!)

335 I don't recommend summoning spirits into devices that you want to keep working.

Steps:

1. Look at the window. Don't look through it; look at the window itself. Focus on the smudges and water droplets.
2. Now, look through the window, out at the world. Feel how the muscles in your eyes move to make this happen. Switch your focus from window to world fast, back and forth, several times, becoming familiar with the movement.
3. Focus on your reflection in the window. This will feel similar but not identical to focusing on the smudges in the window. Switch your focus from reflection to world to smudges several times, becoming familiar with the small muscular movements in your eyes that allow this. You might begin to develop a headache if you do this too long or too fast. Just close your eyes for a little while to let them rest if you need to.
4. Now, try to *slowly* slide your focus from window to the outside world. This will take a little practice, and may feel strange or unfamiliar.
5. *Slowly*, very slowly, slide back and forth from close focus to far focus. This might make your head hurt. Unless the pain is unbearable, just suck it up. You're not damaging your eyes. In fact, this exercise is good for your eyesight.
6. Once you are able to do this, close your eyes, and change their focus from near to far (you might imagine that you are looking *at* your eyelids, or through them).
7. Open your eyes again, and slowly shift focus from near to far. Try to stop at a halfway point, where you are gazing through, but not yet focused on anything. This might take some practice. I find it easier to do this while changing from near to far, but try it both ways.
8. Now, stare (as best as you are able) at the tip of your nose. (If you wear glasses, you might want to take them off for this; the frames can be distracting.)
9. Change focus from your nose to the window, feeling how your eye muscles move. Switch back and forth several times, rapidly.
10. Now, switch from nose to vista—without stopping at the window in between. Feel how your muscles feel in each position. When you've got that, switch back and forth fast several times.
11. Close your eyes, and do all three positions, feeling the motion.
12. Let your eyes relax for a little bit. And then, very slowly, close them, feeling the way that feels in your eyes and eyelids. Open them, and feel what that feels like.

13. With your eyes closed, imagine what it would feel like to close them a second time.
14. Close your "inner eyes."
15. With your eyes double-closed, slide your focus from near to far and back again, slowly. Once you've gotten the trick of that, stop at the "open" focus (midway).
16. Open your eyes, without changing focus.
17. Open your eyes again, without changing focus.

Exercise: Pareidolia

Once you have a facility with the "open eye" state, you still need to learn to see things that aren't there.

1. If you don't already know what *pareidolia* is, start off by reading the Wikipedia article about it.
2. Next, pick a moving surface to watch. When beginning, I believe that by far the easiest thing to start with is clouds. Choose a sunny, pleasant day when there are clouds in the sky, and lie down somewhere with an unobstructed view of the clouds. Because the clouds are far away, it should be easy to focus on them while keeping your eyes relaxed.
3. Try to look through the clouds, to the very edges of the universe.
4. Watch for figures that appear and dissipate in the clouds. For now, don't try to interpret them—just call them out as you see them. You might see animals, faces, or even whole scenes.
5. Do this for at least an hour. It is best to practice this exercise whenever you can, even if only for a minute or two. (You don't have to lie down for short sessions.)

Again, there is no magic to this—it's an inherent skill all humans have, but some adults have forgotten. Once you have retaught yourself this skill of seeing visions in the clouds, move on to a slightly harder version: seeing visions on the ceiling. The ideal ceilings for this are the kind with a texture to the plaster. If you don't have that kind, that's ok too.

1. Lie back on your bed or sofa, and let your eyes drift open.
2. Stare up at the ceiling and let your mind wander. Don't try to empty your mind, or quiet it; just let it chatter on in the background while you ignore it, like a bore at a cocktail party.
3. Put some trippy music on if you want.
4. Watch the ceiling, and look into and through the texture with your

open eyes. Slowly, images will begin to appear and move, crawling and slithering, shifting and morphing.

5. Just watch, mellow and open, and call out the images as you see them, as if describing shapes in the clouds to an invisible lover. (This makes it easier to remember what you have seen, and it helps settle the images, by naming them.)
6. For now, don't try to interpret them or ask any questions. This should be fun! Don't concentrate on trying to make images appear, or they will flee. Just chill out, watch with the mindset of a stoned hippy, laying on a hillside, watching shapes in the clouds.

Dark Mirror Conjuration

Conjuration is more difficult than most of the magic we've learned up until this point. However, you already know how to do most of it. The only hard part is that you need to sustain very close attention for a long time. Thankfully, by creating incenses, evocation scripts, and other tools beforehand, you can minimize how much of that time has to be all in a row.

First, I'll give a brief overview of the technique. After that big-picture view, we'll drill down and I'll show examples of each individual piece. I have very deliberately chosen to show examples with multiple spirits, so you cannot simply ape my practice. You will need to make decisions and develop your own ritual. If you do not feel ready to do that, return to Chapter One, reread the section called "Our First Spell," and write more spells. If you cannot design your own ritual, you are not yet ready to conjure. I'll go over this again after we've filled in all the steps.

1. Choose who you want to conjure. I'll give some suggestions for beginners to conjure in the section on page 322 titled "Who Ya Gonna Call?"
2. Write an evocation script. We'll discuss this in the section titled "Writing Evocation Scripts."
3. Set up the space so that the candles flicker on the mirror. I'll discuss this further shortly.
4. Enter magical space/time/consciousness.
5. Cast a big circle around the space, and then a smaller circle around the mirror.
6. Open the mirror.
7. Read an evocation script.
8. Scry until you know the spirit is there.

9. Have a conversation. If desired, broker and seal a deal.[336]
10. Dismiss the spirit.
11. Close the mirror.
12. Drop the circles.
13. The End.

Making a Magic Mirror

Before we can discuss how to use a magic mirror to conjure spirits, you'll need to have a magic mirror. I'll provide two different methods to create two different kinds of magic mirrors, but there are as many kinds as there are magicians. The type we'll create is a black bowl with a conjuration potion[337] in it. This method is easy, but it requires work to prepare before every conjuration. After this, we'll discuss one way to make a more permanent conjuring mirror.

Black Bowl

First, we'll be creating a conjuration mirror from a black bowl by filling it with a special conjuration potion. You can invent your own based on what you've learned, or use the recipe below, which involves a Greek anise-flavored liquor called *ouzo*. It's relatively cheap, and you can get it at almost any liquor store. We're using it specifically because it will cloud when added to the water (as will most kinds of anise liquor).

Minimally, you'll need enough potion to fully submerge the other ingredients, but it's fine to make extra. Because the potion is mostly alcohol, it will store indefinitely.

You will need:

* A black bowl
* Another bowl, for mixing (I prefer nonmetal)
* Ouzo, or another anise-flavored liquor, or a very strong wormwood tea
* Water
* 1 or more whole nutmegs
* A silver-colored coin
* Dried wormwood

---

336 As a general rule, I recommend against compacting on a first date.

337 Some people would call this kind of potion a "fluid condenser."

* Any other herbs or ingredients you wish to add (you're going to drink some, so nothing too poisonous)
* A small scroll
* A writing instrument with water-soluble ink
* A scarf

Steps:

1. Pour ouzo into the mixing bowl (not the black bowl).
2. Write the following on the scroll in water-soluble ink: "'ΕΡΜΗΣ 'ΕΡΜΗΝΕΥΤΗΣ."[338]
3. Then add the scroll to the ouzo.
4. In the ouzo, soak one or more whole nutmegs,[339] at least one silver-colored coin,[340] and a good amount of dried wormwood.[341]
5. As always, as you add each ingredient, you should talk to it, reminding it of its living essence, extolling its virtues, and asking it to aid you in your magic. For example, you might say something like:

   "Ouzo, sweet liquor of anise and herbs, awaken again to yourself. Born on the Holy Mountain,[342] you are the nectar of the gods and the lion's milk[343] of prophecy. Nutmeg, Myristica,[344] you open the senses and draw mad luck. Awaken to yourself, and bring luck, clarity, and insight into this potion. Silver on my tongue, make me silver-tongued. Wormwood, herb of vision and spirit, open the roads between worlds. Be with me, see with me, O green-leafed Queen. Hermes Hermeneutes, just as your name pervades these waters, so does your vision and voice!"

6. Allow the potion to soak overnight. Soaking it longer is even better; it will get stronger and stronger over time.

---

338 This is the name "HERMES HERMENEUTES" in Greek.

339 Nutmegs are sacred to Hermes, and very mildly entheogenic.

340 So you will be silver-tongued. I like to use Mercury dimes.

341 Wormwood is a classic evocation herb and helps the nutmeg produce visions. If you use absinthe instead of ouzo, you don't have to add extra wormwood (a.k.a. *Artemisia absinthium*).

342 Ouzo was legendarily invented on Mt. Athos, a monastery island in Greece where women are not permitted. Obviously, this makes me very much want to go there.

343 *Lion's milk* (aslan sütü) is a Turkish name for water with raki, a liquor almost identical to ouzo.

344 Myristica is the Latin name for nutmeg. If I had an orange cat, I would name them Myristica, but I'm not into cats, so you should name one that instead!

7. If you make extra, store it in a light-proof container. It's mostly alcohol; it will store indefinitely.
8. We'll discuss how to use this conjuration potion to set up a black bowl conjuration in the section titled "Setting Up the Space."

Making a Pergamon Triangle

The image shown here is of a third-century bronze triangle found in Pergamon. Such triangles appear to have been mass produced; a similar (though simpler) triangle was found in Sardis in 2015, and several others have since been found elsewhere in the ancient world. Of those yet discovered, the Pergamon triangle pictured is of the finest workmanship and contains more writing. The three goddesses each wear a mural crown, and are labeled as Dione,[345] Phoebe,[346] and Nyche.[347] At the top of the picture, Nyx holds a snake and a dagger. Dione holds

345 This name means "goddess" and in this context is probably an epithet of Hekate. It is often associated with Persephone, Demeter, or Aphrodite.

346 Phoebe is another name for Selene, Hekate, or Artemis, as well as the name of their Titaness grandmother. Her name means "Light."

347 This is an alternate spelling of the name Nyx, the most ancient goddess, Night.

a torch and a whip, and Phoebe, a key and torch. At the feet of each goddess is the name Amibousa, which means "She Who Changes," almost certainly a reference to the moon's phases. Around the edges are magical characters I cannot translate.[348] Most of the writing does not form words, but with the goddess labeled Phoebe (bottom right), it says "O Persephone, O Melinoë,[349] O Leucophryne."[350] The function of the original is unclear, but I (and most others) believe it is either a scrying table, with the central disk polished to a mirror finish, or a base for an awakened idol of Hekate.

Based on that ancient example, I have written consecration and opening rituals that can be used for any type of Hekate-based scrying mirror, as well as an illustration you can use as a base for a mirror or crystal ball. Alternatively, you can draw or laser engrave the triangle (or one of your own design) directly onto a mirror. This consecration of a mirror need only be done once when the mirror is first constructed. Thereafter, it should be stored wrapped in cloth or paper so that random things are not casually reflected in it, and rebaptized with moon water from time to time. In addition to being used as a spirit portal, the triangle can also be used to charge lunar or Hekatean talismans or materia.

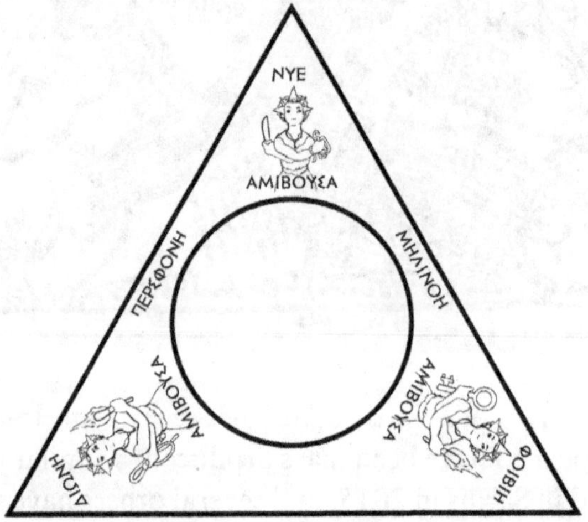

Consecration of the Mirror

This consecration can be performed at any time, but it's best outdoors under a full moon.

You will need:

348 To the best of my knowledge, no one else can either.

349 Melinoë is the goddess of nightmares, a daughter of Persephone by Kronian Zeus.

350 An avatar of Artemis-Hekate worshiped at Leucophrys in Phrygia.

* A Pergamon-style triangle
* A mirror to put on the triangle (or a triangle on a mirror)
* A secret name for the mirror, which you may invent or discover by any method
* About a gallon of moon water (living water infused with moonlight)
* An incense of myrrh, wormwood, and juniper needles
* A white or black cloth big enough to wrap the mirror in
* Three candles
* Cheap[351] silver lipstick[352]

Steps:

1. Put on the silver lipstick. If you like, you can also use it to paint a crescent moon on your forehead, or any other body decorations you like.
2. Enter into magical space, time, and consciousness by any method.
3. Light the candles, placing one at each corner of the triangle.
4. Light the incense and put it somewhere handy, but not in the way.
5. Cast a circle into the ouroboros.
6. Generate an aura of indigo light.
7. Gather it into a ball between your hands, and carefully place it into the central mirror.
8. Speak out loud, saying something like:[353]

"Hekate, Dione, Phoebe, Nyx:
Mistress of mists that mix in betwixt,
That liminal boundary that guards the Between
Artemis, Persephone, Melinöe, Queen,
By key and by torch, by snake, whip, and blade,
I call to you now: Please come to my aid!
Selene, Mene, bright moon shine,
Open this portal as Hekate's shrine!

351 You *do not* want sealed or smudge-proof lipstick, because you're going to lip-print the mirror.

352 Although I rarely wear "normal" makeup, I love lipsticks and eyeliners for drawing signs and sigils on the body, and on mirrors. I especially like Nyx brand pigment crayons (which claim to be for eyes, but also work fine on lips), largely because their brand name is "Nyx," and they're cheap.

353 Very vaguely based on PGM IV:2522–2572.

Triple voiced, triple headed, triple faced, triple necked
Your mirror stands ready, your face to reflect.
Aktiophis,[354] Daeira,[355] give light to true Knowing,
As I bathe this mirror in cold water's flowing,
[Pour the water over the face of the mirror.]
And awaken new life as a portal of insight.
Let darkness disperse, give way to bright light!"

9. Reach up, up, up into the heavens, and pull down the power of the moon, down through the crown of your head, and down into your mouth. (There is no need to fully draw down the moon the way you learned in Chapter Five.)
10. Raise the mirror to your face and kiss it, leaving a silver lip print, and push the entirety of the Moon into the mirror while you whisper her name to her. Do not tell the name to others.
11. Wrap the mirror, and store it undisturbed until the next full moon before using, to allow the power to "settle in."
12. At that time, you can clean off the lipstick[356] before use.

How to Make a Blasting Rod

A blasting rod is a sort of magic ray-gun used to punish spirits for disobedience. I originally learned to conjure with a blasting rod close at hand, but I have never felt it necessary to use one. In fact, I no longer even own one; I gave my last one (pictured) away almost a decade ago. However, having a blasting rod can help ease anxiety for people who are not confident in their ability to command spirits.

The first step in making a Mastros-style blasting rod is to take a walk in the woods and ask the spirits to help you find the right stick. If there is a

---

354 This is an epithet of Hekate which is usually said to be of unknown meaning. I believe it to be ἀκτίς-ὄφις, or "ray snake." I associate it with the Milky Way, and with Hekate's mother (Leto's sister), Asteria, the goddess of "night prophecy."

355 Modern pagans often choose to translate this epithet of Hekate's as "She Who Knows," coming from the root word δα, which means "to learn." However, older commentators often tied it to δαίς, which means "to kindle" (like a torch). If we combine these meanings, we arrive at something like "The Great Teacher, She Who Kindles the Flame of Knowledge" or "Spark of Idea."

356 Use glass cleaner like Windex.

particular forest with whom you have a connection, look there first. Singing or speaking to the forest about your quest will help you seek. The nature of stick wands is that the power will flow along the natural grain of the stick. A very straight stick will produce a very effective laser-like cutting tool, whereas a twisted stick, like the one pictured, produces a more corkscrew/drilling energy, which I personally prefer for blasting rods.

Many people only gather sticks for wands from certain kinds of trees or at certain astrologically significant times, but I do not find that necessary. If you know trees, you know that every tree has its own "personality," but all of them can be mean when they want to be. Particularly for blasting rods, but also for wands and staves more generally, I like to look in cemeteries right after a windstorm. Because cemeteries often have lone trees on hills, they are especially susceptible to wind damage and have lots of limbs down, but they tend to get cleaned up fast.

If you cut from a living tree, remember to get permission first. However, simply from a crafting angle, fallen wood that's had some time to dry out will work better. If you let people know you are wand crafting, they'll often give you cool sticks they find. The stick for the wand I'm holding in the picture was found by my late father, for example. I would never go so far as to say that *all* real witches already have random sticks propped in every corner of their house, but I certainly do, and I imagine you might too.

Choose a stick that feels aggressive. It should be longer than your forearm from elbow to tip and thick enough to feel sturdy as a weapon. Hazel, elder, and blackthorn are all quite traditional for blasting rods, but many kinds of wood work well. Broadly, it's better to work with wood from a tree you know well, or at least a species you know. For blasting rods, I prefer sticks around which vines have grown, so they've grown with a twist in them. The one pictured here is from a quince tree around which morning glory grew. Another practitioner I know has one made from the root[357] of an oak tree from the grove where we used to practice.[358] It was toppled by lightning and wind.

Once you've found the right stick, take it home, and begin crafting your blasting rod.

1. If the stick came off a living tree, let it sit for a week or two to dry out.

357 Root wood is slightly harder to work with energetically; it tends to be slower and lower vibration—"thumpy rather than buzzy," as they might say in a vibrator ad. That kind of energy is good for many things, particularly commanding the Dead, but requires a little more finesse to use.

358 In Frick Park, down the hill from Blue Slide.

2. Spend some time handling your stick (ha ha!). Find the most comfortable spot to hold it. Examine the grain; that's the vasculature through which the tree's vital energy moved.
3. Feel how your power moves through the wood. Generally, it is better to have the handle end of the wand on the part of the stick that was closer to the roots, so the energy will flow through the wand from trunk to tip. If you are using root wood, reverse that, so power flows from the trunk down through the roots.
4. Wash off any loose dirt, and take it outside or somewhere else you don't mind making a mess.
5. Cut the stick to length, and remove any smaller branches that stick out.
6. With a thin-bladed knife, peel off all the bark that will come loose. Try not to slice the wood. Some kinds of trees, the bark will peel right off, and some, it won't. If it won't peel off, that's ok. You can sand it off later.
7. Go to the hardware store and buy a variety pack of sandpapers. Don't cheap out; in sandpaper, as in so many things, you get what you pay for. Starting with the coarsest sandpaper, slowly sand off all the bark.
8. Use long, slow, strong strokes, from the handle end to the tip end. This is important! Try not to sand backward, but if there are small nooks and crannies you can't get to otherwise, that's ok. You'll want to wash off the excess sawdust from time to time.
9. Think about how you'll use the wand as you do this, and imagine energy flowing through it. Speak or sing to the wand as you sand. If you'd like a formal script, you can say something like this, which is adapted from one in *The Grand Grimoire*:

   "I beseech you, Great ONE, by all your mighty names, Adonai,[359] *Elohim,*[360] *Ariel,*[361] *Yehovam,*[362] *to be propitious unto me, and to endow this Wand which I am sanding with the power and virtue of the rods*

359 This means "owner" or "lord" in the feudal sense.

360 This is the same name I mentioned earlier, which means "gods," although many would argue it is an "honorific plural."

361 This means "lion of El" or "lion of God."

362 This is a gross, appropriative, Christian way to say the Most Holy Name, spelled "yod heh vuv heh" For technical magician reasons, I have declined to write any Hebrew Holy Names in this book, because doing do would put additional ritual requirements on the reader.

of Jacob,[363] of Moses,[364] and of the mighty Joshua.[365] I also ask, Holy ONE, that you infuse into this wand the whole strength of Samson, the righteous wrath of Emanuel and the thunders of mighty Zariatnatmik,[366] who will avenge the names of men at the Day of Judgment! Amen!"

10. Slowly work through the various sand papers, until you get to a very fine-grained one that is usually called "finish paper." The stick should be very, very smooth at this point. I like to run it under my nose[367] to make sure there's no rough spots. I don't recommend doing all the sanding at once. I would say that I spend a total of about ten hours sanding a wand, usually spread over at least a week, sometimes over a whole month. This is an important step; the constant rubbing "teaches" the wand which way the energy flows.
11. Once you've completely sanded, and the wand is velvety smooth, wash it lovingly in warm soapy water, and let it completely dry overnight.

For the next step, you'll need paper towels; a small, shallow bowl; and at least an ounce of magical oil. Wear a shirt you don't mind staining, or just forgo a shirt entirely. Choose any oil that feels aggressively compelling. Abramelin and King Solomon oils are nice, but so is bear grease with red ochre or blessed olive oil.

Pour the oil into the dish, and dip your fingers into it.

1. Slowly, rub the oil into the wand. Always run from the handle to the point.
2. Imagine the oil sinking into the wood, impregnating it with its magical essence. The wood will slowly soak up the oil. Depending on the type of wood, the weather, and how dry it is, you can get a surprising amount of oil to soak in.
3. Spend at least an hour lovingly rubbing and polishing your wand. (Ha ha!)

---

363 See Bereshit (Genesis) 32:11, for example.

364 The rod of Moses is a snake. It has a lot of interesting mythology.

365 I am not familiar with any mythology of Joshua's rod, although biblical myth is not my specialty. I'm surprised the third staff here isn't Aaron's. That's who I would have used.

366 According to Aaman Lamba, an expert on *The Grand Grimoire:* "Zariatnatmik basically means 'Powerful or Great person'...he is the archangel who will 'avenge the injuries of mankind on the Great Day of Judgement'...The reference is to the powerful rod or verge foudroyante." (From a Facebook private message, Thursday, August 27, 2020.)

367 *Much* more sensitive than your fingertips.

4. Try to commune with the spirit of the wand and learn its name. However, it probably doesn't have a name yet, so you'll have to give it one.
5. After you've finished oiling your wand, let the wand sit overnight (or longer) to let as much oil as possible soak in, and then rub off any excess oil. If desired, you can rub in some beeswax at this stage to help "seal" the wand.

I re-oil my wands from time to time. More oil sinks in every time, leaving the wand even smoother and smelling lovely. If desired, you can paint, carve, or burn magical symbols onto your wand. Were I going to do that, I'd do it before I applied the oil. I usually leave wands unadorned, but that's just because I like the way the wands look plain.

I'm not going to recommend it as a general practice, but I have also "oiled" some kinds of wands inside my body. If you're going to do that, use lots of olive oil, cocoa butter, ghee, or some other pure, nontoxic, non-perfumed oil as a lubricant. Also, make sure you did a really good job sanding! If you're going to do this, remember to put it in with the handle end first. If it's not clear why, then sticking a magic wand up your twat might not be the right kind of magic for you.

Who Ya Gonna Call?

Now that we've made all our tools, we can get ready to conjure. However, before you can conjure anyone,[368] of course, you have to decide who you want to speak to. If you've never done any direct conjuration before,[369] I recommend that the first spirits you conjure should include at least a few of:

1. Hekate Propylaia, to open the gates of magic
2. Hermes Hermeneutes, to facilitate communication
3. Phoebe Chrysostephanos, to facilitate mystic consciousness
4. Python Drakaina
5. Pasithea
6. Hekate Krokopeplos
7. Lucifer

In this chapter, we'll be using the examples of Hekate Propylaia, Hermes Hermeneutes, and Phoebe Chrysostephanos.

368 Any god, any angel, any demon, any ghost, any spirit. Anyone.

369 If you've been doing everything in this book, you've done several conjurations already.

Writing Evocation Scripts

Now that we've created the mirror and chosen who to call, it's time to write an evocation[370] script. While a potion or mirror can be reused in many conjurations, I find it best to write a new evocation script for every conjuration. Evocation is an alternate name for any kind of conjuration where a spirit is called forth with the voice—it is a magic woven with words and fueled by breath.

Once you get more practice, you can speak directly from your heart to call forth spirits, but when you're first learning, it's better to first prepare a script for yourself. Most evocation-conjurations in Anglophone magic follow a relatively straightforward formula. Some evocations will combine or reorder these steps, and may skip a few, but this is the basic template:

1. Make a small offering, as "bait." Incense, candle, and water is my go-to choice.
2. Call the spirit by many names, titles, and descriptions; be precise but florid.
3. Butter them up with praise.
4. Tell a brief snippet of myth (or a few) relevant to the topic at hand.
5. Explain why you've called.
6. Explain why they should care.

You can either use pre-written evocations or create your own. There's nothing wrong with using a pre-written evocation. The incantations we call "Orphic hymns" are just such pre-written evocations.[371] Next, I'll walk you through writing an evocation for Hermes Hermeneutes as an example, and later in the lesson, I'll provide a fill-in-the-blank template. I like to write my evocation immediately before the conjuration, but you can do it ahead of time. Personally, I find a very mild trance helpful to writing evocations.

The first step in writing an evocation is to do some research about that spirit you want to summon. Learn as much about them as you can. In particular, learn their names and stories.[372] What about them makes you want to summon them? What are their special qualities? What names, titles, and stories relate specifically to the "face" you want to talk to? In this example, we're

---

370 *Evocation* is any kind of conjuration that calls forth spirits using the voice.

371 You can read Thomas Taylor's 1792 translations online, or buy my book of modern translations, *Orphic Hymns Grimoire.*

372 For Greek spirits, I strongly recommend the site Theoi.com for its excellent lists of names and titles.

summoning Hermes. If you don't already know Hermes's "origin story," go read the Homeric hymn to Hermes before proceeding. Here are some names, titles, etc. of Hermes Hermeneutes that feel relevant to learning to communicate better with spirits by means of dark mirror evocation:

* Hermes
* Hermeneutes
* Interpreter
* Well-connected One
* Kharidotes ("Joy Giver")
* Lord of Crossroads
* Signpost
* Guide
* Diaktoros ("Messenger")
* Angelos ("Messenger")
* Messenger
* Clever One
* Quicksilver King
* Caduceus Bearer
* Who Bears the Messenger's Rod
* Herald
* Invented the alphabet
* Gives many gifts
* Speaks every language
* Knows the name of every spirit

Next, we need to make a similar list of names and titles for you. This part I can't write for you; you'll have to write your own. I might say something like: "Sara Mastros, daughter of Ellen and Michael, daughter of the House of Jakob, inheritor of the line of Sarai, Keyholder of the Witch House, Initiate of the Order of the Caduceus, Priestess of the Golden Gryphon, Sister of the Circle of Sibyls, Hermeneutes of Orpheus, Teacher of Witches, Comrade of the Compact of Solomon, etc., etc...." It's kind of like a magical resume; paint yourself in the best possible light. Boast and swagger, but don't outright lie.

Next, figure out why the spirit in question should take your call. There are only a few categories into which these reasons fall:

* You have previously undergone a special initiation into their Mystery and participate in communion with them.[373]
* You have the endorsement of another powerful spirit, and can speak in their name. For example, Christian magicians can use the power of their baptism to call "*In the name of Christ Jesus.*" Blood ancestors make especially powerful endorsers.
* You possess knowledge of their special and secret names. Usually, you would use this method in repeat conjurations, after having first made a conjuration using another method and being given such a "speed dial" name or passcode. You can also learn public "secret" names via research, but they are not as effective as ones you were given directly. This method is very common in Judaism, where we call "*By the power of the Divine Names...*"
* You share traits with a spirit whose call they would want to take. For example, an Egyptian magician might begin: *"I am a truth-speaking magician who is become like Osiris...."* Personally, I usually assume the form of Solomon[374] before summoning Hebrew spirits like angels and demons. You will learn to assume godforms in the next chapter.
* They are especially interested in the topic you would like to talk about: *"I come to you, seeking your wisdom and communication, oh god of wisdom and communication. Oh, Great Hermeneutes, interpreter, teach me to speak with spirits, that I might also serve as hermeneutes."*
* You are calling under a preexisting "service contract" enforced by a powerful spirit. So-called "Solomonic" magic usually works this way. In these cases, it's the spirit's job to take your call. Personally, I find this method the least reliable, because I feel like I tend to get a low-level "answering service" type spirit on the other end much of the time, and treating them like a slave does not inspire good customer service.

Next, you need to weave those things together into a pleasing thing to read. As an example, it might go something like the following. As I've said, it is vastly preferable to write your own scripts, rather than using premade ones.

---

373 For example, several PGM spells call on the power of a chthonic initiation: *"I have gone below and seen many things...."*

374 There are instructions for doing this on pages 53–54 of *The Sorcery of Solomon: A Guide to the 44 Planetary Pentacles of the Magician King.*

Minimally, to use this one, you'll modify the section on offerings to match whatever you're actually going to offer and the type of mirror you're going to use. In the example below, I'm offering coffee, cake, candle flame, and water, and I'm using a black bowl with a conjuration potion.

"Hermes Hermeneutes, Interpreter and Guide, Lord of the Crossroad and the Signpost, I call out to you, blessed Herald, Teacher of Teachers. I, [NAME], child of [NAME, TITLES, ETC.] come before you as a student, eager to learn, eager to know your face and hear your voice. You invented the alphabet; help give form to speech for me. You speak every language; I beseech you to speak to me now in mine. You know every name; I entreat you to speak mine now to me, as I speak yours to you: Hermes, Hermeneutes, Angelos, Kharidotes, lord of Cyllene, Maia's child: O my beloved Quicksilver King. Appear in this mirror, clearly and without complication, appear in this bowl and teach me how to See you. I have brought you coffee with cardamom. I have brought you cake and candle and clean, cool water. I have made this potion for you, smell it with my nose, taste it with my tongue, and allow me to open a portal for you in this bowl. I call you Great Hermeneutes; let me serve as hermeneutes for you. Quick, quick, quick!"

Dream on it at least once, and then reread your evocation script, and make any changes you feel desirable. Once you're happy with what you've written, write or print it very large on a clean piece of paper. You want it to be easy to read by candlelight. If you like, you can decorate it, but it doesn't matter what it looks like. Practice reading it out loud a few times, and make sure it sounds magical. It should feel good in your mouth to say it. This is not about visuals, it's about sound.[375] Magic like this is woven with breath. Not the idea of words, but the *sound* of words.

Prepare Yourself for Magic

Dark mirror conjuration is the first long ritual we've discussed. A conjuration is often an all-day affair and requires tools to be prepared in advance. While each individual step is relatively simple, the actual experience can be a bit grueling if you're not properly "in the zone" before beginning. There are many methods

375 This instruction is for people who are not confident in their skill with words. If you are a writer, you should, of course, focus on both the sound and the visuals.

to prepare for serious magic, but among the most common is fasting as a way of "disconnecting" from the overwhelming drain on our attention that the world constantly demands, as well as anchoring yourself fully into your body. You'll have to decide for yourself exactly what kind of fasting is most appropriate for you and your life. Personally, I recommend a gentle three-day fast, followed by a more intense fast for twelve to twenty-four hours prior to ritual. A gentle fast means no meat, no profanity, no intoxicants, and no sex. A more intense fast might additionally cut out solid food, animal products, social media, paid work, and/or unnecessary speech. It is spectacularly unwise (but also very fun) to dark mirror conjure while on hallucinogens. That is *absolutely not* a practice for beginners. Such practice has a real knack for kicking off long-term psychotic episodes, even in people who have not had such episodes before. But, if you don't go crazy, you do tend to learn a lot of witchcraft very fast. Unless you are 100% confident in your conjuration and containment skills, I do not advise it. Even for experienced magicians, I would strongly recommend against doing it alone. Use the buddy system!

In addition to fasting, I always like a salt bath and casting off immediately before ritual. As I've mentioned before, I like to dress up for ritual. For conjuration, I generally wear either all white or all black. Sometimes, I wear a white, full-body veil that covers me from head to ankle, with only a tiny lattice window for my eyes. It is very effective in aiding dissociation from the body, and it looks showy when I do ritual with an audience. Personally, I do not like any kind of metal on my person when I'm conjuring, although I make exceptions for things like the screws in my plastic spectacle frames. I recommend against dressing up as/for the spirit you are conjuring, unless your goal is a full possessory experience, which is not what I am teaching in this chapter (although you could probably work out how to do it by combining these techniques with those of the previous two chapters).

Prepare the Space for Magic

Just like you should make sure your self is well prepared, the same is true for the space in which you'll be working. Because my lifestyle and housing allow me to leave things set up without danger of them being disturbed, I often set up the space almost the whole way, then go bathe and prepare myself for ritual,[376] and then do the final casting of the circles before beginning the

376 Just so I don't get my pretty whites all mussed before ritual.

conjuration. However, for simplicity of explanation, I'll be describing it as if I fully prepare myself, and then fully prepare the space.

The first step in preparing a space for heavy magic is to decide what space to use. For dark mirror conjuration, you'll probably want to sit directly facing a mirror which is too far away to touch from your seat. Ideally, you'll want a space that can be made completely dark, and then minimally lit with candles. What's most important is that it be a space where you will not be disturbed. If you cannot carve out a full two hours[377] for this work, then I regret to inform you that you do not have space for this kind of magic in your life.

Next, clean up. Do a really good job of it, as if your judgmental grandmother were coming for a visit. Try to avoid strongly scented cleaning products or other artificial smells. Remove any idols, ikons, art, or other images with people, animals, or other "characters" from the space. Next, set up the space so that, when seated, you are looking directly across incense smoke into a mirror barely lit by flickering light. If you're using a bowl as a mirror, fill it about 2/3 full with cold[378] moon water.[379] Do not yet add the conjuration portion. The goal is that you can see your face, reflected but distorted, in the mirror while you are huffing the incense. Make sure that everything is placed completely before ritual. You don't want to "lose your groove" by having to fuss with it during ritual. I like to have a glass of water, pencil, and paper handy in case I want them. I sometimes take notes or make sketches during a conjuration. You can get everything set up well in advance, which is, in my experience, usually easier than doing it immediately before ritual.

Your First Dark Mirror Conjuration

Now that we've prepared everything, it's time for magic! Before beginning, you should already have written and memorized[380] your evocation script, prepared a conjuration potion, prepared yourself, and laid out the candle, incense, and mirror.

---

377 This is just for the conjuration, not the prep or any follow up work.

378 In truth, I don't think there's any reason it has to be cold, but I was taught to do it with cold water, and scrying in warm water just feels weird to me.

379 Or, really, any kind of water will be fine.

380 Even if you have it memorized, it's generally wise to have handy a physical copy written big enough to read by candlelight.

If you like, you can choose an astrologically auspicious time for the conjuration. For example, Wednesdays during an hour of Mercury are best to summon Hermes (whom we'll be summoning in the example below), but anytime will be fine. Personally, I find this type of conjuration easier at night than when the sun is shining.[381]

When you're ready, light the candles and the incense. If you're playing a prerecorded noise, start it. Enter into magical space, time, and consciousness by any method. Center yourself very securely. Ideally, perform a complete Plugging In. Open a circle around you and your working space. The goal is mostly to create a "zone of liminality," an uncanny space where it is easier for spirits to manifest.[382] However, you also want a sort of "clean room" around you, so that things going on outside your immediate environment don't perturb the connection. Cast another circle around the perimeter of the mirror, reinforcing it strongly.

Raise your arms to shoulder height in front of you and make a circle, with your elbows apart and hands open and relaxed. Circulate energy around this circuit: across your heart, from left to right, out your right palm, and back into your left. Once you can feel that energy vortex develop some momentum of its own, to the point where you don't need to consciously direct it anymore, form another, smaller circuit in between your hands: out your right thumb, into your left thumb, out your left middle finger, into your right middle finger. Allow that vortex to build momentum as well. Once it has, slowly move it into the mirror, creating a portal. Shrink or expand it to fit. If you're using a bowl, you may want to stir the water a little with your finger to induce a bit of spinning in the water before you can get it to "click" in. Once it has, detach the mirror-circle from your hands.

Put on your headscarf. Knock back a shot of conjuration potion (I know, it's a little gross), and anoint your third eye with a little more. Splash some on the mirror or pour some into the bowl. In a bowl, it should produce milky streaks in the water. Lean over into the incense, and focus your eyes on the surface of the mirror. There should be enough incense that this is not entirely pleasant, but not so much that you're choking.

---

381 Although, in truth, I find basically everything easier at night than under day glare. I am largely nocturnal.

382 I hate the phrase the veil is thin, but it would be accurate to say that the goal is to thin the veil.

Opening the Mirror

The first step of the actual conjuration (aside from preliminaries like entering magical space/time/consciousness, which precede almost all magic work) is to open the mirror as a portal for spirit communication. In what follows, we'll call upon Hekate Propylaia (Hekate Before the Gates) to open the mirror for dark mirror conjuration. Note that we are not conjuring her in this step. Rather, this is a preliminary step before conjuration to open the mirror into which the spirit will be conjured.

Hekate Propylaia

The Greek word προπύλαιον (propylaion) means literally "(pro) before (pyli) the gates." Today, the word is used by archaeologists to refer to the gated entrance to an ancient temple, flanked by large columns. Throughout the classical world, shrines and statues of Hekate were placed by gateways—the gates of cities and temples—as well as the doors of individual homes. At Lagina, as well as in Miletus, Thasos, and Rhodes, Hekate had shrines at the city gates. At the Acropolis of Athens, a large statue called Hekate Epipyrgidia (Hekate of the Tower) guards the entrance.

Great Greek houses very often had small marble statues of Hekate (called Hekataion) at the doorways. There is good reason to believe that more modest homes also had Hekataion, likely of wood (which rarely survive to the modern day). This association with gates and doorways is primarily as a protective guardian, and helps explain her associations with keys, torches, and dogs, as well.

In addition to her role guarding literal doorways, Hekate Propylaia is also a goddess of the threshold between our world and the Other Place. In mythology both classical and modern, Hekate is unquestionably an initiatrix of all who seek to travel between the worlds. Like every Dweller on the Threshold, Hekate Propylaia can appear fearsome the first time you meet her. This is largely because (if you're reading this book) you grew up in a culture that demonizes the Underworld, and leads us to be afraid of the spirit world. It's true, there are dangers here. Everything worth doing is so, because it has the power to change you, and that is a dangerous and scary thing. Calm your fears, and approach Hekate Propylaia respectfully, but without fear. She will test you; her gateway can appear as a mirror that reflects back all the terrible things we think about ourselves.

Opening the Mirror-Gate of Hekate

When you are ready to begin, say aloud (something like):

"Hekate Propylaia, Who Guards the Gates of the Three Worlds,
I stand before you as a supplicant,
I ask entry into your mystery.
Allow me to pass through the gates of initiation and into your teaching.
I light incense before you. I pay homage to you.
This I will do each Dark Moon, so long as we both shall wish.
Hekate Propylaia, open the gates of my mind to know your truth.
Hekate Propylaia, open the gates of my spirit to feel your presence.
Hekate Propylaia, open the gates of my ears to hear your voice.
Hekate Propylaia, open the gates of my eyes to see your vision.
Hekate Propylaia, open the gates of my body, that I may fly forth safely.
Hekate Propylaia, open the gates of your Temple to me,
that I may enter into your Mystery.
Hekate Propylaia, open the gates of the Other World to me,
that I may fly forth, and return to my body again.
Hekate Propylaia, open every gate to me,
and walk with me as I traverse them."

Take hold of the circle you cast into the mirror, and quickly and without hesitation turn it inside out. This is a similar sensation to when you step through the "waterfall" in trance journey. In some ways, it is the opposite of that operation. There, you entered into the Other Place. Now, you're bringing the Other Place here.

Enter into the Seer's Trance, which you learned in Chapter Four. If you are tempted to turn back to reread that now, you have not yet practiced it enough to be doing a dark mirror conjuration.[383] In your best magician's voice, recite your evocation script, likely several times. You may find yourself slipping into glossolalia. This is a good sign.

As you feel the weird creeping up the back of your back, be quiet, and stare at your reflection in the bowl until it begins to shimmer and morph into someone else. Try to keep your eyes open focused, and look through the smoke into the mirror. If you're having trouble, rapidly switch focus from

383 As always, this book is intended for beginners. If you already have your own style of divination trance, use that.

the incense cloud to the mirror to your eyes reflected in the mirror. Try to focus on all three of them at once, until you're focusing on none of them at all.

Once you see the beginnings of the manifestation, repeat the evocation script again, asking for Hermes (or whoever) to appear clearly and intelligibly in the water. Speak to him, encouraging him to appear, and then stop talking, watch the surface of the water, and listen for his voice in the noise. Once you catch sight of him or hear his voice, *don't panic*. It is genuinely shocking and uncanny the first time you realize that this shit is really, really *real*, and something which is not you is staring back at you from the mirror. If you panic, you'll lose your trance and have to start over. Also, it's very rude to ding-dong-ditch a spirit. If you do it too many times, spirits will stop answering your calls.[384]

Once you've established communication, introduce yourself, and explain why you have called. Ask a question and listen for a response. This part, where you have to maintain trance while interacting with something, is often harder than the initial summoning. Just do your best. It may take several conjurations for you to really get into the swing of it, particularly if you have not yet developed facility with automatic writing or another form of spirit communication.

License to Depart

When you're done conversing, say thank you. If things went well, tell the spirit you will call again (but only if you mean it). Ideally, make an appointment to do so. If things went particularly well, ask them for a "speed dial" name or password to make the conjuration simpler next time, but this is a bit presumptive after a "first date." Bid them goodbye. You should be able to sense their departure. If you cannot, wait a few minutes, but then proceed anyway.

Thank Hekate Propylaia for guarding the gates and ask her to now close them in the reverse order you opened them before. As always, it is better to speak your own words from your heart, but you might say something like:

"Hekate Propylaia, Who Guards the Gates of the Three Worlds,
You have walked with me through every gate,
guarding ever both gate and person.

---

384 If you accidentally get scared and ding-dong-ditch, repeat the conjuration and *apologize.*

I stand before you as a supplicant,
having entered into your mystery.
You have allowed me to pass through the
gates of initiation and into your teaching.
Now we close those gates.
Hekate Propylaia, close the gates of the Other World,
that no more should the mirror be a door.
Hekate Propylaia, close the gates of my body,
that I may live in health and peace.
Hekate Propylaia, close the gates of my eyes,
that I see only with human vision.
Hekate Propylaia, close the gates of my ears,
that I hear with only human hearing.
Hekate Propylaia, close the gates of my spirit,
that I may move through the world as a human.
And yet, beloved Hekate Propylaia,
keep open the gates of my mind to always know Truth."

Next, once again take hold of the circle around the mirror, and turn it right-side-in again. This may require some force if there are spirits holding it open from the other side. If so, ask Hekate to give you the strength, and push witchfire from you heart. Once that is done, spin the circle the other way, closing the vortex. When the mirror is back to reflecting as a normal mirror would, you can drop the circle around the working space. If using a bowl, pour out the water, ideally onto earth, but down a drain is also ok. In either case, follow with quite a bit of clean water. Wrap the mirror and store it respectfully.

Write notes immediately. The experience will fade fast, like a dream. Once you've taken notes, come fully back to yourself. Move your body. Drink some water. Eat something. It is generally wise to bathe after a conjuration and before going to sleep, just in case you got some magical goo on you, but this is less necessary with divine beings, like Hermes, than after conjuring unsavory spirits, like demons.

Compulsive Conjuration

In the previous conjuration, we simply placed a call to the spirit world, and asked nicely for the spirit to appear. If a spirit you are calling fails to take your call, you have the option to try to force them to appear.[385] I do not generally recommend compulsive conjuration to beginners. However, once you develop some facility with conjuration more generally, you might want to experiment with compulsive conjuration. There are four basic options for compulsive conjuration, but in practice, these methods are often combined:

1. Command by Hierarchy
2. Command by Compact
3. Command with a True Name
4. Command by Personal Power

Command by Hierarchy

The first option for compulsive conjuration is to command in the name of a spirit who "outranks" them. For example, Hebraic spirits like angels can be commanded in the name of G-d. Command by hierarchy is particularly common in Christian magic.

What gives you the right to command so? The so-called "Crown of Creation" model teaches that all humans outrank angels (and most other spirits) because humans are the masters of all others. For example, Psalm 8:5 says:

"What is man that You have been mindful of him? You have made him little less than the gods[386] *and adorned him with glory and majesty. You have made him master over Your handiwork, laying the world at his feet, sheep and oxen, all of them, and wild beasts, too; the birds of the heavens, the fish of the sea, whatever travels the paths of the seas."*

I'm not a big fan of this philosophy,[387] but it is very effective with angels and some kinds of demons, though (in my experience) not for many other spirits.

---

385 In general, it is my opinion that if a spirit doesn't answer, they maybe just aren't that into you, and you should find someone who is.

386 While this is often translated as "than the angels," the Hebrew is מֵאֱלֹהִים (m'Elohim), which unambiguously means "than the gods."

387 Because it's imperialist, patriarchal, colonialist bullshit that is literally killing the literal Earth, which is where I live.

Command by Compact

The next option is to operate in the bounds of a specific and prearranged[388] compact. This is my preferred method when I do compulsive conjuration. I work with a few such compacts. Earlier, I mentioned the Circle of Sister Sibyls, which is one such compact. I often operated under the Compact of the Caduceus, which is basically just "don't kill the messenger" and is recognized by most named spirits.[389] When I call Hebraic spirits, I work under the famous compact negotiated by Solomon, the Sorcerer-King. You can learn all about this in my book *The Sorcery of Solomon: A Guide to the 44 Planetary Pentacles of the Magician King* which, in addition to an analysis of the pentacles, includes an "on-ramp" for Solomonic magic more generally.

Command with a True Name

Another option is to compel spirits to appear by speaking their "true" name. In my experience, this isn't *really* a compulsive conjuration at all, but more like the "speed dial" option I mentioned earlier. Those names are more like having their personal phone number. They're not required to answer, but they only give out those names to people they want to hear from. Some of these are known from antiquity, but those are almost always less powerful than ones you learn directly from the spirits. For example, one compelling name of Aphrodite from the PGM is "Nefertiri." A compelling[390] name of Hermes Hermeneutes you can try, which identifies you as my student, is "Enigma Aglossakun." Others are learned as seals of initiation. In my opinion, the best ones are learned.

Command with Personal Power

This method is fun, but dangerous and sometimes a bit ethically questionable; it's what I think of as "real wizard shit." In this method, you just simply throw down with the spirit and see who wins. I *do not* recommend this method to beginners, because it's dangerous to pick fights you can't win. I don't usually recommend it for non-beginners either, except in extremity, because I'm generally opposed to making enemies when you could be making allies. Even when I can't make an alliance, I'd rather have an enemy than a slave.

This type of commanding generally won't work on "big" spirits like gods, but it will often work on small, localized spirits like ghosts or nature spirits,

388 By human magicians.

389 That is to say, spirits with names.

390 Technically, this is more like commanding by compact, with a compact I arranged for you.

and can work on larger spirits like angels and demons if you're savvy and well allied. Command by personal power often uses a blasting rod.

SAFEWORD!

While it's unlikely if you're conjuring someone so friendly and philanthropic[391] as Hermes Hermeneutes, there are times when you'll want to close a conjuration down all of a sudden. That's the nice thing about dark mirror conjuration: it's very easy to shut down compared to some other methods.

Take the scarf off your head, and drape it over the mirror. In most circumstances, just that will be enough to break the connection. If it is not, trace a pentacle in front of the mirror, saying something like, "*By the power of three times three, bound around this work shall be. By the power of four times four, a wall surrounds it with no door. And by the power of the five-point star, I close this portal to all there are!*"

If you're using a bowl, or other temporary mirror, empty it down the drain without looking into it again. Chase it with some salt. If you have a garbage disposal, run a couple of ice cubes and a lemon through after the water and salt. If it's a permanent mirror, wrap it up, tie the wrapping on, and contact me or another, more experienced conjurer. But, really, the chances of this happening are vanishingly small. I'm only teaching you this because I know, for me, having backup plans for the worst possible scenario helps calm my anxieties.

The End

391 Philanthropos, "lover of humans" is a common epithet of Hermes.

What Next?

I hope you have enjoyed reading this book as much as I enjoyed writing it, and have found it valuable. If you did, and would like to deepen and expand your practice, I have a few suggestions. Obviously, if you read the book, but did not actually do the practices, my first recommendation is to start over at the beginning and work your way through. If you would like some extra hand-holding, the opportunity to ask me any questions you like, and a supportive online community of classmates, collaborators, and co-magicians, I encourage you to sign up for the companion course at www.WitchLessons.com, where you will also find a number of options for Intermediate and Advanced Topics classes.

Below, I will recommend some books and other materials to deepen your experience of what you've learned in this book. Please note that my endorsement of a book is not necessarily an endorsement of the character of the writer. While some of the authors I mention below are friends and colleagues, most I know only from their writing. I have roughly organized them by topic.

Other Books by Me

* *The Big Book of Magical Incense*
* *Orphic Hymns Grimoire*
* *The Sorcery of Solomon: A Guide to the 44 Planetary Pentacles of the Magician King*
* *Sefer HaOtot: A Hebrew Book of Seals*

Magical Materia

* *Blackthorn's Botanical Magic: The Green Witch's Guide to Essential Oils for Spellcraft, Ritual & Healing*, by Amy Blackthorn
* *The Witching Herbs: 13 Essential Plants and Herbs for Your Magical Garden*, by Harold Roth
* *Principles and Practice of Phytotherapy: Modern Herbal Medicine*, by Kerry Bone and Simon Mills (this is not entirely beginner accessible)

Divination

* *Tarot for Your Self*, by Mary K. Greer
* *Seventy-Eight Degrees of Wisdom: A Book of Tarot*, by Rachel Pollack
* *The Tarot: A Key to the Wisdom of the Ages*, by Paul Foster Case
* *I Ching, the Oracle: A Practical Guide to the Book of Changes*, by Benebell Wen

Symbol Magic

* *Magic, Power, Language, Symbol: A Magician's Exploration of Linguistics*, by Patrick Dunn
* *Sigil Witchery: A Witch's Guide to Crafting Magick Symbols*, by Laura Tempest Zakroff
* *Amulets and Talismans*, by E. A. Wallis Budge (dated and colonialist)
* *777 And Other Qabalistic Writings of Aleister Crowley: Including Gematria & Sepher Sephiroth*, by Aleister Crowley (read with your critical faculties engaged)

Planetary Magic

* *Arbatel: Concerning the Magic of the Ancients*, author unknown (I specifically recommend the Joseph Peterson edition)
* *Secrets of Planetary Magic*, by Christopher Warnock
* *Seven Spheres*, by Rufus Opus
* *Practical Astrology for Witches and Pagans: Using the Planets and the Stars for Effective Spellwork, Rituals, and Magickal Work*, by Ivo Dominguez

What Next?

Cleansing and Protection

* *Protection and Reversal Magic: A Witch's Defense Manual,* by Jason Miller
* *Psychic Self-Defense: The Definitive Manual for Protecting Yourself Against Paranormal Attack,* by Dion Fortune (dated)

Dreams

* *The Tibetan Yogas of Dream and Sleep,* by Tenzin Wangyal Rinpoche
* *Waking, Dreaming, Being: Self and Consciousness in Neuroscience, Meditation, and Philosophy,* by Evan Thompson
* *Exploring the World of Lucid Dreaming,* by Stephen LeBerge

Trance

* *Trance-Portation: Learning to Navigate the Inner World,* by Diana Paxson
* *Shamanic Trance and Modern Kabbalah,* by Jonathon Garb
* *Shamanic Journeying: A Beginners Guide,* by Sandra Ingerman
* *The Book of Solomon's Magick,* by Carroll "Poke" Runyan

Reference Books (all great for bibliomancy)

* *The Greek Magical Papyri in Translation: Including the Demotic Spells,* edited by Hans Dieter Betz
* *NTC's Classical Dictionary: The Origins of the Names of Characters in Classical Mythology,* by Adrian Room
* *A Dictionary of Angels: Including the Fallen Angels,* by Gustav Davidson
* *Encyclopedia of 5,000 Spells: The Ultimate Reference Book for the Magical Arts, Exploring Folklore, Myth, and Magic from Every Corner of the Earth and Across Millennia,* by Judika Illes (when I was a beginner witch, we played this book like a party game, opening to a page at random and doing whatever spell we landed on)

Miscellaneous

* *How to Solve It,* by George Polya
* *Elements,* Euclid (I recommend the online edition here: https://www.c82.net/euclid/)
* *Psychic Witch: A Metaphysical Guide to Meditation, Magick & Manifestation,* by Mat Auryn (this book has good exercises in it)
* *The Complete Magician's Tables*, by Stephen Skinner